GW01186508

Soldiers, Sailors and Sandalmakers
A Social Reading of Ramesside Period Votive Stelae

Karen Exell

Golden House Publications

Egyptology 10

London 2009

This title is published by
Golden House Publications

© Karen Exell

All rights reserved

No part of this publication may be reproduced or transmitted in any form or by any means, digital, electronic or mechanical, including photocopy, recording, or any information storage and retrieval system, without permission in writing from the author.

Front cover image by Steve Devine: Stela of the Senior Scribe, Ramose, to Ptah and Maat, from Deir el-Medina (The Manchester Museum 1759). © The Manchester Museum.

Back cover image (top): Wooden statue of a king (detail), from Deir el-Medina (Musée du Louvre E. 16277). © 2009 Musée du Louvre / Christian Décamps.

Back cover image (bottom): Stela (verso) of the Sculptor in the Place of Truth, Qen (ii), to Renenut-Mertseger, from Deir el-Medina (Bordeaux, Musée d'Aquitaine 8635). © Mairie de Bordeaux / L. Gauthier.

Printed in the United Kingdom
by

CPI Antony Rowe
Bumper's Farm
Chippenham
Wiltshire SN14 6LH

London 2009

ISBN 978-1-906137-10-6

Giving praise to Amun,
That I may make hymns for him in his name.
I give him praise as high as the sky,
as wide as the earth,
I tell of his power to who(soever) sails north or south,
-beware of him!
Repeat it to son and daughter,
to great and small.
Tell of it to generation (upon) generation,
Who are still unborn.
Tell it to the fishes in the deep,
And to the birds in the sky
...
I shall make this stela in your name, and I shall fix for you in writing this hymn upon it.

From the stela of the Draughtsman in the Place of Truth, Nebre
(Ägyptisches Museum und Papyrussammlung, Staatliche Museen zu Berlin-SPK 20377; Kitchen 2000: 444-446)

Contents

Acknowledgments		vi
List of Figures		vii
List of Plates		ix
Introduction		1
Chapter 1	Votive and Commemorative Stelae	6
Chapter 2	The Deir el-Medina Votive Stelae: Data and Method	15
Chapter 3	The Theban Stelae: Divine Access and Social Display	26
Chapter 4	Festivals, Fertility and Divine Intervention at Deir el-Medina	69
Chapter 5	Beyond Thebes: Soldiers, Sailors and Sandalmakers	99
Chapter 6	Votive Stelae, the Individual and Society	131
Appendix 1	The Votive Stelae	139
Appendix 2	Theban Tombs Cited	187
Appendix 3	Titles Used on the Votive Stelae	188
Bibliography		190
Plate Section		

Acknowledgements

Thanks are due to a number of individuals and institutions who in various ways have contributed to the completion of this book.

The core research is based on my postgraduate work which was completed under the wise guidance of Penny Wilson. John Baines and Ian Shaw commented usefully on the initial work.

Access to unpublished material was kindly granted by Kenneth Kitchen and Glenn Godenho.

Personal maps and images were generously supplied by Ken Griffin, Stephen Harvey and Stephen Snape.

Drawings were beautifully created by Wolfram Grajetzki – and many thanks for all the additional help – and Christiane Müller-Hazenbos.

Images of objects in museum collections were efficiently supplied by Odile Biller (Musée d'Aquitaine, Bordeaux), Catherine Bridonneau, Céline Rebière-Plé and Christiane Ziegler (Musée du Louvre, Paris), Ashley Cooke (World Museum, Liverpool), Steve Devine (The Manchester Museum, University of Manchester), Robert Gray (Kingston Lacy, The National Trust), Adam Jaffer and Tom Heaven (Birmingham Museum and Art Gallery), Luc Limme and Dominique Hoornaert (Musées royaux d'Art et d'Histoire, Brussels), Stephen Quirke and Richard Langley (Petrie Museum of Egyptian Archaeology, UCL), Bettina Schmitz (Roemer-Pelizaeus Museum, Hildesheim), and Sabine Schumann and Klaus Finneiser (Ägyptisches Museum und Papyrussammlung, Staatliche Museen zu Berlin-SPK).

Chris Naunton at the Egypt Exploration Society deserves special thanks for his swift handling of bibliographic - and many other! - requests, as do Scott Harder and Jamie Woodward for cheerful proofing.

List of Figures

Figure (i)	Chronology of the Late New Kingdom	4
Figure (ii)	Map showing the sites discussed	5
Figure 1.1	Plan of North Abydos (after Richards 2005: figure 6)	11
Figure 2.1	The Deir el-Medina votive stelae findspots	23
Figure 3.1	Chart showing the number of stelae dedicated in the 19th and 20th Dynasties at Deir el-Medina	27
Figure 3.2	Deir el-Medina stelae by reign	27
Figure 3.3	Compositional form of the Deir el-Medina stelae	28
Figure 3.4	Compositional form of the Deir el-Medina stelae by dynasty	28
Figure 3.5	Recipients of the Deir el-Medina votive stelae	29
Figure 3.6	Recipients of less than 10 stelae on the Deir el-Medina votive stelae	30
Figure 3.7	Stela of Bek depicting a criosphinx and a statue of Khonsu in the upper register, and Bek adoring a ram statue in the lower register (DB280; Pushkin Museum of Fine Arts, Moscow I.1.a.5607; © Wolfram Grajetzki)	31
Figure 3.8	Forms of Amun-Re on the Deir el-Medina stelae in total and in the 19th and 20th Dynasties	32
Figure 3.9	Cult images of Amun-Re	32
Figure 3.10	Identified forms of Amun-Re and the titular rank of the dedicators	36
Figure 3.11	Forms of Mertseger on the Deir el-Medina stelae in total and in the 19th and 20th Dynasties	37
Figure 3.12	Cult images of Mertseger	38
Figure 3.13	Identified forms of Mertseger and the titular rank of the dedicators	42
Figure 3.14	Forms of Amenhotep/Queen Ahmes Nefertari on the Deir el-Medina stelae in total and in the 19th and 20th Dynasties	43
Figure 3.15	Cult images of Amenhotep I/Queen Ahmes Nefertari	44
Figure 3.16	Identified forms of Amenhotep I/Queen Ahmes Nefertari and the titular rank of the dedicators	47
Figure 3.17	Cult images of Ptah	49
Figure 3.18	Identified forms of Ptah and the titular rank of the dedicators	52
Figure 3.19	Forms of Hathor on the Deir el-Medina stelae in total and in the 19th and 20th Dynasties	52
Figure 3.20	Cult images of Hathor	53
Figure 3.21	Reliefs DM87 (Louvre E.16276 a/b) and DM88 (Cairo JdE 72017) from the Khenu-chapel at Deir el-Medina (© Wolfram Grajetzki)	54
Figure 3.22	Identified forms of Hathor and the titular rank of the dedicators	58
Figure 3.23	Percentage of stelae dedicated in each Theban subset in the 19th and 20th Dynasties	59
Figure 3.24	Percentage of each compositional form dedicated by Deir el-Medina and non-Deir el-Medina residents in the 19th and 20th Dynasties	59
Figure 3.25	Cult images of Amun-Re (Thebes)	60
Figure 3.26	Cult images of Amenhotep I/Queen Ahmes Nefertari (Thebes)	62
Figure 3.27	Cult images of Osiris (Thebes)	63
Figure 4.1	Images of Ramesses II from Deir el-Medina	71
Figure 4.2	Amenhotep 'of the Forecourt' carried in his palanquin in oracular procession as part of the Valley Festival, in TT19 of Amenmose (after Foucart 1932 IV, *Le Tombeau d'Amonmos*)	75

Figure 4.3	Oracular representations on stelae dating to the reign of Ramesses II	76
Figure 4.4	Private stelae from the Queens' Valley chapels dating to the reign of Ramesses III depicting the Vizier, To	80
Figure 4.5	Years of known active service of the individuals on the stelae listed in Figure 4.4	81
Figure 4.6	Offerings depicted on the Deir el-Medina stelae	85
Figure 4.7	Stela of Irynefer (i) and his wife Mehykhati (ii), Deir el-Medina, r. Ramesses II, first half (DB33; The British Museum EA 284; © Trustees of the British Museum)	85
Figure 4.8	Large columnar bouquet (left), mid-size bouquet (centre) (after Dittmar 1986: Abb. 100, Abb. 105) and small bouquet (right), not to scale (© Wolfram Grajetzki). These examples are from stelae dating to the reign of Ramesses II	86
Figure 4.9	Attendance at state festivals/oracle stelae	89
Figure 4.10	Deir el-Medina individuals with three or more stelae, showing the stelae categorised according to life events	96
Figure 5.1	Plan of the temples at Abu Simbel (after Fouchet 1965: 207)	99
Figure 5.2	King's Sons of Kush during the reign of Ramesses II (after Reisner 1920: 39-47; Raedler 2003: 132-133)	100
Figure 5.3	Plan of the temple-fort at Zawiyet Umm el-Rakham (© Steven Snape)	104
Figure 5.4	Dated stelae from the comparative dataset	107
Figure 5.5	Recipients of the votive stelae in the comparative dataset	109
Figure 5.6	Location of the majority of the rock cut stelae at Abu Simbel (after Porter and Moss VII 1951: 111)	110
Figure 5.7	Offerings depicted on the Qantir votive stelae	122
Figure 5.8	Sketch of the stela of the Standard-bearer, Amenmessu, showing Ramesses II smiting, Zawiyet Umm el-Rakham, r. Ramesses II, first half (DB430; ZUR 2; © Christiane Müller-Hazebos)	124

List of Plates

Plate 1a The Middle Kingdom mud brick features, including cenotaphs, at the Ramesses II 'Portal Temple' at Abydos (© Stephen Harvey)

Plate 1b Stela of Sankhptah (top section), from Abydos, 17th Dynasty (The British Museum EA 833; © Trustees of The British Museum)

Plate 2a The New Kingdom mud brick chapels within the Ptolemaic Hathor temple enclosure wall, Deir el-Medina (© Ken Griffin)

Plate 2b The Queens' Valley Chapels ('L'Oratoire de Ptah et Mérseger'), Deir el-Medina (© Ken Griffin)

Plate 3a Stela (recto) of the Sculptor in the Place of Truth, Qen (ii) to Renenut-Mertseger, Deir el-Medina, r. Ramesses II, first half (DB80; Bordeaux, Musée d'Aquitaine 8635). The verso (see back cover) depicts Mertseger as anthropomorphic (© Mairie de Bordeaux / L. Gauthier)

Plate 3b Stela of Henut to Mertseger, Deir el-Medina, Ramesside Period (DB239; World Museum, Liverpool M13830; © National Museums Liverpool (World Museum))

Plate 4a Stela of the Wab-priest of the Prow of Amun, Huy, to Khonsu-em-Waset Neferhotep (?), Ptah (?), an unidentified god and goddess (upper register), and Amenhotep I in the blue crown and Queen Ahmes Nefertari (lower register), from the West Bank Mortuary Temple of the High Priest Nebwenenef, Thebes, r. Ramesses II (DB270; Petrie Museum of Egyptian Archaeology UC14212; © Petrie Museum of Egyptian Archaeology, University College London)

Plate 4b Wooden statue of a king found beneath the Khenu-chapel at the Hathor temple, Deir el-Medina, r. Ramesses II (Musée du Louvre E. 16277; © 2006 Musée du Louvre / Christian Décamps)

Plate 5a Stela of the Lady of the House, Bukhanefptah (i) to Nebethetepet (Hathor), Deir el-Medina, r. Seti I-Ramesses II, first half (DB13; Bankes Collection 7; © Bankes Collection (Kingston Lacy), The National Trust)

Plate 5b Stela of the Workman in the Place of Truth, Karo/Kel (i) to Ptah, Deir el-Medina, r. Ramesses II, first half (DB39; The British Museum EA 328; © Trustees of The British Museum)

Plate 6 Stela of the Senior Scribe, Ramose (i) to Hathor, 'Lady of the Southern Sycamore', from Pit 1414, Room 9 of the Khenu-chapel at the Hathor temple, Deir el-Medina, r. Ramesses II, first half (DB89; Musée du Louvre E. 16345; © 2007 Musée du Louvre / Georges Poncet)

Plate 7 Stela of the Foreman in the Place of Truth, Khons (v) to Mertseger and Ramesses III with the Vizier, To, *in situ* in Chapel A, The Queens' Valley Chapels, Deir el-Medina, r. Ramesses III (DB188; © Ken Griffin)

Plate 8 Stela of the Workman of the Lord of the Two Lands, Hesysunebef (i) to Mut and the Foreman in the Place of Truth, Neferhotep (ii), from the area of the Ramesseum, Thebes, r. Ramesses III (DB183, The Manchester Museum 4588; © The Manchester Museum, University of Manchester)

Plate 9 Stela of the Draughtsman of Amun/in the Place of Truth, Nebre (i) and his son, the Outline Draughtsman, Khay (ii), to Amun-Re, from the area of the Ramesseum, Thebes, r. Ramesses II, first half (DB60; Ägyptisches Museum 20377; © Ägyptisches Museum und Papyrussammlung, Staatliche Museen zu Berlin-SPK)

Plate 10 Stela of the Quarryman, Huy and his son Mose, to Ptah, Deir el-Medina, early 19th Dynasty (DB153; Birmingham Museums and Art Gallery 1969W2978; © Birmingham Museums & Art Gallery)

Plate 11a Stela of the Workman in the Place of Truth, Neferabu (i), to Ptah, Deir el-Medina, r. Ramesses II, mid (DB116; The British Museum EA 589; © Trustees of The British Museum)

Plate 11b Stela of the Workman in the Place of Truth, Khabekhenet (i), to Hathor, Deir el-Medina, r. Ramesses II, first half (The British Museum EA 555; © Trustees of The British Museum)

Plate 12a Rock-cut stela of the First Royal Cupbearer of his Majesty, Ramesses-Asha-Hebu-Sed to Ramesses II, *in situ* at Abu Simbel, r. Ramesses II, early (DB321, Abu Simbel 9; © Karen Exell)

Plate 12b Rock-cut stele of the Royal Scribe, Usimare-Asha-Nakhtu to Ramesses II in his chariot, *in situ* at Abu Simbel, r. Ramesses II (DB337; Abu Simbel 8; © Karen Exell)

Plate 13 Rock-cut double stela of the King's Son of Kush, Setau to Ramesses II, *in situ* at Abu Simbel, year 38 of Ramesses II (DB327; Abu Simbel 24; © Karen Exell)

Plate 14 Stela of the Infantryman of the Great Regiment of (Ramesses Meryamun) Beloved of Atum, Mose to Ptah and the statue of Ramesses II as Sun-of-the-Rulers, Qantir, r. Ramesses II (DB379; Pelizaeus-Museum 374; © Roemer- und Pelizaeus-Museum Hildesheim)

Plate 15a Stela of the Singer of Montu-em-tawy, Isis to the statue of Ramesses II as User-Maat-Re Setep-en-Re Montu-em-Tawy, Qantir, r. Ramesses II (DB370; Pelizaeus-Museum 380; © Roemer- und Pelizaeus-Museum Hildesheim)

Plate 15b Stela of the Draughtsman of Amun, Userhat to Ptah and an unidentified statue of Ramesses II, Qantir, r. Ramesses II (DB408; Musées royaux d'Art et d'Histoire E. 3049; © Musées royaux d'Art et d'Histoire, Brussels)

Plate 16 Stela of the Overseer of the Goldworkers and Greatly Favoured one of the Great God, Penweret to Sobek-Re, Qantir, r. Ramesses II (DB391; Pelizaeus-Museum 398; © Roemer- und Pelizaeus-Museum Hildesheim)

INTRODUCTION

This book sets out to explore the meaning of votive stelae to the individuals who dedicated them, and the nature of the events that they commemorate, during the Ramesside Period (1295-1069 BC). All stelae can be described as commemorative, utilised to record a variety of types of information, from royal decrees, participation in expeditions and votive activity, to funerary texts securing offerings for the deceased. The Egyptian word for stela is *wḏ*, which also has the meaning 'proclamation, declaration, order', and the stelae allow the information proclaimed to be commemorated eternally (Schneider 1971: 8). The stelae in this discussion commemorate votive activity by private individuals. They take the form of round-topped or rectangular slabs of stone, most commonly limestone, though granite and sandstone occur, or, more rarely, wood. Decorated in painted sunk or raised relief, or simply painted, a votive stela typically depicts one or more individuals interacting directly, or by means of a higher-ranking individual, with a divine hypostasis, which could take the form of a deity statue or relief, or a piece of symbolic ritual paraphernalia such as a sistrum. The decoration takes the form of either a single scene with labels, or is arranged in two registers, often with a longer text in the second register. Both representations and text are in most cases extremely formulaic. The stelae were erected in and around temples and local chapels, and also in domestic contexts.

Traditional interpretations of votive stelae have regarded them as representing the abstract relationship of an individual with a deity, and, as such, as a material manifestation of 'personal piety' (see Chapter 1), and as sources for genealogical and prosopographical information. Such interpretations leave largely unexplored their complex multivalent nature. The pietistic interpretation addresses the form the information takes (Morris 1992: 165), whilst ignoring less obvious - to the modern viewer - , but no less central, messages regarding the individual and his/her society. The votive stelae are the material manifestation and record of a select repertoire of social practices, and act as markers of social identity. As inscribed private monuments, conveying information via text, iconography and materiality, the stelae display a multi-layered message about the dedicator, his/her place in society, and the structure of that society. The stelae are an aspect of Egyptian 'self-presentation', defined by Baines as a genre that encompasses both visual and textual media, and reflects social practice: such monuments 'existed in a social context that must have included ceremonies and performances in which a person's self was presented' (Baines 2004: 35). In order to discover the original event or process that inspired the production of a stela, an attempt must be made to identify the decorative conventions in operation, and understand the rules on which the conventions are based. Given our almost complete lack of social and historical context for the use of private votive monuments, such an approach must frequently begin with the monument itself. A stela, as the material marker of a set of social processes, has to be deconstructed to reveal the social processes that it encapsulates, and the social position or role of its dedicator in society.

This study can be situated within discussions of identity and agency, and archaeology and text, of the last 20 years. Recent archaeological debate has drawn attention to the role of archaeologists and historians in historical periods, and the need for collaborative working, rather than the institutionalised separation of past evidence into artefact/archaeology and text/history (see, for example, Moreland 2001; Woolf 2002; Sauer 2004; Richards 2005). The division of evidence has resulted in 'cross-boundary' artefacts, such as inscribed, ritual monuments, remaining relatively unexamined (Morris 1992: 165; Meskell 2002: 8). Inscriptions, and to a lesser extent representations, are often perceived as supplying the meaning of the artefact (Moreland 2001: 98), with inscriptions and representations often studied separately, and the artefactual context, the materiality, often ignored. Such decontextualisation at the level of genre or form can lead to overemphasis on individual elements of the whole, in particular in relation to inscriptions, which have traditionally been afforded an elevated position in academia (Woolf 2002: 53; Sauer 2004: 24) - the inscriptions do not serve simply to convey information, in the way that language and texts are often used today. In the case of Egyptian monuments, the inscriptions are frequently either so generic as to convey minimal specific information (Pinch 1993: 98), or they are inscribed on artefacts in locations which would have been hard to read, or, indeed, invisible (Baines 2004: 35). Related to this is the fact that few of the individuals who viewed the inscriptions at any point in their production or installation would have been able to read them - though this is perhaps less the case in relation to the Deir el-Medina stelae discussed in this book, whose owners were more likely to have been literate (see Section 2.1). Some stelae texts do record specific information, for example, regarding an individual's confessions of 'sin' and requests for forgiveness (Borghouts 1982b). Borghouts' study of manifestations of divine *b3w* illustrates the dense religious landscape inhabited by the ancient Egyptians (Baines 2001), and the variety of means available to interact with the divine, or overcome negative divine influence on an individual's life. Borghouts cites a number of stelae that he believes relate to interaction with divine *b3w*, alongside various other artefacts, spells and so on, that were used in the same context. The stelae, therefore, are not the only medium through which an individual could interact with the divine, but will have been chosen as a record of divine interaction for other reasons, such as the material form of the stela, its enduring nature, and the cultural or symbolic value of its form and content, the text and images.

In addition, the inscriptions may relate to an oral, public presentation at their installation (Baines 2004: 35), that is, to formal social and ritual practice (see Kessler 1999). Gilchrist (2004: 150) divides ritual activity into two categories: performance and inscription; the votive stelae are the 'inscription' that relates to ritual practice. Baines has noted that such a concept is easy to envisage in texts relating to tombs, given our understanding of funerary rituals, 'but is unknown in detail for statues and stelae set up in temples' (2004: 5), where no contemporary comparative context exists. These practical uses of text, as record and message, should not, however, be privileged over symbolic uses of writing (Beard 1991: 37). The use of text was as an indicator of status: writing in ancient Egypt was almost wholly restricted to elite contexts (Baines 1983: 580). Discussing the function of the written word in Roman religious contexts, Beard (1991) stresses the importance of the naming of the individual and the deity in the inscriptions found in chapels, both as graffiti and on portable artefacts. She defines the function of these inscriptions as assertions of membership of paganism, which would be expressed in practice (participation in ritual), but made permanent through inscription. The naming of the individual and the deity make a statement regarding an individual's own enduring position in relation to the deity, a relationship extending beyond the needs of a particular occasion - hence the frequent lack of specificity. In the majority of cases, the primary purpose of the inscription was neither to record a specific act, though they were inspired by a specific act of devotion, nor to be read, but to fix one's relationship to the divine (Beard 1991: 47-48) in an elite, exclusive, permanent, magical medium.

This book focuses on the representations, rather than the texts, on votive stelae. As with the use of text, access to, and use of, images relating to the central ideology, the king and the gods, was traditionally limited to elite contexts. Such images were not freely available, and, when they appear on private monuments, they carry a great cultural weight. They are also indicative of a change in decorum in relation to the use of restricted images, a phenomenon that has been noted for the Ramesside Period. Much of the discussion is based on the proposition that, on one level, the representations on votive stelae can be related to specific events, though this is only one of their many meanings (see Chapter 4), and an understanding that the scenes on stelae are frequently closer in content to private tomb representations than to temple decoration, though still controlled by representational decorum. The combination of strict convention and freer content forces a careful reading of the iconography to elucidate the event or process commemorated, bearing in mind that the stelae representations are complex iconographic messages rather than 'photographic' representations of single events (see Pinch 1993: 336-339). The pictorial content may also, and simultaneously, operate as part of a meaningful internal discourse (J. Baines, *pers. comm.*). One of the messages conveyed by the representations on votive stelae is an individual's level of 'divine access', that is, access to the central ideology, or ability to display such access, represented by their interaction with a deity (Podeman Sørenson 1989b; see Chapter 1), which is closely linked to their social status. At this individual level, we can begin to see examples of choice, or agency, in how an individual presented their identity and social status.

Agency is defined as the motivations and actions of agents (Dobres and Robb 2000: 8), who may be individuals or social groups, which can be discerned in the archaeological record by means of the material culture (see Dobres and Robb 2000: 9 and Chapman 2003: 65-66 for further definitions of the term). Contemporary analysis of identity focuses on the concept of 'self-identity', that is, of identity at an individual, and psychological, level. In the archaeological record, in both pre-historic and historic archaeology, it is almost impossible to discern individual identity at such a level of precision (for an attempt, see Meskell 1999). In this discussion, identity means social identity and the marking of social status, referring to two concepts: individual identity at the superficial level of name, title and family relations; and formal group identity within a community (Meskell and Preucel 2004: 125; see also, Dìaz-Andreu and Lucy 2005: 1). Social structure is the normative, ideal constitution of society, created and recreated by beliefs, practices and their material manifestation in iconography, architecture, institutions and language. Social organisation is the everyday reality of social relationships, which may not have an official context for expression, and is, as a result, harder to discern in the archaeological record.

Agency and structure have been central to the theoretical archaeological debate since the 1980s' reaction to processual archaeology and its adherence to systems theory (Meskell and Preucel 2004: 7; Babić 2005: 73).

At the centre of the debate is the work of the social theorists, Pierre Bourdieu and Anthony Giddens. Giddens' structuration theory (1984) proposed that the action, and its manifestation in material culture, of individuals and social groups, is constrained by, and contributes to, social structure (Dobres and Robb 2000: 5; Cowgill 2000: 51; Chapman 2003: 65; Hodder 2004: 51). Giddens (1984: 17) suggested that social systems do not have 'structures' but that their structure exists in practices, and as memory traces which orient the conduct of knowledgeable human agents. He also makes an important distinction between what an agent does, and what he or she intended, which can have very different consequences (Giddens 1984: 10). Bourdieu's theory of 'habitus' (1980: 88-91) foregrounds everyday social practice as central to shaping society (Dobres and Robb 2000: 5; Gilchrist 2004: 146; Babić 2005: 75). The structure/agency debate has, to date, mainly focused on prehistoric archaeologies but is especially relevant to historical archaeologies where the actions of the individual can be 'seen' by means of inscribed monuments (Woolf 2002: 54). Both Giddens and Bourdieu emphasise the role of agents in shaping and maintaining the society in which they live, by means of social, symbolic and material structures, institutions, habitation and belief (Dobres and Robb 2000: 8; see also Turner 1969: 117). In ancient Egypt, two-dimensional representation was controlled by a set of conventions, termed decorum, which 'bar certain types of representation from associating freely and occurring freely in different contexts' (Baines 1985: 277). The system of representational decorum was defined in the context of temples, which represented, architecturally and by means of iconography, the Egyptian state ideology of the centrality of the kingship: the king is represented within the sacred spaces repeatedly offering to the gods, in his role as intermediary between the people and the gods. The system of representational decorum also occurs in tombs and on portable monuments of private individuals, upholding and disseminating the ideological centrality of the kingship. Decorum does not act as a structure imposed from outside, but rather represents a constant (re-)enactment and (re)assertion of ideology (Baines 1990: 21; 1994b: 88). Use of such conventions by private individuals on their monuments can be set within the context of Giddens' duality of structure: the conventions support and maintain social structure. The stelae 'connect with the collective past, are active in the present and actively create the future' (Gilchrist 2002: 150). The level of convention displayed on a stela is a public statement of the dedicator's relationship *vis-à-vis* the central ideology. It indicates that the dedicator has knowledge of such conventions, as well as licence to use them.

The use of material culture has been termed 'consumption' (Miller 1995). Miller notes that '[t]he structure of consumption is the key to the reproduction of class relations' and that this, conversely 'provides a novel mechanism by which analysts could study social relations in some objectified form' (1995: 267). The aspect of an individual's social identity that is clearly marked on votive stelae, on every level, from the explicit (the inclusion of the title) to the implicit (the form and content), is his, less frequently her, social status. Differentiating social groups, relationships between them, and influential individuals within them, creates the network of social relationships that constitutes social structure (Service 1971; Chapman 2003: 34); the stelae express the co-existence of a number of different structures, or hierarchies, both state and local, and the elite systems that operated at the different levels (Richards 2005: 16). A recent definition of social status in relation to contemporary society defines it as 'an individual's position in society, in the narrow sense referring to one's legal or professional standing within a group (as married, as a lieutenant), and in a broader sense as referring to an individual's value and importance in the eyes of the world' (de Botton 2004: 3). This succinctly describes the two aspects of social status marked by votive stelae in ancient Egypt.

Votive stelae are a material manifestation of agency working within emphatic social constraints. Identity at an individual, superficial, level can be discerned in the personal content of the stelae - inclusion of name and title, family, colleagues, the divine hypostasis. In many past societies, ancient Egypt included, to be individual in the contemporary sense of different, 'other', was not a desired state. There was little or no public context for the expression of desires or activities contrary to the social norm (but see Baines 1986). Rather, people desired to be successful participants in normative society: individual identity was exhibited in terms of sameness, rather than difference (Meskell and Preucel 2004: 151). Votive stelae as public monuments belong to the realm of state ideology; it is unlikely that they will deliberately reference alternative structures. Within this ideology individuals used votive stelae, and other private monuments, in particular mortuary monuments (Morris 1992: 165; Meskell and Preucel 2004: 125) as a means of negotiating their social position, or status, both for their contemporary audience, and for the hereafter (Baines 1994: 75; Foxhall 1994, 1995; Woolf 1996). The votive stelae discussed in this book record, commemorate and display the public achievements of individuals, from viziers to royal workmen, soldiers to sandalmakers, living in Ramesside Egypt.

A note on the dating of the stelae

Ramesside Period votive stelae are principally dated on stylistic grounds and by identifying the kings and individuals depicted on them. Many individuals from Deir el-Medina are well-known through the extensive extant texts and monuments from this site, and their period of service securely dated (see Davies 1999). The inclusion of representations of royal statues is not an effective tool for dating, given that many of the stelae depict cult statues of dead kings. In this light, one group of stelae remains problematic: the stelae from Pi-Ramesses/Qantir. The majority of the stelae from Qantir depict one or more colossal statues of Ramesses II, and have been dated to the king's reign, based on the assumption that the cults of these statues were primarily active during the reign. This may well prove to be incorrect, as the cults of various statues of Ramesses II from elsewhere are known to have continued long after his reign (see, for example, Černý 1969). However, until further evidence to the contrary is discovered, the assumed date will stand for this group. More precise dating using a more extensive set of criteria (for example, changes in palaeography, orthography, the writing of formulae) along the lines of the dating that is now possible for Middle Kingdom stelae (see Obsomer 1993), is not at this stage possible as New Kingdom stelae have not yet received the same level of attention, though there has been some recent palaeographic work that is beginning to address this (Moje 2007). The dating of the stelae has been based on the above mentioned criteria, together with a consideration of the date given by the museum or publication. As a result of the research carried out for this book a number of stelae have been given more precise dates, by means of secure identification of the owner, comparison with similar examples, or their clear association with known or surmised historical events. This is the date that is used in the discussion.

Figure (i) Chronology of the Late New Kingdom*

Dynasty and king	Dates
Late 18th Dynasty	
Horemheb Djeserkheperura	1319-1295 BC
19th Dynasty (1295-1185 BC)	
Ramesses I Menpehtyra	1295-1294 BC
Sety I Menmaatre	1294-1279 BC
Ramesses II Usermaatra Setepenra	1279-1213 BC
Merenptah Baenra	1213-1203 BC
Sety II Userkheperura	1200-1194 BC
Amenmesse Menmira	(1203-1200?) BC
Siptah Akhenra Setepenra	1194-1188 BC
Tausret Sitrameritamun	1188-1186 BC
20th Dynasty (1186-1069 BC)	
Sethnakht Userkhaura Meryamun	1186-1184 BC
Ramesses III Usermaatra Meryamun	1184-1153 BC
Ramesses IV Hekamaatra Setepenamun	1153-1147 BC
Ramesses V Usermaatra Sekheperenra	1147-1143 BC
Ramesses VI Nebmaatra Meryamun	1143-1136 BC
Ramesses VII Usermaatra Setepenra Meryamun	1136-1129 BC
Ramesses VIII Usermaatra Akhenamun	1129-1126 BC
Ramesses IX Neferkara Setepenra	1126-1108 BC
Ramesses X Khepermaatra Setepenra	1108-1099 BC
Ramesses XI Menmaatra Setepenptah	1099-1069 BC

*Based on *The British Museum Dictionary of Ancient Egypt* (1995)

Definition of terms

Personal piety: individual rather than corporate piety centred on one or more of the state gods (Pinch 1993: 325), and incorporating domestic versions of such cults.
Popular religion: beliefs and practices of the Egyptian people themselves, outside of the endowed, state-run, secluded official temple cults (Sadek 1987: 2).
Private: non-royal.
Public: referring to civic or communal contexts.
Votive stela: a stela dedicated during an individual's lifetime to a deity or deities, living or deceased kings, or high-ranking individuals, in the hope of accruing benefits in this life and the next (after Pinch 1993: 83), and acting as a record of access to the deity in various contexts. In this sense they are also commemorative, and should perhaps be primarily regarded as such.

Figure (ii) Map showing the sites discussed

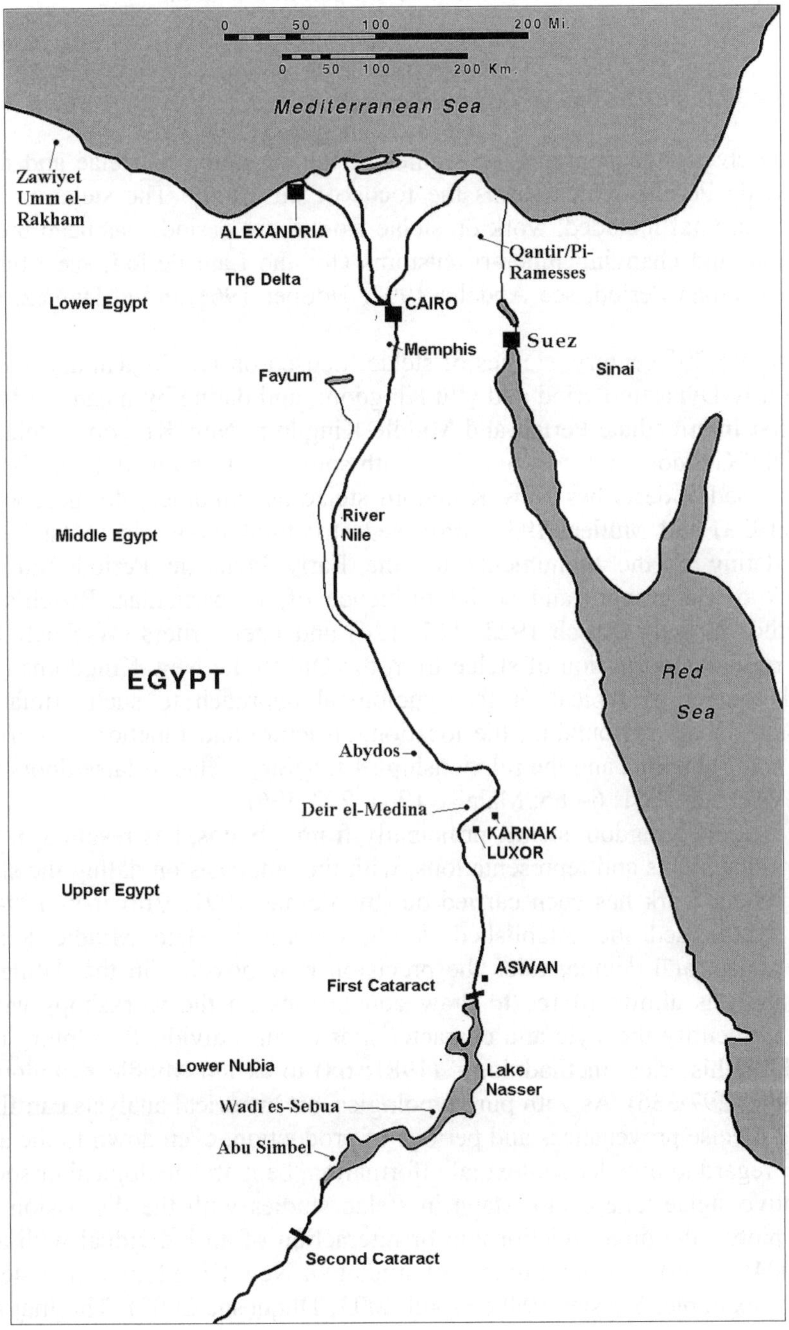

1. VOTIVE AND COMMEMORATIVE STELAE

Chapter 1 outlines the different approaches to stelae: typological, religious, social, individual (in the sense of detectable agency) and political, with an extended discussion of the Middle Kingdom Abydos stelae, which provide one of the richest pre-New Kingdom corpuses of material. Early writers frequently did not differentiate between votive and funerary stelae, and between funerary stelae and false doors, resulting in confusion in the terminology. In this discussion, 'false door' refers to the large architectural proto- and actual false doors found in Early Dynastic and Old Kingdom tombs; 'funerary stela' refers to stelae from a funerary context, decorated with representations of the deceased, the offering formula, and, by the later Middle Kingdom and New Kingdom, depictions of afterlife deities; 'votive stela' refers to Middle and New Kingdom stelae from civic and domestic contexts (for example, temple precincts, local chapels and houses), most commonly depicting an individual adoring or offering to a (predominantly) non-afterlife deity, the majority of which do not include the offering formula. Many of the votive stelae may, in fact, be defined as commemorative, particularly those from Abydos (Simpson 1974; O'Connor 1985; Kessler 1999: 176, n. 8; see Section 1.2), a proposal central to the argument developed in this book.

1.1 Approaches to funerary, votive and commemorative stelae

The discussion in this chapter concentrates on studies of the evolution of stelae and false doors up to and including the Ramesside Period, which forms the focus of this study. The stelae of the Late Period and Graeco-Roman Period are not included; work on stelae from these periods has been predominantly directed towards funerary stelae and changing funerary customs (for the Late Period, see Munro 1973 and Leahy 1977; for the Graeco-Roman Period, see Abdalla 1992; Hooper 1961 and el-Hafeez, Grenier and Wagner 1985).

During the early to mid 20th century, studies of stelae focused on typological analyses of stelae and false doors dating to the Early Dynastic Period and Old Kingdom, and dating by means of iconography and texts of stelae from the First Intermediate Period and Middle Kingdom. New Kingdom stelae were regarded as a continuation of Middle Kingdom stelae in function, with some small innovations in form (see, for example, Vandier 1954: 498) - Sadek describes New Kingdom stelae as 'innumerable merely conventional stelae' (1987: 43). Rusch (1923) and Müller (1933) proposed structural typologies of stelae and false doors to establish sequence dating of the monuments for the Early Dynastic Period and Old Kingdom. The inflexibility and lack of geographic and social influence of, in particular, Rusch's system, have been critiqued, by the author himself (Rusch 1923: 115; 124) and later writers (Wiebach 1981: 21; Strudwick 1985: 8). Vandier's rigid categorisation of stelae from the Old to the New Kingdoms (1954 II.1: 389-523), based on form and content, is typical of the typological approach to such artefacts. The typological discussion fed into the debate surrounding the location, structure and function of Early Dynastic funerary stelae from Abydos and Memphis, and the relationship of funerary stelae to false doors (Vandier 1952: 724-774; Shoukry 1958; Wiebach 1981: 64-65; Malaise 1984: 393-396).

The abundance of Middle Kingdom stelae, principally from Abydos, has resulted in numerous studies of the iconography, formulae, texts and representations, with the emphasis on dating the stelae (for a summary see Obsomer 1993; recent work has been carried out by Vernus 1991; Brovarski 1994 and Spanel 1996). Marée (1993) has synthesised the established dating criteria for late Middle Kingdom and Second Intermediate Period stelae, and demonstrates the precision now possible in the dating of stelae from this period. Such close analysis allows Marée to draw conclusions on the workshops where the stelae were produced, and even to identify the style and characteristics of an individual sculptor (1993: 16). Similarly, Freed has employed 'art historical methodology' (1981: 68) to assign Middle Kingdom Abydene stelae to workshop groups (1996: 297-336). As with pure typologies, art historical analysis can fix an artefact in time or place, determining precise provenances and periods of production, even down to the artist's hand, but it is less informative with regard to broader contextual information, be it archaeological or social.

New Kingdom votive stelae take centre stage in stelae studies with the discussion of the phenomenon known as 'personal piety', the direct relationship or interaction of an individual with a god (Quirke 1992: 135-138; Morgan 2004: 57-65). A small number of studies of New Kingdom votive stelae have focused on social issues (see, for example, Kessler 1999; Frood 2003; Duquesne 2005). The majority of votive stelae commonly regarded as expressing 'personal piety' are provenanced to Deir el-Medina. These votive stelae have been interpreted as symbolic representations of a personal relationship with a deity, and are said to indicate a new level of personal piety (Assmannn 2001: 231ff.) or give expression to an existing concept that had previously lacked appropriate articulation (Gunn 1916: 93-94; Quirke 1992: 135; Kessler 1999: 174, 181; Baines 2001: 2; 4). Posener (1975) discusses pre-Amarna expressions of personal piety on ostraca (see also Sadek 1987: 293).

Gunn's 1916 article, 'The Religion of the Poor in Ancient Egypt,' is one of the earliest treatments of the concept of personal piety, and of the votive stelae from Deir el-Medina. The article discusses the texts of a number of the stelae and sets them within a biblical construct of sin and humility, interpreting them as purely religious documents. The texts on the stelae are not treated as products of their own society, but are set within an abstract and implied religious framework drawn from an overtly western Christian tradition. Gunn states that '[i]n these memorial and votive stones we find the manifestation of a religious emotion for which we shall look in vain at any earlier or later period in Egypt, until Christian times' (1916: 93). A traditionally religious interpretation of New Kingdom votive stelae can be seen in the work of Sadek (1987) who surveyed New Kingdom votive stelae to establish the existence of 'popular' as opposed to state cults throughout Egypt. Sadek focuses on identifying the cults, and the forms of expression of worship. He does not discuss the stelae dedicators, or owners, apart from a brief note on rank (pp. 45-46), nor any social context for the scenes represented on the stelae.

Social and historical influences, such as the prevailing political situation, an individual's status, and agency in the form of expressions of identity and personal choice, have been identified by some scholars as influential in the development and use of stelae and false doors. In addition, analysis of the monuments has been set within the context of social convention, genre and representational decorum (Baines 2002: 4). Such an approach forms the partial context for the analysis of Ramesside Period votive stelae in the following chapters.

The influence of an individual's social status on the form of their personal monumental record has been discussed in relation to tomb size, particularly of the Early Dynastic Period and Old Kingdom. Tomb size has often been assumed to have an absolute correlation with social status: the larger the tomb, the more important the individual. Saad (1957) found 25 slab stelae set into the ceilings, rather than into a niche in the superstructure, of the 2nd Dynasty tombs at Helwan. Haeny (1971: 150-151; see also Kees 1958; James 1962) suggested that these stelae could not be *in situ,* because of their unexpected location, and also because there was no correspondence between the social status of the individuals, indicated by the titles on the stelae, and the size and complexity of the tomb. This assumed correspondence of tomb size and social status has formed the basis for Kanawati's discussion of Old Kingdom tombs (1977). In his analysis of Kanawati's data, Strudwick (1985: 6) points out that there appear to be large numbers of men of the same status at Giza/Saqqara who have different tomb sizes. Though doubting that there is 'really any consistent pattern' Strudwick concedes that 'in general there must have been some correlation between wealth and lavishness of tomb' (1985: 4-5).

Wiebach's assessment of the function and development of the form of the false door (1981; 2001) takes into account aspects of social status such as gender. She notes, for example, that '[t]he cornice element - as a status symbol at the beginning - was used mainly for men; the first attested occurrence in a female tomb is that of Queen Nebet, wife of Unas' (2001: 498). Wiebach's analysis makes the important point that, though social status may well affect the form, design and size of tombs (2001: 500), the most revealing aspect of a tomb in terms of social status is its proximity to the royal burial (1981: 221; see also Roth 1991: 111); the proximity of private monuments to state/royal monuments is central to social status in ancient Egypt. Hermann's study of 18th Dynasty funerary stelae (1940) attempted to prove that it was the content of the stelae, that is, the inclusion of a representation of a deity, which correlated with the status of the individual (Hermann 1940: 45-48). Deities had first appeared on funerary and Abydene votive/commemorative stelae in the Middle Kingdom (Klebs 1915; Evers 1929: 74-84; Müller 1933: 196-199; Hermann 1940: 50-53; Pflüger 1947; Peterson 1965-1966; Malaise 1984). Their appearance has traditionally been interpreted as representing a democratisation of religion, or the afterlife (Malaise 1984: 416; Quirke 1992: 155 ff.; Assmann 2001: 231 ff.), and indicating a functional change of the funerary stelae from memorials of the deceased to indicators of worship of the divine (Malaise 1984: 416). Using funerary and votive stelae from the Old Kingdom to the Third Intermediate Period, Podemann Sørensen (1989b: 109-125) traces an increase in defined types of divine access, or ritual participation, which demonstrate religious status. During the Old Kingdom, royal and religious status were one and the same; by the Middle Kingdom, religious status, or divine access, had become a separate phenomenon that could be acquired by private individuals through rank or profession (Podemann Sørensen 1989b: 117), and displayed on votive monuments. It has long been recognised that, in ancient Egypt, as in comparable ancient societies, religious activity cannot be separated from secular social activity (see for example, Baines 1987; Carless Hulin 1989; Morris 1992: 16; Stevens 2003: 168). Finnestadt has argued that religion is integrated into culture at all social levels 'and differentiated according to these' (1989a: 73). Votive stelae, though outwardly religious in function and intent, also record social status within the constraints of the genre (Simpson 1982: 266-271; Baines 2002: 4).

In relation to expressions of individual identity, Wiebach (1981: 160; 163) argues, after Hermann (1940: 54), that the inclusion of wedjat-eyes on false doors (see also Fischer 1964: 40; 1968; 226; 1976: 46) indicates that the deceased was regarded as immanent within the monument, and that the false door 'condenses and concentrates the personality of the deceased forever' (2001: 499). Vandier noted that 'les stèles égyptiennes sont, avant tout, des marques de propriété, qui précisent la personnalité du mort, et dans lesquelles l'esprit de généralisation n'a aucun rôle à jouer' (1952: 724). Both the multiple functionality (Frankfort 1948: 4; Wiebach 1981: 68) of such monuments, and the concept of the false door or funerary stela as representative of the identity of an individual extend to the later votive, or commemorative, stelae of the Middle and New Kingdoms.

That funerary stelae and false doors may have been partially designed according to the personal taste of the owner has been suggested in relation to the varied style of Old Kingdom false doors from Giza (Hassan 1944: 81) and the non-standard content of their offering lists (Hassan 1933-1934: 124). These false doors manifest an interaction of royal favour, which granted the use of a false door, and elements of personal choice in their design. Reisner (1936: 306) suggests that such a combination may be the reason for the inclusion, or not, of the palace façade decoration in 3rd and 4th Dynasty tombs. Strudwick (1985: 19) argues that the expression of individuality, and of social status, on the false doors is the stimulus for variants in the panel scene, where family or sculptural traditions introduce unusual poses, or include the tomb owner's wife as a mark of special affection (Malaise 1977: 193). Malaise attempted to discover whether the pose of the women on Middle Kingdom funerary stelae reflected their status. He identified (1977: 185) three positions that the women could take on the stelae: seated or standing, the man touching the woman; not touching; or facing (sometimes in separate compartments), which indicated degrees of emancipation. However, he concludes (1977: 188) that aesthetic values, rather than status related considerations, were the more likely influence on the final form, and that personal affection could influence the pose in which a woman was shown (1977: 193). Malaise also suggests that individuals could take centre stage on their monuments in a way that they did not in reality, thus presenting an alternate desired, or ideal, existence (1977: 189; compare Morris 1992: 165).

In the discussions of funerary architecture, false doors and funerary stelae, structural differences are related to social status and decoration is associated with personal choice or local tradition. However, in his study of First Intermediate Period funerary stelae from Naga ed-Deir, Dunham states that 'there seems to be no relation between the rank of the owner, as indicated by his titles, and the quality of the workmanship of his stela' (1937: 119). Returning to the same corpus of material for his PhD thesis, Brovarski (1989) demonstrated that, by accurately dating the stelae by means of both epigraphic and iconographic criteria (1989: 161 ff.), the apparent inconsistency of rank and quality can be related to the prevailing political situation and not to personal choice or disregard for quality. It seems that private monuments were at any one period created to the highest quality attainable dependent on available resources, not least access to court-trained craftsmen. Periods of political stability produced higher quality monuments (Brovarski 1989: 971-976). Freed states that 'private stelae from the reigns of Amenemhat I, Sesostris I, and Amenemhat II provide a rich illustration of the art historical creativity of the time and mirror its political changes' (1996: 334). The work of Brovarski and Freed demonstrates that, whilst personal choice cannot be ruled out in relation to the quality and style of a private stela, other factors are clearly influential on perceived variations.

Historical context or a single historical event may impact on New Kingdom votive/commemorative stelae in a more direct way. Schulman (1988: 4-5) has argued that at least two of the scenes found on New Kingdom votive stelae are representations of actual events: the royal smiting-scene and the giving of reward gold by the king. Schulman interprets the royal smiting-scene as follows: 'While [the smiting-scenes] obviously presented the timeless truth of the triumph of the king at all times over all of his foes, they must also have illustrated a specific act in a specific ceremony at a specific point in time' (1988: 47). He goes on to assert (1988: 194–196; see also 1980: 101-102) that many more popular scenes from the New Kingdom votive stelae repertoire could also be recordings of historical events - additional scenes which include a king, as his examples do, and scenes without a king. Schulman's work has been critiqued by Baines (1991; see also Müller-Wollermann 1988), who prefers to see the stelae as having a religious context or as works of art, or to combine these approaches, rather than as solely commemorative of historical events, an interpretation which he regards as reductive. Stelae are 'more complex works of art than Schulman would allow…they merge categories of time and space, and… in many cases one should not seek literal connections between text and picture' (1991: 92). The following chapters explore the notion that, whilst votive stelae are indeed complex works of art, merging 'categories of time and space', the motive for their creation, which may be a single event, may often be discerned by a careful reading of their iconography and associated social context.

It is useful at this point to look at approaches to epigraphic monuments in related disciplines in order to analyse and draw upon potentially relevant and applicable methodologies. Classical Studies presents an interesting comparison in the similarity, to a certain extent, of the inscribed data, and the difference in approach to, and interpretation of, the material. Egyptology and Classical Studies share a traditional divide between language scholars and archaeologists, which has led to a split between scholars focusing on linguistic analysis and those working with material culture, and a consequent lack of focus on the contextual information that may be discernible on inscribed monuments (Meskell 2002: 8). Morris (1992: 165) has observed that, for Archaic Greek material, the ritual context of burial monuments, such as stelae, or other inscribed markers, falls into the gap. Egyptian votive/commemorative stelae also fit this category.

Over the last 30 years, Classical scholars have begun to use inscribed private monuments as sources of information for social and economic histories (see, for example, Austin and Vidal-Naquet's *Economic and Social History of Ancient Greece: An Introduction*, first published in France in 1972). Both the writing of such histories for Egypt and the use of private epigraphic sources have been regarded as problematic by Egyptologists (Richards 2005: 18). Meskell (2002: 14) notes that there are numerous books creating an overarching social history of ancient Egypt, portraying daily life in taxonomic frameworks, with little focus on individual life experience and inequality. Social approaches have been largely nomothetic, focusing on classes or groups, such as women (Meskell 2002: 14). Such histories of Egypt draw on sources covering wide time periods and geographical areas to produce a homogeneous picture of Egypt that little reflects the duration and complexity of the civilization (but see Szpakowska 2008 for a gender- and period-specific social history of Middle Kingdom Lahun).

The reluctance to write histories of ancient Egypt other than the traditional 'ordering of kings and listing of their deeds' has been discussed by Häggman (2002: 3). Häggman's approach to the administration of Deir el-Medina attempts to use new historical methodologies, such as 'The New History', a 'total history' regarded as a deliberate reaction against traditional history with its political concerns - the state, war and the church (Burke 1991: 2), concerned with everyday life and human activity. It takes as central to our understanding of ancient society that social activities are not unchanging but are in fact cultural constructions subject to variation over time and space (Burke 1991: 3). The New History encompasses 'History From Below', a history written from the ordinary person's perspective of social change - Le Roy Ladurie's *Montaillou* (1975), a description of a medieval village in southern France in the 1300s, based on inquisition records, is the best known example of this kind of work - , and 'Microhistory', a historiographical practice focusing on small scale analysis of documentary material (Häggman 2002: 3-9). Häggman (2002: 3) cites *Ancient Egypt: a social history* (Trigger *et al* 1983) as one of the first examples of a 'new and less traditional' history of Egypt, though this volume is still reticent with regard to using all available sources. Introducing the chapter on the New Kingdom, O'Connor notes the mass of available data - settlements, temples, tombs - that reflect a wide range of socio-economic status and professions (p. 185). Despite the richness of the data, there are gaps, and he observes that 'the total complexity of Egyptian society and history cannot be appreciated without fully representative samples of all the types of archaeological data' (O'Connor in Trigger *et al* 1983: 185). He goes on to make a distinction between two types of textual data - archival material (papyrus and ostraca) and monumental texts (temple and tomb walls, and inscribed artefacts). He says:

> "The complementary character of the two main sets of textual data is vital for the reconstruction of Egyptian history. Despite frequent and useful inclusion of historical and biographical information, the fundamental purposes of most monumental texts are limited and religious. They are not concerned with the details of civil and religious government or of the ordering of social relationships (all of which are richly represented in papyri and ostraca). Addressed primarily to the gods, the monumental texts present a highly idealised version of Egyptian history and life." (O'Connor in Trigger *et al* 1983: 186)

Whilst the idealised nature of monumental texts cannot be denied (see Richards 2005: 19-25), in their very construction and expression they carry information on the society and individuals who created them. In ancient Egypt religion is politics: temples act as architectural expressions of the king's role as intermediary between the people and the gods, and the maintainer of Maat; private monuments create, recreate and reflect social structure and status, and living social networks of patronage and association (which equate to social organisation). Arguably, inscribed monuments are intimately linked to civil and religious government and the ordering of social relationships, albeit created within a strictly controlled set of conventions that may, to modern eyes, initially conceal more than they reveal. The controlled form and conventions of stelae and other monuments are in themselves an expression of the existing social structure (Morris 1987: 32-43), and these can form the object of a revealing study (Bodel 2001: 46). Egyptian private votive stelae inhabit a less official realm than that of the state temples, where fixed rules governed representation of the king and the gods to ensure the daily maintenance of Maat (Baines 1985: 277 ff.), yet they show remarkably little variation. In his study of New Kingdom votive stelae, Sadek (1987: 200-201) found only seven examples of people shown not raising their arms in the conventional 'adoring' posture. This suggests that rules of decorum governing two-dimensional representation were in operation, upheld by belief but also by social pressure (Meskell 1999: 178).

In his studies of Archaic Greek burials, Ian Morris (1987; 1992; 1994; 2000) treats private monuments as status related social artefacts, perhaps partly as a result of the lack of overt religious content. Such an approach has prompted an interpretation of the archaeology of the Greek and Roman world that emphasises the secular, that is, the economic, political and social. There is an absolute awareness of the methodological problems inherent in dealing with epigraphy and its often brief and formulaic manifestation: inscriptions (particularly epitaphs) are unrepresentative of society as a whole (Saller 2001: 100); such monuments will naturally present an ideal, due to their permanent nature, expense and the fact that they are public, if not always state, monuments (Bodel 2001: 46); and there is little or no information on the ritual or archaeological context (Morris 1992: 156). However, Saller (2001: 100) states that such caveats are true of almost all genres of evidence for the ancient world and should not deter historians from attempting to use this type of evidence to describe and analyse the broad characteristics of ancient society, characteristics such as social status, structure and organisation (see also Morris 1987). Bodel (2001: 5) comments that, as long ago as 1815, Barthold Georg Niebuhr stated that inscriptions were essential primary sources for studying ancient society. More importantly the onus is on archaeologists to interrogate the different types of texts, bearing in mind the significance of the monument as well as the message of the text.

Saller (2001) applies a broad social interpretation to brief and formulaic Roman epitaphs, and demonstrates that, if interrogated, they can provide a wealth of information on the structure of families and society in the ancient world. He states that '[t]he fact that ancient Greeks and Romans habitually chose to represent themselves and their social relationships to posterity through the medium of inscribed texts offers the social historian special opportunities…[I]nscriptions provide a range of evidence over space, time and social class that classical literature cannot match. As a result, epigraphy is especially valuable in helping the social historian to understand the margins of society (actually the majority) as defined by literate aristocratic men…' (2001: 117). An example of a social interpretation of private inscribed monuments can be found in the work of Ruth Leader (1997). Leader interprets Greek burial stelae from the 5th and 4th centuries BC as one of a range of visual constructions of gender. She rejects traditional approaches to stelae, wherein either the imagery is taken as expressing beliefs about death (the Christian influence) or where death and associated rituals are taken as a rite of passage (the influence of anthropology). Both of these approaches have led scholars to use funerary art to define the meaning of death (1997: 683). Leader states that, '[w]hile funerary art reveals a society's beliefs about the nature of death, many other social issues are raised by Athenian funerary monuments of the Classical Period' (1997: 683). Similarly, in studies of ancient Egyptian private votive monuments, the religious content has heavily influenced interpretations of the monuments.

Greg Woolf (1996) discusses the motives behind setting up a private inscribed monument in the Roman world, and the function of that monument within its own cultural and historical setting. For him, identity emerges as the primary function: 'No simple formula exists for explaining why inscriptions were set up, but the desire to fix an individual's place within history, society, and the cosmos provides a plausible psychological background to "the epigraphic impulse"' (1996: 29). The inscriptions were intended to defy change and entrench a particular view of the self, for that individual's lifetime and for posterity (see also Beard 1991). Monuments preserve identities in terms of qualities or virtues: conjugal affection, loyalty or patriotism; or personal achievements: embassies performed, military successes, magistracies or priesthoods held (1996: 32). The most obvious reason to set up a private monument is fear of oblivion, loss of the self (1996: 32), a common theme in ancient Egyptian thought. For example, in the Middle Kingdom story, 'A Dispute between a Man and his Ba' (Lichtheim 1975: 163-169), the Ba threatens to leave when the man longs for death, which would result in the man's annihilation. The Ba points out that if he stays with the man, 'Though you are dead, your name lives' (Lichtheim 1975: 165). In addition, Woolf (1996: 32) observes that the Roman world was one in which one's worth was publicly measured, that is, not by conscience or god. In ancient Egypt, tomb autobiographies record an individual's career achievements, reflecting what was regarded as a successful life. An individual could place himself within the cultural (and religious, social and sometimes political) tradition by means of the form of monument and form of the formula; the location and format act as a claim to authority by association, and an assertion of conformity within accepted norms: 'Epigraphy, with its highly formulaic presentation of social personae standardised yet at the same time individualised, offered a partial remedy to the problem of how to surpass and conform at the same time' (Woolf 1996: 32; see also Baines 2004).

Greek and Roman inscribed funerary monuments are directly related to identity and social position. This is also the case for Egyptian private votive stelae of the Ramesside Period, and perhaps also for the Middle Kingdom commemorative stelae, set within the context of political changes and royally sanctioned modifications to decorum. Government reforms are known from the ancient Greek world where their affect on funerary and votive monuments has been well documented, but scholars have not felt the need to link such changes to alterations in levels of religious feeling (Morris 1987: 50-51; 1994; Cannon 1989: 445). Approaching the private votive stelae of the Ramesside Period as social artefacts in the manner of Classical scholars allows an interpretation of the stelae that contextualises religious activity as a cultural and social phenomenon. Analysis of the conventions (decorum) and content can inform us of aspects of personal choice, social status and by extension social structure and organisation. Such a methodology, which takes the perspective of the individual in society, is a form of 'History from Below'. This does not mean that the information gleaned is too specific or parochial to be of use in a wider analysis of ancient society. As Sharpe notes, 'the history of the 'common people'...cannot be divorced from wider considerations of social structure and social power' (1991: 27).

1.2 Abydos in the Middle Kingdom

By the Middle Kingdom an independent stela had emerged that contained and represented the individual. The stelae are represented in their hundreds at Abydos (see, for example, Mariette 1880; Lange and Schäfer 1925). The Abydene Middle Kingdom stelae function as the prototype for the Ramesside votive/commemorative stelae and are the starting point for the discussion.

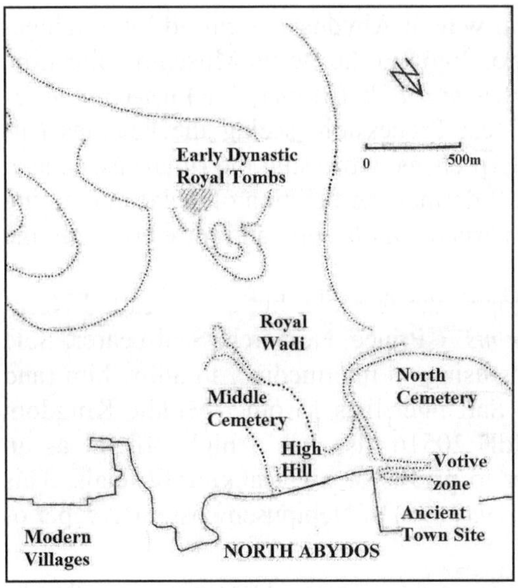

Figure 1.1 Plan of North Abydos (after Richards 2005: figure 6)

Ancient interest in Abydos stemmed from its function as the cult centre of first Khenty-imentyw and then Osiris, and the association of the living king with the dead Osiris, believed from the Middle Kingdom to be buried in a tomb of Djer on the Umm el-Qa'ab (Otto 1968; Richards 2005: 39). In the 19th century Abydos became one of the principal targets of treasure hunters such as Anastasi, d'Athanasi, Drovetti and Passalacqua (Leahy 1977: 9 and references; also, Simpson 1974: 5-6 and references), resulting in the loss of context for many of the stelae. In addition, during early scientific excavations, neither Mariette, nor his deputy, Gabet, were normally present during work at Abydos (Leahy 1977: 12), allowing less than precise records of artefact provenance to be kept.[1] Frankfort noted that the stelae he discovered 'were all found loose in the drift sand or re-used as paving stones in Late tombs but never in connection with the tomb for which they were intended' (1928: 235). Of note is the fact that Mariette recorded removing stelae that had been found leaning against the temple enclosure wall. Maspero, continuing the work, confirmed their location (Maspero 1916: 336-337; Simpson 1974: 10, n. 43). O'Connor believes that these stelae had in fact been reused, and were not free-standing votive stelae, as the enclosure wall post-dates the Middle Kingdom (O'Connor 1985: 166, n. 9; 167-168, n. 18). However, Ramesside Period votive stelae have been discovered leaning against temple enclosure walls at Wadi es-Sebua in Lower Nubia (Barsanti 1911) and Zawiyet Umm el-Rakham in the Western Desert (Snape and Wilson 2007). The work of Simpson (1974) and O'Connor (1985) as part of the Pennsylvania-Yale Archaeological Expedition to Abydos (1967-present) has demonstrated that hundreds of stelae from the site are commemorative, in that they represent an individual's visit, or stand in lieu of that person's actual presence. This has led to the question of who was erecting monuments at Abydos, that is, who had this very real 'divine access'. By extension, it may be possible to examine what controls, if any, there might have been on commemoration at Abydos, and how such controls may be detected.

Simpson (1974), taking up Müller's observation (1933: 193), that inscriptions and formulae relating to single individuals were spread across more than one Abydene stela, explored the concept of stelae groups associated with chapels ('cenotaphs') rather than tombs. He put together groups of stelae that may have come from single chapels, constructed in the area, 'outside of and abutting on the northern end of the western enclosure wall of the Osiris-Wepwawet precinct', referred to in the inscriptions as the *rwdw n nṯr ꜥ3* in the *wꜥrt ꜥ3t n hm-hmt* ('Terrace of the Great God' in the 'District Great of Renown' (?); Simpson 1974: 1-2). This area stands at one end of the processional way which extends along the wadi from the temple to the Umm el-Qa'ab (Leahy 1977: 267-285; 1989: 52-54; Wegner 2001: 9-10) and would have allowed actual or metaphorical viewing of the Osiris mysteries that took place along this route (Schäfer 1904; Satzinger 1969: 129; Leahy 1989). In the 1969 season, the Pennsylvania-Yale Expedition discovered a 12th Dynasty chapel/cenotaph with its stela still in place and no associated burial structure, though Simpson (1974: 9) suggested that a shaft may be located outside of the chapel. O'Connor (1985: 164 ff.) argued for the existence of such cenotaphs in the mud brick structures discovered below the Portal of Ramesses II in the same area as the Middle Kingdom stratigraphic level (Plate 1a). He states that 'the "cenotaphs" ... are not associated with burials' (1985: 170) - two test pits did not discover a burial shaft - and he believed the structures to be too crowded together to allow for burials.

The issue of access to commemoration close to the processional way at Abydos was raised by Satzinger (1969) in his publication of the early 12th Dynasty stela of Ipuy, no. 26/66 in the Berlin Museum collection. This stela contains the classic Abydos formula of *sn t3 n ḫnty-imntyw m prt ꜥ3t m33 nfrw* (*nw*) *wp-w3wt m prt tpt* (*in NN*) ('Kissing the ground for Khenty-Imentyw in the Great Procession, seeing the beauties (of) Wepwawet in the First Procession (by NN)'), which Satzinger interprets as witnessing the rituals associated with the Abydene gods (1969: 126; 129-130). Satzinger (1969: 127) defines the function of stelae containing this formula as representing their dedicators and allowing them to partake, *in absentia* and for eternity, in the rites.

On the Berlin stela it is not Ipuy, the dedicator, who is the actor in the formula, but a man called Nesu-montu who has the titles *iry-pꜥt ḥ3ty-ꜥ sḏ3wty-bity smr-wꜥty imy-r mšꜥ* ('Prince, Nomarch, Seal-bearer, Sole Friend, General'); Ipuy has the title *wḥmw* (='Courtier'), and he is using an intermediary to allow him (and his family, who are listed on the stela) to partake in the rituals. Satzinger lists 15 other Middle Kingdom stelae with the formula *m33 nfrw* (*nw*) *wp-w3wt*. Stela Cairo JdE 20516 also has a high official as an intermediary for a man of lower rank; the other 14 belong either to priests or high-ranking officials. This same formula occurs on the stela BM EA 101 (Porter and Moss V 1937: 96) of Nebipusenwosret ('Keeper of

[1] See Leahy 1977: 9-18; 255-285 for a summary of excavation work at Abydos to date, and a discussion of the topography of the site.

the Diadem and Henchman of the House'; Blackman 1935: 4), a resident of Memphis who had the stela (perhaps granted by royal favour?) sent from Thebes at the time of a royal festival (Blackman 1935: 5). The stela has a pair of wedjat-eyes inscribed centrally on it enabling Nebipusenwosret 'to witness the Osirian mysteries' (Blackman 1935: 7). The stela of Sankhptah (BM EA 833; Plate 1b), a chamberlain (*ỉmy-ḫnt*) in the reign of Rahotep (17th Dynasty) depicts the king as the intermediary, the earliest known example of the king in this role, in the ceremony of *mȝȝ nfrw* (*nw*) *wp-wȝwt* for the stela owner and his family (Clère 1982).[2] These Abydene stelae demonstrate the use of intermediaries of varying statuses to allow access to restricted rituals. They also demonstrate status by association with the intermediaries for the stelae dedicators.

Mediation, or patronage, on stelae can also take a different form. Leprohon (1978) discusses the individuals mentioned in Simpson's ANOC (Abydos North Offering Chapel) group 1, and disentangles a group of people linked, either through family or profession, to the Overseer of the Treasury (*ỉmy-r pr-ḥḏ*), Ikhernofret. He interprets Ikhernofret as generously allowing a man of lesser rank, Minhotep, to set up a stela for himself in his patron's chapel, and, in return, Minhotep dedicates the offering formula (*ḥtp-di-nsw*) to Ikhernofret. The pattern is repeated with a large group of other officials, as well as craftsmen (Leprohon 1978: 34). A similar situation occurs at Wadi es-Sebua in the 19th Dynasty (r. Ramesses II), where a group of soldiers dedicate stelae with the King's Son of Kush, Setau, as the beneficiary of the offering formula (Pamminger 1996: 296-297; Raedler 2003; see Chapter 5).

There are well-documented examples of sculptors adding their names to the stelae which they had produced for others (Miller 1937: 1-6; Leprohon 1978: 36; Snape 1986: 103-104). Craftsmen may have reduced the 'cost' of a stela if they were included (Leprohon 1978: 36, with examples; Snape 1986: 103). This raises the question of the status of craftsmen working, in this case, in the funerary industry at Abydos. Faulkner (1952) published the large, good quality stela of the master sculptor (*ỉmy-r gnwty*) Shen, and his family (Los Angeles County Museum A.5141.50-876; Porter and Moss 1937 V: 67), dating to the 12th Dynasty. According to the inscription, Shen was buried at Abydos despite probably having originally come from the 18th Upper Egyptian nome. His Abydene burial suggests that the profession of sculptor was regarded as fairly high status, granting him the privilege of burial at Abydos.

The second formula discussed by Satzinger, *sn tȝ n…*, occurs on two stelae whose owners do not have titles, suggesting a disparity in status requirements for the use of the two Abydene formulae (Satzinger 1969: 127-129). Satzinger (1969: 129) notes that there are many stelae of high ranking officials from Abydos that do not have this formula, and suggests that criteria other than titular rank, such as birth, profession or priestly office, may have allowed access to some of the Osiris mysteries.

In terms of control of physical access to the sacred areas at Abydos, stela Cairo JdE 35256 (Randall-McIver and Mace 1899-1901: 64, 84, 93, pl. XXIX) contains a royal edict protecting an area sacred to Wepwawet (Leahy 1989: 41). The edict is in the name of Neferhotep I, but Leahy (1989: 41; 46-49) has argued for the monument belonging to the reign of Khutawyre Ugaf, an earlier king of the 13th Dynasty. The edict states that anyone found within the protected area, which may be the wadi/processional way leading to the royal tombs (Leahy 1989: 52-54) or the North Cemetery area (Simpson cited in Snape 1986: 91), will be burnt (Leahy 1989: 43). Snape suggests that this stela is one example of a practice of policing the cemeteries at Abydos - a stela belonging to a Guardian of the Terrace of Abydos (*sȝw rwdw n Wsir*) was discovered by Garstang in tomb 316 A'07 (Snape 1986: 91). If this area is reserved for cenotaphs rather than burials, this title may relate to the issue of commemorative access to the Osiris rituals at Abydos. Less official commemoration is evident in the small, low-quality stelae from the subsidiary cenotaphs, indicating a very wide socio-economic diversity amongst the individuals dedicating monuments. These small stelae resemble ostraca, but are inscribed with the offering formula and were found *in situ* set up against the rear wall of a miniature cenotaph (O'Connor 1985: 175-177; Richards 2005: 39-42 and fig. 9).

The use of intermediaries and the inclusion of family and colleagues on stelae are phenomena related to divine access, and social status. Restricted official access to the Abydene cemeteries may have meant that the only way to be officially commemorated at Abydos, on a stela or in a chapel, was to include someone with 'Abydene status', such as a high-ranking official or a priest, on the stela (Leprohon 1978: 36). Some individuals, whether by rank or some other means, had more divine access than others and could mediate for less fortunate individuals; the inclusion of family and colleagues allowed them to share in this mediated

[2] The king, Rahotep, offers the *nmst*-vase to Osiris. Behind him stands the Chamberlain (*ỉmy-ḫnt*), Sankhptah, and the Lector-priest of the Funerary Workshop (*ḫry-ḥbt n pr-nfr*), Besi. The lower section of the stela, depicting Sankhptah's relatives, is in the Musée du Louvre (E. 6167, 10).

access and related social status. Leprohon's suggestion (1978: 36) that 'simple piety, the real desire of a truly devout people to see close friends share in one of the most important religious acts of their time' hints at the social complexity of ritual participation in ancient Egypt.

1.3 Summary

Egyptian stelae studies have focused on form and function, typological studies, structural evolution and dating of Early Dynastic to First Intermediate Period/Middle Kingdom funerary stelae and false doors. The Abydos Middle Kingdom votive/commemorative stelae are precursors of the votive stelae of the Ramesside Period, both in their commemorative function, and in aspects of their use. The stelae commemorate participation in the Abydos rituals and represent an individual in perpetuity at Abydos, publicly demonstrating a certain level of divine access in a restricted domain, both actual (the installation of a chapel or stela in a sacred area) and metaphorical (perpetual virtual participation in the rites). At Abydos, this divine access seems to have been granted either in full or via a higher-ranking intermediary, who could either participate in ceremonies on behalf of a lower ranking individual, and his family, and as such he is represented on the stela in the upper register, or allow such a person to set up their own stela in his chapel. Such chapels may be related to the use of similar structures, or temple precincts, by high-ranking individuals of the Ramesside Period, such as the construction of a Khenu-chapel at the front of the Hathor temple at Deir el-Medina by the Senior Scribe, Ramose (see Chapter 4), the activity of the Commander, Nebre, at Zawiyet Umm el-Rakham, and that of the King's Son of Kush, Setau, at Wadi es-Sebua in Lower Nubia (see Chapter 5).

Ramesside Period votive stelae are complex artefacts that function on multiple levels. Earlier interpretations have sought to define them as primarily religious artefacts indicative of increased religious feeling among a demographic group previously silent in the historical record. Such an interpretation is reductive and ignores the social background behind the creation of the stelae, and the social practices and conventions that are referenced by them. Drawing on the social approach of Classical scholars, the forthcoming discussion will demonstrate that the stelae use religious expression to articulate social concerns, such as status, identity and personal choice. Social status is embedded within these monuments in the form, content and location of the stela; the stelae owners' identity - or those aspects which they chose to exhibit - is preserved for all eternity on the stela. Personal choice may be discerned in this, and in the motives behind commissioning or making a stela. No two stelae are identical though the variations in design fall within a limited repertoire; however, it is in the limited and often deliberate variation that the tension between the individual and society is expressed. This can be interpreted as an example of Bourdieu's 'habitus' (1980: 88-91) - individual freedom acting within limits set by culture (Burke 1991: 18). The limited diversity makes it possible to begin the task of interpreting the social meaning of the stelae; the variations in design are the window through which the actions of the individual in the past can be viewed. Though deemed 'private,' (i.e. non-royal) these monuments exist in the public domain and reflect social and political changes. Analysis of the stelae and the light they throw on the royal policy of, for example, Ramesses II, demonstrates the validity of recent alternative historical methodologies such as 'History from Below'.

2. THE DEIR EL-MEDINA VOTIVE STELAE: DATA AND METHOD

The hundreds of votive stelae extant from Deir el-Medina form the primary dataset in this discussion. The large and fairly consistent group of stelae is contrasted with the smaller and more diverse group from the wider Theban area. Section 2.1 discusses the site of Deir el-Medina and the archaeological context of the stelae, Section 2.2 outlines the method used to assess the stelae, and Section 2.3 summarises the aims and method of the forthcoming investigation.

2.1 Deir el-Medina

> "Nestling in a small and secluded valley in the shadow of the Theban hills lie the remains of the New Kingdom settlement of Deir el-Medina. The 'Village', as it was known to its ancient occupants..." (Davies 1999: xviii).

Deir el-Medina is located on the West Bank at Thebes, between the Valley of the Kings and the Valley of the Queens, close to the Ramesseum and Medinet Habu, and well away from the cultivation. It was known to its inhabitants as the Village (*p3 dmi*) located in the Place of Truth (*m st m3ʿt*) (Černý 1973: 29-67; Ventura 1986: 38-63; Häggman 2002: 56). The settlement was established under Tuthmosis I, expanded during the 19th and 20th Dynasties, and deserted in the reign of Ramesses XI, perhaps due to civil unrest (Meskell 1998: 212-213; Häggman 2002: 57-59; 319-325).

The walled village is in the form of a trapezoid roughly $5,600m^2$, containing 68 houses separated by a road running the length of the village, with a gate at the north end (Porter and Moss 1964 I.2: plan XIII; McDowell 1999: 9-10). Houses were constructed of plastered mud brick on stone foundations. Each house consisted of a first room ('Room 1') with an 'enclosed bed' ('lit clos'; Bruyère 1934-1935 (1939) III: 54-64; Meskell 1998: 222; McDowell 1999: 11), a central room ('Room 2') with a 'divan' (Bruyère 1934-1935 (1939) III: 65-69; Meskell 1998: 229-233), and, in the back of the house, a group of smaller rooms and the kitchen space, with cellars beneath. The roof offered additional living space (McDowell 1999: 12 and fig. 3). Room 1 assemblages include stelae, anthropomorphic busts, offering tables and statues, leading Meskell (1998: 226, fig. 9) to conclude that the household cult took place in this room. Room 2 had a niche that probably held a stela (Bruyère 1934-1935 (1939) III: 193; Meskell 1998: 231). Archaeological evidence has shown that the *3ḫ iḳr n Rʿ* ('Excellent Spirit of Re') stelae, which demonstrate ancestor worship (Bruyère 1934-1935 (1939) III: 151-174; Demarée 1983; Schulman 1986; Sadek 1987: 77-79; McDowell 1992b: 106-107; 1999: 104-105; Friedman 1994: 111-117) were set up in Room 2, probably in these niches. Anthropomorphic busts, libation basins and offering tables have also been found in these rooms (Meskell 1998: 232-3). Houses of a different design lay outside the walled enclosure (McDowell 1999: 12).

The village is surrounded by its necropoleis. To the east lies the 18th Dynasty cemetery (Bruyère 1934-1935 (1937) II; Meskell 1999: 145-146; Andreu 2002: 22), which has a predominance of simple shaft tombs and a hierarchical layout, with children in the lower section, adolescents in the middle and adults in the top section. No superstructures remain (Meskell 1999: 145-146; Andreu 2002: 22). The Western cemetery (Bruyère 1922-1923 (1924); 1923-1924 (1925); 1924-1925 (1926); 1926 (1927); 1927 (1928); 1928 (1929); 1930 (1933); 1931-1932 (1934)) contains a small number of 18th Dynasty tombs but is predominantly 19th and 20th Dynasty in date. The majority of tombs have large single vaulted substructures, and, above the tomb chapel, superstructures consisting of a courtyard entered through a pylon and a pyramid, crowned with a pyramidion which held a lucarne-stela (McDowell 1999: 13-14, fig. 4; Andreu 2002: 30, fig. 12). Some tombs had rock cut chambers. The tomb chapels contained funerary stelae, both on the façade and within.

To the north-east of the village lies the Ptolemaic temple to Hathor (Du Bourguet 2002), and, beyond, the Great Pit (Bruyère 1945-1947 (1952); 1948-1951 (1953); McDowell 1999: fig 5; Andreu 2002: fig 3). The pit may be the result of an attempt by the community to dig down to the water table, but it was subsequently used as a rubbish dump (McDowell 1999: 18). Between 1949 and 1951, over 5,000 ostraca were excavated from the pit (Andreu 2002: 41), which provided the primary source of information on the purpose of the community, and the lives of the residents of Deir el-Medina in the Ramesside Period (Andreu 2002: 41): the translation of the ostraca allowed Jaroslav Černý to identify the fact that the village was the residence of the men who built and decorated the royal tombs, and their families (Černý 1929a; Bierbrier 1982a: 144; Ventura 1986: 40; Meskell 1998: 212). Early excavations (see Andreu 2002: 36-39) were directed by

Bernadino Drovetti from 1811 to 1815 and the material found at this time forms the basis of the collection of the Museo Egizio, Turin (Bierbrier 1982a: 127; 132). Turin's collections were further enhanced by the work of Ernesto Schiaparelli from 1905 (Bierbrier 1982a: 140), one of whose major finds was the intact tomb of Kha and Meryt. Emile Baraize excavated the Ptolemaic temple to Hathor from 1909 to 1912 (Baraize 1913), and, in 1917, the concession was given to the French Institute (Institut Français d'Archéologie Orientale (IFAO)), and the work directed by Bernard Bruyère from 1922-1940 and 1945-1951 (Bierbrier 1982a: 141; Andreu 2002: 39-41; Häggman 2002: 1). He described the site as a 'véritable champ de bataille' (quoted in Andreu 2002: 36) due to its disturbed nature. Bruyère published his work in a series of *Rapports* (1924-1953) which form the basis of any study of the site to this day. More recent work has included a reassessment of the archaeology of the village itself by Valbelle and Bonnet (1975) for the IFAO. The authors summarise excavation work at Deir el-Medina and critique Bruyère's conclusions on the chronology and layout of the village as oversimplified, proceeding to re-examine the evidence for the 18th Dynasty village.

The Ptolemaic temple to Hathor stands on the site of a temple constructed by Ramesses II replacing an earlier 18th Dynasty shrine (Bruyère 1935-40 (1948); Sadek 1987: 60; McDowell 1999: 14). Very little remains of either of the New Kingdom structures, with reliefs and inscriptions extant only from the associated chapel attached to the front of the temple (Kitchen 1996: 465). One of these inscriptions describes the chapel as the 'Khenu of Ramesses II' (*ẖnw n* (*Rˁ-ms-sw mry-Ỉmn*); Bruyère 1935-1940 (1948): 216; Sadek 1987: 60). Mud brick chapels dating to the Ramesside Period are located in and around the Hathor temple. Of the 32 chapels identified by Bruyère (1929 (1930a)), Bomann dismisses three as tombs or domestic structures (Bomann 1991: 40). She divides the remaining 29 into five groups: 14 located west and south-west of the main temple, one north-east of the village enclosure wall, five within the enclosure wall of the main temple (Plate 2a), two east of the temple's enclosure wall and seven north of the temple's enclosure wall (Bomann 1991: 40-51, fig. 25; see also Bruyère 1929 (1930a), pls. I, IV, V; Sadek 1987: 83-84). The plan of the chapels generally follows the standard Egyptian temple/chapel model: an open court, one or two covered halls and an inner sanctuary, laid along a straight axis. The majority of the sanctuaries have a triple shrine along their rear wall (McDowell 1999: 15).

When working in the Valley of the Kings, the workmen seem to have spent the working week sleeping in a series of small huts located above the Valley, perhaps to avoid the long walk there and back daily (Andreu 2002: 35). A chapel attributed to Amun 'of the Happy Encounter' (*n ṯḥn*(*i*) *nfr*) is built up against the rock face here (McDowell 1999: 17). In addition, along the path to the Valley of the Queens lies a sanctuary traditionally described as being dedicated to Ptah and Mertseger, consisting of seven natural and man-made grottos (Plate 2b), containing stelae of the workmen and their superiors (Bruyère 1930b; McDowell 1999: 17). Vernus (2000) has tentatively identified a further sanctuary at the western end of the Valley of the Queens, mentioned on a stela of the Workman, Qenhirkhopshef (iv)[1] (BM 278 = DB196 in this catalogue) by the toponym *mnt*, dedicated to Hathor.[2]

Approaches to Deir el-Medina

Bruyère's excavation reports (1924-1953) and Černý's *A Community of Workmen at Thebes in the Ramesside Period* (1973), the latter aptly described by Davies (1999: xx) as 'seminal', have been the starting point for numerous studies of the community and its surroundings, covering administration, economy, religion, social life, prosopography, Theban topography, law, women, kinship, language, palaeography and literacy.[3]

The site of Deir el-Medina has been the focus of Egyptological attention since the mid 20th century for a number of reasons: it is one of the few extant settlement sites from ancient Egypt; it has produced a wealth of written documents in the form of ostraca and papyri; and it is the source for hundreds of private monuments,

[1] Throughout, Davies' (1999) numbering system for individuals from Deir el-Medina has been used.
[2] See Porter and Moss I.2 1964: plan III for the layout of the site.
[3] At date of publication, a systematic bibliography of Deir el-Medina can be found at http://www.leidenuniv.nl/nino/dmd/dmd.html. Also relevant is Deir el-Medina online which can be accessed from the University of Munich's webpages at http://obelix.arf.fak12.uni-muenchen.de/cgi-bin/mmcgi2mmhob/mho-1/hobmain.

particularly stelae, which have formed the primary corpus for the study of the phenomenon known as 'personal piety'. This is one of the few sites that provides an insight into the daily lives of the non-elite, and into the workings of local administration, law and religious beliefs (Davies 1999: xxii). By extension, the data from the village can reveal social structure and organisation within the community, and in the outside world.

However, the fact that the Deir el-Medina community was inhabited by specialist royal craftsmen has led to the criticism that, as a community, it was atypical and cannot be said to reflect life in ancient Egypt, though this is often how it is used. However, Meskell (1994: 193; 212) argues that, due to its prolonged occupation and thus differentiated population, Deir el-Medina can be used as a valid case study for social life in Egypt, and it is as such that it is used in this discussion. One of the most anomalous aspects of the village is the high rate of literacy. Baines and Eyre (1983: 65-72) suggest that, during the Old Kingdom, less than 1% of the Egyptian population was literate. In contrast, the New Kingdom inhabitants of Deir el-Medina appear highly literate, but the precise level of literacy has provoked debate. One school of thought argues that only those required to read and write, in order to carry out their duties, were literate, that is, no more than 25-30% of the villagers and associated workers (the *smdt* - the water carriers, washermen and so forth who serviced the community and lived outside the walled village) (Baines and Eyre 1983: 90). The other suggests that literacy was much higher, and included the majority of the workmen and some of the women (Janssen 1992; Lesko 1994: 135). Janssen (1992: 86; 89) argues that a high level of literacy is apparent in the high percentage of literary ostraca which would have required both writers and readers, and the notes written by workmen to their wives. Lesko (1994: 134-135) suggests that such evidence may not be proof that Deir el-Medina is anomalous as an example of settlement and society in ancient Egypt, rather that the same quantity of written documents has not survived at other settlement sites, though this is a difficult claim to substantiate.

The data from Deir el-Medina can connect us, at least partially, with the lives of individuals, whose biographies are populated by the extant inscribed monuments, letters, administrative references and graffiti. Janssen (1982) describes the characters of two inhabitants of Deir el-Medina, which he has reconstructed from a number of documents: a workman called Hesysunebef who was active under Seti I and Siptah in the early 19th Dynasty, and Merysekhmet (iii), active in the mid-20th Dynasty. In addition, the Foreman, Paneb (i), is well known to us as a result of Papyrus Salt 124 (BM EA 10055; Černý 1929b) where the alleged misappropriation of his post is detailed (Bierbrier 2000). These glimpses into the activities and careers of individuals constitute no more than 'brief vignettes' but 'can often be exploited as a unique source for the study of human beliefs and attitudes in an ancient settlement' (Davies 1999: xxii-xxiii). Zivie (1979: 125) sounds a note of caution against assuming that such data constitutes an individual's life: '[q]uoi qu'on en dise, la personnalité précise et la vie des ouvriers de Deir el-Médineh ne sont pas des mieux connues, ou du moins ne peuvent pas être bien connues que lue la masse de la documentation le laisserait d'abord croire'.

Meskell has attempted to discover evidence for the individual and for agency/personal choice in the Deir el-Medina mortuary and domestic data (1994; 1998; 2000; 2002). Her approach can be contextualised as 'History from Below', where the perception and study of social strata within one settlement site is a result of the focus of archaeology 'upon the lives of ordinary people…rather than those of an élite minority' (Meskell 1994: 195). Meskell herself chooses to situate her work within the theoretical models of anthropological, gender and social studies of the 19th and 20th centuries (Meskell 2002), as she attempts to reveal the lives 'of the silent majority, namely the middle and lower classes, women, children, slaves and foreigners' with an 'holistic' approach to text and data (Meskell 1994: 195). Meskell's theories of individuality and gender mapping are laid out in *Archaeologies of Social Life* (1999), expanding on her statement that 'it is possible to identify how specific individuals and groups functioned with[in] a domestic context, taking into account the complex vectors of social inequality - age, sex, class, status, and life experience' (Meskell 1998: 209). However, the data has not substantiated the theory (Morris 2002: 264-265; see also, Babić 2005: 76), and Meskell's studies have identified groups or roles of a more traditional nature, such as defining male and female domestic activity and space (1998), rather than individuals at the level of definition she suggests may be possible (1998: 139-241).

Moving beyond the individual to social groups, some studies of the villagers of Deir el-Medina have treated the community as a single social unit (Meskell 1999: 141). McDowell (1999: 7) notes that the Deir el-Medina workmen were initially regarded by scholars as lower class, but recent studies have shown that 'the workmen were well-off by Egyptian standards', and that, 'the officials of the gang [were] in the top 2 per cent of the population...on the basis of economic status...the social strata at Deir el-Medina ranged from the upper middle to the lower middle class'.

The formal hierarchy of the Gang was as follows: the royal workmen were overseen by two foremen (*ʿ3 n iswt*/*ḥry iswt*), one for the right side and one for the left side (Meskell 1994: 202), and a senior scribe (*sš n p3 ḫr*). These men were known collectively as the chiefs of the gang (*ḥwtyw n p3 ḫr*) (Černý 1973: 231). The senior scribe reported directly to the vizier (Černý 1973: 114-116; Bierbrier 1982: 29; Ventura 1986: 98-103; Davies 1999: xix; McDowell 1999: 6-7; Häggman 2002: 116-130; 176-178; 231-248). The gang itself included chief craftsmen (*ḥry ḥmww*), (chief) draughtsmen ((*ḥry*) *sš ḳdw*), sculptors (*ḳstyw*), guardians (*s3wty-s3w*) and doorkeepers (*iry-ʿ3*) (Černý 1973: 149-174). On monuments the title *sš*, scribe, is often a shortened form of *sš ḳd*, draughtsman. Scribes were also attached to the *smdt*, the external support staff who serviced the Village. The workmen acted as lay priests and on monuments could take the titles wab-priest (*wʿb*), servitor (*b3k*) and god's servant (*ḥm-nṯr*). They were represented by their deputy (*idnw*), who may have been elected from amongst them and served as their representative (Černý 1973: 147; Bierbrier 1982: 37; Lesko, B. 1994: 20).[4]

Janssen (1975: 536) identifies three 'classes': the upper class of chiefs and scribes, the middle class of ordinary workmen, and the *smdt*. Ward (1994: 168, n. 23) defines a separate stratification, that of function, with the administrators (the foremen and senior scribe) as the most important, and the workmen as the least, that is, the most easily replaced. In between were the specialists: artists, physicians, priests.

Status differentiation within an ancient community can be articulated and identified in a number of ways, for example, according to wages, private monuments and personal influence - 'wages' here has the sense of rations or dues. Economic studies have identified the different amounts paid to the workmen, the highest wages going to the two foremen (Janssen 1975: 455 ff.; Lesko, B. 1994: 20; McDowell 1999: 231-233). The senior scribe is included as one of the chiefs of the gang but his income is surprisingly low. It has been suggested that either the figures indicate the payment from only half of the gang, so must be doubled (Ventura 1986: 72), or that the senior scribe made up his income from extensive private commissions (Lesko, B. 1994: 21). The deputy of the gang is differentiated from the workmen by his title but not by his income.

House and tomb size, and other personal material wealth, have been correlated with the prestige of the individual and family, and thought to act as symbols of status (Crocker 1985: 52; Kemp 1991: 298; 301; McDowell 1999: 7; Babić 2005: 69-70; Richards 2005: 16). Sennedjem (i) and his son Khabekhenet (i), both owners of richly decorated tombs, owned large houses in the south-west corner of the village (Meskell 1994: 203, fig. 6). The Foremen of the Gang, Paneb (i), Anhurkhawy (ii), and Qaha (i), have impressively large tombs (respectively, TT5, TT359, TT360; Bruyère 1923-1924 (1925): 60; 1930 (1933): 33ff.; 71ff.). It may be true that in some, or perhaps most, cases, there was a direct correlation between social status and material wealth, but the material record can be biased by a number of ancient and modern factors. Ancient factors include active manipulation of the funerary record to award an individual a higher status in death than they had in life (Malaise 1977: 189; Meskell 1999: 129; 177; Bierbrier 1982: 60; Morris 1992: 165; Baines 2002: 4-5), and fashion and personal choice influencing the richness of a burial (Cannon 1989). Modern factors include current theoretical thinking which can bias our interpretation of the data (Morris 1987: 9-10; 212-216), and the accident of preservation (Morris 1987: 97 ff.). Lesko (B.) notes that '[t]he monuments - tombs, statues and stelae - left by the village families vary considerably in size and refinement and some individuals known from the ostraca seem not to have left so much as a stela behind them' (1994: 23).

Social status may have been expressed through the holding of religious titles, an example of Ward's functional status (1994), or through veneration of gods with restricted cults. Both of these are forms of divine access and can indicate an individual's social status. Certain leading families, those holding the posts of foremen and scribes (Černý 1973: 126; 146; 223; Janssen 1992: 84), held the monopoly on admission to the lay priesthood of Amenhotep I (Lesko, B. 1994: 23; see Chapter 3). The majority of women who cited a religious rank alongside their names were married to either scribes or foremen (Lesko, B. 1994: 25). Bruyère (1923-1924 (1925): 21) proposes that a number of foremen had a special devotion to the cataract divinities.

---

[4] There have been many detailed studies of the organisation of the workforce at Deir el-Medina. For a general overview of life in the village and aspects of its organisation, see Della Monica (1975), Bierbrier (1982), Valbelle (1985), Gutgesell (1989), Lesko (1994) and McDowell (1999). For more detailed studies of organisation, titles, roles and individuals, see Černý (1973), Ventura (1986), Davies (1999) and Häggman (2002). For information on individual titles, see Bogolovsky (1980) and Janssen (1997).

All the foremen known to him represent Khnum, Anukis and Satis in their tomb chapels. He suggests that this was either because these men had overseen workshops at Aswan creating monuments for Ramesses II, or that Khnum was venerated as a southern version of the creator god, and patron of craftsmen, Ptah.

The hundreds of votive stelae that have come from Deir el-Medina (see, for example, *Hieroglyphic Texts from Egyptian Stelae etc. in the British Museum*, vols. V-XII, 1914-1993; Tosi and Roccati 1972) have prompted numerous studies of popular religion and personal piety at Deir el-Medina. Sadek's analysis of popular religion (1987) dedicates two chapters (V and VI) to Deir el-Medina, the site which provides the majority of evidence for local cults at this period. His emphasis is on the identification of the deities worshipped in the chapels located in and around the village of Deir el-Medina, rather than the individuals involved in the ritual activity and depicted on the stelae. Typical articles by Clère (1975), and Bierbrier and de Meulenaere (1984), use the votive stelae in question to discuss the genealogy of the owner, the other known monuments of the individual, and, briefly, the aspect of religion demonstrated. The underlying concern is with the identification of the individual within the Deir el-Medina community, and their expression of piety. Davies quotes Frandsen as saying, 'it was becoming increasingly clear that it is high time that more extensive studies were undertaken of the so-called religious texts as well, in that without material bearing upon the religious dimension, our understanding of Deir el-Medina will inevitably remain rather imperfect' (Davies 1999: xxi, n. 19, from Frandsen 1992: 48-49). Although generally accepted as a Ramesside phenomenon, the motives and the rules governing the expression of 'personal piety', and its social context by individuals in the Ramesside Period remain largely unexplored (Vernus 2000: 331).

The perceived generic nature of the representations and texts on votive stelae has dissuaded scholars from attempting to glean any additional information from them, though in a limited number of cases a non-standard element of the text or iconography allows a motive to be discerned for erecting a stela. For example, a group of stelae contain the phrase 'seeing darkness' (*m33 kkw*), which has been interpreted in a number of ways: as referring to actual blindness or blurred vision, inflicted as divine punishment (Rowe 1940-1941: 47-48; Pinch 1993: 257); indicating a loss of contact with the deity, that is a spiritual blindness, whilst the dedicator is alive (Pinch 1993: 257); or, metaphorically, as meaning the dedicator, when dead, cannot see the deity (Galan 1999: 20-21). Stelae texts using this phrase belong to a category of texts where a dedicator seeks forgiveness from the deity. The stela of the Workman, Neferabu (i) (Turin 50058 = DB115), is the best-known example, where he says 'I made a transgression' (*iw.i ḥr irt p3 sp*) against the Peak (=Mertseger). Demarée (1982) proposes a secondary practical reason for erecting a stela. The document O. Petrie 21 (= Hier. Ostr. 16, 4) is the text of a dispute where a man has installed a stela in a building in a wrongful claim of ownership. In this case, the content of the stela is only relevant in that it functioned as the representation of an individual, a routine version of the function of Middle Kingdom Abydene stelae which actively represent individuals at the rituals of Osiris. The owner of the stela was deemed present in the building by means of his stela - it acts as a kind of legal claim to ownership.

Additional events, or motivations, other than the seeking of forgiveness, or the use of a stela to establish ownership, as motives for setting up a stela have received little attention, despite the fact that a number of stelae depict statues of deceased kings that have been linked to the processions associated with the Beautiful Festival of the Valley (Redford 1986: 52; McDowell 1992b: 100; 103; see Chapter 4). Festival attendance at one of the great state festivals may well have been an event worthy of commemoration on a stela (Cabrol 2001: 761; see also Kessler 1999: 176-178; 184-185; Morgan 2004: 53-54), especially given that such attendance was marked in tombs (Cabrol 2001: 608-616). Schulman's arguments (1988: 194-197) for the historical nature of stelae are relevant here, where it may be the case that stelae were erected to mark significant events in an individual's life.

In addition to individual events, the prevailing political situation may have influenced stelae production. Votive stelae are generally regarded as a Ramesside Period phenomenon, but it may be the case that they were produced in greater numbers at certain periods throughout the Ramesside Period, rather than being typical of the period as a whole, and that their production can be related to royal activity.

2.2 Developing a method of analysis

Stelae from Deir el-Medina are held in museum collections throughout the world, with only a handful remaining *in situ* (for example, Bruyère 1930b: 14-18, fig. 10; see Plate 7). Early non-scientific 'excavation' at the site allowed hundreds of the stelae to be removed without record of their provenance (Andreu 2002:

36). Stelae were also removed from their original context in antiquity: a large number of stelae and other monuments were cleared from the area of the New Kingdom temple to allow for the construction of the Ptolemaic temple (Bruyère 1948-1951 (1953): 20-21). Identification of Deir el-Medina stelae is facilitated by the similarity in their representational content, and by the identification of names and titles of many of the individuals who lived and worked at Deir el-Medina (see, for example, Černý 1973; Bierbrier 1975; Bogoslovsky 1980; Davies 1999), thus making stelae provenance and attribution relatively secure. In addition, the use of the epithet *m st m3ʿt* ('in the Place of Truth') after titles, referring to the necropolis area in which the men worked (Černý 1973: 29-67; Ventura 1986: 48ff.; Häggman 2002: 56-57), aids the attribution of the stelae to Deir el-Medina individuals.

The discussion in this book is based on a dataset of 436 stelae from five sites: Deir el-Medina, the wider Theban area, Abu Simbel and Wadi es-Sebua in Lower Nubia, Qantir/Pi-Ramesses in the Delta and Zawiyet Umm el-Rakham in the Western Desert. 319 of the stelae come from the Theban area, and of these 264 have been provenanced to Deir el-Medina.[5] The criteria for the inclusion of a stela are that it is private (non-royal), retains the title of the owner, an indication at least of who the deity is, and that it is possible to distinguish the representation of the individual in relation to the deity on the stela. The *3ḫ iḳr n Rʿ* stelae are not included, as they do not, as a rule, contain an individual's titles, and do not express devotion to a deity, but rather ancestor worship (Demarée 1983: 288). Hundreds of stelae and stelae fragments that do not retain the necessary information have been excluded. There are in addition stelae in museum collections that remain too briefly published, unpublished, or as yet unidentified as Deir el-Medina stelae. Ongoing publications (for example, Martin 2005) are rectifying this situation, but it has not been possible to include all such stelae. The decision to use only clearly published or accessible stelae retaining the relevant criteria reduces the sample size considerably, and for this reason it is acknowledged that the sample may not be fully representative.[6] However, the dataset is large enough to produce representative results, and the use of fully or almost fully preserved examples increases the accuracy of the analysis.

The emphasis in cataloguing of the stelae was to record as much intrinsic and extrinsic information as possible to allow a varied and evolving approach to the data. The stelae data from Deir el-Medina and the comparative sites were input into a flat field Microsoft Access database that is suitable for text based searches and quantitative analysis. An edited version of the database for reference can be found in Appendix 1, where the stelae are listed by site and arranged chronologically and, within the time periods, alphabetically according to the principal dedicator. The stelae are numbered consecutively 1-436, and are prefixed in the text by DB (=database). Henceforth all stelae from the dataset will be referred to by their database number; repository/site numbers and primary publication references can be found in the tables in Appendix 1.

One of the principal aims of this study was to establish whether aspects of the design and content of a stela were related to the social status of the dedicator. The criteria chosen as possible expressions of social status were:

1. The 'compositional form' of the scene;
2. The cult image (hypostasis) depicted;
3. The original location of the stela.

The term 'compositional form' has been coined to describe the representational relationship of the dedicator to the deity. There are three basic variants: the dedicator stands directly in front of the deity (type A; see, for example, Plate 10); the dedicator uses a higher-ranking intermediary (type B; see, for example, Plate 5b); or the dedicator is depicted in the lower register (type C; see for example, Plate 6). Types A and C may simply be aesthetic variations, though some of the patterning in use that emerges suggests that the type C stelae, defined as indirect access to the deity hypostasis, relate to a more formal or traditional use of iconographic representation; as a result these two groups have been maintained. Sadek (1987: 201) has argued that the lower part of the stela, which in Egyptian representational terms is spatially further from the deity, is reserved for the less important people, which may be the case when a group of individuals is depicted, and is certainly validated on stelae depicting individuals of a variety of ranks. Compositional form, or the two-dimensional depiction of the relationship of the dedicator and the deity, is influenced by a number of factors, not least decorum. Rules of decorum are different for individuals of different status, for example, the king

[5] Many more stelae that may be from Deir el-Medina are coming to light in the ongoing Porter and Moss VIII publication of unprovenanced stelae.

[6] Notable exclusions include the following stelae held in the Cairo Museum, which I have been unable to view: JdE nos. 2020, 27785, 36347, 36349, 36671, 36716, 36717, 36718, 36913; Temporary nos. 3.3.25.1, 19.6.24.2, 30.1.15.13.

has full divine access; in the Ramesside Period, private individuals gain similar privileges on their own monuments (Podemann Sørensen 1989a; 1989b; Finnestadt 1989b; Baines 1983: 591; Quirke 1992: 135-138; Pinch 1993: 349; Frood 2003: 74-75).

The term 'intermediary' in the context of Egyptian religion denotes 'the individual mediating between god and man' (te Velde 1982: col. 161). In terms of official religion and society, the king is the intermediary between the gods and the rest of society (Radwan 1969: 41; te Velde 1982: col. 162; Myśliwiec 1985: 11). Other forms of intermediaries are the manifestations of deities in intermediary forms, often zoomorphic, for example, the Mnevis Bull of Re, or, less officially, Amun-Re as the Good Goose (*smn nfr*). Such intermediaries have been regarded as more approachable versions of the deity, and are objects of veneration themselves (Sadek 1987: 85; Baines 1991: 197; Pinch 1993: 183). Statues of private individuals can also act as intermediaries. In this discussion the term 'intermediary' refers to the first definition, a god, king or higher ranking individual depicted on a stela participating in cult activity on behalf of a lower ranking individual (Pinch 1993: 95). Podemann Sørensen (1989b: 120) argues that typically 18th Dynasty stelae with royal intermediaries maintain the concept of the king as the *nb ỉrt ỉḫt*, 'Lord of Rites', 'who alone could officiate in temple ritual and confront the gods'. In the Ramesside Period an individual could be shown on stelae face to face with the god (type A), as a result of both changes in decorum and the related process which Podemann Sørensen terms 'secularisation', where private individuals use royal prerogatives which have, over time, become detached from royal status (1989b: 123).

However, if direct divine access was permissible and desirable by the Ramesside Period, what was the purpose of using an intermediary? There are three possible interpretations of the use of intermediaries on private votive stelae at this period:

1. An intermediary allowed an individual representational access to a restricted divinity or sacred space from which they would have been normally excluded (Baines 1985: 277-286; Podemann Sørensen 1989b: 120; Pinch 1993: 349). This has been documented at Abydos in the Middle Kingdom (Satzinger 1969; Simpson 1974; Clère 1982);
2. The depiction of an intermediary may indicate that the stela records an actual cult ceremony (Schulman 1988: 42; Pinch 1993: 95);
3. In both cases, the intermediaries represented by the dedicator may indicate a relationship with a higher ranking individual, and, as a result, reflect or elevate the dedicator's social status. In addition, the intermediary chosen may share in the spiritual and economic benefit from the stela.

An institution such as the Amun-Re temple at Karnak, a state temple representing and promulgating the role of the king as central to society, will have exerted a powerful influence on the form private monuments took in relation to their proximity to the temple proper. No stelae depicting private individuals interacting directly with the god could have been erected in close proximity to the Amun-Re temple. Stelae where the king acted as intermediary would have been acceptable, as these demonstrated the accepted ideological role of the king as intermediary between the people and the gods. A high-ranking individual may have dedicated such a stela in close proximity to a state temple, displaying his own relationship to the king and perhaps recording a ceremony at which the dedicator was present.

The display of access to deities by individuals of the social status of the Deir el-Medina workmen, the aspirational middle class, was not part of the traditional ideology, and may have been an iconographic innovation reflecting a Ramesside Period loosening of decorum. The innovative quality of such stelae may not have been so readily acceptable to high-ranking individuals, who may have preferred to continue to display the concept of the king alone having direct access to the gods. It is simplistic to assume that there is a direct link between represented direct divine access (type A) on private monuments, and high social status, or that such stelae represent increased divine access as a linear chronological evolution. 'Compositional form' may also have been influenced by aesthetic considerations, the location in which the stela was set up, and the type of cult activity or icon depicted.

The cult images depicted on stelae represent actual hypostases, ranging from temple reliefs and statues to votive statuettes and sacred animals (Pinch 1993: 94-95, 98). Cabrol (2001: 723) notes that at Memphis a number of stelae depicting the royal smiting-scene were found at the entrance to the Ptah temple and she interprets the stelae as a direct copy of the temple pylon scene (*contra* Schulman 1988; 1994; see Chapters 4 and 5). The phenomenon of temple decoration influencing the representation of popular cult activity is evident throughout the dataset. Much of Schulman's work has centred on the premise that stelae depict historical events (1980; 1981; 1984a; 1985; 1988; 1994). He has attempted to construct a methodology for identifying which cult statue might be depicted, focusing on the cults of Ptah (1981) and Reshep (1981;

1985). He concludes (1981: 164) that a particular cult statue can be more easily identified by epithets, much as Habachi had done for the four cult statues of Ramesses II at Qantir (Habachi 1954; see also Pinch 1993: 98; see Chapter 4), than iconography, which may be vulnerable to the personal idiosyncrasies of the sculptor carving the representation. Schulman states, '[t]hus it is clear that the variety of general statue types does not automatically imply that each type or variation within it represents a distinct cult statue of the god' (1981: 164; see also 1985: 92). However, when the iconography is very specific it may aid the identification (Schulman 1985: 95-96). As for the use of epithets, Schulman dismisses as too generic those that are too frequent and accompany more than one form of the cult statue (1981: 165-166), though ess common epithets can be of use in the identification process.

The *Lexikon der ägyptischen Götter und Götterbezeichnungen* (Leitz 2002-2003) has been used to match temple images with the same epithets as representations of deity hypostases on stelae. If the temple image was of a contemporaneous date and may have been accessible at the time, it has been included in the discussion as a possible source for a stela image. The second, and perhaps more practical and valid approach, was to identify temple hypostases that show evidence of secondary use as cult images beyond the primary state function of the temple.

This latter approach draws primarily on the work of Borchardt (1933), Fischer (1959), Traunecker (1979; 1987; 1991), Guglielmi (1994), Cabrol (2001) and Brand (2003) who have identified and discussed augmented temple reliefs. An exhaustive survey of such images at Thebes is a task that remains to be completed. Evidence for the use of temple reliefs as cult images can be found in sanctioned additional decoration of, and alterations to, exterior, and some outer court, reliefs of deities (Fischer 1959: 196-198; Traunecker 1979; 1987; 1991: 88-90; Guglielmi 1994: 58; Cabrol 2001: 722-725). Borchardt (1933: 1) discusses the regular drill holes that can be found on obelisks and lintels, and surrounding two-dimensional images on exterior temple walls. He argues that these are the nail holes used to attach sheets of metal to the stone to augment the carving (see Traunecker 1991: 88-89 for further interpretations of these drill holes; also Cabrol 2001: 724). Whilst the former appear to have been part of the initial design process when the temple was being constructed, the latter, the holes surrounding reliefs, may have been added later. The discussion of the Ramesses III temple at Karnak notes that the 'figures of the gods are frequently surrounded by the plugholes common to Empire reliefs' (*Reliefs and Inscriptions at Karnak* 1936 I: vii). Larger holes sunk into temple walls above and around reliefs may be sockets for holding awning supports (Borchardt 1933: 4; Brand 2003). The tradition of adapting images on the exterior walls of temples for popular cult usage begins in the Ramesside Period and extends down to the Roman Period (Traunecker 1999: 91; Cabrol 2001: 720-725; Brand 2003). Clear examples of sockets and drill holes around images on temple walls can be found in Ptolemaic and Roman Period temples, such as at the Hathor temple at Dendera, where the large Hathor head on the rear exterior wall has deep sockets and drill holes around it to support an awning and some kind of covering across the relief (Borchardt 1933: 8-9, fig. 19 on pl. 5). Awnings and veils over reliefs may be a less formal version of 'Gegenkapellen', which also appear in the New Kingdom. Such small subsidiary chapels were built against temple exterior walls to allow access to the deity for those excluded from the temple interior. An example of one of these chapels is Ramesses II's Chapel of the Hearing Ear at Karnak (Sadek 1987: 46; Guglielmi 1994: 55-56; 60), at the rear of the temple, on the site where Tuthmosis III had also constructed a similar chapel. The date of the augmentation of temple reliefs, and the addition of secondary epithets such as the one added to an Amun-Re relief figure on the Karnak temple exterior wall (Helck 1968: pl. 49), is hard to ascertain (Fischer 1959: 197-198). Secondary use of the images raises the issue of temple access: these images are on the exterior walls of temples, but within the enclosure walls, or on the inner walls of the first courts before the temple proper. Access seems to have been allowed for non-priestly and non-high-ranking individuals at certain times, perhaps for a special plea or on the occasion of a festival. An example of evidence for such festival access for the non-elite can be found in TT2 of Khabekhenet (i), where Khabekhenet (i) and his family are clearly shown worshipping in the precinct of Mut (Cabrol 1995b: 53; 2001: 262-266).

A few of the stelae depict what are clearly large temple statues, for example, the stela of Nebre (i) (DB60; Plate 9), or criosphinx and ram statues. A number of the original criosphinx and ram statues statues show signs of secondary use, most often in the form of gouges where stone dust has been removed (Cabrol 1995a: 3-4, pl. 1; 1995b: 35; 2001: 246; 633-634; 721). Stelae can also depict portable statues and sacred barks. These images may depict the deity statues in festival procession (Schulman 1980), where they could also act as oracular deities (Kruchten 2001: 609). Objects from ritual ceremonies, such as sistra, may be included on stelae as representative of the deity and of part of a ceremony. On the whole, ritual and processional paraphernalia have not survived in the archaeological record, though there are some exceptions, such as Hathor masks (Pinch 1993: pls. 27-30) and sistra (Pinch 1993: 139-159). A staff with a ram's head, which may have been a form of Amun visible in processions, occurs on stelae; an example of one of these was found by Bruyère at Deir el-Medina (Guglielmi and Dittmar 1992: 123). Stelae that depict groups of animals may represent actual living animals (Bierbrier and de Meulenaere 1984; Pinch 1993: 94; 173; Guglielmi 1994: 57); those that depict single animals on plinths or barks represent statues of the animal forms of the deity (Pinch 1993: 196). Bruyère discovered a large number of statuettes of snakes, geese and other animals at Deir el-Medina, which may be the source for such depictions on stelae (for example, 1929 (1930a): 68; 1945-1946 (1952): 39; 1948-1951 (1953): 37; 1948-1951 (1953): 76). Stelae that depict more than one form of a deity can be construed as conflated depictions of a temple visit where the deity was evident in a number of forms.

The hypostasis represented on the stela demonstrates occasions and levels of temple or ritual access, as well as being a form of social display: the king has full temple access, as do certain priests when officiating in the role of the king; high officials and lay priests have access at some or all of the time to inner parts of the temple; non-priestly individuals may have access on certain occasions such as festivals (Bell 1985: 271 (notes); 275; Pinch 1993: 350-351; Brand 2003). Such divine access is also applicable to the location where a stela was erected. It can also be indicative of the possible existence of patronage, with whosoever oversaw the setting up of private stelae in relation to state temples allowing certain individuals such dispensation, similar to the 'sumptuary control' which may have existed at Abydos in the Middle Kingdom (see Chapter 1). It is ostensibly the king who would have exercised this control, but, in practice, it may have been the first god's servant (*ḥm nṯr tpy*) of a temple; at the Hathor temple at Deir el-Medina, the highest-ranking individual in the community may have been responsible. The Amun-Re temple in the Karnak temple complex would have maintained a restricted level of access to all but the highest-ranking priests, dignitaries such as the vizier, and the king. The dedication of private monuments in or near the Amun-Re temple would in turn be limited to these people. By plotting the findspots of private monuments in relation to state temples, it is possible to determine a broad social hierarchy which should reflect the vertical hierarchy of social structure in Egypt. In relation to non-state sanctuaries, such as the mud brick chapels at Deir el-Medina, or smaller state-funded institutions such as the Deir el-Medina Hathor temple and the attached Khenu-chapel, the find spots of the private monuments dedicated in or near them will reflect the social hierarchy operating within the local community. What may be revealed is something closer to the 'empirical distribution of relationships in everyday experience' (Morris 1987: 39), i.e., social organisation, with the stelae reflecting social groups whose status is linked to their involvement in the local cults. This is an example of Ward's functional status (1994: 61-85).

Figure 2.1 The Deir el-Medina votive stelae findspots

Toponym		Porter and Moss reference
Hathor temple and precinct		Porter and Moss I.2 1964: 695-700
Votive chapels		Porter and Moss I.2 1964: 689-695
Queens' Valley chapels		Porter and Moss I.2 1964: 706-709
Workman's col station		
Village		Porter and Moss I.2 1964: 702-706
Western cemetery		Porter and Moss I.2 1964: 686-688
Mortuary temples:		
	Deir el-Bahri	Porter and Moss I.2 1964: 628-650; II 1972: 340-400
	Medinet Habu	Porter and Moss I.2 1964: 771-778; II 1972: 460-537
	Ramesseum	Porter and Moss I.2 1964: 678-684; II 1972: 431-443
Valley of the Kings		Porter and Moss I.2 1964: 490-491
Karnak temple complex		Porter and Moss II 1972: 1-339

However, the criterion of location, or findspot, is perhaps the most problematic to map, in that it is rare indeed for a stela to be found *in situ*, or, if it was, to have had the precise findspot recorded. Due to the frequent lack of precision, in this assessment a stela with a known findspot has been recorded as coming from a general area, for example, the Hathor temple precinct, with a more specific context recorded if known. Within the temple precinct there are a number of different contexts: tombs, houses, votive chapels, the temple proper and the Khenu-chapel. It is the general area that has been the basis of queries; the precise context is discussed where relevant. The table in Figure 2.1 lists the findspots of the Deir el-Medina stelae with the Porter and Moss reference (see Porter and Moss I.2 1964: map I for a map of Thebes showing the various locations).

2.4 Summary

Deir el-Medina, located on the West Bank at Thebes, is one of only two examples of New Kingdom settlement sites extant from ancient Egypt, the other being Amarna, the site of Akhenaten's 18th Dynasty capital in Middle Egypt. The site of Deir el-Medina includes a walled village, necropoleis, a temple and a number of chapels. The discovery of large amounts of written material in the form of ostraca and some papyri, and hundreds of inscribed monuments, has prompted numerous studies of social life and popular religion in ancient Egypt, despite the potentially anomalous highly literate and specialised nature of the community. The dense nature of the epigraphic and archaeological material has allowed scholars to access individuals to an unprecedented level, although attempts have sometimes been more ambitious than the data allows. The community's social structure and the status of certain individuals have been plotted by means of an economic analysis of wages and monumental wealth. However, status may be more closely related to an individual's function within the community.

Personal piety has been taken as the principal motive for the creation of the hundreds of votive stelae extant from the site, and the stelae regarded as too generic to allow closer analysis of additional motive. More recently, stelae have been related to festivals, suggesting that they may have been set up to mark significant events in an individual's life, utilising the festival context. Access to certain deity hypostases, the erection of stelae in certain places, the recording of an individual's presence at a festival, and the use of priestly titles, are all aspects of divine access, and may allow the stelae to serve as indicators of an individual's social status. The three chosen criteria of compositional form, hypostasis and location are closely interlinked. The location of the dedication influences the compositional form, and the depiction of the relationship between the dedicator and deity. As Baines states, 'high-cultural artefacts cluster around temples, exhibiting a maximum of order and aesthetic ideals' (1997: 219).

In discussing the purpose of royal and private monuments, Simpson notes the importance of bearing in mind 'the function, the *raison d'être*, of the object, and to determine, if possible, the nature of the message, statement or communication it makes' (1982: 271). Discussing the use of grave markers in ancient Greece, Morris observes that '[t]he use of symbols in ritual depends on sumptuary rules, in the sense of sanctions laying down what is right and proper in the given circumstances for people occupying particular places in the ideal social structure' (1987: 154). The three criteria utilised in this analysis have been chosen because they reflect wider manifestations of decorum and divine access known from temple decoration, use and access (Bell 1985: 271 and notes; Baines 1985, 1995, 1997) and tomb decoration and location (Podemann Sørensen 1989b; Roth 1991: 111). Whilst neither the intent, nor the controlling decorum of the genre behind the processes involved in the commissioning and dedication of stelae are fully understood (Morris 1987: 155; 2000: 12; Baines 2001: 4; 1994: 5), an analysis of stelae using such criteria can begin the process of revealing the social processes at work in their creation.

Chapters 3 and 4 focus on the Deir el-Medina, and other Theban stelae. In Chapter 3, the first part of the assessment of the Deir el-Medina stelae comprises an analysis of the dates of stelae production and their compositional form, in order to trace patterns in iconography that may relate to political and social changes. The second part focuses on the five most frequently occurring deities - Amun-Re, Mertseger, Amenhotep I/Queen Ahmes Nefertari, Ptah and Hathor, the sources of their cult images, and their forms and epithets. Part 2 also contains a discussion of the stelae dedicated to each of the deities in terms of date, compositional form, location dedicated and titular rank of the dedicator, in an attempt to reveal patterns in the use and popularity of specific hypostases, and the context of their utilisation. The third part compares the Deir el-

Medina stelae with the stelae from the wider Theban area, to ascertain whether the former group reflect social phenomena restricted to the workmen's community, or to Ramesside Thebes in general.

Bearing in mind the aims of this study, which are to examine an individual's social status based on the form, content and location of the stela, to attempt to reveal the motives for the commissioning and erection of votive stelae, and to determine whether stelae can be linked to actual historical events, a number of other associated issues can be assessed. For example, it may be possible to establish the rules of representational decorum that control content on private votive stelae, and to assess the extent to which stelae reflect social structure and/or social organisation within a community or on a pan-Egyptian scale - hence the discussion in Chapter 5 of votive stelae from additional sites. Such a comparative approach allows broader trends in stelae production to be traced across the Ramesside Period, and presents a more comprehensive picture of patterns, motives and influences in private votive stelae production at this time.

3. THE THEBAN STELAE: DIVINE ACCESS AND SOCIAL DISPLAY

3.1 The Deir el-Medina stelae

The analysis of the Theban stelae aims to establish patterns in stelae use and production which can then be linked to social and historical motivations for the dedication of stelae. In Giddens' concept of Signification, or 'theory of coding' (1984: 30), iconography acts as a symbolic mode of discourse, transmitting accepted social practice. The forthcoming analysis of the stelae interprets the iconography as a form of coding informed, or shaped, by cultural constraints, or representational decorum. The iconography also encodes information on specific events, which aspect is explored further in Chapter 4. The bulk of the forthcoming chapter discusses the stelae from Deir el-Medina; the Theban (non-Deir el-Medina) stelae are dealt with separately at the end.

The Deir el-Medina subset consists of 264 votive stelae, all of which meet the necessary criteria, that is, that they are private (non-royal), retain the title of the owner, an indication of who the deity is, and an indication of the relative location of the individual to the deity on the stela (see Table 1 in Appendix 1). Stelae dedicated by viziers at Deir el-Medina are included as Deir el-Medina stelae. Although the viziers were not formally part of the workmen's community, they were directly responsible for the its administration (Bierbrier 1982: 29; Ventura 1986: 98-103; McDowell 1999: 6-7; Häggman 2002: 116-130; 176-178; 231-248) and are the only non-Deir el-Medina individuals, other than kings, to dedicate stelae at locations specific to Deir el-Medina cult activity. The workmen themselves viewed the vizier as an extension of their community and as their link to the king (Eyre 1980: ch. IV; Valbelle 1985: 138). In the early 19th Dynasty, the monuments co-dedicated by the Senior Scribe, Ramose (i), and the Vizier, Paser, indicate a close relationship that it would be perhaps unwise to separate.[1] By the 20th Dynasty there is some evidence that some viziers may have been drawn from the community (Bruyère 1930: 16; Edgerton 1951: 137-145; Eyre 1980: 116; *contra*, Häggman 2002: 168).

The Deir el-Medina stelae represent individuals belonging to a closely-knit community linked by a common purpose, the construction and decoration of the royal tomb. This community was socially and geographically distinct from the other communities in the Theban area: the workmen had a relatively elite status, and the village was situated on the West Bank at a distance from the cultivation. The wealth of data and resulting research into the Deir el-Medina community, and, in particular, the genealogical and prosopographical work of Davies (1999), has meant that it is relatively easy to identify an individual named on a stela and fix his period of service, or, in the rarer case of a stela dedicated by a woman, to date her according to her husband or father's period of service.

Extrapolating from Davies' work, some stelae, which have previously only been given a general Ramesside Period date, but which have titles and filiations that can be connected to individuals identified by Davies, have been attributed to dated workmen and their families. The detailed level of knowledge of an individual's activity has made it possible to date monuments to parts of the long reign of Ramesses II. This ease of dating allows the identification of trends in the dedication of stelae during the Ramesside Period.

The dates of the stelae

Figure 3.1 shows the number of stelae produced in each dynasty. By plotting the 198 stelae that are dated to a reign or reigns, it is possible to obtain a more precise picture of the rate of stelae production over the Ramesside Period. The figures plotted in Figure 3.2 below exceed the 198 stelae as many of the stelae are dated across a number of reigns, reflecting a workman's period of service, and each reign has been counted as a 'hit', giving a total of 288 hits. Figure 3.2 shows a clear peak in the reign of Ramesses II, with 123 hits, and a second smaller peak across the reigns of Ramesses III (27 hits) and Ramesses IV (30 hits). 123 stelae date to Ramesses II's long reign (c. 66 years), which can partially be explained by the length of the reign, though such an interpretation does not account for the marked peak of stelae production during the first half of the reign: 96 stelae can be dated to this period, 11 to the middle period, 5 to his later years and 11 cannot be placed at any particular period within his reign. The possible reasons for this focused production of stelae

[1] See Davies 1999: 79-80 and n. 38 for a list of monuments dedicated by Paser and Ramose (i).

are explored and discussed in Chapter 4. The second peak in stelae production is across the reigns of Ramesses III and Ramesses IV. The shorter reigns and relative lack of genealogical and prosopographical information available for this period have not allowed stelae to be so easily placed within parts of the reigns. The majority of the Ramesses III stelae (18/27) date from this king's reign and into the subsequent reigns, suggesting that they may have been dedicated by individuals active towards the end of the reign and thereafter.

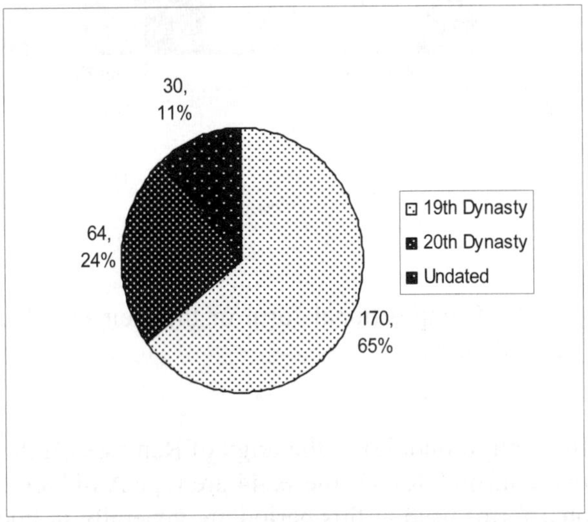

Figure 3.1 Chart showing the number of stelae dedicated in the 19th and 20th Dynasties at Deir el-Medina

Figure 3.2 Deir el-Medina stelae by reign (total stelae: 198 = 288 hits)

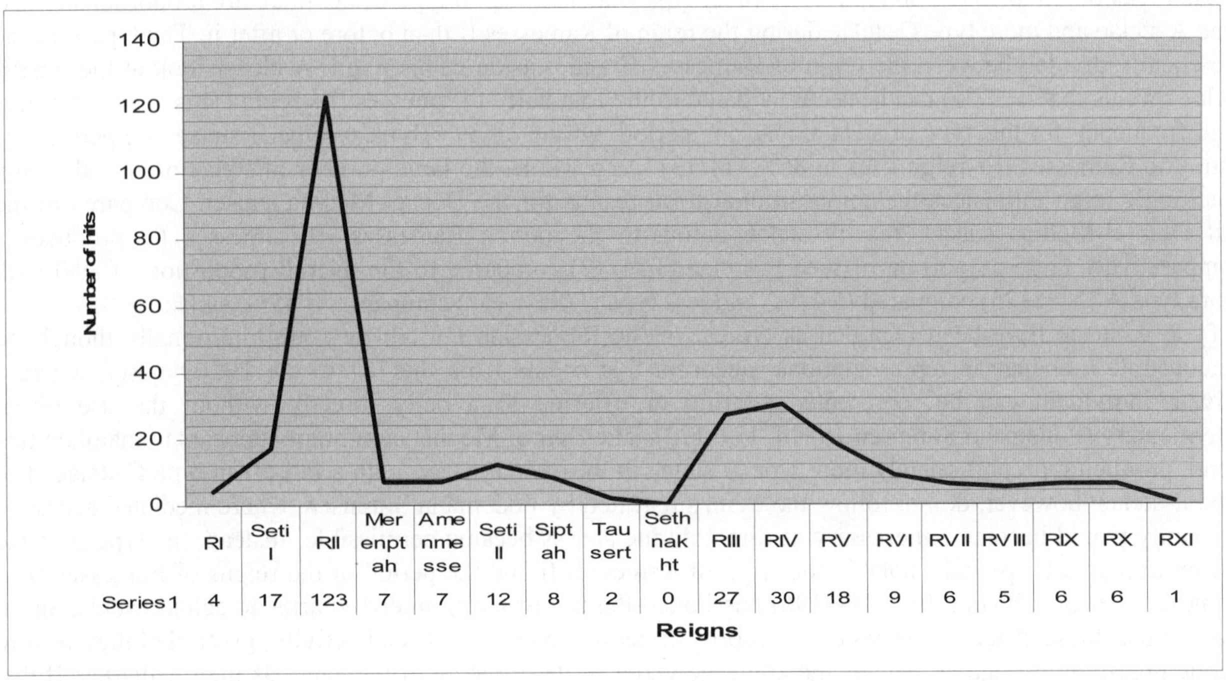

Compositional form

The Deir el-Medina residents utilise an almost equal proportion of compositional forms A and C. When presented as percentages according to dynasty, it is clear that there is a proportional increase in the use of type A stelae and corresponding decrease in type C stelae into the 20th Dynasty. There is also a slight increase in the use of type B stelae in the 20th Dynasty (see Figures 3.3 and 3.4).

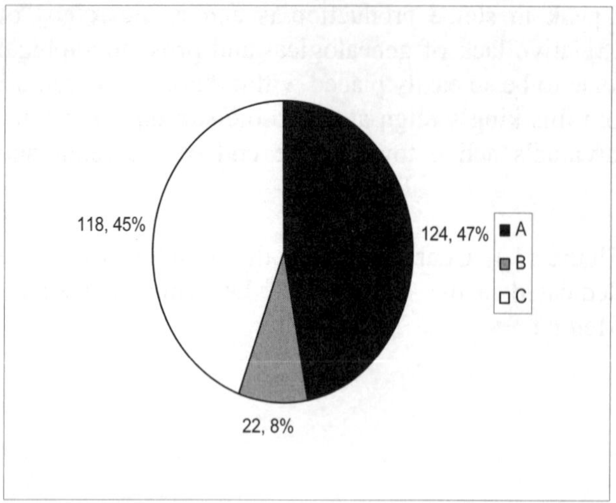

Figure 3.3 Compositional form of the Deir el-Medina stelae

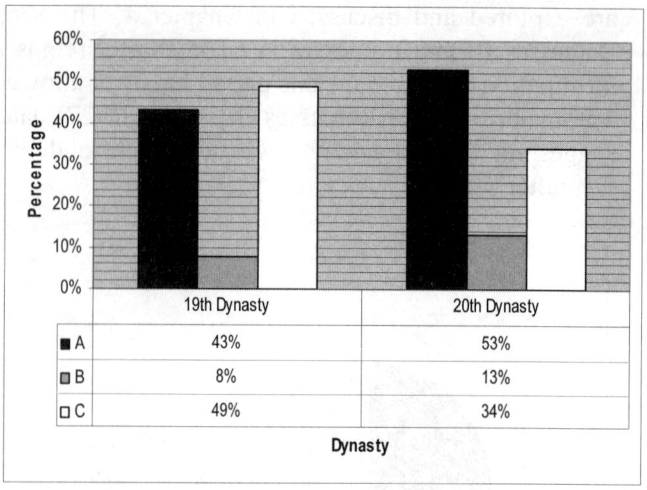

Figure 3.4 Compositional form of the Deir el- Medina stelae by dynasty

There is a clustering of stelae dating to the first half (or first half to middle) of the reign of Ramesses II (99 stelae; 96 dating to the first half of the reign and 3 to the first half/middle). Of these, 44 are type A (44%), 6 are type B (6%) and 49 are type C (50%). The compositional forms used at this period are generally in line with the overall proportion of stelae forms used (A: 47%; B: 8%; C: 45%), with a slightly larger proportion of type C stelae. However, when the Ramesses II stelae are removed from the subset, the remaining 141 stelae break down to 75 (53%) type A, 11 (8%) type B and 55 (39%) type C, i.e. there are proportionally less type A stelae and more type C stelae during the reign of Ramesses II than before or after it. The type B stelae are equally divided between the reign of Ramesses II and outside of his reign. A closer look at the type B stelae reveals that 6 (27%) can be securely dated to the first half of Ramesses II's reign. This is an extremely high frequency for this type of stela at any one period. Of the 13 19th Dynasty type B stelae, the percentage dating to Ramesses II's reign rises to 85% (11/13). As a whole, the large number of stelae produced within this king's reign influences the compositional form results for the Deir el-Medina subset. Compared to the full Deir el-Medina subset, the 49 stelae dating to the period Ramesses III-Ramesses IV produces a comparatively large proportion of type B stelae (14% (7) compared to the overall proportion of 8%) with more type A (51% (25) compared to 47%) and less type C (35% (17) compared to 45%) stelae.

Type A stelae have been regarded as typical of the Ramesside Period: they are traditionally thought to demonstrate a change in representational decorum that occurs from the 18th to the 19th Dynasty, where a private individual can be represented adoring or offering to a deity directly without the use of an intermediary (Podemann Sørensen 1989b: 121-122). The Deir el-Medina community appears to maintain this trend, producing proportionately more type A stelae in the 20th Dynasty, with a fall off in type C stelae. The type B stelae, however, do not follow the trend suggested by Podemann Sørensen, where mediated access to a divinity would become unnecessary as direct divine access became permissible. Instead, the type B stelae cluster at particular periods, notably the reign of Ramesses II and the period of the reigns of Ramesses III – Ramesses IV. Schulman (1988: 194-196) has linked the use of living intermediaries to actual events, and it may be that these stelae were created as records of certain events or official activity, given that they feature public high-ranking figures such as the king, the vizier or the foreman of the gang, as intermediaries. If this is the case, and the event can be identified, then the stelae can be more precisely dated and the nature of the event explored.

A closer look at the stelae from the first half (to middle) of the reign of Ramesses II reveals that 21 of the 99 stelae (21%) are the monuments of one man: the Senior Scribe, Ramose (i). 18 of these stelae are type C, therefore Ramose (i)'s type C stelae account for 21% (18/84) of the type C stelae from the 19th Dynasty, 29% of the type C stelae from the reign of Ramesses II (18/63) and 37% of the type C stelae from the first half of the reign of Ramesses II (18/49) - Ramose (i)'s prolific monuments influence the proportion of type C stelae for this period. Given his high status and aristocratic background (Malek 1974: 165; Davies 1999: 79, n. 31), Ramose (i)'s choice of stelae design, at odds with the proposed typical Ramesside type A design, may have influenced the choice of stelae of his contemporaries at Deir el-Medina, thus aggravating this anomaly. Individual influence on aspects of private monuments may be more of a factor than has previously been understood. Without Ramose (i), type A stelae would dominate the subset and may more accurately reflect stelae design choice within the community at this period, closely following Podemann Sørensen's proposed New Kingdom trends (1989: 121-122). Ramose (i) may have deliberately chosen a more traditional design that reflected the accepted ideology, that of private individuals having only indirect access to the deity, thus using stelae design to diplay a conventional position in the traditional social hierarchy.

3.2 Deir el-Medina cult trends

The deities

Figure 3.5 gives the number of appearances on stelae of deities that appear 10 times or more and the number of times the deity appears alone on a stela. The most prominent deities in the Deir el-Medina subset, in terms of the number of their appearances on stelae, are, in order of popularity, Amun-Re, Mertseger, Amenhotep I/Queen Ahmes Nefertari, Ptah and Hathor. There are occasional overlaps of stelae between the groups when more than one god is represented on one stela. The gods are either fully anthropomorphic, mixed (anthropomorphic with animal heads, or in the case of Mertseger, a snake/serpent body with a woman's head), or appear in the form of one of their zoomorphic intermediaries, for example, Amun-Re as the good ram Rehni. The majority of the stelae texts express devotion to the deity in the form of a generic hymn, request benefits from the deity (for example, a long life or a good burial), offer thanks for a perceived divine intervention, articulate guilt for a misdemeanour, or, rarely, explicitly record an event. In some cases the inscription simply consists of identifying labels for the deities and the individuals represented. The texts will not be studied in detail, but will be mentioned if relevant to the discussion.[2]

Figure 3.5 Recipients of the Deir el-Medina votive stelae

Deity	Frequency of occurrence	Number of stelae dedicated to this deity alone (percentage in brackets)
Amun-Re	51	20 (39%)
Mertseger	44	25 (57%)
Amenhotep I and Queen Ahmes Nefertari	43	Couple: 14 (33%); AI: 13; QAN: 5
Ptah	40	20 (50%)
Hathor	34	13 (38%)
Mut	20	3 (15%)
Forms of Horus (total):	17	8 (53%)
Re-Harakhti	8	4 (50%)
Harsiesi	4	2 (50%)
Haroeris	2	2 (100%)
Harmachis	2	0 (0%)
Horus	1	0 (0%)
Near Eastern Gods	14	13 (93%)
Osiris	14	7 (50%)
Taweret	10	4 (40%)

Amun-Re features on the largest number of stelae, though in over 61% of cases the deity is depicted either with members of the Theban triad, or local West Bank deities such as Mertseger, or Amenhotep I and Queen

[2] See Assman 1975, and Sadek 1987: 199-244, for discussion of the texts on votive stelae.

Ahmes Nefertari. The other members of the Theban triad, Mut, Khonsu or Khonsu-em-Waset Neferhotep (there are just seven stelae in the subset dedicated to Khonsu in both these forms) do not have strong individual cults. Of the five most frequently occurring deities, it is Mertseger and Ptah who have stelae dedicated to themselves alone most often (Mertseger: 57%; Ptah: 50%), indicating that these deities do have strong individual cults in the Deir el-Medina community. The Near Eastern gods appear as the triad Qadesh, Reshep and Min (or Min-Amun-Re), occasionally with Astarte and Anat, but only on one occasion (DB8, where Isis is depicted) with indigenous Egyptian gods other than Min. This cult appears to be extremely exclusive (Hulin 1989: 92).

There are smaller numbers of stelae dedicated to other gods, kings (living or deceased) and private individuals (Figure 3.6). These deities and venerated individuals are discussed in conjunction with the five major deities if and when they appear in association with them.

Figure 3.6 Recipients of less than 10 stelae on the Deir el-Medina votive stelae

Deities	**Kings and members of the royal family**	**Private individuals**
Anubis	Tuthmosis IV	An unnamed King's Son of Kush
Atum	Horemheb	The Vizier, Parahotep
Bau-Neteru	Ramesses I	The Foreman, Nebnefer (i)
Isis	Seti I	The Foreman, Neferhotep (ii)
Khonsu, Khonsu-em-Waset Neferhotep	Ramesses II	
Khnum, Satis and Anukis (the cataract deities)	Ramesses III	
Maat	Ramesses IV	
Meret	Wadjmosi	
Montu	Nefertiti and Iretnofret	
Nebmaat (a form of Ptah) and Net		
Ratawy		
Thoth, Iah-Thoth		

The sources for the cult images

The representations of deities on stelae are depictions of cult images, or hypostases, which were extant at Thebes during the Ramesside Period, and were accessible to the Deir el-Medina community. Cabrol (1995b: 53-54; 2001: 238; 386-413) and Schulman (1981; 1985; 1988) propose that stelae representations can record locations and events identifiable through architectural features and cult statues. Cabrol (1995a; 1995b; 2001) uses tomb representations to reconstruct the architecture and layout of, and changes to, the outlying parts of the Theban temples at any one period. She extends this methodology to a number of stelae, for example, describing the stela of Bek (DB280 - non-Deir el-Medina), which depicts a ram statue and a criosphinx[3] (Hodjash and Berlev 1982: 141 [81]; see Figure 3.7), as a kind of geographical map of a part of Karnak temple (Cabrol 2001: 236-238). Stela DB183 of the Workman, Hesysunebef (i) (r. Ramesses III), depicts a similar scene to that found in TT2 of Khabekhenet (i) of festival activity in the Mut complex at Karnak South (Cabrol 1995b: 53); Stela DB196 of the Workman, Qenhirkhopshef (iv) (r. Ramesses III – Ramesses V), contains a long and much discussed text recording the owner's presence in a number of temple areas (Bierbrier 1982a: 105 [73]; McDowell 1999: 100; Andreu 2002: 239-243 [92]; Bierbrier 1982b: 37-38, pl. 8); Stela DB60 of the Draughtsman, Nebre (i) (active during the first half of the reign of Ramesses II) depicts a colossal statue of Amun before a temple pylon (Plate 9).

[3] Guglielmi (1994: 65) takes both statues to be criosphinxes.

Figure 3.7 Stela of Bek depicting a criosphinx and a statue of Khonsu in the upper register, and Bek adoring a ram statue in the lower register (DB280; Pushkin Museum of Fine Arts, Moscow I.1.a.5607; © Wolfram Grajetzki)

The following discussion focuses on aspects of the stelae dedicated to the five most popular deities in the subset in terms of form and iconography in order to determine and identify the original hypostasis, if possible, or to suggest a hypostasis should a suitable one not be extant, through matching iconography and epithets and/or evidence of popular cult activity on the original hypostasis. The constantly evolving nature of the temples in ancient times and the vast span of time since any such activity took place have erased much of the evidence, so the suggestions for popular cult hypostases are tentative at best.

Amun-Re (51 stelae)

By the New Kingdom, Amun-Re was the state god *par excellence*. His cult had been active at Thebes since the Middle Kingdom, brought to prominence by the Theban 12th Dynasty, and overshadowing that of the local war god Montu. The Amun temple at Karnak and the rituals carried out there were closely related to the concept of the kingship, and as a result most subsequent rulers patronised the cult of Amun-Re (the creator god version of Amun), and built extensively at his temple. There were numerous festivals celebrated in the name of Amun-Re, the most important Theban state festivals being the Opet festival and the Valley festival, in which the king participated.[4] The Opet festival was celebrated in the second month of the inundation season (Myśliwiec 1985: 19) and lasted for up to 27 days (Bell 1997: 158). The festival celebrated the renewal of the royal Ka and the gods Amun-Re of Karnak and Amun of Luxor (Bell 1997: 157), and involved transporting the statues of the Theban triad from Karnak to Luxor temple (Bell 1997: 160-162). The Valley festival was celebrated in the second month of the harvest season (Myśliwiec 1985: 19). The statue of Amun-Re was brought across from Karnak to the West Bank to visit the Hathor shrines at Deir el-Bahri and the active mortuary temples (Schott 1952: 32; Otto 1975: col. 242; Myśliwiec 1985: 21). The level of public participation in the Opet festival is open to debate.[5] Public participation in the Valley festival is suggested by the depictions of the event in tombs (Schott 1952; Myśliwiec 1985: 21; Cabrol 2001: 608-616).

[4] For royal participation in the Opet festival, see Myśliwiec 1985: 20; in the Beautiful Festival of the Valley, see Schott 1952: 8.
[5] For a limited level of public access to Luxor temple, see Sadek 1987: 47; Bell 1997: 163-168; for none, see Baines 2001: 31, n. 86.

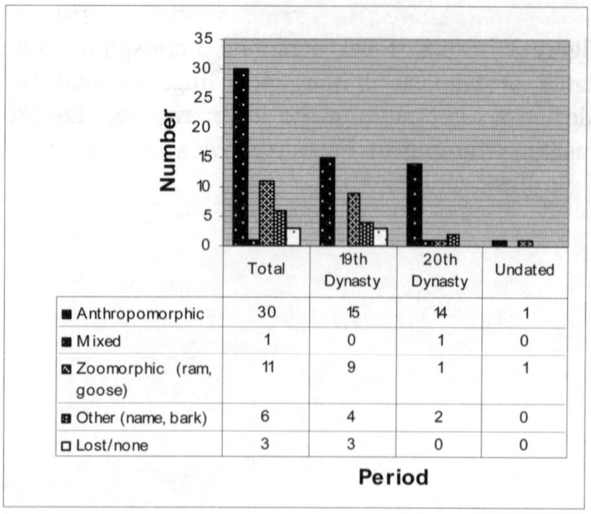

	Total	19th Dynasty	20th Dynasty	Undated
Anthropomorphic	30	15	14	1
Mixed	1	0	1	0
Zoomorphic (ram, goose)	11	9	1	1
Other (name, bark)	6	4	2	0
Lost/none	3	3	0	0

Figure 3.8 Forms of Amun-Re on the Deir el-Medina stelae in total and in the 19th and 20th Dynasties

Amun-Re can be depicted as a man, often enthroned, with deep blue skin and wearing double plumes; or as a ram, a goose, a criosphinx or a bark (Hart 1986: 4; Sadek 1987: 86). Amun-Re is depicted anthropomorphically and as a ram both within the state temples and elsewhere; his goose form is not part of the official temple iconography. Figure 3.8 gives the number of occurrences of different forms of Amun-Re in total, and compares the figures for the 19th and 20th Dynasties. These figures demonstrate a proportional increase in the use of the anthropomorphic representations of Amun-Re and a dramatic fall off of other forms (zoomorphic, bark) from the 19th to the 20th Dynasties. Of particular note is the fall off of zoomorphic forms from nine instances in the 19th Dynasty to only one in the 20th Dynasty. As a percentage, where Amun-Re is represented, he is anthropomorphic on 59% of the stelae and takes another form on 35%; on 3% of the stelae there is no representation or it is lost.

Figure 3.9 Cult images of Amun-Re

Epithet	No. of stelae	Form/ iconography	Related stelae
The Good Rehni	4	Ram statue	DB17, DB20, DB77, DB229, B255 (ram stelae, different epithets)
The Good (Goose)	3*	Goose statue	
The Eastern One	1	Mixed form (man with a ram's head)	
Lord of the Gods/August God	6	Anthropomorphic (2), bark (1), name (1), lost (2)	DB22 and DB171, depicting barks
Of the Happy Encounter	5	Anthropomorphic	

**One of these stelae features the Ram of Amun and is also included in the Good Rehni section.*

Amun-Re's anthropomorphic iconography is generally unvarying and specific versions of him must be identified by means of his epithets. He has a number of standard epithets that relate to his status as a national god: 'King of the Gods', 'Lord of the Sky', 'Lord of the Thrones of the Two Lands', 'Lord of Appearances', 'Great God' (*nsw nṯrw, nb pt, nb nsw tꜣwy, nb ḫꜥw, nṯr ꜥꜣ*), to his cult centre at Thebes: 'Ruler of Thebes', 'Lord of Thebes' (*ḥkꜣ Wꜣst, nb Wꜣst*) and specifically to Karnak temple: 'Foremost in Karnak' (*ḥry-ib ipt swt*). The functional epithets, 'Lord of the Gods' (*nb nṯrw*) and 'August God' (*nṯr špsy*), occur, as well as epithets referring to specific forms of Amun located at Karnak, for example, the 'Eastern One' (*(i)ꜣb*), and West Bank forms such as 'of Deir el-Bahri' (*n ḏsrt*) and 'of the Happy Encounter' (*n ṯḥn(i) nfr*). The stelae also refer to zoomorphic forms of Amun: the 'Good Rehni' (*rhni nfr*), the 'Good Goose' (*smn nfr*). Extended epithets articulate his role as one who listens to prayers and aids individuals. Sadek notes that 'throughout Western Thebes…Amun is most often given his commonest epithets by ordinary people, just as much as in the great temples of the kings - King of the Gods, Chief in Karnak, Lord of Heaven, Great God, Ruler of Thebes…' (1987: 88). In other words, access via private monuments to Amun-Re of the official pantheon is apparently unrestricted. For a full list of Amun-Re's epithets, see Sadek 1987: 90-92.

There are 25 stelae outstanding from the table in Figure 3.9, due to the frequent use of standard epithets and iconography in relation to representations of Amun-Re. Representations of an anthropomorphic Amun-Re abound at Thebes. Ramesside Period relief depictions of Amun-Re appear on exterior walls of temples, a number of which have signs of secondary use. For example, drill holes surround an Amun-Re representation on the external wall of the Amun temple at Karnak (Helck 1968: pls. 26, 35, 49, 75, 80 and 86; see also Guglielmi 1994: 59; Borchardt 1933: 4; figs. 11 and 12), on figures from the temple of Ramesses III in the first court of the Amun temple at Karnak (at least two separate examples: Borchardt 1933: 6, figs. 13 and 14 on pl. 3; *Reliefs at Karnak* 1936 I: pls. 7B, 9E), and on a figure on the exterior south wall of the Luxor temple (Borchardt 1933: 5, fig. 10). Doorways are traditional locations for secondary cult images, whose function is indicated by epithets and original inlays. On the staircase of the eighth pylon at Karnak, a graffito records an 'Amun-Re of the wall-thickness (*wmt*) who is in the Wabet (*wꜥbt*)' (Guglielmi 1994: 59; Cabrol 2001: 724), which may refer to one of the images decorating the wall of the processional way (Traunecker 1979: 27-28; Cabrol 2001: 724). At Medinet Habu, a figure of Amun-Re with indications of secondary cult usage is located in the doorway through the second pylon (Medinet Habu 1936 V: pl. 254; Fischer 1959: 196; Wildung 1977: col. 673; Guglielmi 1994: 59).[6] Given the proliferation of anthropomorphic images and their standardisation, the section on Amun-Re is limited in its identification of such cult images depicted on the votive stelae.

(i) The 'Good Rehni' (*rhni nfr*) (4+5)
Stelae DB12, DB63, DB117, DB151+ DB17, DB20, DB77, DB229, DB255

The 'Good Rehni', from *rhn*, to rest upon, or to travel on water, or to support, raise up (Guglielmi and Dittmar 1992: 119-120; Guglielmi 1994: 61; Cabrol 2001: 392-394), is the epithet applied on four stelae to Amun-Re as a ram. There are no depictions of criosphinxes. There are five additional stelae with representations of the ram of Amun, with different epithets, or none at all: DB17: 'Lord of the Sky'; DB20, with extensive epithets;[7] DB77: 'Lord of the Thrones of the Two Lands'; DB229: 'Ruler of Beauty for Eternity' (*ḥḳ3 nfrw n ḏt*), and DB255 with none. The Good Rehni ram stelae are of compositional form A (one) and C (three); the additional ram stelae are of compositional form A (four) and C (one). There are no type B stelae, indicating that this cult did not receive official attention. Of the nine, two are undated, one dates to the 20th Dynasty, and the remaining six to the early 19th Dynasty, no later than the middle of the reign of Ramesses II. The five type A stelae are 19th Dynasty (four) or undated (one).

During the Ramesside Period the only visible criosphinxes at Karnak were those before the tenth pylon. Ram statues were located along the dromos to the temple of Mut, installed by Amenhotep III (Cabrol 2001: 237-238), and were moved to the front of the Khonsu temple, where they stand to this day, during the reign of Ramesses II, to allow for his construction work, and inscribed with his titulary (Cabrol 2001: 207; 268). These ram statues occur in the representations of parts of the Karnak temple complex in the tombs of Khabekhenet (i) (TT2) and Neferabu (i) (TT5) (Cabrol 1995b; 2001: 262-269). Khabekhenet (i) was active in the first half of the reign of Ramesses II, Neferabu (i) in the middle of the same reign. The stela of Bek (DB280 - non-Deir el-Medina; see Figure 3.7) depicts one each of these statue types. These ram statues and criosphinxes are restricted to the Karnak temple complex and do not appear on the West Bank (Cabrol 2001: 342). Their appearance on Deir el-Medina stelae indicates that Deir el-Medina residents visited the East Bank and its temples, at least occasionally. If, as Cabrol argues, the ram statues were moved during the reign of Ramesses II, the men who depicted the statues in their tombs and on stelae may have been involved in the operation, or present at the concluding ceremony.

The heads of the extant ram statues (and criosphinxes) have been worn smooth as if frequently touched, and there is evidence of 'cupules' on the bodies (Cabrol 2001: 246; 722) - oval or circular indentations

[6] See Fischer 1959 for a further 14 images of Amun-Re in this temple which may have received secondary cult attention.

[7] 'Bull who is amongst them (?); Bull, Lord of Thebes and Heliopolis (?) Chief of the Sky, the Elder of the Entire Land, Foremost of the Ennead, King of Heliopolis, Ruler of Thebes, Source of Holiness (?) in the Sanctuary of the Ben-Ben, Numerous of Forms in the Sky and in the Land, Foremost of the Two Chapels (of Upper and Lower Egypt), Lord of everything which he causes to exist (?)'.

caused by rubbing the stone to create dust (Traunecker 1987). The base of one of the criosphinxes in front of the tenth pylon has a niche which may have served as a small chapel (Cabrol 2001: 234; 721). Cabrol (2001: 722) concludes that this archaeological evidence together with the frequent depictions of ram statues and criosphinxes on stelae indicate that such statues were indeed the focus of cult attention (see also Guglielmi 1994).

(ii) The 'Good Goose' (*smn nfr*) (3)
Stelae DB66, DB163, DB255

Guglielmi and Dittmar (1992: 121) suggest that the goose was chosen as a representation of the god Amun through wordplay on that god's name: *imn*/*smn*. Of the three sacred geese stelae, two are type A and one type C. Only one stela can be dated, DB66, type A, to the first half of the reign of Ramesses II. Guglielmi and Dittmar's survey (1992) of such stelae places them all in the 19th Dynasty. Again the lack of type B stelae suggests this was a popular rather than official cult, the use of type A stelae indicating accessibility. The findspots suggest that the stelae were dedicated to secondary cults in the West Bank temples. Bruyère (1946-1947 (1952): 56) discovered an ebony *smn*-goose statuette base in TT1443, dedicated by a workman called Amennakht. The majority of Leitz's references (2000 VI: 342) for the *smn*-goose come from Deir el-Medina,[8] but Guglielmi and Dittmar (1992: 128 and pl. 14) record a ram and goose stela which has been provenanced to Hermopolis (Ashmunein).

(iii) The 'Eastern One' ((*i*)*3b*) (Stela DB193)

There is only one Deir el-Medina Amun-Re stela using the epithet (*i*)*3b*, DB193, a type C stela dating to the 20th Dynasty. There are two non-Deir el-Medina stelae with this hypostase (DB280 dating to the 19th Dynasty and DB312, Ramesside Period, dynasty unknown), both type A. The three stelae in the database that have this epithet apply it to different forms of Amun: the mixed form, a criosphinx and a ram (this latter on stela DB312, non-Deir el-Medina). The epithet has been discussed by Hodjash and Berlev (1982: 140-141), Guglielmi (1994: 65) and Cabrol (2001: 395), and taken to indicate either a geographical location (*i3b*, 'eastern') or as the word 'desire', based on a stela from El Bersheh which depicts the ram of Amun with the epithet *3b Kmt*, 'who desires Egypt'. Discussing the stela of Bek (DB280; Figure 3.7), Cabrol (2001: 203) suggests that the epithet might indicate that the criosphinx depicted with this epithet could be one located on the east of the dromos approaching the tenth pylon, east of the temple of Khonsu, as the stela also depicts Khonsu. The epithet also occurs in the Medinet Habu geographical list (E103; Nims 1952: 42) where an anthropomorphic Amun-Re is described as *3b st nb pt* ('Who desires the throne/place(?), Lord of the Sky'). A version of this list was inscribed on the façade of the plinths of the criosphinxes that now stand before the tenth pylon at Karnak (Cabrol 2001: 203), which were moved further north by Ramesses II (Cabrol 2001: 207). The criosphinx with this epithet, depicted on the stela of Bek, may refer to the particular criosphinx that has Amun-Re *3b*...from the geographical list inscribed on the front of the plinth. In general, the small number of stelae with the Amun goose, lack of findspots[9] and variable factors make it hard to draw any firm conclusions about the original hypostasis.

(iv) 'Lord of the Gods'/'August God' (*nb nṯrw*/*nṯr šps*y) (6 + 2)
Stelae DB55, DB60, DB86, DB114, DB126, DB131 + DB22, DB171

Kruchten (2001: 609) has argued that the epithet 'Lord of the Gods' (*nb nṯrw*) refers specifically to the form of Amun-Re that gave oracles, and that the term 'august god' (*nṯr šps*y) can refer to any deity who gives oracles. On this basis, these epithets have been taken as identifying an oracular form of the god Amun-Re on the stelae. This oracular form can take the form of the portable statue of the god carried in a sacred bark, and depictions of such images have also been taken as oracular forms. Seven of the eight stelae date to the reign of Ramesses II, with four dating to the first half of his reign. Of the six principal stelae, two are type A and

8 No provenances are given in Leitz (2002 VI: 342) for stela Avignon A60 and the stela of Ptahmay in New York.

9 Stela DB312 may be from Karnak temple, but nothing more precise is known.

four are type C. The two additional stelae, which, due to their depiction of divine barks, may belong to this group, are both type C. The seven stelae dating to the reign of Ramesses II suggest that oracles or festival processions involving the giving of oracles, were a particular feature of this reign. The one stela, DB171, dating to the 20th Dynasty belongs to the Senior Scribe, Amennakht (v), and depicts a procession but with no oracular epithets. The lack of type B stelae in the Deir el-Medina group suggests that these stelae represent personal petitions that took place during festival processions, rather than official oracles involving the king or his representative. The proportionally high use of type C stelae suggests that these stelae are semi-official, perhaps set up in the vicinity of a local temple, and, indeed, two of them were found in or near West Bank temples.

Of the two type A stelae, DB114 depicts a festival procession which is not necessarily oracular, and DB60, belonging to the Draughtsman, Nebre (i), is unusual in both its representation and text (Plate 9). This stela, described as 'unique' by Schulman (1988: 44), depicts a statue of Amun-Re before temple pylons, and invokes the god as 'Lord of the Thrones of the Two Lands, Great God, Foremost in Karnak, the august god who hears prayers…; Amun of the City, Great God, Lord of the Forecourt, great of grace; Lord of the Gods' (*nb nsw tꜣwy nṯr ꜥꜣ ḥry-ib ipt-swt pꜣ nṯr špsy sḏm nḥwt…; ꞽImn n niwt nṯr ꜥꜣ nb n pꜣy wbꜣ ꜥꜣ ꜥny; nb nṯrw*). The stela has been extensively published in the context of its perceived encapsulation of 'personal piety' (Gunn 1916: 83-85; Erman 1907: pl. 5; Bierbrier 1982: 97; Kitchen 1982b: 200-202; Schulman 1988: 44-45; Davies 1999: 153-154). The epithets used are oracular, suggesting that this statue was approached as part of a festival or oracular ceremony, and the unique nature of the representation suggests that this kind of access was unusual. The text records an expression of gratitude to Amun-Re for curing Nebre (i)'s son Nakhtamun (iii). In the text Nebre (i) states 'I shall make this stela in your name, and I shall fix for you in writing this hymn upon it' (*iw.i r irt ꜥḥꜥw pn ḥr rn.k mtw.i smn n.k pꜣy sbꜣyt m sš ḥr ḥr.f*), explicitly linking the making or commissioning of the stela to the event of Nebre (i)'s temple visit. The stela is recorded as coming from the Ramesseum Area, Brick Building A (Porter and Moss I.2 1964: 683; see McDowell 1994: 56 for a discussion of the provenance of this stela), and may represent a colossal statue of Amun-Re from the Ramesseum.

(v) 'Of the Happy Encounter' (*n ṯḥn(i) nfr*) (5)
Stelae DB158, DB196, DB203, DB230, DB232

This epithet only occurs on stelae dedicated by members of the Deir el-Medina community. Of the five stelae in this group, two are type A, one is type B and two are type C. The two type C stelae have findspots, at Medinet Habu and the Queens' Valley Chapels. Given that this is a local form of Amun-Re, it is perhaps surprising to find a type B stela in the group. On closer inspection, it is revealed that the intermediary is a statue of the deified king Amenhotep I brought before Amun-Re 'of the Happy Encounter', together with Mut and Khonsu, perhaps as part of a festival.

Four of the stelae date to the 20th Dynasty. DB158 of an unidentified Workman, Nebnefer, has been dated to the second half of the 19th Dynasty (Bierbrier 1982b: 39; Quirke 1992: 40), but given the dates of the other stelae in this group, it may be that this stela should be re-dated to the 20th Dynasty. This form of Amun-Re may well be a late Ramesside form only, and depict a statue of the god resident at Deir el-Medina during this period.

The dedicators of the Amun-Re stelae

The stelae dedicators have been divided into five broad titular groups: Chiefs of the Gang and Viziers (the two foremen and the senior scribe), Priests (those using lay priesthood titles), Workmen (members of the gang), women and male individuals not using titles.

In addition, the Vizier, Panehsy, dedicates a stela, DB137, found in the temple of Tuthmosis III at Deir el-Bahri, to Amun-Re, 'Lord of the Thrones of the Two Lands, Residing in Karnak'. The ram and 'of the Happy Encounter' forms receive proportionally the most attention from workmen, therefore access to the temple complex at Karnak to visit the ram statues must have been possible, and not restricted to their chiefs. The lack of priestly titles in this group may be indicative of the fact that this was not a cult local to the Deir el-Medina community. No women dedicate stelae to these forms of Amun-Re, or, indeed, across the whole subset of 51 stelae. This reflects women's restricted access to 'monumentality' - public, long-term representation (Foxhall 1994: 135-136), and is a feature of the subset. Women do not dedicate stelae themselves to any forms of Amun-Re, appearing only as relatives on a small number of stelae and on one of the ram stelae, indicating that cult access for women to Amun-Re was extremely restricted.

Figure 3.10 Identified forms of Amun-Re and the titular rank of the dedicators

	Chiefs of the Gang and Viziers	Priests	Workmen	Women	No Title	Total
The Good Rehni	2	0	6	0	1*	**9**
The Good Goose	1	0	1	0	1*	**3**
The Eastern One	0	0	1	0	0	**1**
Lord of the Gods/August God	3	1	4	0	0	**8**
Of the Happy Encounter	1	1	3	0	0	**5**

**The same stela.*

A look at the compositional form of the stelae in this subset reveals that type A stelae cluster at the official cult centres and the West Bank. The majority were dedicated by the Chiefs of the Gang and Viziers group and the Workmen group, with none left by individuals using religious titles. The overall number of type A stelae drops off by the expected proportion, but are sustained in the same number by the Chiefs of the Gang and Vizier group into the 20th Dynasty. The three provenanced type B stelae are from official locations: the Hathor temple or the Queens' Valley chapels - the Karnak provenance is dubious (see note 18 in this chapter). The type B stelae are dedicated by the Chiefs of the Gang and Viziers group, and those using religious titles, and their use increases into the 20th Dynasty, contrary to the suggested trend for increased direct divine access, indicated by type A stelae, as the Ramesside Period progressed (Podemann Sørensen 1989b: 120-123; see Chapter 1). The fact that these stelae are dedicated at official cult locations by high-ranking individuals, supports the theory that type B stelae with representations of living intermediaries are connected with actual events at official cult locations. The Hathor temple precinct attracts type C stelae in the 19th Dynasty, the majority dedicated by the Chiefs of the Gang and Viziers' group. The decline in type C stelae from the 19th to the 20th Dynasty is slightly less than expected.

Mertseger (44 stelae)

The principal work on Mertseger is Bernard Bruyère's publication (1930b) of the excavations carried out in 1926 by the French Institute of the seven natural and man-made grottos on the path to the Valley of the Queens (1930b: plan II). Bruyère (1930b: 6; 43) argues that these chapels, which he labeled A-G, were the location of a popular cult to Ptah and Mertseger, and that the stelae found in museum collections representing the goddess can be proven to come from here, taken from the stelae niches cut into the walls of Chapels F and G (see Section 4.1(iii) for a discussion of the name and function of the Queens' Valley chapels). Yoyotte identifies two distinct Mertsegers: Mertseger as a cosmic Hathor and Mertseger, the Peak of the West, the local cult: 'Méreseger, divinité féminine fort locale, piusqu'elle est pratiquement confinée sur la rive ouest de Thèbes, en vient à faire la synthèse en sa personne de toute grande déesse égyptienne' (Yoyotte 2003: 288). A graffito in Tuthmosis III's Deir el-Bahri temple,[10] where the majority of the inscriptions are addressed to Hathor, invokes Mertseger, explained by Marciniak (1974 I: 96 [39]) as a result

[10] The location is given as the north face of the third column.

of her fusion with Hathor. Mertseger begins to appear in royal tombs in the late 19th Dynasty. Her earliest appearance on an official monument may be her depiction in the tomb of Tausert (KV8) in the Valley of the Kings, where she appears, as a winged undulating serpent with female head, as 'Mistress of the West' (Champollion 1835-1845 [1970] III: pl. CCXXXV, 1; Bruyère 1930b: frontispiece). The sarcophagus lid of Ramesses III, now in the Fitzwilliam Museum, Cambridge, carries a carving of a serpent goddess (E.1.1823; Porter and Moss I.2: 526 (66); Hart 1986: 119), who may be Mertseger.

Mertseger can appear anthropomorphically as a woman wearing the horned sun-disc, or, occasionally, the double plumes and sun-disc. She has mixed forms such as a woman with a serpent head or a serpent with a woman's head, zoomorphic forms such as a single rearing ureaus-serpent, a group of serpents, or a sphinx with a serpent/woman's head. Mertseger can also take the form of eggs. She can appear in up to three forms on a single stela; as a result, the total number of occurrences of different forms in Figure 3.11 is 50 rather than 44. Mertseger appears as eggs on one of the stelae, but as she also takes another form on the same stela the egg form has not been included as a separate category. As a percentage, Mertseger appears equally zoomorphically and in mixed forms (42% of the subset each). She is only fully anthropomorphic on 8% of the stelae (an additional 8% of the subset have lost the representations). This is an extremely low percentage when compared to the percentage of anthropomorphic Amun-Re stelae (59%), and may relate to the popular nature of the cult throughout the 19th Dynasty. The use of different forms of Mertseger is consistent in number across the period.

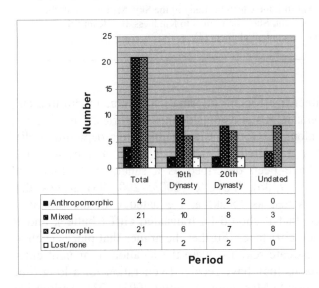

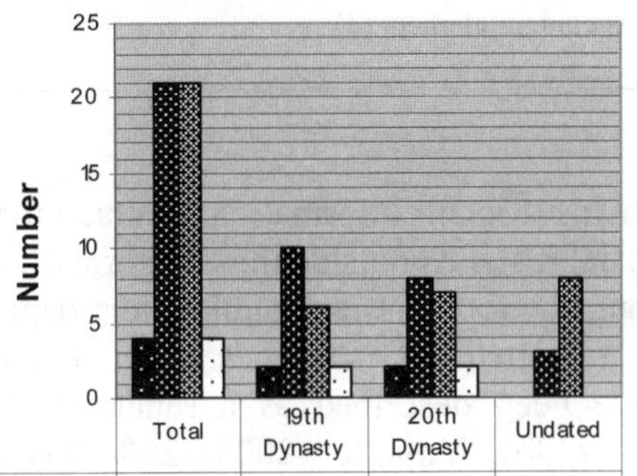

	Total	19th Dynasty	20th Dynasty	Undated
■ Anthropomorphic	4	2	2	0
Mixed	21	10	8	3
Zoomorphic	21	6	7	8
□ Lost/none	4	2	2	0

Period

Figure 3.11 Forms of Mertseger on the Deir el-Medina stelae in total and in the 19th and 20th Dynasties

Mertseger receives a limited repertoire of epithets and often none at all. She appears without epithets most frequently when she is depicted in the company of other gods who receive numerous epithets. Her nature as the personification of the 'peak' or 'cliff' may have rendered the use of identifying epithets unnecessary: she was always the same deity. On 25 occasions Mertseger is described as the 'Mistress of the West' (*ḥnwt ỉmnt*), which can be extended to 'Lady of the Sky, Mistress of all the Gods' (*nbt pt ḥnwt nṯrw*). She is identified as the 'Peak' (*dḥnt*) on two occasions, on two occasions as 'Mistress of the Two Lands' (*ḥnwt tꜣwy*) and once as the 'Mistress of Offerings' (*ḥnwt ḏfꜣw*). On eight stelae she has no epithets, and four have lost the relevant text. Two of the stelae have unusual epithets. Stela DB164 identifies her as being 'Excellent of Every Writing, One who Knows the Divine Words' (*iḳr sš nb nty rḫ md(w)t nṯr(yt)*). On stela DB80 (Plate 3a), where she is identified as Mertseger-Renenut and is depicted in three different forms, she has a long string of epithets: 'The Beautiful, the Clement' (*nfr ḥtpy*); 'Lady of the Sky, Mistress of all the Gods, the Clement, She who returns to Kindness, the Beautiful Mistress who is content/clement' (*nbt pt ḥnwt nṯrw nb(w)t ḥtpy ꜥnn ḥtp nwt nfr ḥtpy*). Mertseger's epithets are often generic (for example, 'Mistress of the West, Lady of the Sky') and applied to various different forms. The categories are defined by forms rather than epithets.

Figure 3.12 Cult images of Mertseger

Form/iconography	No. of stelae	Epithet
Anthropomorphic (twice with the 'west'-glyph on her head)	4	Mistress of the West (3); Lady of the Peak who is before her Lord (1); The Beautiful, the Clement, Mistress of all the Gods, the Clement, She who returns to Kindness, the Beautiful Mistress who is content/clement (1)
Mixed: woman with serpent head	17	Mistress of the West (10); Lady of the Sky (3); Mistress of all the Gods (2); Mistress of the Two Lands (1); Excellent of Writing, One who Knows the Divine Words (1); None (5); Lost (1)
Mixed: serpent with a woman's head	3	Lady of the Sky (2); The Beautiful, the Clement, Mistress of all the Gods, the Clement, She who returns to Kindness, the Beautiful Mistress who is content/clement (1); Peak of the West (1); Mistress of the West (1); Mistress of the Two Lands (1)
Sphinx statue (serpent head (1); human head (2))	3	Mistress of the West (1)
Single serpents	12	Mistress of the West (5); Lady of the Sky (3); Mistress of the Gods (1); Mistress of Offerings (1); Mistress of the Two Lands (1)
Groups of serpents	7	Mistress of the West (6); Lady of the Sky (6); Mistress of all the Gods (3); The Beautiful, the Clement; Lady of the Sky, Mistress of all the Gods, the Clement, She who returns to Kindness, the Beautiful Mistress who is content/clement (1)

There are five outstanding stelae for which there is either insufficient information to attach them to a cult image, or, as in the case of stela DB23, the image is so unusual it stands outside the categories. This stela has four serpent heads carved in the round facing forward, along the top of a rectangular stela depicting a cliff face, and shows Isis the Great as an anthropomorphic deity. Yoyotte (2003: 291) has interpreted the stela as a representation of the Queens' Valley chapels which have been described as a sanctuary to Ptah and Mertseger ('L'Oratoire de Ptah et Mérseger'; Bruyère 1930b). Yoyotte (2003: 290-293) argues that Mertseger's identification as the *dḥnt*, traditionally translated as 'peak' and equated with the mountain overlooking the Valley of the Kings is incorrect; rather, that it should be translated cliff ('butte'), and is linked to representations of Mertseger emerging from such cliff faces. Further, he argues that places such as the cliff housing the Queens' Valley chapels, which demarcate regions, were the location of ancient cults. The rocky cliff face on the way to the Valley of the Queens may have received veneration for a long time before the ancient serpent cult took the form of the Ramesside Mertseger (Yoyotte 2003: 293). Andreu has taken up this argument suggesting that the form of the rocks here represents a serpent 'prêt à bondir' (2002: 275).

(i) Anthropomorphic (4)
Stelae DB80, DB140, DB172, DB192

The four stelae with representations of Mertseger or Renenut-Mertseger as fully anthropomorphic are type A (two) and type C (two) stelae, indicating the popular/semi-official nature of this cult. On three of the stelae she has the epithet 'Mistress of the West', with two representations depicting her with the 'west' hieroglyph on her head. One of these stelae comes from the Hathor temple precinct. The stelae with the anthropomorphic representations range in date from Ramesses II (first half) to Ramesses III; the examples with the 'west' hieroglyph are Seti II and Ramesses III. The Ramesses II example is Renenut-Mertseger, with the extended epithet. This suggests that the anthropomorphic Mertseger as 'Lady of the West' is a later Ramesside form of the deity, from the period when she had evolved from the popular snake goddess into a form of the cosmic Hathor (Yoyotte 2003: 288).

The epithet 'who is before her lord' (*ḫft-ḥr nb.s*) is also employed on one of the 'Mistress of the West'/'west'-hieroglyph headdress stelae. The epithet is more commonly applied to Hathor or to a generic

Goddess of the West (Leitz 2002 V: 725), though Leitz lists one example of the epithet applied to Mertseger, in the Valley of the Queens (QV43; Leitz 2002 V: 725). On the stela it is applied to Mertseger taking either or both of these roles. The two stelae that have the 'Mistress of the West' epithet and the 'west'-hieroglyph were dedicated by men using priestly titles: DB140 by a Wab-priest of the Lord of the Two Lands, and DB192 by a Wab-priest of Amun and Lector-priest of all the gods. Mertseger appears on both these stelae in the company of Amenhotep I, and other gods, to whose lay priesthood the dedicators belong. The anthropomorphic form of Mertseger is rare and in three of the four cases in the subset she is depicted as such when merged with another deity, for example, here, as the personification of the West (i.e. Hathor) and in the case of stela DB80, as Renenut. On stela DB172 she is depicted as an 'excellent spirit of Re' (*ꜣḫ iḳr n Rꜥ*; see Demarée 1983).

There are no known anthropomorphic statues of Mertseger from Deir el-Medina (Bruyère 1930b: 225). Mertseger may have been represented in the reliefs at the Hathor temple, or statues or reliefs of Hathor may have been adopted by the workmen as personifications of Mertseger. Hathor and Mertseger share a number of aspects, in particular the association with the West and their (later) nurturing function. A fragment of a 'Hathor' statue survives whose base is incised with both a rearing and undulating serpent, discovered in the north east angle of the Ptolemaic temple court (Bruyère 1935-1940 (1952) II: 115, fig. 194 on pl. XX [269]), which may represent the amalgamation of Hathor and Mertseger. Mertseger is present at the Queens' Valley chapels in her anthropomorphic form on the 20th Dynasty royal stelae of Sethnakht and Ramesses III. In Chapel B, on the stela of Ramesses III, she offers papyrus-plants to Osiris (Bruyère 1930b: pl. III). In Chapel C, she suckles the young king (Bruyère 1930b: pl. IV). In both cases, she is fully anthropomorphic and wears the double plumes and sun-disc on a vulture headdress. In Chapel E, she may again suckle the king in the almost destroyed second register of the royal stela, where a goddess is depicted wearing the horned sun-disc (Bruyère 1930b: pl. VI). She does not appear in the extant decoration in the popular cult chapels known as Chapels F and G.

(ii) Mixed: woman with a serpent head (17)

Stelae DB45, DB61, DB81, DB104, DB143, DB157, DB164, DB166, DB185, DB188, DB193, DB198, DB218, DB228, DB230, DB251, DB261

Mertseger as a woman with a serpent head is the most popular form in the subset, occurring 17 times across the period from Ramesses II to Ramesses IX. The compositional form is equally balanced between A and C (eight of each), with one type B. The type B stela, DB188, was dedicated by the Foreman, Khons (v), in Chapel A at the Queens' Valley chapels (it remains *in situ*), and depicts the Vizier, To, adoring the cartouches of Ramesses III, and Mertseger holding the *rnpt*-signs (Plate 7). In Chapel B the stela of Ramesses III depicts Mertseger, fully anthropomorphic, offering papyrus-plants to Osiris while Ramesses III makes offerings above, and a vizier makes offerings below. The stela of Khons (v) may relate to images on this stela, or a related ceremony (see Section 4.1(iii)). The two stelae from the Valley of the Kings are DB143 of the Foreman, Paneb (i) (r. Seti II-Siptah), and DB185 of the Chief Draughtsmen, Hori (ix) (r. Ramesses III).

The stelae employ Mertseger's generic epithet 'Mistress of the West' ten times. On five of the stelae she has no epithets at all. According to the subset, the focus of the cult appears to move from the Hathor temple in the 19th Dynasty to the Queens' Valley chapels in the 20th Dynasty. The 19th Dynasty stelae are predominantly type A (six), and the 20th Dynasty type C (eight). This might indicate that the cult became more official and less accessible in the 20th Dynasty, perhaps when it became linked with the 20th Dynasty royal patronage of the Queens' Valley chapels. The evolution from popular to official cult follows the pattern discussed in the section on the anthropomorphic Mertseger above.

There are no extant source hypostases for Mertseger as a woman with a serpent's head. The stelae images may, in the 19th Dynasty, have been based on accessible versions of Hathor from the Hathor temple, and, in the 20th Dynasty, on images in the Queens' Valley chapels, where Mertseger emerges as an integrated state deity in a nurturing Hathor-esque role.

(iii) Mixed: serpent with a woman's head (3)

Stelae DB80, DB115, DB258

There are just three stelae with this image, one type A and two type C, all dating to the first half of the reign of Ramesses II. Two of the individuals dedicating stelae are identified: the Sculptor, Qen (ii) (DB80) and the Workman, Neferabu (i) (DB115). Both of these individuals inscribe their stelae with long texts. The dedicator of the remaining stela, DB258, has no title and only part of his name ('...pahapi') survives; his stela is unfinished. The text on Neferabu (i)'s stela asks forgiveness and warns of the power of the Peak of the West (see Sadek 1987: 233; 236); the text is similar to that on another of his stelae, DB116 (Sadek 1987: 236) dedicated to Ptah. Qen (ii)'s stela depicts three forms of the goddess: anthropomorphic as Renenut, as a serpent with a woman's head, and as a group of serpents (see Plate 3a and back cover). It also employs a set of unusual epithets relating to the (hoped for?) clemency of the goddess, as well identifying a feast day on which beer (to placate?) must be offered to Renenut (Clère 1975; Davies 1999: 176). This form of the cult was restricted to relatively high status male individuals in the early 19th Dynasty, and is distinguished by the utilisation of epithets and hymns requesting clemency and forgiveness. The lack of type B stelae indicates the cult was accessible without official intermediaries.

The relative rarity of this type of stela in the subset is of note given that zoomorphic forms of deities are generally regarded as having been the accessible version of the deity. There are extant statues and statuettes from Deir el-Medina that match the depictions on the stelae, including large limestone statuettes up to 68 centimetres in height depicting an undulating serpent on a base, with a woman's head,[11] and wooden examples with coiled tails.[12] The largest serpent statue, Turin 118, is inscribed for the Ka of the Workman, Pashedu. This Pashedu may be one of a number of individuals with this name, including Pashedu (x), one of the foremen during the first half of the reign of Ramesses II, who perhaps dedicated the statue prior to his promotion. Other candidates are the Workmen, Pashedu (i) and (xiv), and the Chief Draughtsman, Pashedu (vii). House SEIX in the Village contained an offering table dedicated by a Workman, Pashedu, together with a number of other items which can be termed 'magical' or 'ritual' (amongst a number of fragmentary offering tables, lintels and naoi): two Bes masks, a flint carved to represent a crocodile, and another carved in the form of an obese woman (Bruyère 1934-1935 (1939) III: 276-277). It may be that such statues of Mertseger were invoked on special occasions when divine forgiveness was required. Either an individual of some importance owned/had guardianship of the active cult statue that was petitioned, and only certain individuals could access this statue, or the statues themselves were costly offerings given in exchange for clemency.

Bruyère has argued that such serpent statues came from household shrines and, indeed, he discovered lintels invoking Mertseger in houses in the Village.[13] However, the majority of these household shrine fragments are inscribed for Renenut.[14] The household shrines inscribed to Mertseger may have held the large limestone or wooden female-headed statuettes of the goddess, or, alternatively, they may have housed fully serpentine statuettes, to which many more stelae are dedicated, one of which had a findspot in the Village (see below).

(iv) Sphinx statue (3)

Stelae DB190, DB234, DB250

Three stelae depict a sphinx statue of Mertseger with either a human or serpent head. An ostracon design for a stela with such a depiction is extant from Deir el-Medina (Leipzig 1660; Brunner-Traut 1956: 90-91, pl. 32 [90]), and there are graffiti images of similar versions of Mertseger on the Western Mountain (Cabrol 2001: 378, n. 628). One of these stelae, DB234, depicts the sphinx on a naos carried by three men in nemes headdresses, similar to the much later representation in the southern chapel of the Ptolemaic Hathor temple at Deir el-Medina where three men in blue crowns carry the bark of Sokar (Du Bourguet 2002: 58, 304 [60]).

---

[11] For example, Bruyère 1930: 225-226, fig. 114 = Museo Egizio, Turin 118 [old number?]; 1930: 226 = Museo Egizio, Turin 3; Bruyère 1935-1940 II (1952): 34, 60, fig. 107 [36]; 47, pl. XX [186]; Andreu 2000: 281 [228] = Museo Egizio, Turin 957.

[12] For example, Bruyère 1935-1940 II (1952): 102, pl. XXXI [230], from Chapel 1 near the Hathor temple.

[13] For example, Bruyère 1934-1935 (1939) III: 248, house NEIII, part of a lintel to Renenut completing one to Mertseger discovered in 1930; pp. 287, 293, house NOXII, a right jamb inscribed to Mertseger.

[14] For example, Bruyère 1934-1935 III (1939): 267, house SEII; 293, house NOXII; 320, house SOIII.

Cabrol (2001: 379) suggests that this unique stela image may express Mertseger's role as the dominating Peak of the West. Two of the three stelae date to the 20th Dynasty, the third is undated. The stelae are either type A or C. The dedicators are a Wab-priest, a Workman and a Sculptor.

The lack of epithets (only one stela has any, and then only 'Mistress of the West') and findspots, hinders the establishment of any firm conclusions regarding this cult image, other than it seems to date to the 20th Dynasty and may relate to a cult image carried in festival processions.

(v) Single serpents (12)

Stelae DB7, DB47, DB144, DB159, DB169, DB197, DB185, DB223, DB235, DB244, DB249, DB256

Of the 12 stelae depicting serpent figurines, three are type A and nine are type C. There are no type B stelae. Six of the stelae are 19th Dynasty, three are 20th Dynasty and three are undated. Mertseger has either no epithets or the standard 'Mistress of the West', sometimes replaced by or extended to 'Mistress of all the Gods', and 'Lady of the Sky'. On one occasion she is designated 'Mistress of Offerings'. One of the 19th Dynasty stelae was found in the Village, a 20th Dynasty example, where Mertseger also appears as a woman with a serpent head, in the Valley of the Kings, and an undated example in the Hathor temple precinct.

These depictions of serpent figurines seem to represent a purely popular and perhaps domestic cult image, restricted to male dedicators of workman rank with one foreman in the 19th Dynasty, and extending to include women in the 20th Dynasty. Three of the stelae are dedicated by women, two dating to the 20th Dynasty and one undated. The one man who dedicates a stela to this cult image in the 20th Dynasty is the Chief Draughtsman, Hori (ix), whose stela includes an image of Mertseger as a woman with a serpent head. This stela was found in the shaft, or in the huts, above KV53 (Reeves 1984: 232 and pl. 30a).

Small limestone and wooden snake figurines have been found at Deir el-Medina.[15] That stelae can depict such figurines as cult images is supported by a comparable discovery in a house at Amarna of a stela depicting two ureai-serpents facing each other, with an offering bowl between them. Adjacent to the room in which the stela was found is the findspot of the British Museum clay cobra EA 55594 (Szpakowska 2003). The clay cobras discussed by Szpakowska are far cruder than the Deir el-Medina serpent figurines, and yet may have functioned as, amongst other things, domestic cult images. The high quality of the Deir el-Medina figurines may be a result of their production by trained artisans, rather than indicating a functional difference. Serpent figurines have also been found at Karnak. Three cobra heads were discovered at the level of the Amenhotep III ramp at Karnak North, and additional examples were located at Karnak West and at the entrance to the Mut temple (Cabrol 2001: 101-102; 672-691; pls. 30; 31). The Amenhotep III examples, however, may have been used in an apotropaic ritual (Cabrol 2001: 682-684), rather than serving as cult foci; the other examples post-date the Ramesside Period.

(vi) Group of serpents (7)

Stelae DB80, DB166, DB197, DB217, DB239, DB256, DB261

Within this category there are two distinct groups: three stelae dedicated by men, two of which date to the 19th Dynasty, one to the first half of the reign of Ramesses II, and one undated, which include two or more forms of Mertseger; and four stelae dedicated by women, two dating to the 20th Dynasty and two undated, which depict the group of serpents alone (see Plate 3b). The latter stelae all have the epithet string 'Mistress of the West, Lady of the Sky, (Mistress of all the Gods)'. In both groups there are type A and C stelae.

The representations may be of the actual serpents or of figurines discovered in the Village. The dedication of stelae by women to the serpent figurines may bear witness to both a change in access to stelae as personal monuments, and to the evolution of a domestic cult of a local protective serpent deity separate from the more formal cults patronised by the male members of the community.

[15] See, for example, Bruyère 1929 (1930a): 68; 1930b: 7; Bruyère 1945-1946 (1952): 39 [87]; Bruyère 1948-1951 (1953): 37 and 76 [J].

The dedicators of the Mertseger stelae

A Vizier appears as an intermediary on DB188 of Khons (v) but otherwise viziers do not feature in this subset. There are relatively few chiefs of the gang and individuals using priestly titles; those that do use such titles are attached to the lay priesthood of Amenhotep I. Women dedicate stelae exclusively to the serpent forms of Mertseger.

Figure 3.13 Identified forms of Mertseger and the titular rank of the dedicators

	Chiefs of the Gang and Viziers	**Priests**	**Workmen**	**Women**	**No Title**	**Total**
Anthropomorphic	0	2	2	0	0	**4**
Mixed: woman with a serpent head	2	0	15*	0	0	**17**
Mixed: serpent with a woman's head	0	0	2	0	1	**3**
Sphinx	0	1	2	0	0	**3**
Single serpents	1	0	8	3	0	**12**
Groups of serpents	0	0	3*	4	0	**7**

**One of these stelae uses the title 'Child of the Tomb' (ms-ḫr; Černý 1975: 117-120), known from the Village documentation but not usually found on monuments.*

There are 16 findspots for the Mertseger stelae, with seven examples from the Hathor temple precinct. Only two stelae come from the Queens' Valley chapels, where it has been thought that the cult of Mertseger was practiced (Bruyère 1930b; Valbelle 1982: col. 80; Sadek 1987: 83-84). The other findspots are scattered across the Village, the Votive Chapels, the Valley of the Kings and the West Bank mortuary temples. The lack of clustering other than at the Hathor temple makes it difficult to draw any but the obvious conclusion that this cult had a focus at the Hathor temple, as the dominant local cult centre, but may have also been practiced in different forms at different locations. The type B stelae follow the expected pattern of high-ranking individuals dedicating stelae at official cult locations; in the case of Mertseger these stelae appear to reflect the increasingly official nature of her cult into the 20th Dynasty. Otherwise, the use of type A and type C stelae reveal no definite patterns, except that the type A stelae are, by the 20th Dynasty, not used by the high-ranking groups.

Amenhotep I/Queen Ahmes Nefertari (43 stelae)

The cult of Amenhotep I was a popular cult, originating from the establishment during this king's reign of the workmen's village to house the workers who constructed his tomb (Černý 1927: 160; Tosi 1988: 174) and the belief in the Ramesside Period that it was Amenhotep I who established the 18th Dynasty (Sadek 1987: 131). His cult was centred on the West Bank, but was not exclusive to Deir el-Medina (Wente 1963; Hornung 1975: col. 202); as such it contrasts with the Amun-Re cult at Deir el-Medina which demonstrates secondary use of state hypostases located across the river. The tracing of original Amenhotep I hypostases is problematic as the majority seem to have been portable statues or small chapel statues that have not survived. Both Sadek and Černý locate chapels to Amenhotep I in the village of Deir el-Medina (Černý 1927: 133; Sadek 1987: 83; 133).[16]

[16] Sadek (1987) identifies three chapels, which are also dedicated to Queen Ahmes Nefertari: chapels C+D, north of the Hathor temple precinct; chapel II, inside the southern half of the Hathor temple precinct, and chapel 1190, in the northwest angle of the cliffs west of the Hathor temple precinct.

Amenhotep I has two principal iconographic forms. In the first, he wears a cap crown (*ibs*), with a head band and uraeus serpent. This headdress can be plain, or surmounted by the atef crown. He carries one or more of the heka-sceptre, flail and ankh-sign. In the second, he wears the blue crown (*ḫprš*), and can also carry the aforementioned attributes (Černý 1927: 165-166; Redford 1986: 53; Tosi 1988: 174). Based on two paintings in TT2 of Khabekhenet (i) (Černý 1927: figs. 13 & 14), dating to the first half of the reign of Ramesses II, which depict Amenhotep I in one each of these two headdresses, one identified as Amenhotep 'the Favourite (of Amun)' (*pꜣ ib ib/pꜣ ḥꜣty (n ỉmn)*)[17] wearing the blue crown, and one as Amenhotep 'of the Village' (*n pꜣ dmỉ*) wearing the cap crown, Černý (1927: 168) has argued that there existed simultaneously two distinct cult statues of the king. The Deir el-Medina blue crown representation is the rarer of the two (Myśliwiec 1976: 38) and seems to appear on stelae and in tombs dating to the reign of Ramesses II only (Černý 1927: 168; Tosi 1988: 174; Quinn 1991). Often described as a military crown, Davies (1982: 75) has argued that this crown has associations with the coronation (see Hardwick 2003). The epithet 'of the Village' does not appear on stelae.

As deified humans, Amenhotep I and Queen Ahmes Nefertari are always represented anthropomorphically, with only slight iconographic differences, for example, wearing different crowns, and the use or not of a palanquin. In Figure 3.14 the 'forms' of Amenhotep I are categorised according to the crowns and the use of a palanquin, with some overlap between crowns and palanquin groups. The representation of Queen Ahmes Nefertari without her son is treated here as a separate 'form'. Amenhotep I in the cap crown is by far the most popular form, and increases relatively in use into the 20th Dynasty. The blue crown and nemes headdress only occur in the 19th Dynasty. The palanquin is rare, with one occurrence in each dynasty. Queen Ahmes Nefertari alone enjoys a more popular cult in the 19th Dynasty than in the 20th Dynasty.

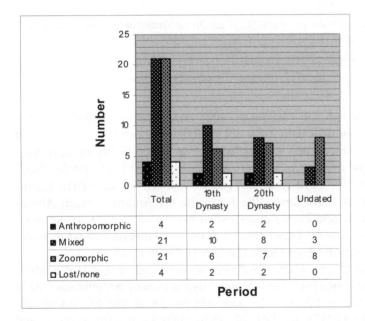

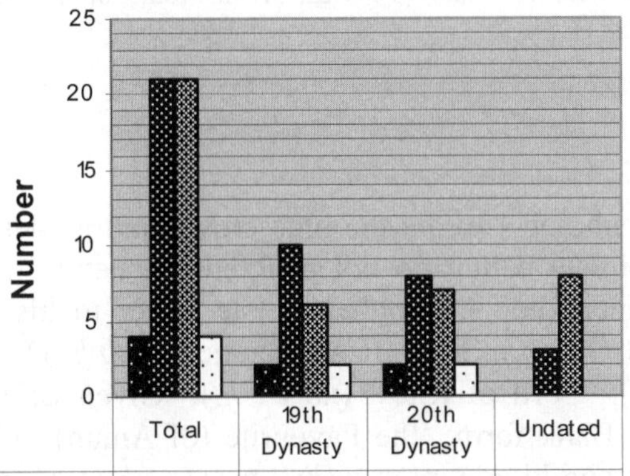

	Total	19th Dynasty	20th Dynasty	Undated
Anthropomorphic	4	2	2	0
Mixed	21	10	8	3
Zoomorphic	21	6	7	8
Lost/none	4	2	2	0

Figure 3.14 Forms of Amenhotep I/Queen Ahmes Nefertari on the Deir el-Medina stelae in total and in the 19th and 20th Dynasties

Textual evidence refers to numerous forms of Amenhotep I in addition to those found in TT2 of Khabekhenet (i). The sources list Amenhotep 'of the Garden', Amenhotep 'of the Forecourt' (Papyrus Abbott; BM 10221 (20th Dynasty); Černý 1927: 162) and Amenhotep 'who navigates on water' (Lepsius 1900 III: 282, cited in Černý 1927: 162; see also Cabrol 2001: 614-615). Papyrus Abbott goes on to identify cult temples belonging to the forms of Amenhotep I mentioned (Černý 1927: 163). Only one cult temple has been located, that of the mortuary temple of Queen Ahmes Nefertari and Amenhotep I, Men-Aset, located at Dra Abu el-Naga'a and excavated by Spiegelberg in 1896 (Spiegelberg 1898; Černý 1927: 163; Porter and Moss II 1972: 422-423; Sadek 1987: 132; Cabrol 2001: 40; 546 and n. 227). In addition, there existed an

[17] See Hovestreydt 1997: 109, n. b, for a discussion of similarly constructed (*mrwt mi* (god) NN) statue epithets mentioned in Ramesside Period donation texts.

Amenhotep 'Pakhenty' (lintel BM EA 369 [153]; Porter and Moss I.2 1964: 737) and an Amenhotep 'favoured of Hathor' (Papyrus Bologna 1094, 10, 1.9-11, 1.4; Černý 1927: 164; Sadek 1987: 133). The cult of Amenhotep I and Queen Ahmes Nefertari was not restricted to the West Bank. A chapel to the pair has been identified at Karnak (Andreu 2002: 252) and two stelae, DB271 and DB273, are dedicated to Amenhotep I by high-ranking military (non-Deir el-Medina) men, who depict Ramesses II as the intermediary. Černý (1927: 163) has suggested that certain cult images of Amenhotep I may have originated in Karnak and transferred and flourished on the West Bank, though this cannot be proven (see also Sadek 1987: 133).

Figure 3.15 Cult images of Amenhotep I/Queen Ahmes Nefertari[18]

Form/iconography	No. of stelae	Epithets
Amenhotep I in the blue crown	5	Lord of the Two Lands (2); Lord of Appearances (1); Given Life like Re for Eternity (2); Son of Re (1); Perfect God (1); The Favourite (1)
Amenhotep I in the cap crown	23	Lord of the Two Lands (and/or) Lord of Appearances (12); Perfect God (3); Great God (1); Son of Re (3); Given life (like Re) (4); Lord of Rites (2); Lord of Strength (1)
Amenhotep I in the nemes headdress	1	Good God, Lord of the Two Lands, Son of Re, Given Life like Re
Amenhotep I in the palanquin	2*	Lord of the Two Lands, Lord of Appearances (2); Given Life like Re for Eternity (1)
Queen Ahmes Nefertari	6	God's Wife (of Amun) (3); Great Divine Mother of the Lord of the Two Lands (1)

**Also occur in the local statue sections.*

On all the stelae but one, stela DB79 where Amenhotep I wears the blue crown and is identified as 'the Favourite', Amenhotep I receives only generic epithets which do not differentiate between the different forms of the deity known from other sources. Amenhotep I's epithets relate either to his identity as a deceased and divine king: 'Lord of the Two Lands' (*nb tꜣwy*), 'Lord of Appearances' (*nb ḫꜥw*), 'Perfect God' (*nṯr nfr*), 'Son of Re' (*sꜣ Rꜥ*), 'Great God' (*nṯr ꜥꜣ*), 'Lord of Rites' (*nb ỉrt ḫt*), 'Given Life (like Re for Eternity)' (*dỉ ꜥnḫ (mi Rꜥ n ḏt)*); or to a local West Bank form: 'the Favourite (of Amun)'. Queen Ahmes Nefertari's epithets relate to her role as a royal wife and king's mother (*ḥmt nsw (n nb tꜣwy), mwt nṯr wrt n nb tꜣwy*), her royal status as 'Mistress of the Two Lands' (*ḥnwt tꜣwy*), her divine status (*dỉ ꜥnḫ mi Rꜥ n ḏt*), and her role as a God's Wife of Amun/of the Lord of the Two Lands (*ḥmt nṯr (n ỉmn/n nb tꜣwy)*).

On the majority of the stelae Amenhotep I and Queen Ahmes Nefertari have strings of standard epithets that are attached to a variety of forms, so that identification of the original hypostases of Amenhotep I must be by iconography rather then epithets. The table in Figure 3.15 accounts for 35 of the 43 Amenhotep I/Queen Ahmes Nefertari stelae. Two of the stelae, DB128 and DB174, occur in the local statue sections and again in the palanquin section. The outstanding eight stelae retain insufficient information to attach them to a group. Two of these, DB125 and DB178, were dedicated by foremen and one, DB98, by the Senior Scribe, Ramose (i), and their omission from consideration is unfortunate.

[18] Stelae DB121 and DB124, dedicated, respectively, by the Foremen, Anhurkhawy (i), and Neferhotep (ii), both in post in the latter stages of the reign of Ramesses II and after, have traditionally been provenanced to a 'Chapel of Hatshepsut' at Karnak (Porter and Moss II 1972: 455, 456). James (1976: 7-10; see also Bierbrier 1982b: 27) has convincingly argued that this 'chapel' never existed, but that the finds recorded as coming from here were in fact gathered and buried by the antiquities dealer Mohamed Mouhassib, from whom Wallis Budge purchased them. That these are the only two stelae in the Deir el-Medina subset to have a Karnak provenance supports James' argument.

(i) Amenhotep I in the blue crown (5)
Stelae DB54, DB79, DB127, DB128, DB162

Amenhotep I is identified as 'the Favourite (of Amun)' on stelae DB128 of the Wab-priest of Amenhotep I, Atumnakht, dating to the reign of Ramesses II. The epithet in association with the blue crown also occurs in TT2 of Khabekhenet (i), and on DB270 (Plate 4a) of the Wab-priest of the Prow of Amun, Huy. This stela has been designated as non-Deir el-Medina, although this is not certain. Otherwise, Amenhotep I's epithets are standard royal epithets that relate to the deceased king's royal and divine status. There are two type A and two type C stelae; the type B stela, DB127, depicts Ramesses II as an intermediary in relation to Amun-Re and Mut, while the dedicator, the unidentified Wab-priest and God's Father of Amun, Anhotep, adores Re-Harakhti, Amenhotep I and Queen Ahmes Nefertari. Four of the stelae date to the reign of Ramesses II, with two dated to the first half of this king's reign. In the light of the other stelae dates, stela DB162, dated to the 19th Dynasty, may be dated more specifically to the reign of Ramesses II. None of these stelae have findspots.

A form of Amenhotep I in the blue crown is known from outside Deir el-Medina at this period: Amenhotep I 'of the Forecourt' (*n pꜣ wbꜣ*).[19] This version appears in TT19 (Foucart 1932 IV, pls. 28-32; Černý 1962: fig. 9; Wilkinson and Hill 1983: 139 [31.6.5]; Cabrol 2001: 552-553; 608-609; pl. 33) whose owner is a priest in the deified king's priesthood. Amenhotep I 'of the Forecourt' may pre-date Ramesses II if TT19 dates to Ramesses I-Seti I (Quinn 1991: 174; see Černý 1962: 42 for a date in the 20th Dynasty). Representations of Amenhotep I in the blue crown are known from the 18th Dynasty, for example, royal representations at Karnak from the reign of Amenhotep I (Quinn 1991: 172-175). The majority of these representations seem to be actual portraits of the living king, as may be the Girton College stela discussed by Quinn (1991: 173) which is dated on stylistic grounds to the early 18th Dynasty. There is a representation of Amenhotep I in the blue crown from the tomb of Nebamun (TT181) which dates to the reigns of Amenhotep III-Amenhotep IV (Wilkinson and Hill 1983: 130).

Bruyère excavated a large wooden statue of a standing king wearing the blue crown (Louvre E. 16277; Porter and Moss I.1: 698; Plate 4b and back cover) in the Khenu-chapel of Ramesses II attached to the Hathor temple. He identified this statue as Ramesses II and associated it with the royal cult that he took to be the focus of this chapel (Bruyère 1935-1940 (1952) II: 42 and pl. XXXII [112]). In the exhibition catalogue for the 2002 exhibition of material from Deir el-Medina, *Les artistes de Pharoan: Deir el-Medinéh et la Vallée des Rois,* this same statue is tentatively identified as Amenhotep I (Andreu 2002: 255 [202]) which identification fits well with the depictions of Amenhotep I in the blue crown from Deir el-Medina, dating to the reign of Ramesses II (see Hovestreydt 1997 and Section 4.1(ii) for a discussion of the identification of this statue).

(ii) Amenhotep I in the cap crown (23)
Stelae DB9, DB42, DB77, DB82, DB112, DB124, DB132, DB136, DB140, DB141, DB145, DB168, DB174, DB176, DB182, DB187, DB199, DB206, DB207, DB218, DB225, DB231, DB236

The epithet group 'Lord of the Two Lands' (and/or) 'Lord of Appearances' occurs on 12 of these stelae. All of the epithets refer to Amenhotep I's royal and divine status. This form of Amenhotep I occurs in almost evenly balanced numbers across the period, with 12 dating to the 19th Dynasty and 10 to the 20th Dynasty; one is undated. This indicates a proportional increase in these stelae into the 20th Dynasty. In terms of representational types, 12 are type A, evenly spread between the 19th and 20th Dynasties, three are type B, one 19th Dynasty, two 20th Dynasty, and seven are type C, five in the 19th Dynasty and two in the 20th Dynasty. The two type B stelae dating to the 20th Dynasty are dedicated by individuals using priestly titles, and one, DB187, comes from the Queens' Valley chapels where Amenhotep I shares the stela with Ptah. In both these cases the intermediary is a vizier. The 19th Dynasty type B stela, DB42, comes from one of the votive chapels (Chapel 1190) in the Village where an unidentified queen shakes sistra before the couple. It is not clear whether the sistra-player is a real person or a statue. Stela Cairo JdE 43649 (Porter and Moss V 1937: 93) from Abydos depicts a bark with an oracular statue of Ahmose hidden from view in a kiosk. In front of the kiosk is a small statuette of a queen shaking sistra (Legrain 1916: 161-167, pl. XVI). The

[19] See Quinn 1991: 174-175 for a list of representations of Amenhotep I wearing the blue crown.

proportion of these stelae including family members and colleagues is high, and this may be related to Amenhotep I and his mother's accessibility as popular funerary and ancestor cult deities.

Though findspots are few, the occurrence of these stelae in the Village and Votive Chapels fits with the popular nature of the cult. In the subset, the cult seems to have been practised from the reign of Ramesses II, initially alongside the blue crown statue cult and then continuing into the 20th Dynasty when it seems to evolve into something more official. In the 20th Dynasty, foremen continue to patronise the cult, whilst the number of priests dedicating stelae increase. Two out of the three 20th Dynasty priests clearly identify themselves as belonging to the cult 'of the Lord of the Two Lands' (*n nb tꜣwy* = Amenhotep I). The use of such titles indicates the existence of a more established and organised priesthood evolving later in the Ramesside Period,[20] coinciding with the inclusion of Amenhotep I in the decorative scheme of the Queens' Valley chapels (Chapel B, second room: Bruyère 1930b: 21-22; Chapel F, rear naos: Bruyère 1930b: 42-45). Perhaps the statues of the royal couple paid a visit here as part of the coronation celebrations that are recorded in Chapels A-E (Bruyère 1930b: 13-42).

Amenhotep I in the cap crown is identified as 'of the Village' in TT2 of Khabekhenet (i) (Černý 1927: 168 and fig. 14), an epithet that does not appear on stelae. It may be that Khabekhenet (i) was differentiating the original Village statue from the new blue crown statue, 'The Favourite', in the painting. On stelae it may have not been thought necessary to specifically identify such a well-known local statue. A number of statuettes of Amenhotep I in the cap crown survive from Deir el-Medina (see, for example, Andreu 2002: 255 [203]), some of which may have served as the source for the stelae images.

(iii) Amenhotep I in the nemes headdress (Stela DB27)

Only one stela, dating to the first half of the reign of Ramesses II, depicts Amenhotep I in the nemes headdress. It represents Ahmose in the blue crown with Ahmes Nefertari as a matching pair to Amenhotep I and his mother. Amenhotep I has the standard royal epithets, 'Good God, Lord of the Two Lands, Son of Re, Given Life like Re'. The stela is type C. Redford (1986: 51-54) suggests that the deceased kings depicted on monuments are images of cult statues carried in festival processions on the West Bank (see also McDowell 1992b: 101-102). A cult image of Tuthmosis II in the nemes headdress certainly existed on the West Bank – temple reliefs record the transport of the statue in this king's mortuary temple (Bruyère 1926 (1952): 43, fig. 23, pls. 5, 6, 7; Redford 1986: 54). One of the dedicators on the stela, Smentawy, who may be the Guardian, Smentawy (i), active at this period (Davies 1999: 190), chooses to use the title wab-priest, which may indicate a priestly function at a festival ceremony recorded on the stela. No family or colleagues are represented.

(iv) Amenhotep I in the palanquin (2)
Stelae DB128, DB174

There are two stelae, DB128 and DB174, depicting Amenhotep I carried in a palanquin. Both have the epithets 'Lord of the Two Lands' and 'Lord of Appearances', the latter epithet being a standard royal and divine epithet for kings and Amun-Re (Leitz 2002 III: 712), but on the stelae the epithets may also relate to the role of this cult statue as a portable festival hypostasis. The stelae are type A. Stela DB128 was dedicated by the unidentified Wab-priest of Amenhotep I, Atumnakht; active during the first half of the reign of

[20] Though earlier lay-priesthoods of Amenhotep I certainly existed. The column base Cairo JdE 25111/51512 (Černý 1927: 194-195; Porter and Moss I.2 1964: 739) gives a list of 10 members of the priesthood of Amenhotep I in the middle of the reign of Ramesses II. Some of the male members of two prominent families are represented, those of the family of Sculptor, Qen (ii), and of the Draughtsman, Nebre (i), together with other individuals. Černý (1927: 196) suggested that this column base relates to the erection of a column in a sanctuary of Amenhotep I to mark 'une occasion solennelle', though without further evidence the nature of the occasion remains obscure. It may be that this priesthood was linked to the Amenhotep I, 'The Favourite', statue that dates to the reign of Ramesses II. The following individuals are listed: Qen (ii), Servitor of Djesekare (also, Sculptor), his sons, Huy (xiii), Wab-priest of Amenhotep I (also, Sculptor), Tjauenhuy (i), Wab-priest (Davies 1999: 176), and Pendua (i), Wab-priest (Davies 1999: 206); Nebre (i), Lector-priest of Amenhotep I (also, Draughtsman of Amun) (Davies 1999: 153-155), his brother, Pendua (iii), Workman (Davies 1999: 65); Amenwia (i), *ꜥꜣ n ꜥ* (Davies 1999: 207); Penshenabu (ii), Workman (Davies 1999: 181); Apehty, Fanbearer (also, Workman) (Davies 1999: 205); Neferronpet (ii), Wab-priest (also, Sculptor) (Davies 1999: 88-89; 183).

Ramesses II; stela DB174 by the Foreman, Anhurkhawy (ii), active during the reigns of Ramesses III - Ramesses VI.

The statue on the 19th Dynasty stela wears the blue crown; that on the 20th Dynasty stela the cap crown; both statues are protected by Maat. There are two further dataset stelae, DB271 and DB273, non-Deir el-Medina, that depict Amenhotep I in the palanquin protected by Maat, dedicated by high-ranking military men. On these stelae Ramesses II offers to his deified ancestor, and in both cases Amenhotep I wears the blue crown.

These stelae may depict festivals of Amenhotep I, of which nine are known from Deir el-Medina (Sadek 1987: 135-138; see also Černý 1927: 182-183). Amenhotep I in the palanquin has also been linked to his role as an oracle giver at Deir el-Medina (Černý 1962: 43-46; McDowell 1999: 172). Analysis of the dates on which the Village court (*ḳnbt*) gathered, which were followed by consultations of Amenhotep I, and the known festival days of Amenhotep I have revealed that oracular consultations could and did occur on days other than the festival days of Amenhotep I (Vleeming 1982; McDowell 1990: 114). In TT19 of Amenmose, Amenhotep I 'of the Forecourt' is depicted with the text recording an oracular decision (Foucart 1932 IV: pls. 28-32; Černý 1962: fig. 9). It is unclear whether the stelae, which do not have such texts, depict Amenhotep I in the role of oracle giver or Amenhotep I simply in festival procession.

(v) Queen Ahmes Nefertari (6)

Stelae DB73, DB121, DB149, DB155, DB210, DB240

Queen Ahmes Nefertari is primarily defined by her role as 'God's Wife of Amun', and as the mother of Amenhotep I. The majority of these stelae are type A and include family members, indicating the popular and accessible nature of this cult - of note is the fact that stela DB240 is dedicated by a woman. The type B stela, DB121, dedicated by the Foreman, Anhurkhawy (i), has a statue of Tuthmosis IV as the intermediary. The source for the images of Queen Ahmes Nefertari may have been statues or statuettes of the deified queen, a number of which are known from the Village (Andreu 2002: 260-263 [211-213]).

The dedicators of the Amenhotep I/Queen Ahmes Nefertari stelae

Figure 3.16 Identified forms of Amenhotep I/Queen Ahmes Nefertari and the titular rank of the dedicators

	Chiefs of the Gang and Viziers	Priests	Workmen	Women	No Title	Total
Blue crown	1	2	1	0	1	**5**
Cap crown	4	4	13	0	2	**23**
Nemes headdress	0	1	0	0	0	**1**
Palanquin	1*	1**	0	0	0	**2**
Queen Ahmes Nefertari	1	0	4	1	0	**6**

* *A cap crown stela.*
***A blue crown stela.*

No viziers dedicate stelae to Amenhotep I. One stela, DB48 to Queen Ahmes Nefertari, is dedicated by a woman, the Lady of the House, Hori, together with the Lady of the House, Iyi (dynasty unknown). In general, a high proportion of chiefs and individuals using priestly titles dedicate stelae - Queen Ahmes Nefertari is the only cult form in this group to not receive stelae from priests, which may indicate that her cult had no lay priesthood at Deir el-Medina. Gitton (1975a: 91-92) has argued that Queen Ahmes Nefertari had an official cult in the 18th Dynasty based at her funerary temple Men-Aset, with cult personnel, but by the Ramesside Period she had developed a popular cult at Deir el-Medina, where she was associated with Amenhotep I.

The frequency of priestly titles, three of which use the epithet 'of the Lord of the Two Lands' and one 'of Amenhotep', indicates the existence of a lay priesthood of this god, which is known from other sources (see Černý 1927: 192-197; Lesko, B. S. 1994: 23). The blue crown stelae are dedicated by a high proportion of priests and chiefs of the gang, and there is a marked tendency to dedicate the stela alone or with one other colleague, not with family members. The small number of stelae, and the high or religious rank of the majority of the dedicators, indicates limited access to this particular cult statue. The same may be the case for Amenhotep I in the palanquin, suggesting that either festivals or oracular occasions of this god had restricted access, or that the god is shown being carried in procession as part of a larger state festival in which only chiefs of the gang or members of the god's priesthood could participate, or represent participation. On the cap crown stelae, the one priestly title dates to Seti II, the rest are 20th Dynasty. In addition, foremen continue to patronise the cult into the 20th Dynasty, which may relate to the establishment of a more organised or formal priesthood later in the Ramesside Period.

Ptah (40 stelae)

Ptah was one of the state gods during the Ramesside Period. At Thebes, Ptah was worshipped on the East Bank in a temple reconstructed as part of the Theban temple complex by Tuthmosis III (Porter and Moss II 1972: 195-202; Hart 1986: 174; Strudwick and Strudwick 1999: 48). Here he was co-templar with Hathor, as he was at Deir el-Medina. On the West Bank, his cult was active at the Hathor temple and the Queens' Valley chapels at Deir el-Medina, as well as at mortuary temples such as that of Tuthmosis II and Ramesses III (Medinet Habu). In all of these cult locations there is an overt connection with the royal cult, whether at a royal mortuary temple or at a cult temple patronised by the king.

Ptah is always depicted anthropomorphically and mummiform (Sandman Holmberg 1946: 12-17; te Velde 1982: col 1178). He is shown wrapped in a close-fitting garment similar to mummy wrappings and wears a blue skull cap, or is shaven headed (Sadek 1987: 100), and a straight beard - the only one of the gods to do so. The straight beard is often described as the royal beard, and it has been argued that Ptah may therefore be characterised as a king; alternatively, the king may have adopted the beard of Ptah (te Velde 1982: col. 1179). Ptah can be shown wearing a menat-necklace and holding either a was- or a composite-sceptre (ankh, was and djed; te Velde 1982: col. 1178-1179; Hart 1986: 173). There are occasional slight variations in iconography: he can hold either of the sceptres, and be shown in a shrine, standing or enthroned (Sandman Holmberg 1946: 13-17). These variations cannot with any certainty be linked to distinct cult images of Ptah, as such slight variations occur with regularity in depictions of the same original hypostasis of other gods (Schulman 1981: 164).

Ptah's epithets can be divided into the following groups: generic, state-god epithets: 'King of the Two Lands', 'Lord of the Sky', 'Great God', 'Lord of Eternity' (*nsw t3wy, nb pt, nṯr ꜥ3, nb nḥḥ*); epithets relating to his role as the patron of craftsmanship: 'Overseer of Craftsmanship', 'Chief (of) Craftsmen [in Upper and Lower Egypt]',[21] 'Creator of Craftsmanship' (*ỉmy-r ḥmwt, ḥry ḥmwt* [...], *msw ḥmwt*); epithets relating to his role as a creator god and the creator of kingship and thus harmony: 'Who Creates the Gods, Unique God in the Ennead, Beautiful of Face on the/his Great Place (=throne), Who loves Truth, Who carries out Maat having established the Two Lands, Lord of Fate, Fosterer of Fortune, Who Sustains the Two Lands by his Skills, Favourite as the King of Both Lands' (*ms nṯrw nṯr wꜥ m-ẖnw psḏt nfr ḥr ḥry st(.f) wrt mr m3ꜥt ỉr m3ꜥt smn.tỉ t3wy nb šꜥy sẖpr rnnt sꜥnh t3wy m ḥmwt.f mry m nsw t3wy*); geographically specific epithets: 'Of the Place of Beauty' (*n t3 st nfrw*; the Valley of the Queens, Bruyère 1930b: 48-52; Černý 1973: 88-89; Ventura 1986: 6; 19; 56, n. 129; 186), 'Who is at the South of his Wall' (*rsy ỉnb.f*; the Memphite Ptah; Sandman Holmberg 1946: 204-220; Hart 1986: 175-176), and the difficult to interpret 'Chief in his Opening' (*ḥry m ḥpd.f*), which may relate to the Opening of the Mouth ceremony (Hannig 1995: 525). See Sadek 1987: 104-107 for a full list of Ptah's epithets. Not included in this list is the Ptah called 'of the Great Door' (*n p3 sb3 ꜥ3*). This epithet occurs on two stelae in the full subset dedicated by non-Deir el-Medina residents, stelae

---

[21] The translation is taken from the publication (Botti and Romanelli 1951: 91-92, pl. LXV [136]) where the original hieroglyphs are not clear.

DB296 and DB303 of 20th Dynasty Wab-priests and God's Servants. The stelae were discovered under the tell of the Temple of Tuthmosis II, not far from Medinet Habu.

It is the epithets rather than the forms of Ptah that define original hypostases (see Figure 3.17). However, certain epithets or strings of epithets occur with such regularity that they cannot be used to firmly define cult images. Variants of the epithet string 'Lord of Truth, King of the Two Lands, Beautiful of Face in the/his Great Place' occur on 30 of the stelae, and are attached to the majority of the accessible and inaccessible images of Ptah in the East and West Bank temples and shrines. The epithet string 'Beautiful of Face on his/the Great throne' occurs on 22 of the stelae and has been included as a hypothetical group, as there appear to be patterns in terms of dated stelae and find locations.There are seven outstanding stelae with insufficient information to attach them to a group. One of these, DB264, contains the epithet 'Chief of his Opening'. The stela owner's name is lost and the stela is undated and has no provenance, so little can be gleaned from it.

Figure 3.17 Cult images of Ptah

Epithet	No. of stelae	Form/iconography
Beautiful of Face in the/his Great Place	22*	Anthropomorphic, mummiform; shrine (6)
Of the Place of Beauty	5	Anthropomorphic, mummiform; scales or feathers (1)
Creator/Overseer/Chief of Craftsmen/Craftsmanship	4	Anthropomorphic, mummiform
Who is at the South of his Wall (+ Unique God in the Ennead, Beloved One)	1**	Anthropomorphic, mummiform, in shrine
Who Creates the Gods, Great God, Lord of Eternity; Fosterer of Fortune, Who Sustains the Two Lands by his Skills	1**	Anthropomorphic, mummiform

**The three B stelae in this group are also in the Craftsmanship group.*
***These stelae also have the epithet 'Beautiful of Face in his/the Great Place' and are included in the relevant section.*

There are a number of extant images of Ptah on the East and West Bank that show evidence of secondary use, but have not, as yet, been linked to Deir el-Medina stela images. A block from the enclosure wall of the Ptah temple at Karnak depicts a now headless standing figure of Ptah, epithets lost, while a king offers to him (de Lubicz 1999: 672, pl. 301). De Lubicz notes that the undecorated portion of the block is outlined with 'dots' (drill holes?) and that the king is partially cut off, and suggests that the image was intentionally reused. He dates the king shown to the Ramesside Period (Lubicz 1999: 672). This may have been an important Ramesside cult image reused later, perhaps visible on an exterior wall when first in use. At Medinet Habu, an originally inlaid image of Ptah 'of the Great Door', located in the doorway through the Eastern High Gate, is surrounded by drill holes (Bruyère 1930b: 38; Medinet Habu IV: pl. 245). The image has the epithet, 'who hears prayers' (*sḏm nḥwt*). This cult image is referred to in the temple by further images of Ptah 'of the Great Doorway', for example, on the left jamb of the doorway through the first pylon (Medinet Habu IV: pl. 245; Guglielmi 1994: 58), and on column 33 in the second court (*Medinet Habu* V: pl. 262; Yoyotte 1960: 45 and n. 86). Fischer also identified an image of Ptah, 'who is in the temple' (*ḥry-ib tꜣ ḥwt*), enclosed by six square holes, on the west wall of the second court in the middle register (*Medinet Habu* V: pl. 290; Fischer 1959: 197); this same Ptah also occurs on the exterior south wall, west of the second pylon in the frieze above the second calendar (Medinet Habu VII: pl. 574 D; 576 D).

(i) Beautiful of Face in the/his Great Place' (22)
Stelae DB11, DB19, DB24, DB26, DB31, DB39, DB43, DB53, DB61, DB69, DB72, DB84, DB88, DB105, DB116, DB135, DB138, DB170, DB179, DB250, DB262, DB264

This is the largest group, consisting of 22 stelae. Many of the stelae also have the epithets 'Lord of Truth, King of the Two Lands' (*nb mȝʿt nsw tȝwy*), with a few having in addition 'Lord of the Sky' (*nb pt*) or 'Great God' (*nṯr ʿȝ*). Where there are further extended epithets the stelae have been included again in the relevant sections below. There are 12 type A, four type B, and six type C stelae. Three of the type B stelae occur again in the Craftsmanship section (below); the other stela, DB39 dedicated by the Workman, Karo/Kel (i), depicts Ramesses II offering Maat to Ptah followed by his Vizier, Paser, which may be a depiction of an official (royal) ceremony (see Section 4.1(i); Plate 5b).

The majority of the stelae (16) date to the early 19th Dynasty, (Seti I) - Ramesses II, with 12 dating to the first half of the reign of Ramesses II. Six out of the eight with findspots come from the Hathor temple precinct. Stela DB88 (see cover image) comes from the Ramesseum area and was dedicated by the Senior Scribe, Ramose (i); it includes a number of extended epithets and is discussed below. The findspots suggest that the original hypostasis may have been a relief or statue, now lost, from the Hathor temple. An image of 19th Dynasty date with this epithet can be found in Queens' Valley Chapel G. The epithet occurs again in the 20th Dynasty Chapels B, D and E (see below; Bruyère 1930b: 21-22; 38-44).

(ii) 'Of the Place of Beauty' (5)
Stelae DB208, DB221, DB230, DB245, DB254

Other than stela DB230, which has the additional epithet 'Great One', all of these stelae use only this epithet. The three dated examples are 20th Dynasty, with varied findspots: Medinet Habu, the Hathor temple and the Queens' Valley chapels. Four of the five are type A and this, together with the lack of type B stelae, indicates a popular accessible hypostasis.

The topographical term 'Place of Beauty' has been identified as the Valley of the Queens (Bruyère 1930b: 48-52; Černý 2001 (1973): 88-89; Ventura 1986: 6; 19; 56, n. 129; 186), and one of the stelae was discovered in the area of the Queens' Valley chapels. It is tempting to conclude that these stelae depict a relief or statue of Ptah housed in the Queens' Valley chapels, despite the fact that the majority of the stelae were discovered elsewhere and that there is no extant image in the Queens' Valley chapels with the epithet 'Of the Place of Beauty'; the original hypostasis may have been a statue, now lost. The Queens' Valley chapels do provide a number of images of Ptah. The 19th Dynasty chapels (F and G) both include Ptah in the tableaux of deities decorating the walls. In Chapel F the seated Ptah has lost his epithets; in Chapel G, he is standing and identified as Ptah 'Lord of Truth, King of the Two Lands, Beautiful of Face in the Great Place' (*nb mȝʿt nsw tȝwy nfr ḥr ḥry st wr*(*t*)). Ptah '[in the] Great [Place]' ([*ḥry st*] *wr*(*t*)) appears on the stela of Ramesses III in Chapel B, and Ptah, 'Lord of Truth, King of the Two Lands, Beautiful of Face in the Great Place' (*nb mȝʿt nsw tȝwy nfr ḥr ḥry st wrt*) on the stela of Sethnakht in Chapel E. Perhaps the most likely source hypostasis is that found in Chapel D, on the right wall, where the 75 centimetres high image was originally inlaid with 'turquoise enamel' (faience?) (Bruyère 1930b: 38). He is called Ptah 'South of his Wall, Lord of Memphis, Beautiful of Face who is in the Great Place' (*rsy inb.f nb ʿnḫ tȝwy nfr ḥr ḥry st wr*(*t*)). These epithets indicate that this may be the source hypostasis of another of the stelae images, perhaps in addition to this one.

(iii) 'Creator/Overseer/Chief of Craftsmen/Craftsmanship' (4)
Stelae DB135, DB138, DB179, DB205

These stelae span the Ramesside Period. The two 19th Dynasty examples were discovered in the Hathor temple precinct; the Ramesses III example in Chapel E at the Valley of the Queens. These three stelae are type B and were dedicated by a Foreman, a Senior Scribe and the Vizier, Panehsy, the highest ranking individuals in the community. The type A stela, findspot unknown, was also dedicated by a Foreman.

The epithet may relate to a cult image housed in the Hathor temple or the adjacent Seti I chapel. The fragmentary stela of the Vizier, Panehsy (DB138), depicts Merenptah offering Maat to Ptah, enthroned, with the goddess Maat standing behind him protecting him with her wings (Bruyère 1935-1940 (1952) II: 143, fig. 233). This was discovered in the Eastern Sector of the Hathor temple precinct, and probably formed one of a pair of façade stelae from the Seti I Hathor chapel (Sadek 1987: 62). Ptah is called 'Lord of Truth, King of the Two Lands, Beautiful of Face, Creator of Craftsmen'. Ptah, 'Overseer of Craftsmanship', occurs in TT3 of the Foreman, Pashedu (x), dating to the early 19th Dynasty (Zivie 1979: 42-43 and pl. 18). This form of Ptah also has the epithet 'Who creates the Gods' (see below). Other possible accessible images with this epithet include an image on the exterior north wall of the Qurna temple of Seti I (Osing 1977: pl. 13), and on the external wall of Karnak temple decorated by Ramesses II. The wall carries a number of images of Ptah: on the south wall there is a representation of Ptah '[...] Creator of the Gods' ([...] *ms nṯrw*; also 'South of his Wall' and 'Great of Strength', *ꜥꜣ pḥty*) standing in a shrine holding the composite sceptre (Helck 1968: pl. 53).

(iv) 'Who is South of his Wall' (+ 'Unique God in the Ennead, Beloved One') (DB116)

There is just one stela with this epithet, DB116 of the Workman, Neferabu (i), identifying the Memphite form of Ptah (Plate 11a). This stela is also the only Ptah stela to employ the epithets 'Unique God in the Ennead, Beloved One'. It is a type C stela and dates to the middle of the reign of Ramesses II. The stela is of note in that it includes a number of epithets that do not occur on any of the other stelae, and the text informs us that the dedicator, the workman Neferabu (i), swore falsely by Ptah which resulted in him 'seeing darkness' (Galan 1999). The stela's text is elaborate and non-generic (for translations of the text see Gunn 1916: 88-89; Lichtheim 1976: 109-110; Kitchen 2000: 517-518; also, Morgan 2004: 98-100) and indicates that Neferabu (i) was making a personal approach to the god, unrelated to official cult or festival activity. Neferabu (i) also dedicated a stela, DB115, to Mertseger, which is also notable for its non-generic text, a plea for clemency and a warning of the power of the 'peak' (Tosi Roccati 1972: 94-96, 286; Sadek 1987: 233-236; Kitchen 2000: 518-519).

The epithet 'South of his Wall' occurs in Chapel D at the Queens' Valley chapels (Bruyère 1930b: 38) and at Medinet Habu in the Eastern High Gate (Medinet Habu IV: pl. 245); both images were originally inlaid, and the latter is surrounded by drill holes. Given that much of the decoration of the temple of Medinet Habu is copied from the Ramesseum, there may have been a 19th Dynasty Ptah figure in the Ramesseum gateway that is now lost. Ptah, 'South of His Wall', occurs again on the north exterior wall of Medinet Habu, west of the second pylon, in the frieze above the Sea Peoples battle (Medinet Habu VII: pl. 582C). This version of Ptah occurs in the tomb of the Workman, Khabekhenet (i) (TT2) (Bruyère 1952: 44-45 and pl. V), dating to the reign of Ramesses II, indicating that this form of Ptah was known and accessible to the workman in service during the 19th Dynasty. Ptah, 'South of his Wall', also occurs on the girdle wall at Karnak (Helck 1968).

(v) 'Who Creates the Gods, Great God, Lord of Eternity; Fosterer of Fortune, Who Sustains the Two Lands by his Skills' (Stela DB88)

'Who Creates the Gods' occurs uniquely on stela DB88 of the Senior Scribe, Ramose (i) (front cover). The epithet is extant on an image of Ptah from the girdle wall of Karnak temple decorated by Ramesses II (Helck 1968: pl. 53) and also occurs in TT3 of the Foreman, Pashedu (x) (Zivie 1979: 42-43 and pl. 18; see above), of the same period. The stela, which comes from the Ramesseum area, includes a string of epithets unknown from extant monuments or other stelae. 'Great God' occurs on an image from the Karnak girdle wall (Helck 1968: pl. 81).

The dedicators of the Ptah stelae

Given the nature of the Ptah cult at Deir el-Medina, with its associations with the professional lives of the workmen, it is unsurprising that no women dedicate stelae to the deity. The table in Figure

3.18 also demonstrates the exclusive nature of Ptah as the Chief of Craftsmanship, where type B stelae proliferate, and the popular nature of Ptah as 'Beautiful of Face on his/the Great Throne'.

Figure 3.18 Identified forms of Ptah and the titular rank of the dedicators

	Chiefs of the Gang and Viziers	Priests	Workmen	Women	No Title	Total
Lord of Truth, King of the Two Lands, Beautiful of Face on the/his Great Throne	7	0	16	0	0	**23**
Of the Place of Beauty	0	0	5	0	0	**5**
Creator/Overseer/Chief of Craftsmen/Craftsmanship	4	0	0	0	0	**4**
Who is at the South of his Wall (+ Unique God in the Ennead, Beloved One)	0	0	1	0	0	**1**
Who Creates the Gods, Great God, Lord of Eternity; Fosterer of Fortune, Who Sustains the Two Lands by his Skills	1	0	0	0	0	**1**

Hathor (34 stelae)

The cult of the goddess Hathor at Thebes dates back to the First Intermediate Period, receiving royal attention from the 11th Dynasty - reliefs survive of Nebhepetre Mentuhotep II being suckled by a cow goddess (Pinch 1993: 4). The temple constructed by this king at Deir el-Bahri (Akh-isut) served as a cult centre for the goddess in the New Kingdom. The 18th Dynasty kings Amenhotep I, Hatshepsut and Tuthmosis III also built at Deir el-Bahri, the latter two definitely incorporating Hathor shrines into their constructions, the former possibly (Pinch 1993: 4-12; 25). The form of the goddess worshipped at Deir el-Bahri was the cow, depicted suckling the king (Pinch 1993: 8; 25; 175-6; Blumenthal 2000: 35-38). Hathor participated in the Valley festival, where the king brought the statue of Amun-Re of Karnak to the Hathor cult sanctuaries at Deir el-Bahri (Schott 1952: 5-7; 108-9; Pinch 1993: 6; 95).

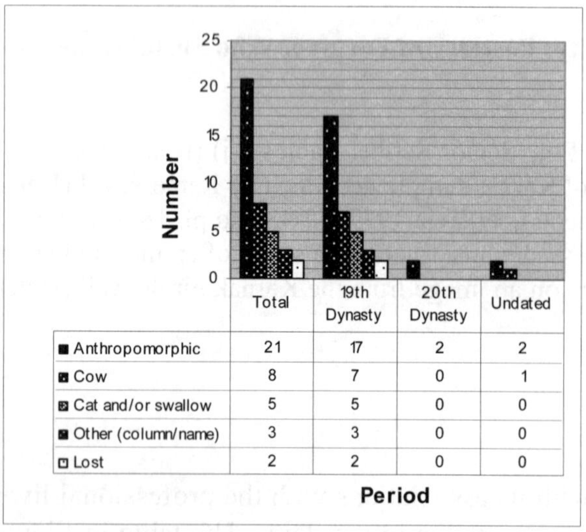

	Total	19th Dynasty	20th Dynasty	Undated
Anthropomorphic	21	17	2	2
Cow	8	7	0	1
Cat and/or swallow	5	5	0	0
Other (column/name)	3	3	0	0
Lost	2	2	0	0

Period

Figure 3.19 Forms of Hathor on the Deir el-Medina stelae in total and in the 19th and 20th Dynasties

On the stelae, Hathor can appear anthropomorphically as a woman, usually wearing the horned sun-disc, zoomorphically as a cow, cat and swallow, and as a Hathor-headed column. This latter form is here recorded as 'other'. The cow incorporates a number of roles: the nurturer of the king, a motherly goddess nurturing individuals, and a funerary deity emerging from the Western Mountain (Hart 1986: 76-79; Pinch 1993: 175-183; Blumenthal 2000: 35-49). There are no mixed examples in this subset. The anthropomorphic form of Hathor is the only one that continues into the 20th Dynasty. As a percentage, Hathor appears anthropomorphically on 55% of the stelae and zoomorphically on 32% of them, comparable to the Amun-Re figures of 59% and 35%.

Hathor's epithets can be divided into generic, national or state god epithets: 'Mistress of (all) the Gods', 'Lady of the Sky', 'Mistress/Lady of the Two Lands', 'Great Divine Mother' (*ḥnwt nṯrw (nb(w)t), nbt pt, ḥnwt/nbt tꜣwy, mwt wrt ntryt*); funerary epithets: 'Lady of the West', 'She who presides over the Western Desert' (*nbt imnt, ḥry(t)-tp ḫꜣst imntt*); form specific: 'The Good Cat', 'Established for Eternity' (applied to the cat and the swallow form; *miw nfr, smn(.ti) n ḏt*); geographically specific: 'Residing in Thebes', 'Who is in Djesret (Deir el-Bahri)', 'Lady of Dendera', 'of Gebelein', 'Lady of Mededu', 'Sycamore of the South/Lady of the Southern Sycamore' (*ḥry(t)-ib Wꜣst, ḥry-ib ḏsrt, nbt Iunt, nbt Inrty, nbt Mḏd(n)y, nht rsy/nbt nht rsy*) and the processional or oracular form, 'who hears prayers' (*sḏm nḥwt*). For a fuller list of Hathor's epithets see Sadek 1987: 116-118.

Figure 3.20 Cult images of Hathor

Epithet	No. of stelae	Form/iconography	Related stelae
Residing in Thebes	8	Anthropomorphic	
Residing in Thebes	3	Cow	Additional cow stelae: DB101, Ramesses II (first half), epithets lost, Type C, Queens' Valley chapels; DB246, undated, epithets lost, type A.
Residing in Thebes	2	Form lost	
Lady of the West/Mistress of the West (Lady of the Sky, Mistress of (all) the Gods/of the Two Lands)	10	Cow (3); Anthropomorphic (7)	
Lady of Djesret/Lady of Dendera	3*	Anthropomorphic	
Of Gebelein; Lady of Mededu; Lady of the Southern Sycamore	3*	Anthropomorphic	
The Good Cat/Swallow/votive offerings	4**	Cat and/or swallow	

* *One each of these stelae is included in the 'West' section.*
** *One of these stelae is in the 'West' section and one is the 'of Gebelein' stela.*

There are three outstanding stelae: DB74 which has an anthropomorphic Hathor as Hathor-Isis, the Great Divine Mother; stela DB108, which is an ear stela with only the name of Hathor as the 'Lady of the Sky, who hears prayers' (*nbt pt sḏm nḥwt*); and DB241, which has an anthropomorphic Hathor and has lost its epithets. Stela DB251, undated, has Hathor 'in her good name of Mertseger' (*m rn.s nfr n mrt-sgr*) alongside a representation of Mertseger, demonstrating the conflation of these two deities.

The Hathor temple and associated royal chapels at Deir el-Medina must have provided a rich source of images of Hathor, though little remains today other than fragmentary reliefs from the Khenu-chapel, and cow statues in various states of preservation. These are discussed in the relevant sections below. In addition, the Queens' Valley chapels contained images of the deity. Of particular note is the 61 centimetres high anthropomorphic image in Chapel D, balancing the 75 centimetres inlaid image of Ptah, where Hathor is called 'Lady of Chemmis, Mistress of all the Gods' (Bruyère 1930b: 37-39; Porter and Moss I.2 1964: 707). Hathor also appears, less prominently, in Chapel B on a stela of Ramesses III, as Hathor, 'Lady of Djesert', and in Chapel E on a stela of Sethnakht as Hathor, 'Lady of the West' (Bruyère 1930b: 21-22; 39-42).

(i) 'Residing in Thebes' (13)

Stelae DB10, DB11, DB15, DB28, DB32, DB40, DB55, DB76, DB77, DB79, DB105, DB110, DB227

The epithet 'Residing in Thebes' occurs on 13 stelae in total, eight of which carry anthropomorphic representations of Hathor, three depict her as a cow statue either on a sledge in a shrine, emerging from the Western Mountain or in a papyrus marsh. The latter representation is on stela DB76 of the Guardian, Penbuy (i), where the cow statue protects a statue of Ramesses II. Two stelae have lost the representations. There are eight type A stelae, two type B stelae (both with an anthropomorphic Hathor) and three type C stelae. Eleven of the stelae, and one of the possibly related stelae, date to the first half of the reign of Ramesses II. Where findspots are known, the stelae come from the Hathor temple precinct (DB15 and DB40 with anthropomorphic representations), the Western Cemetery and the Queens' Valley chapels.

The two type B stelae, DB28 and DB40, are of the anthropomorphic 'Residing in Thebes' group; in both cases the intermediary is Ramesses II, and on stela DB40, he appears with his Vizier, Paser. These stelae, whose representations are very similar, may depict a ceremony at which the dedicators were present, perhaps when Ramesses II (or his statue) visited the Deir el-Medina temple (see Section 4.1(i)). The dedicators, the Workman, Huy (iv) and the Guardian, Khawy (ii), are prominent in the subset in terms of monuments - the guardians seem to have enjoyed a certain status in the community (Janssen 1997: 31-33; McDowell 1990: 46-49). The inclusion on six of the type A stelae of numerous family members perhaps indicates a record of a festival of some kind, and festival access to the cult image for either the principal dedicator alone or with his family. The type B stelae include only male family members - the name Nebre is incised on DB40, who is possibly to be identified as the Draughtsman (of Amun), Nebre (i), another individual with numerous extant monuments.

Figure 3.21 Reliefs DM87 (Louvre E.16276 a/b) and DM88 (Cairo JdE 72017) from the Khenu-chapel at Deir el-Medina (© Wolfram Grajetzki)

Brovarski (1976: 69-70; see also Pinch 1993: 7-9) has suggested that the portable cult image of Hathor, Residing in Thebes', in her cow form, normally resident in the Ptah temple at Karnak,[22] visited Deir el-Bahri during festivals. A relief on the northern wall of the entrance hall of the Djeser-djeseru shrine, the 18th Dynasty temple of Hatshepsut, depicts the barks of Amun and Hathor on the river in the New Year (*tp-rnpt*) festival; in the outer sanctuary of the shrine the Hathor cow statue rests on a bark (Brovarski 1976: 70, n. 35; Porter and Moss II 1972: 352 (48)). Pinch illustrates a cloth with an image of the Hathor cow on a bark, where the king is protected and nurtured by her, on water, which may indicate the same Nile crossing (Pinch 1993: fig. 11B and p. 106; location unknown), and another textile (Huntington, Long Island HM 59.294; Pinch 1993: 5; 111; pl. 25b) discovered in Akh-isut, the 11th Dynasty temple of Nebhepetre Mentuhotep (Pinch 1993: 4-6), depicts a Hathor cow statue with a statue of a king before her standing in a shrine with the epithet, 'Residing in Thebes'.

The epithet 'Residing in Thebes' falls out of use at Deir el-Bahri at the end of the 18th Dynasty (Pinch 1993: 8), only to resurface at Deir el-Medina in the extant reliefs in the Khenu-chapel of the Hathor temple. On relief DM87 from room 4 of the Khenu-chapel (Louvre E.16276 a/b; Bruyère 1935-1940 (1952) II: 39; 66-68 and pl. XXXVI; Porter and Moss I.2 1964: 696; Figure 3.21) Hathor is depicted in her cow form as a portable statue on a sledge with a lotiform prow, in a papyrus thicket, with a statue of the king protected by the menat-necklace, identified as Ramesses II by a cartouche. The cow is identified as '[Hathor], Residing in Thebes'. The Ptolemaic temple to Hathor that now stands on the site includes a relief on the southern end of the west wall of the pronaos of Hathor, 'Residing in Thebes', as a cow in a shrine on a bark, wearing the menat-necklace, before whom Ptolemy VI Philometer offers incense (Porter and Moss II 1972: 403 (13); Du Bourguet 2002: 102-103 [109]). Anthropomorphic forms of Hathor are identified as Hathor, 'Residing in Thebes', throughout the temple (Du Bourguet 2002: 203). Given that there are stelae dedicated to Hathor, 'Residing in Thebes', in both her anthropomorphic and cow forms, and that Ramesside and Ptolemaic reliefs depict both these forms, it may have been that statues of both of these forms of the deity were housed in the Hathor temple. Perhaps the anthropomorphic Hathor statue was housed in the temple proper and the (portable) cow statue in the Khenu-chapel, where the reliefs depicting such a statue were located.

There are at least seven fragmentary cow statues extant from Deir el-Medina, any of which may have served as source hypostases. When Bruyère was excavating the Hathor temple precinct in the seasons 1935-1940 he unearthed and catalogued the statues and other artefacts deposited in three cachettes by Baraize in 1912. These included a fragment of a cow statue, and a large statue fragment that may have been part of another cow statue. Bruyère mentions various fragments of two other similar statues which had been held in the excavation stores for a long time, and which had no provenance. These fragments can be reconstructed to form the cow statues with the king standing in front (Bruyère 1935-1940 (1952) II: 15-16, fig. 87; Porter and Moss I.2 1964: 700; Vandier 1969: 167 (c - α)). During the same 1935-1940 excavations, Bruyère excavated a cow statue in the northern section of the temple precinct. This 65 centimetres high statue has lost the head and has a Hathor mask attached to the front (Bruyère 1935-1940 (1952) II: 106 [248], pl. XIX, fig. 181, 182; Porter and Moss I.2 1964: 713; Vandier 1969: 168, fig. 6, 1). In his discussion of the various aspects of Hathor, Vandier includes two cow statues from Deir el-Medina now in the Louvre (Vandier 1969: 167, figs. 4 and 9).

Other possible, though less likely, sources for the cow statue images are the permanent cow forms of Hathor housed in the Hathor chapels at Deir el-Bahri, often identified by epithets invoking the temple name (see Pinch 1993: 4-12). From the 11th Dynasty to the reign of Ramesses II in the 19th Dynasty, Akh-isut, housed a cult to a cow form of Hathor. Images of the statue have survived on two late 18th Dynasty objects, a stela (BM EA 689; Porter and Moss II 1972: 396; Pinch 1993: 5; 86; pl. 9.1) and a votive cloth (Huntington, Long Island HM 59.294; Pinch 1993: 5; 111; pl. 25b). A life size calcite cow's head was discovered in the debris on the north side of the temple platform (BM EA 42179; Porter and Moss II 1972: 394; Pinch 1993: 5; pl. 9, centre). Hathor was known as 'Hathor who is in Akh-isut' (*Ḥwt-ḥr ḥry*(*t*)*-ib ꜣkh-iswt*), and 'Lady of Djeser who is in Akh-isut' (*nbt ḏsr ḥry*(*t*)*-ib ꜣkh-iswt*). Pinch (1993: 5) suggests that Nebhepetre Mentuhotep may have originally constructed a separate chapel dedicated to Hathor, but, later in the New Kingdom,

[22] The epithet 'Residing in Thebes' applied to Hathor is known from the southern chapel of the Ptah temple in the Karnak temple complex, where the deity is depicted anthropomorphically (Brovarski 1976: 69). This form of Hathor can be dated here as far back as the 12th Dynasty where Hathor accompanies Senwosret I on a basalt dyad (Cairo JdE 42008; Porter and Moss II 1972: 108; Brovarski 1976: 69).

Hathor was worshipped in the main part of the temple. Stelae demonstrate that this temple was in use until the reign of Ramesses II - Ramesses II and Siptah carried out restoration work here (Pinch 1993: 11). Hatshepsut's temple, Djeser-Djeseru, had a partly rock-cut Hathor shrine located at the south end of the colonnade. Reliefs depict a statue of Hathor as a cow suckling and protecting Hatshepsut, versions of which Pinch suggests may have stood in the empty niches within the sanctuary (Pinch 1993: 8).[23] Hathor is known as 'Lady of Dendera', or, most frequently, 'Residing in Thebes' (Pinch 1993: 8). The shrine continued in use into the Late Period and was remodelled by the Ptolemies (Pinch 1993: 9). Djeser-Akhet, the temple constructed by Tuthmosis III between the two existing temples, included a speos at the back forming a Hathor shrine in which the excavators discovered a life-size sandstone Hathor cow statue nurturing and protecting the king, inscribed with the cartouches of Amenhotep II (Cairo JdÉ 38574; Naville 1907: 63-67, pls. XXIX-XXXI; Porter and Moss II 1972: 380; Pinch 1993: 11; pl. 41B). Hathor is shown in the reliefs in both cow and human form, and identified as 'Lady of Dendera' and 'Residing in Thebes', but it is not clear whether each epithet was applied to a specific form of Hathor (Pinch 1993: 10). The statue is identified as Hathor, 'Lady of Djeser, Foremost in Akh-isut' (Brovarski 1976: 71). Stelae dating from the mid 18th Dynasty to the late 19th Dynasty, and 20th Dynasty graffiti, testify to the continued use of this shrine, which was restored by Horemheb and Ramesses II (Pinch 1993: 10). A rock fall sealed off the speos in the late 20th Dynasty (Pinch 1993: 12).

(ii) 'Lady/Mistress of the West' (10)
Stelae DB18, DB37, DB64, DB89, DB99, DB118, DB130, DB165, DB196, DB251

The 10 stelae with the epithet 'Lady/Mistress of the West' define Hathor as the divine ruler of the Theban necropolis. She appears anthropomorphically seven times and as a cow three times. Three of the anthropomorphic stelae come from the Hathor temple precinct. There are four type A, one type B and five type C stelae. The type B stela, DB118, belongs to the Workman, Nekh(em)mut (i), who later became a foreman of the gang, and depicts Ramesses II as the intermediary.

The findspots suggest that the anthropomorphic stelae at least may depict a Hathor temple statue, defined by different epithets, or a secondary statue or relief from the temple. The stelae depicting cows may relate to the cow statue perhaps housed in the Khenu-chapel. Blumenthal (2000: 40-44) differentiates between a cow form of Hathor as the divine ruler of the Theban necropolis where she is represented emerging from the Western Mountain (see also Pinch 1993: 179-182), and the Deir el-Medina Hathor cow, shown on a bark (actually, a sledge), both with a statue of a king before them. Of the three cow stelae, only one, DB18, depicts Hathor emerging from the Western Mountain. This stela has a provenance of TT292 in the Western Cemetery and therefore has an overtly funerary context. Stela DB79 depicting the Hathor cow, 'Residing in Thebes' (discussed in the section above), also depicts the cow emerging from the Western Mountain. The other two stelae in this section depict the cow statue in a papyrus swamp (DB64) and in a shrine (DB99), and were dedicated respectively by the Vizier, Paser, and the Senior Scribe, Ramose (i) (on behalf of his servant Ptahsankh (i)). The high rank of these men suggests that the statue depicted may have had fairly restricted cult access. There is no clear differentiation in iconography and epithets to define a cow statue in the Western Mountain as 'Lady/Mistress of the West' or a cow statue on a bark/in a shrine as 'Residing in Thebes' and located in the Hathor temple/Khenu-chapel.

In addition to the 'Lady/Mistress of the West' and 'Residing in Thebes' cows, a third cow is known from the Hathor temple Khenu-chapel reliefs as Hathor, 'Lady of the Southern Sycamore' (DM88; Cairo JdE 72017; Bruyère 1935-1940 (1952) II: 39; 66-68 and pl. XXXVI; Porter and Moss I.2 1964 : 697; see Figure 3.21). The sources for the images may be the Hathor temple statues and reliefs, and the cow statues listed in the previous section.

[23] See Arnold 1962: 10 ff. for a discussion of how the temple reliefs reflect the statuary held within the chapel.

(iii) 'Lady of Djesert'/'Lady of Dendera' (3)
Stelae DB126, DB134, DB196

The three stelae with the epithets 'Lady of Djesert'/'Lady of Dendera' are all type C; two come from official cult locations, one of the 19th Dynasty examples from the Hathor temple, and the 20th Dynasty example from the Queens' Valley chapels. Two of the stelae, DB126 and DB196, describe the anthropomorphic Hathor as 'Foremost in Djesret' - on stela DB126 Amun is also called 'of Djesret', referring to the form of the deity worshipped at Deir el-Bahri in the chapels built by Nebhepetre Mentuhotep, Hatshepsut and Tuthmosis III (Pinch 1993: 4; 8; 10). Stela DB134 describes Hathor as 'Lady of Dendera', a form of Hathor found in the chapels of Hatshepsut and Tuthmosis III (Pinch 1993: 8; 10).

The original source hypostases may have been the images and statues located in the Deir el-Bahri chapels, which had become the centre for popular worship by the Ramesside Period, but no stelae of the workmen in the subset have a provenance here. Stela DB137 of the Mayor and Vizier, Panehsy (r. Merenptah), comes from room A of the Tuthmosis III temple, and depicts Amun-Re and Maat, with an inscription of the Wab-priest, Penamun, on the verso. A man of the rank of Panehsy would have had access to a wider variety of cult centres than the royal workmen. Stela DB82 of the Sculptor, Qen (ii), has been provenanced to Deir el-Bahri by Porter and Moss (I.2 1964: 723), but an alternative provenance has been suggested by Scott (1962) as TT4, Qen (ii)'s tomb, discovered during the 1862 excavations of the German consul B.W. König. This stela depicts Amenhotep I and Queen Ahmes Nefertari, and a funerary context is possible. Given that the cult of Hathor, 'Residing in Thebes', seems to have transferred from Deir el-Bahri to Deir el-Medina during the reign of Ramesses II, it may be that the Hathor temple restored by Ramesses II was decorated with forms of the deity that referred to her Deir el-Bahri forms, and that these were the source hypostases.

(iv) 'Of Gebelein' (DB13); 'Lady of the Southern Sycamore' (DB89); 'Lady of Mededu' (DB107)

The three stelae in this group date to the early 19th Dynasty, and probably to the first half of the reign of Ramesses II. The epithets refer to specific geographical forms of Hathor which would have been extant on temple reliefs at this time.

Stela DB13 (Plate 5a) of the Lady of the House, Bukhanefptah (i), depicts the anthropomorphic Hathor (here called Nebethetepet, the Heliopolitan Hathor; Vandier 1965: 161-166),[24] 'of Gebelein', plus a Hathor-headed column and two cats. The epithet 'of Gebelein' is a form of the goddess found at E145 in the Medinet Habu Ramesses VI geographical list (Nims 1952: 40; Leitz 2000 I: 399). Another stela, DB37, dedicated by the Workman, Kasa (i), husband of Bukhanefptah (i), depicts a similar anthropomorphic Hathor as 'Lady of the West', as well as the column and cats (this stela is included in both the relevant sections). Both stelae depict numerous relatives with 'tambourines' and bouquets of flowers, and must record a festival of Hathor and access to a specific image of the deity, also depicted in the Ramesseum geographical list, perhaps accessible to certain visitors whilst the official rituals took place within the temple. That two stelae of one family record this event suggests that the festival itself, as well as attendance at the festival, was of some importance. These stelae have no findspots.

Stela DB89 of the Senior Scribe, Ramose (i), found in pit 1414 of room 9 of the Khenu-chapel attached to the Hathor temple, depicts an anthropomorphic Hathor, 'Lady of the Southern Sycamore', the Memphite form of the goddess (Malek 1974: 163; Plate 6). This form of Hathor is depicted in the Ramesseum (Leitz 2000 IV: 79), but not in the Medinet Habu geographical list. This Hathor in her cow form occurs in the Khenu-chapel: relief DM88 (Cairo JdE 72017; see Figure 3.21) which depicts Ramose (i) kneeling on the right hand side before a Hathor cow figure on a sledge. Ramose (i)'s personal connection to this cult is discussed in Section 4.1(i).

Stela DB107 of the Workman, Tusa (i), depicting Hathor, 'Lady of Mededu', and Wepwawet may relate to scene E119 of the geographical list of Ramesses VI (= B24 of Ramesses III) where the same two deities are depicted (Nims 1952: 43-44; Leitz 2000 III: 477). The stela includes Tusa (i)'s family with offerings. Tusa (i) went on to become a guardian and is included in the representations in TT250 constructed by the Senior Scribe, Ramose (i), perhaps indicating a close relationship with Ramose (i), and relatively high social status in the community. The stela has no findspot.

---

[24] See Vandier 1964: 91-97 for a discussion of Hathor Nebethetepet at the Ramesseum and Medinet Habu.

These stelae are informative with regard to state temple access, and the importance of such access to the dedicators to define their social status, both through actual participation and the monumental record of such participation.

(v) The Good Cat/Swallow/Hathor-headed column (4)

Stelae DB13, DB37, DB59, DB152

The stelae in this group either depict symbols of Hathor in the form of cats, swallows and Hathor-headed columns alongside anthropomorphic representations of Hathor, as is the case on stela DB13 of Bukhanefptah (i), and stela DB37 of her husband Kasa (i), or alone, as is the case on stela DB59 of the Draughtsman, Nebre (i), and stela DB152 of the Weshbet-mourner, Hemtneter. Stelae DB13 and DB37, discussed above, include numerous relatives and may represent a festival visit. The cats, swallows and Hathor-headed columns represent votive offerings or ritual paraphernalia; the stelae depicting both the anthropomorphic hypostases and votive offerings may be a conflation of the various parts of a temple visit.

The two stelae depicting only the votive offerings or ritual paraphernalia do not depict the primary dedicators: stela DB59 was dedicated by the Draughtsman, Nebre (i), on behalf of his sons who are represented in the lower register, with only Nebre (i)'s name appearing in the upper register; stela DB152 was dedicated by a female Weshbet-mourner and her daughter, with their names only on the stela. Stelae representing such images may be restricted to women and children, and can perhaps be linked to the fertility or nurturing aspect of Hathor. Conventions may have precluded stelae dedicated by, or on behalf of, women and children, from depicting Hathor as anthropomorphic, or in her cow form, or such hypostases were simply inaccessible to them.

The dedicators of the Hathor stelae

Figure 3.22 Identified forms of Hathor and the titular rank of the dedicators

	Chiefs of the Gang and Viziers	Priests	Workmen	Women	No Title	Total
Residing in Thebes (anthropomorphic)	2	0	6	0	0	**8**
Residing in Thebes (cow) + 2 additional	1	0	4	0	0	**5**
Residing in Thebes (form lost)	0	0	2	0	0	**2**
Lady of the West/Mistress of the West	3*	0	7	0	0	**10**
Lady of Djesret/Lady of Dendera	0	1	2	0	0	**3**
Lady of Gebelein; Lady of Mededu; Lady of the Southern Sycamore	1	0	1	1	0	**3**
The Good Cat	0	0	2	2	0	**4**

* *One of these stelae is dedicated by the Mayor of Thebes and Vizier, Paser.*

At Deir el-Bahri, Pinch (1993: 96) noted that of the six stelae where the donor is depicted, two were women, and that women left the majority of the textiles. At Deir el-Medina women dedicate only two stelae out of the 34 in the subset. This suggests two things: firstly, that stelae may not have been the form of votive offering utilised by women, who may have preferred, or traditionally had access to, other types of votive offerings, such as the Deir el-Bahri textiles, or uninscribed statuettes and amulets; secondly, if stelae record public events, women may not have been present at such ceremonies - their approach to a deity may have been of a more informal nature, relating to less official aspects of the cult, such as Hathor as a fertility goddess. The Hathor venerated on the Deir el-Medina stelae is a state form of the deity, not a popular fertility cult. The votive offerings discovered at Deir el-Bahri, for example, the stone, wood, faïence and pottery phalli (Pinch 1993: 235-238) suggest that this was the location for the popular fertility form of the cult in the Ramesside Period.

Three Foremen dedicate stelae during the reign of Seti I and the first half of the reign of Ramesses II. The Senior Scribe, Ramose (i), dedicates three stelae: DB89 to the anthropomorphic Hathor as 'Lady of the Southern Sycamore'; DB99 on behalf of his servant Sankhptah (i); and DB101 to the cow form, indicating his close connection to the cult, which is also indicated by the reliefs depicting Ramose (i) before the goddess in the Khenu-chapel of the Hathor temple. There is just one priestly title, the Wab-priest and Servitor, Amennakht, who dedicates DB126 to Amun and Hathor of Djeseret, though his cult affiliation is not indicated. Otherwise the Hathor cult is practised predominantly by workmen. The unusual predominance of workmen dedicating type B stelae at official locations highlights the importance of the event recorded. The official nature of the Hathor cult is indicated by the provenance of type B and C stelae to local official cult locations, such as the Hathor temple.

3.3 Theban non-Deir el-Medina stelae

The term non-Deir el-Medina refers to the Theban area excluding Deir el-Medina. There are 55 stelae in this subset (see Appendix 1, Table 2), which equates to 17% of the 319 stelae in this study dedicated at Thebes in the Ramesside Period. The non-Deir el-Medina stelae belong to a very broad demographic group, the sample is much smaller, and the genealogies of the individuals are largely unknown, with the result that their stelae are much harder to date precisely. Only monuments belonging to high-ranking individuals such as known first god's servants of Amun, or stelae with inscriptions containing dates, can be securely dated. In some cases, stylistic analysis can provide a general date within the Ramesside Period. The result is that trends outside of Deir el-Medina, in the Theban area, are harder to identify. 31 stelae date to the 19th Dynasty, 13 to the 20th Dynasty and 11 are dated only to the Ramesside Period (see Figure 3.23). There is a relative similarity in proportion of stelae for each dynasty compared to the Deir el-Medina subset indicating that, while stelae production is a particular feature of the workmen's Village, general production in the whole Theban area followed a downward trend over the course of the late New Kingdom. Only 15 stelae can be assigned to a reign, with seven dating to Ramesses II, and four to Ramesses III/IV, which can be seen as a slight parallel with the peaks of stelae production at Deir el-Medina.

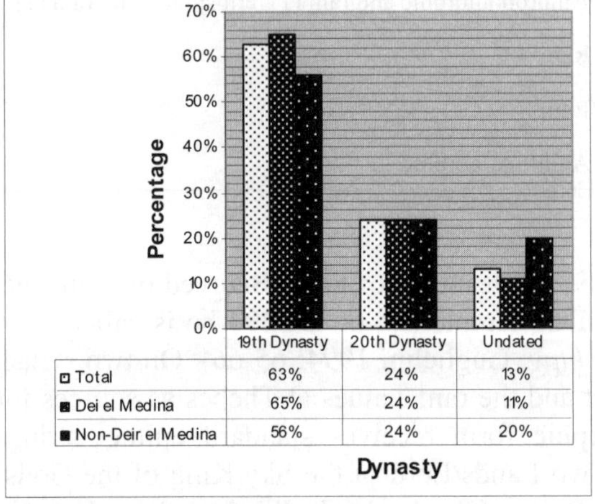

Figure 3.23 Percentage of stelae dedicated in each Theban sub-set in the 19th and 20th Dynasties

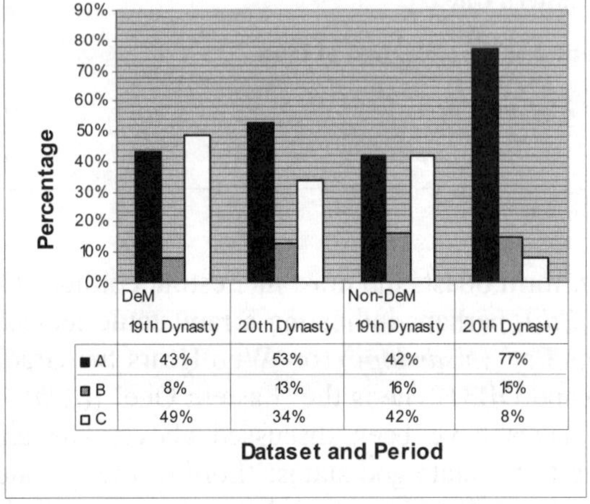

Figure 3.24 Percentage of each compositional form dedicated by Deir el-Medina and non-Deir el-Medina residents in the 19th and 20th Dynasties

With respect to compositional form, 20 (51%) are type A, seven (13%) are type B and 28 (36%) are type C. At Deir el-Medina, the percentages are type A, 47%; type B, 8%; and type C, 45%. The non-Deir el-Medina residents use a far larger proportion of type A stelae (51%) compared to type C stelae (36%). Figure 3.24 gives the percentages of each compositional form in each dynasty; the stelae that are dated only to the Ramesside Period as a whole have been omitted. There is a marked increase in the use of type A stelae at Thebes in the 20th Dynasty. The number of stelae is, however, small: 10 out of the 13 are dated to the 20th Dynasty, and the apparent sharp increase may be the result of accidents of preservation or collecting rather than a true reflection of choice and practice at the time.

Deities

The deities who receive the highest number of stelae dedications are Amun-Re (14), Amenhotep I/Queen Ahmes Nefertari (13), and Osiris (13). These are the only gods receiving a significant number of stelae.

Amun-Re (14)

Stelae DB274, DB275, DB280, DB287, DB294, DB295, DB300, DB301, DB302, DB304, DB307, DB308, DB312, DB316

There are 14 stelae dedicated to Amun-Re alone or in the company of other deities, most frequently the other members of the Theban triad. The stelae are evenly spread across the Ramesside Period (six are 19th Dynasty and four are 20th Dynasty; four are undated), and the choice of compositional form A and C across the subset and across the period is also balanced. There are three type B stelae in this group, a relatively high proportion. Amun occurs nine times anthropomorphically, five times as a ram (on one stela he is both anthropomorphic and a ram) and once as a bark. The anthropomorphic form of Amun occurs in the 19th and 20th Dynasties, the ram forms that are dated occur only in the 19th Dynasty.

Figure 3.25 Cult images of Amun-Re (Thebes)

Epithet	No. of stelae	Form/iconography
Foremost of Karnak	3	Anthropomorphic (2); Ram (1)
Ruler of Thebes	2	Anthropomorphic
Lord of the Thrones of the Two Lands/Lord of the Sky/King of the Gods	3	Anthropomorphic
In his Good Festival of the Opet	1	Bark
The Eastern One	2	Anthropomorphic and ram (1); criosphinx and ram (1)
Beautiful of Face, Beloved of Ptah	1	Ram
The Gracious Ear	1	Ram
Lost	1	Anthropomorphic

The ram form boasts the most interesting epithets. On DB287 he is 'Beautiful of Face, Beloved of Ptah' (*nfr ḥr mry Ptḥ*), perhaps indicating a ram statue located near the Ptah temple (?); on DB294 he is called 'The Gracious Ear' (*msḏr ḥtpy*) (or 'Who Hears the Gracious', *sḏm ḥtpy*; Guglielmi 1994: 65-66). On two stelae, DB280 and DB312, he is the 'Eastern One' (*(i)ꜣb*); this epithet and the ram statues at Thebes as sources for these images have been discussed above. His anthropomorphic form receives standard epithet strings referring to his state god status: 'Lord of the Thrones of the Two Lands/Lord of the Sky/King of the Gods' (*nb nswt tꜣwy/nb pt/nsw nṯrw*), his pre-eminence in Thebes as 'Ruler of Thebes' (*ḥkꜣ Wꜣst*), and residence in Karnak (*ḥry-ib/ḫnty ipt swt*). These images may relate to a number of the external reliefs of Amun-Re that received secondary attention at Karnak or elsewhere in Thebes. On one dated stela, DB300, the bark of Amun is depicted with the other barks of the Theban triad, and the epithet, 'in his Good Festival of the Opet' (*m ḥb.f nfr ỉpt*) confirms the depiction of the Opet festival (see Kitchen 1983: 282 for the text; Kitchen calls this the 'Oracle Stela'). This stela is dated to year 7 of Ramesses VI and is clearly commemorative; it was dedicated by the Wab-priest, Divine Scribe and Overseer of the Temple of Maat (in the Karnak temple complex), Merymaat. It can be related to the proposed function of other stelae depicting barks as records of festivals.

The majority of individuals dedicating the stelae with anthropomorphic images of Amun-Re are connected in some way with the temple or estate of Amun: the First God's Servant, Mahuhy (Lefebvre 1929: 154-156; 259-260; Bierbrier 1975: 17; DB274); the Overseer of the Draughtsmen of Amun, Dedia (DB275); the God's Father of Amun, Fanbearer and Mayor of Thebes, Paser, with the Overseer of the Treasury of Upper and Lower Egypt, Amen[…] (DB301); the Sandalmaker of Amun, Amenemhat (DB307); and the Guardian of the Temple of Amun, Anenna (DB308). In addition, there is a Sculptor, a Ka-servant of Tuthmosis I, a Scribe of the Divine Offerings and a Chief of the Medjay, whose status in relation to the Amun temple is not clear - the Medjay were stationed on the West Bank and more closely associated with the Deir el-Medina community (Bierbrier 1982a: 39). Stela DB312 of the Chief of the Medjay, Pagar, is, in fact, principally dedicated to a ram of Amun. The ram stelae are dedicated by a looser group of lower ranking individuals: the Medjay chief, a woman with the titles Follower of Re, Great Singer of Hathor, and a Workman (*sḏm ꜥš*) of Amun; two have no titles. These stelae may in fact belong to unidentified members of the Deir el-Medina community, and, if this is the case, it may be that they all date to the early part of the reign of Ramesses II, when the ram statue cult seems to have been active in the Deir el-Medina community.

Of note is the fact that three of the stelae are made of sandstone and one of granite. This latter stela, DB275 of Dedia, the Overseer of the Draughtsmen of Amun, was dedicated at Akh-isut, the Mentuhotep temple at Deir el-Bahri, and is fairly elaborate in design, with the Theban triad on one side, and two sub-registers of deities on the other. The sandstone stelae have no findspots and are more conventional in design. The use of more costly material may indicate a difference in function or intent of the stelae, with the material acting as an additional expression of status. Of the Deir el-Medina Amun-Re stelae, only two of the 51 were not made of limestone: DB186 of sandstone and DB229 of wood, both 20th Dynasty in date.

There are few known findspots. The only stelae dedicated within the Karnak temple complex belong to high-ranking temple officials: the Overseer of the Temple of Maat, Merymaat, and the God's Father of Amun, Fanbearer and Mayor of Thebes, Paser. This latter stela, DB301, is catagorised as a type B stela with Paser as both beneficiary and intermediary for his lower-ranking colleague, the Overseer of the Treasury, Amen[...] and his wife. It fits the pattern of type B stelae dedicated in the vicinity of official cult locations by high-ranking individuals. Of the other two type B stelae, the First God's Servant of Amun, Mahuhy has Seti II as his intermediary, and the Ka-servant of Tuthmosis I (name lost) has the statue of the deceased king, Tuthmosis I. The other two certain findspots are on the West Bank, at Deir el-Bahri and Men Aset, the funerary temple of Queen Ahmes Nefertari.

Amenhotep I/Queen Ahmes Nefertari (13)

Stelae DB265, DB268, DB269, DB270, DB271, DB273, DB277, DB279, DB282, DB305, DB308, DB315, DB317

There are 13 stelae dedicated to Amenhotep I/Queen Ahmes Nefertari, nine of which date to the 19th Dynasty, one to the 20th Dynasty with three undated. The group is evenly balanced in compositional form with five type A and six type C. The subset includes two type B stelae, both depicting Ramesses II before the palanquin carrying Amenhotep I, dedicated by high-ranking officials (DB271 and DB273). This event, where Ramesses II offers to the deified royal ancestor (and in fact may be involved in an oracular ceremony), may be associated with the rise in importance of the cult of Amenhotep I at Thebes in the 19th Dynasty. The appearance of a new statue of Amenhotep I in the reign of Ramesses II at Deir el-Medina is certainly discernible in the record.

Amenhotep I is most frequently given epithets that refer to his status as a king: 'Perfect God', 'Lord of the Two Lands', 'Son of Re', 'Lord of Appearances' (*nṯr nfr, nb t3wy, s3 Rꜥ, nb ḫꜥw*). On stela DB273 of the Captain of the Bowmen and Architect, Penre, where the statue of Amenhotep I appears in the palanquin to which Ramesses II offers, the epithets are lost from the upper register, but in the lower register the deity receives the following epithet string: 'Son of Amun, His Excellent Image, whom He Loved more than any King, Divine Sperm, Holy Egg, Begotten of Amun himself' (*s3 ỉmn tit.f ỉḳr mr.n.f r nsw nb mw nṯry swḥt ḏsrt ỉr.n ỉmn ḏs.f*). On stela DB270 of the Wab-priest of the Prow of Amun, Huy, Amenhotep I is called 'The

Favourite' (*pꜣ ỉb ỉb/pꜣ ḥꜣty*). This is the epithet that is more commonly found at Deir el-Medina, in the reign of Ramesses II, applied to statues of Amenhotep I in the blue crown, as is the case here. The stela was found under the mortuary temple of the First God's Servant, Nebwenenef, on the West Bank. Huy may, in fact, be an unidentified member of the royal workforce, or it may be that this form of Amenhotep I transferred from the East Bank at Thebes to the Village during the reign of Ramesses II. Queen Ahmes Nefertari is identified as the 'God's Wife (of Amun)' (*ḥmt nṯr (n ỉmn)*).

Figure 3.26 Cult images of Amenhotep I/Queen Ahmes Nefertari (Thebes)

Form/iconography	No. of stelae
Blue crown	4
Cap crown	5
Nemes Headdress	1
Queen Ahmes Nefertari	1
Lost	2

Two of the stelae may have come from the Karnak temple complex: DB268 and DB317. DB317 has no recorded provenance but depicts Amenhotep I and Queen Ahmes Nefertari seated with a dom-palm behind them; on the Temple of Khonsu at Karnak there is a representation of Amenhotep I 'of the Dom Palm' (Guglielmi 1994: 55). Whether the stela would actually have been set up near this image is another question; the unknown Measurer who dedicated the stela could have paid his respects at the temple and set up the stela elsewhere. Stela DB268 is given a Karnak provenance in Porter and Moss (II 1972: 294). Eight have no provenance and the remaining three come from West Bank locations.

The dedicators are all male. Six of the stelae are dedicated by individuals connected to the temple or cult of Amun in some respect: the First God's Servant of Amun, Roma, with the Guardian of the Treasury (DB269), two Guardians of the Amun temple (DB277 and DB308), a Measurer (DB317), and two men calling themselves Wab-priests of the Prow of Amun (DB270 and DB279). DB271 and DB273 have already been discussed, the dedicators are high-ranking military men, holding the title Overseer of Foreign Lands, amongst other titles. The remaining five stelae are dedicated by Sculptors, a Scribe, Workmen (*sḏm*), and one man with no title. The two individuals whose stelae have been given a Karnak temple provenance are a Scribe and the Measurer, whose rank is uncertain. The Amun temple Guardians and one of the Wab-priests of the Prow of Amun dedicate stelae at West Bank mortuary temples. The use of type B stelae by high ranking-individuals fits the expected pattern.

The Theban Amenhotep I and Queen Ahmes Nefertari cult is predominantly early 19th Dynasty; a number of stelae can be dated to the reign of Ramesses II. For example, the palanquin stelae both date to the 19th Dynasty, reign of Ramesses II, and there are two additional stelae where Amenhotep I wears the blue crown, which can also be dated to this reign. The cap crown is worn on five occasions, the three dated examples are 19th Dynasty. Amenhotep I (and Queen Ahmes Nefertari) frequently share the stelae with funerary deities or deceased kings. In TT19 of Amenmose, Amenhotep I is depicted being carried to his bark in a palanquin, and he and Queen Ahmes Nefertari are also shown in their portable barks as part of the Valley festival, alongside seated statues of deceased kings. The festival activity takes place at the temple of Tuthmosis III on the West Bank (Cabrol 2001: 608-609; 612-616; pl. 33). It is tempting to link stelae with representations of deceased kings and funerary deities with this festival, in particular where the dedicators use the title Wab-priest of the Prow of Amun, indicating their role as principal bark-carriers in festival processions. The carrying of Amenhotep I in the palanquin could well have been a part of such a festival (as shown in the TT19 of Amenmose), a ritual less accessible to individuals of lower rank. On stela DB277, dedicated by the Guardian of the temple of Amun, Amenmose, and found in the temple of Mentuhotep, Akh-isut, at Deir el-Bahri, Amenhotep I (his figure is lost) is seated opposite the Hathor cow emerging from the mountain. This temple was the focus of the Valley festival during the New Kingdom, and the stela suggests that the statue of Amenhotep I was carried to the Hathor sanctuary. Interestingly, although Amenmose is the named dedicator, his wife, Amenhotep, and son, precede him on the stela; his rank may have allowed his family this instance of divine access (Robins 1994).

Osiris (13)
Stelae DB265, DB269, DB276, DB278, DB279, DB288, DB291, DB293, DB297, DB304, DB305, DB309, DB313

Osiris is new to the discussion of deities on votive stelae; he did not figure significantly enough in the Deir el-Medina stelae to warrant a section of his own. His stelae are numerically almost evenly spread between the two groups, but not proportionately: 14 Deir el-Medina and 13 non-Deir el-Medina. Osiris' iconography varies so little it is not possible to differentiate cult forms of the god using these as criteria. His epithets are also standard, referring either to his role as a funerary deity: 'Foremost of the Westerners', 'Wennenefer', 'Lord of the Living', 'Lord/Ruler of Eternity', 'Lord of the Necropolis' (*ḫnty imntyw, wnnfr, nb ꜥnḫw, nb ḥkꜣ nḥḥ ḏt, nb r-stꜣw*); or as a state god: 'Great God', 'Lord of the Sky' (*nṯr ꜥꜣ, nb pt*).

Figure 3.27 Cult images of Osiris (Thebes)

Co-deities	No. of stelae
Alone	8
With deceased kings	4
With the Theban triad	1

In Figure 3.27, the stelae are categorised according to those on which Osiris appears alone, those on which he appears with members of the Theban triad, and those on which he appears with deceased kings. This latter group overlaps with the stelae from the Amenhotep I group discussed in the previous section.

The Osiris cult represented on these stelae is predominantly 19th Dynasty. The majority are type A, indicating the popular nature of the cult; there are no type B stelae. Distinguishing votive from funerary stelae when funerary deities are included is not always straightforward. In this study, stelae are regarded as funerary when they depict aspects of the funerary ritual, and as votive when they depict a funerary deity, such as Osiris, alone or with other deities, receiving adoration or offerings from dedicators in the same format as other deities on votive stelae. Two stelae, DB276 and DB305 include the offering formula; the latter is dedicated to Osiris in the company of deceased kings, the former to Osiris alone. DB293 to Osiris alone includes the request for funerary offerings of 'everything good and pure' (*ḫt nbt nfrt wꜥbt*). As Duquesne has noted in relation to the Ramesside Period votive stelae dedicated principally to Wepwawet and Anubis from the tomb of Djefaihapy III at Assiut, by the New Kingdom, the offering formula had 'ceased to have exclusively funerary associations' (2004: 6; see also Pinch 1993: 99). Stela DB278 is provenanced to TT149, the tomb of the dedicator, the Royal Scribe of the Altar/Table of the Lord of the Two Lands, Overseer of the Huntsmen of Amun, Amenmose; this stela is a reuse of another stela and is much damaged, but its findspot suggests an overtly funerary function.

An image of Osiris is extant on the girdle wall (east section) at Karnak, decorated by Ramesses II, where he stands mummiform wearing the white crown, and is called Osiris 'Wennenefer, the True One, King of the Gods, of Coptos, Foremost of the Mansion of Gold near the Temple of Osiris in the Great Place' (*wnnfr mꜣꜥ nsw nṯrw Gbtyw ḫnty ḥwt-nbw m-hꜣw pr-Wsir m st ꜥꜣt*). This image has drill holes above and behind it indicating secondary use (Helck 1968: 67 [89]).

No women dedicate stelae to Osiris, though they appear with other family members on a number of the stelae. The highest ranking individuals dedicate stelae to Osiris with deceased kings: the Prince, Nomarch, Overseer of the God's Servants of all the Gods and the God's Servants of Amun, First God's Servant of Amun, Roma (DB269), and the Scribe of Troops of the Estate of Amun, Wab-priest of the Prow of Amun, Overseer of Works of all the Monuments of Amun, Amenemopenakht (DB279). A Royal Scribe and Huntsman of Amun (DB278) and an Overseer of the temple of Medinet Habu (DB297) dedicate stelae to Osiris alone. Otherwise the stelae are dedicated by Scribes, Craftsmen, a Soldier of the Ship and an Overseer of the Chamber, whose relative rank is hard to establish.

The Osiris stelae may be linked to the Valley festival both when the deceased kings are depicted alongside Osiris, and when they are not. The funerary associations of the Valley festival meant that Osiris was an integral part of this celebration. The high rank of a number of the dedicators, and the West Bank focus of the dedications (the findspots of the stelae and work places of a number of the dedicators) supports this theory:

the festival procession took place on the West Bank, and attendance, or at least the record of attendance, was restricted to the elite and local dignitaries. Stela DB78 from Deir el-Medina depicts Ramesses II and his Vizier, Paser, offering flowers to Osiris while the Foreman, Qaha (i), and his wife kneel below. The stela was found in the court of Qaha (i)'s tomb, TT360. The content of the stela, the king offering flowers to a funerary deity on behalf of a high-ranking member of the Deir el-Medina community, suggests that this stela is connected with the Valley festival (see Section 4.2).

The Theban stelae group: findspot, rank and compositional form

Within this group of 55 stelae, 22 have findspots. Six of these are from the East Bank temple complex of Karnak, though three are not of definite provenance. Of the three that are definite, two are dedicated by an Overseer of the Temple of Maat, Merymaat (the same man?; DB300, DB310), and one by the First God's Servant of Amun, Mahuhy, active in the reign of Seti II (Lefebvre 1929: 154-156; 259-260; Bierbrier 1975: 17; DB274). Of the other 17, three were dedicated at Deir el-Medina sites and, although their titles indicate that their dedicators were not an integral part of the workmen's community, their findspots suggest that they were associated with the community in some way, and perhaps should properly be included in that subset: stela DB278, found in TT149, was dedicated by the Royal Scribe of the Altar/Table of the Lord of the Two Lands and Overseer of the Huntsmen of Amun, Amenmose; stela DB298, from the Great Pit, was dedicated by the Scribe of the Lord of the Two Lands, To; and stela DB299, discovered at the Workmen's Col Station, was dedicated by the Royal Scribe and Overseer of the Treasury, Montuemtawy (r. Ramesses IV). The 14 remaining stelae were dedicated at various West Bank mortuary temples.

It is possible to discern some patterns in the titles and dates of the provenanced stelae. At the temple of Tuthmosis II, all the dedicators use priestly titles, indicating that their role at the temple allowed them the privilege of erecting stelae here. At the Ramesseum, the two 19th Dynasty stelae dedicated by individuals with titles belong to military men, reflecting the military emphasis of the cult of this king.[25] The Deir el-Bahri stelae are all 19th Dynasty, and their dedicators are of a range of ranks.

Some additional patterns are discernible in the choice of compositional form. The three stelae definitely dedicated at Karnak are one type B, stela DB274 of the First God's Servant of Amun, Mahuhy, and two type A, stelae DB300 and DB310 of the Overseer of the Temple of Maat, Merymaat. Stela DB274, discovered in the area known as the 'Fowl yard' (Porter and Moss I.1 1960: 222), is a classic type B stelae where the king, Seti II mediates to the god of the temple, Amun-Re, while Mahuhy kneels below. No other form of stelae could be erected at such proximity to the temple deity, and the stela exactly reflects the ideal political/ theological hierarchy. Of the two Karnak stelae from the Temple of Maat, DB300 is Kitchen's 'Oracle Stela' and commemorates the Opet festival in year 7 of Ramesses VI (Kitchen 1983: 282), depicting the barks of the Theban triad and that of Maat; DB310 depicts priests adoring Maat and Thoth for the benefit of the Ka of the Overseer of the Temple of Maat, Merymaat. At the Deir el-Medina sites the high-ranking individuals who had contact with the community through their administrative duties use type A stelae (both are 20th Dynasty), reflecting the looser decorum on this side of the river, and contrasting with the Senior Scribe, Ramose (i)'s earlier 19th Dynasty reluctance to use anything but type C stelae. This may be due to the later date of these two stelae, and the choice of deities: on stela DB298, To adores Thoth of Hermopolis on a crude stela that appears very unofficial indeed, and on stela DB299, Montuemtawy adores a serpent-headed goddess (Mertseger?) with the cartouches of Ramesses IV above. At the Ramesseum, the stelae dedicated by military men are type A and seem to belong to personal popular cults rather than to a restricted state cult. Stela DB286 of Nebwa, the Scribe of the Army of the Two Lands, includes a list of temple personnel (see Haring 1997: 457; 458) and is dedicated to Wenut and Sobek-Re of 'Hut [...]' (*ḥwt* [...]) - perhaps images from a Ramesseum geographical list. The stela depicts individuals involved in a festival. At Deir el-Bahri, the majority of the stelae are type C.

---

25 Witness the Qantir/Pi-Ramesses stelae, many of which were dedicated by soldiers to colossal statues of Ramesses II (Roeder 1926; Habachi 1954; see Chapter 5).

3.4 Discussion and conclusions

There are a number of general points relating to patterns in production and function of votve stelae that emerge in the analysis of the Deir el-Medina and Theban non-Deir el-Medina subsets. Of obvious note is the marked peak of stelae production in the first half (to middle) of the reign of Ramesses II, amounting to 99 of the 264 stelae in the Deir el-Medina subset, with a second smaller peak occurring in the period Ramesses III-Ramesses IV. These peaks of production are reflected to a less marked extent in the Theban non-Deir el-Medina subset. Type B (mediated divine access) stelae also cluster at these periods, in particular during the first half of the reign of Ramesses II.

It has been possible to link some of the hypostases depicted on the stelae with known archaeological examples of statues and reliefs. A good example is the ram form of Amun-Re, which has an extant original hypostasis in the ram statues now standing in front of the Khonsu temple at Karnak, originally located in front of the Mut temple. The identification allows a discussion of cult access and activity around the Karnak temple complex, with the implication that there may have been a particular link between the Deir el-Medina workmen and the Mut temple complex (Cabrol 1995b: 54), and that the workmen may have been significantly affected, or involved, with Ramesses II's alterations at Karnak, in particular the moving of the ram statues. The identification of specific cult forms helps differentiate groups with varying levels of cult access and affiliation. The question of differential cult access to forms of Amenhotep I arises in relation to the new statue in the blue crown (possibly statue Louvre E. 16277), introduced during the reign of Ramesses II. The appearance of Ramesses II on non-Deir el-Medina stelae, offering to Amenhotep I in the blue crown in the palanquin, is possibly related to the introduction of the new statue in the image of Ramesses II, a statue which gave oracles, and whose cult access delineates a higher-status social group at Deir el-Medina. Ptah has a variety of epithets that have been used to attempt to define forms of the cult, the most popular of which is 'Beautiful of Face who is on his/the Great Throne', which may have been a popular 19th Dynasty cult centered on the Hathor temple, later moving to the Queens' Valley chapels. A second popular cult is that defined as Ptah 'of the Place of Beauty'. The official and more exclusive Ptah cult was that of Ptah as 'Creator/Overseer of Craftsmen/Craftsmanship'. The Hathor cult at Deir el-Medina dates primarily to the early 19th Dynasty, consistent with the restoration work of Ramesses II at the Hathor chapels at Deir el-Bahri and the reconstruction of the Hathor temple at Deir el-Medina, which must have taken place during the first half of his reign: the Senior Scribe, Ramose (i), who, in the Khenu-chapel reliefs DM87 and DM88 (Figure 3.21) associates himself with the construction of the Khenu-chapel attached to the front of the Hathor temple, and dedicates three stelae to the Hathor cult, was in post years 5-40 of Ramesses II; the Vizier, Paser, in post from the reign of Seti I through to the first half of the reign of Ramesses II (Donohue 1988b: 106-107; Pamminger 1996a: 288-290; 1996b: 185), is also depicted in the chapel. Ramesses II also appears on three Hathor stelae, DB28, DB40 and DB118, as an intermediary, where, unusually for this type of stela, the dedicators are all of workmen rank, no higher. Some of the Hathor stelae may relate to a specific historical event - perhaps the restoration and inauguration of the Hathor temple at Deir el-Medina - and define a social group centred on Ramose (i) (see Section 4.1(i)). Access to the Hathor cult, and the use, not only of the image of the king, but that of Ramose (i), as the royal representative and overseer of the Hathor cult, is a status indicator for those individuals using such representations on their stelae.

Mertseger's cult at Deir el-Medina has traditionally been interpreted as a domestic cult and therefore centered on the women in the community, or at the Queens' Valley chapels. However, the serpent cult of the 19th Dynasty in the form of serpent statues with a woman's head is restricted in the subset to men socially central to the community, and to particular pleas and requests. There appears to have been at least one magical statue of Mertseger as a serpent with a woman's head, in use during the first half of the reign of Ramesses II, to which certain individuals had access when clemency from the goddess was required. During the 20th Dynasty, women began dedicating stelae to groups of serpents, a form which had previously only appeared on stelae dedicated by men alongside other forms of the deity. That women do not noticeably utilise votive Mertseger stelae until the 20th Dynasty may be a result of changes in either decorum or cult accessibility, or both. The appearance of stelae dedicated by women to the serpent cult of Mertseger is a rare example of female access to the predominantly male monumental record, highlighting the infrequent records of female ritual social practices, and acting as a reminder of the bias of the stelae as social records towards elite adult males. In relation to the Hathor cult, another cult traditionally associated with women due to Hathor's associations with fertility, there is a clear distinction in cult access for men and women: Hathor's anthropomorphic and cow form represent official versions of her cult and the stelae to these forms are dedicated by men; her cat, swallow and column forms are depictions of statuettes and votive offerings and may represent the paraphernalia associated with a temple visit, and women as stelae dedicators only occur in relation to such indirect depictions. The conspicuous lack of female dedicators overall underlines the overtly masculine public and professional domain that the stelae reflect.

The non-Deir el-Medina stelae have been presented in a less detailed and more discursive manner than the Deir el-Medina stelae, justifiable on the grounds that they are comparatively few in number and, as a result, do not form a subset that can be unpicked to the same level of detail. This is clear when attempting to identify patterns in terms of the compositional form of the stelae, the deity and the original location of the stelae, the factors that were chosen as status related. The non-Deir el-Medina stelae are simply too few, and the cult images too problematic to locate, to allow the identification of clear patterns. Status identification is hampered by the fact that we know so little about the relative status of the majority of the titles.

The cults of Amenhotep I and Osiris in the non-Deir el-Medina group are predominantly 19th Dynasty; the Amun-Re stelae span both dynasties. The ram/criosphinx of Amun-Re and the Amenhotep I in the palanquin stelae are the only iconographic groups that emerge with any clarity. These stelae are dedicated by individuals that fit the pattern established by the Deir el-Medina dedicators: the ram statue/criosphinxes are an accessible popular cult; Amenhotep I in the palanquin is a restricted elite cult. Both are 19th Dynasty, and both may date to the reign of Ramesses II, though there are no reign dates for the ram statue/criosphinx stelae. There are a number of representations of other deceased royal ancestors at Deir el-Medina, for example those depicting Tuthmosis IV. Stela DB121 of the Foreman, Anhurkhawy (i), depicts a statue of Tuthmosis IV as the intermediary to Amun-Re and Queen Ahmes Nefertari. Tuthmosis IV also occurs in the text of stela DB128 (Amenhotep I in the palanquin). The Senior Scribe, Ramose (i), includes the cartouche of Tuthmosis IV on the relief DM88 (Cairo JdE 72017; see Figure 3.21) along with that of Ramesses II and Horemheb. All of these instances date to the reign of Ramesses II, and suggest that Tuthmosis IV had a cult statue in the Village and it is this that appears on stela DB121,[26] just as there may have existed a cult statue of Tuthmosis II on the West Bank (Redford 1986: 54). Alternatively the depictions are of festival processions where statues of deceased kings were paraded (Redford 1986: 51-54). This would explain the representation of Amenhotep I in the nemes headdress, a cult processional statue, on stela DB27, dating to the first half of the reign of Ramesses II, which may be a non-Deir el-Medina festival statue. Stela DB121 has the names of Anhurkhawy (i) and his wife added in ink (Edwards 1939: 54, pl. XLV), suggesting that this stela may have been a generic artefact perhaps available at a festival event, which Anhurkhawy (i) personalised. Ramesses II's involvement with the cult of Amenhotep I (Ramesses II does not appear on any of the other Theban stelae), and at Deir el-Medina, together with tomb paintings of festival occasions dating to this reign, suggests that, early in his reign, Ramesses II took part in a large festival, perhaps the Valley festival or Opet festival, which made a lasting impression on the Theban community at this time. A high-profile, dramatic festival, early in the reign of Ramesses II, coupled with a change in decorum allowing a broader demographic to create public records of royal events, may have been the impetus behind the numerous stelae and tomb paintings recording festival activity that can be dated to Ramesses II's reign, in particular to the first half of the reign. In addition, some or all of the non-Deir el-Medina Osiris stelae may be related to such a festival.

The high proportion of stelae dedicated on the West Bank reflects the nature of this area of Thebes as the centre for acts of private devotion manifesting, during the Ramesside Period, as votive stelae. Devotional acts on the East Bank have not left such a permanent record, perhaps due to sumptuary controls that limited an individual's freedom to record his devotion at close proximity to a state temple, and/or to frequent clearances of temple areas. It is interesting that a number of anepigraphic Amun stelae have been found at Karnak (Porter and Moss II 1972: 171) which suggests that such artefacts were considered to be a different class of votive object (Pinch 1993: 94), perhaps because of their anonymous nature - they could not act as personal status indicators if the dedicator was not recorded.

That cult activity manifested itself in the apparent production of such a contrasting proportion of stelae at Deir el-Medina and amongst the other residents of Thebes cannot be explained away simply with the belief that 'personal piety' was the prerogative of the workmen. The numerous Deir el-Medina stelae bear witness to royally sanctioned, innovative artistic behaviour by the workmen, who were well-placed to make such artefacts: stelae would not have been so easy to come by if one were not a craftsman by trade. Cult activity

[26] See McDowell 1992b: 98 for a discussion of why Tuthmosis IV in particular may have been prominent in the Village.

amongst non-Deir el-Medina individuals may have manifested itself in more transient activities, or anepigraphic or less permanent artefacts. The relative importance of stelae to each community could well have been very different - the higher proportion of stelae made of more costly materials in the Theban non-Deir el-Medina group suggests that stelae were regarded as more significant to non-Deir el-Medina dedicators.

There are a number of instances of innovative cult practice and use of the monumental record dating to the reign of Ramesses II which can be summed up as follows:

- The Hathor cult at Deir el-Medina dates predominantly to the reign of this king (25/34 stelae), and, in particular, the cow cult, the 'Residing in Thebes' cult, and the geographical list versions of Hathor;
- At Deir el-Medina, zoomorphic and emblemetic forms of Hathor and Amun-Re occur frequently during this reign, and not at all in the 20th Dynasty. In this group are the ram statues, whose depiction on early 19th Dynasty stelae is also paralleled in the Theban non-Deir el-Medina stela;
- Representations of Amun-Re with oracle related iconography or epithets date exclusively to the first half of the reign of Ramesses II;
- Representations of Amenhotep I in the blue crown are exclusive to the reign of Ramesses II; the depiction of Amenhotep I in the nemes headdress also dates to this reign;
- Representations of the statue of Mertseger as a serpent with a female head date exclusively to the reign of Ramesses II;
- The majority of the Ptah stelae with the 'Beautiful of Face' epithet date to the early 19th Dynasty;
- In the Theban subset, the majority of the Amenhotep I and Osiris stelae are 19th Dynasty and may in fact date to this king's reign, though this cannot be proven at this stage.

Such phenomena, together with the large number of stelae produced at this period, and the relatively high frequency of type B stelae, can be linked to Ramesses II's policy in relation to popular cult activity, to Theban building projects and to the attempt at re-establishing the authority of the kingship across as broad a demographic as possible (Kitchen 1982b: 178).

Some stelae are clearly records of events, i.e. they have an explicit commemorative rather than a purely votive function, such as the stelae depicting Ramesses II offering to the gods at the Deir el-Medina Hathor temple on behalf of the workmen. The stelae dedicated one each by Bukhanefptah (i) (DB13) and her husband Kasa (i) (DB37), with comparable representations of an anthropomorphic Hathor, ritual paraphernalia and family members with offerings and musical instruments, record a festival occasion. The text on the stela of Nebre (i) (DB60) depicting, uniquely, a colossal statue of Ramesses II before temple pylons overtly links a temple visit or pilgrimage with the making of a stela. It may be the case that other stelae record temple visits or festival events, such as the oracle or festival stelae of Amun-Re and the depictions of Amenhotep I in his palanquin. Depictions of visits to East Bank hypostases such as the ram statues at the Khonsu temple may record a festival occasion where temple access was granted, and the depictions of deceased kings, such as Amenhotep I in the nemes headdress, can be linked to parts of state festival processions where such statues were paraded. In the Theban non-Deir el-Medina subset there are a number of specific instances of commemoration: stela DB300 of the Wab-priest and Divine Scibe, Merymaat records part of the Opet festival of year 7 of Ramesses VI; stelae DB271 and DB273 depict Ramesses II offering to Amenhotep I in the presence of high ranking military men; stela DB286 of the Army Scribe, Nebwa, from the Ramesseum, depicts Nebwa with colleagues and family holding musical instruments and offerings, indicating the event of a festival, before Wenut and Sobek-Re 'of Hut', possibly a version of Sobek-Re from the Ramesseum geographical list.

The stelae can record, through iconography, format, and on rare occasion directly in the text, access to temples at particular times, allowing an assessment of the social status of the dedicator. Stelae were not always dedicated in the vicinity of the original hypostasis, for example, the ram statue stelae were discovered at Deir el-Medina when such statues only existed on the East Bank, suggesting that records of visits to state temples were set up within the community of the dedicator to record such a visit for posterity and display the fact of the visit, with the concomitant effect this would have had on his status within his own community. As with tomb paintings, the stelae record presence at events as a single occasion that would benefit the owner for their lifetime and beyond - presence at state festivals altered the status of an individual. This is comparable to modern day participation in the Hajj, where on completion an individual can take the title Hajji. Paintings of the pilgrimage can be found on Egyptian village houses to mark that the owner is a Hajji.

Compositional form is frequently linked to the rank of the dedicator. The type B stelae are most often dedicated by individuals of high rank such as viziers, foremen and senior scribes, in particular when the intermediary is a living individual such as the king or his vizier. The depiction of a living king as intermediary, traditionally interpreted as a two-dimensional representation of the concept the king as *nb irt ḫt*, 'Lord of Rites' (Podemann Sørensen 1989b: 120), or of the offering formula (*ḥtp-di-nsw*) (Radwan 1969: 41; Myśliwiec 1985: 11), functions on the stelae as the record of the presence of the dedicator at a royal or state ceremony, as is equally the case when viziers appear as mediators carrying out a ceremony in lieu of the king. Type C stelae are a more traditional mode of representation where the dedicator does not have, or does not choose to display, direct representational access to the deity. The Senior Scribe, Ramose (i), chose type C for his stelae design, reflecting his relationship to the traditional social order. Innovative forms of monumental record (e.g. type A stelae) may have conflicted with the royal theogamy; rather, Ramose (i) displayed his higher social status by choosing traditional modes of representation, closer to the authorised decorum. Such choices of form and content, as well as the constraints within which such choices operate, act as a symbolic mode of discourse which can be related to the ongoing construction of social structure.

***

The analysis of the core subset has identified a number of events and hypostases to which the stelae refer, providing the context (the social practices) for the commissioning of some of the stelae. In addition, there appears to be a level of correlation between compositional form and individual social status, and compositional form and the nature of the event recorded. This correlation allows the stelae to serve as a mechanism for studying social relations (Miller 1995: 267), hierarchy, structure and organisation, in an individual's immediate and wider society. Chapter 4 takes a closer look at some of groups of stelae that have emerged through the discussion in Chapter 3.

4. FESTIVALS, FERTILITY AND DIVINE INTERVENTION AT DEIR EL-MEDINA

The data analysis in Chapter 3 suggested that patterns in the form and content of the Deir el-Medina/Theban votive stelae could be related to specific events of either a public or a private nature. Public events can be defined as events which took place in the larger community, such as royal ceremonies, which the dedicator attended or witnessed, and which affected or involved a group of people beyond his (never her) immediate family. Private events can be defined as events that directly involved or affected him (less frequently her) or his (or her) family. We may include in private events activities such as promotion at work or entry into a wab-priesthood.

In Section 4.1, stelae from the dataset that relate to public events are set within the context of other textual and representational data relating to the same event. The three historical events that can be identified from the Deir el-Medina private votive stelae are: a visit of Ramesses II in person or in statue form to the Hathor temple in the Village; the use of oracles in the reign of Ramesses II, in particular the oracle of the deified Amenhotep I; and a visit of the Vizier, To, to the Queens' Valley chapels in the reign of Ramesses III. In Section 4.2, stelae are grouped into categories relating to private events, or desires, according to defined criteria and an attempt is made to interpret the motivating event. Some of the events which are here termed 'private' may be defined as 'rites of passage'. In Section 4.3, a number of Deir el-Medina stelae belonging to a small group of individuals are placed within the suggestd framework of public and private events, creating a form of individual monumental biography.

4.1 Public events on votive stelae

Woolf sees Roman monuments as permanent and enduring symbols, 'important not in themselves but for what they were reminders of... The eternity of monuments guaranteed not lasting things but rather momentary events of lasting significance - treatises, virtuous acts, acts of public generosity, acts of religious devotion' (1996: 27). This statement can be compared to Schulman's arguments for the event-related nature of Egyptian votive stelae (1980: 101-102; 1988: 194). This section discusses the historical nature of some private votive stelae that record three sets of public events of lasting significance for their owners. The choice of events is based on existence in the dataset of iconographically coherent groups of stelae linked with contemporary dedicators. In addition, in the latter two cases, documentary records in the form of ostraca and graffiti provide supplementary evidence for the occurrence of the event.

4.1(i) A visit of Ramesses II to the Hathor temple in the Village

Bruyère (1935-1940 (1948) I: 84-85; see pl. II) established that an 18th Dynasty stone-built chapel stood where the Ptolemaic temple to Hathor, and Maat, now stands, north of the Village. He hypothesised (1935-1940 (1948) I: 8) that the Ptolemies would only have built a temple to an existing cult, and thus it was Hathor to whom the fragmentary 18th Dynasty remains were dedicated. Ventura (1986: 47-48) defines this Hathor as an aspect of the goddess Maat. It is as Hathor that this goddess is given royal attention in the 19th Dynasty at Deir el-Medina, while, in the 20th Dynasty, Mertseger takes on this role on royal monuments. Stelae dating to the reigns of Horemheb, Ramesses I and Seti I (Bruyère 1935-1940 (1952) II: 16 [3A], 17 [3A], 149 [414] and [422]) demonstrate the continuation of royal patronage at the site in the early Ramesside Period, to Hathor, and other gods, in particular Ptah and Amun-Re. In addition, Bruyère discovered reliefs of Horemheb below the Ramesses II Hathor chapel (Bruyère 1935-1940 (1948) I: 20). Ramesses II rebuilt the Hathor chapel and constructed a chapel to Amun-Re to the south-east (Bruyère's Eastern Sector; Bruyère 1935-1940 (1948) I: 121-125). Merenptah and Seti I built Ka-chapels to the north-east (Bruyère's Sector 3 (Merenptah) and Northern Sector (Seti I)) of the Hathor chapel (Bruyère 1935-1940 I (1948) I: 91; 97; 101-104).

Stelae dedicated to Hathor as a cow, and to Hathor in her anthropomorphic form, have been discovered at Deir el-Medina, indicating that there were hypostases in both forms at Deir el-Medina. Fragmentary cow statues are also extant (p. 55). There are no extant reliefs from the Hathor temple proper. Sadek (1987: 64; 83) identified a mud brick chapel (Chapel III; Porter and Moss I.2 1964: 691) in the temple precinct as dedicated to Hathor, amongst other gods, on the evidence of relief dedicated to Hathor and Harsomtus and the royal Ka, as well as other fragments mentioning the goddess. If this is the case, this chapel may have been dedicated to a popular anthropomorphic cult image of Hathor separate from the official temple cult, to whom some of the stelae may have been dedicated.

The monumental evidence in the form of reliefs from the Khenu-chapel attached to the front of the Hathor temple reveals that the Vizier, Paser, and the Senior Scribe, Ramose (i), constructed this chapel for the cult of the living king in association with the goddess Hathor (Davies 1999: 80). Ramose (i) held the post of Senior Scribe from year 5 of Ramesses II's reign to around year 40 (Černý 1973: 321; Davies 1999: 79 and nn. 33, 34). He was appointed from outside the Village, having previously held scribal posts at the memorial temple of Tuthmosis IV and perhaps at the memorial temple of Amenhotep son of Hapu, both on the Theban West Bank (Davies 1999: 79). His father held a courtier's post, indicating an aristocratic family background and links to the king (Malek 1974: 165; Davies 1999: 79, n. 31). Ramose (i) claimed responsibility for building the Khenu-chapel and may have been involved with Ramesses II's restoration of the main temple. He recorded the building of the Khenu-chapel in inscriptions extant from that building: reliefs DM87 and DM88 (Figure 3.21; Bruyère 1935-1940 (1952) II: 39; 66-68 and pl. XXXVI) from room 4 of the Khenu-chapel. In DM87 (Louvre E.16276 a/b; Porter and Moss I.2 1964: 696; Figure 3.21) a Hathor cow statue stands on a sledge with a lotiform prow in a papyrus thicket, with a statue of the king, identified as Ramesses II by a cartouche, protected by the menat necklace. The inscription tells us that this is Hathor, 'Residing in Thebes', and states below, '[Made by] this servant (according to) the instruction of his lord, the Royal Scribe in the Place of Truth to the West of Thebes, Ramose, justified' ([*ir.n*] *b3k im sb3 n nb.f sš nsw m st m3ˁt ḥr imntt W3st Rˁ-ms m3ˁ ḫrw*). Relief DM88 (Cairo JdE 72017; Porter and Moss I.2 1964: 697) depicts the Senior Scribe, Ramose (i), kneeling before a Hathor cow statue, identified as Hathor, 'Lady of the Southern Sycamore', on a sledge, with a statue of a king protected by her menat-necklace, and the cartouches of Ramesses II, Thutmosis IV and Horemheb above. The four columns above Ramose (i) read, 'Receiving the good place by Hathor, Lady of the Southern Sycamore, by the hand of the Royal Scribe, Ramose, justified' (*šsp bw nfr Ḥwt-ḥr nbt nht rsyt m-dt sš nsw Rˁ-ms m3ˁ ḫrw).* According to these reliefs, the Khenu-chapel houses two Hathor cults: one identified as Hathor, 'Residing in Thebes', the Hathor that transferred from Deir el-Bahri (Pinch 1993: 8) and one as Hathor, 'Lady of the Southern Sycamore', the Memphite Hathor (Malek 1974: 163).

Blumenthal (2000: 48) suggests that the Hathor cow cult at Deir el-Medina may have been an invention of Ramesses II. The monumental evidence discussed in Chapter 3 indicates that the cult of Hathor, Residing in Thebes, originally located at Deir el-Bahri, was transferred to Deir el-Medina, possibly by Ramesses II, emphasising his association with Hathor who as a cow suckles and protects the legitimate king.

A group of stelae from Deir el-Medina, depicting Ramesses II making offerings before Hathor, Ptah and perhaps Amun-Re, may record a royal visit on the occasion of the inauguration of the cult temple of Hathor, 'Residing in Thebes', at Deir el-Medina, following the restoration work. The reliefs from the Khenu-chapel may support such a reading of the stelae (see the table in Figure 4.1). Three of the stela have an almost identical representation of Ramesses II offering to the gods of the official pantheon (Ptah, Hathor or Amun-Re) followed by his Vizier, Paser, carrying the royal Ka-staff (DB39, DB40, stela Turin Museum Suppl. 6189+6193). In the second register male members of the community kneel in adoration. Stela DB135 has lost most of the upper register but the text contains a hymn to Ptah and the royal Ka by an unnamed Foreman. Stelae DB28 and DB118 carry similar depictions of the king offering or censing to an anthropomorphic Hathor seated holding the was-sceptre and ankh-sign, but lack the Vizier (neither has a find spot). Stela DB65 depicts the Senior Scribe, Ramose (i), following the Vizier, Paser, adoring a statue of Ramesses II (the lower register only remains). On this stela, Ramesses II is in the role of beneficiary rather than active participant/intermediary, and this stela may relate to a different event. The king is depicted in the cap crown, more commonly worn by Amenhotep I at Deir el-Medina.

The representation of Paser carrying the royal Ka-staff found on the stelae is also found on the limestone doorjamb discovered by Bruyère in Pit 1415 in the Khenu-chapel (Bruyère 1935-1940 (1952) II: 40 [94], fig. 116). Ramesses II's association with the Khenu-chapel and Hathor as a cow worshipped within it is supported by relief DM70 (Bruyère 1935-1940 (1952) II: 38; 63-65 [70], pl. XXX; Porter and Moss I.2 1964: 697) from the doorway between rooms 2 and 3. The relief shows Ramesses II, followed by his Vizier, Paser, offering a cow to the goddess Hathor (the figure of the deity is lost). A man who may be the Senior Scribe, Ramose (i), kneels below with a broken text, part of which reads, 'I will make a Khenu within the [house] of this statue of my lord which rests within it' (*iw iry.i ẖnw m-ẖnw*[. ..] *twt pn n nb.i ḥtp m-ẖnw.f).*

Figure 4.1 Images of Ramesses II from Deir el-Medina

Database/Repository number	Dedicator	Find spot	Description
Stela DB28	Workman, Huy (iv)	Unknown	Ramesses II censes to an anthropomorphic, seated Hathor
Stela DB39	Workman, Karo/Kel (i)	Hathor Temple: Khenu-chapel, Room 2	Ramesses II offers maat to Ptah, with the Vizier, Paser carrying the Ka-staff
Stela DB40	Guardian, Khawy (ii)	Unknown	Ramesses II offers to Hathor, with the Vizier, Paser, carrying the Ka-staff
Stela DB65	Senior Scribe, Ramose (i)	Hathor Temple: Hathor Chapel of Seti I: Shrine of Bukentef	The Vizier, Paser, followed by Ramose (i), adore a statue of Ramesses II in the cap crown
Stela DB118	Workman, Nekh(em)mut (i)	Unknown	Ramesses II offers to an anthropomorphic, seated Hathor and Mut
Stela DB135	Unnamed Foreman	Outside the north wall of the Ptolemaic temple enclosure	[Ramesses II offers to ?Ptah]
Stela Turin Museum Suppl. 6189 + 6193 (=Tosi and Roccati 50095)	Dedicator lost	Queens' Valley chapels?	Ramesses II offers maat to ?Amun, with the Vizier, Paser, carrying the Ka-staff
Relief DM70		Hathor Temple: Khenu-chapel, doorway between rooms 2 and 3	Ramesses II, followed by Paser, offering a cow to the goddess Hathor (figure lost) with a male figure below
Doorjamb DM94[1]		Hathor Temple: Khenu-chapel, Pit 1415	Paser carrying the royal Ka-staff

The content of these stelae suggests that they represent a royal ceremony that took place within the Hathor temple, and that they may have originally been set up in or near the temple or Khenu-chapel. Ramesside Period private stelae depicting royal ceremonies have been found lined up around the temple at Zawiyet Umm el-Rakham and set up against the wall in a row in the sphinx forecourt at Wadi es-Sebua (see Chapter 5). The fragmentary stela, DB135, of the unnamed Foreman, discovered outside the north wall of the Ptolemaic temple enclosure, could have been moved here during a general temple clearance at any period after the reign of Ramesses II. The Ptolemies certainly cleared out much of the temple area to make room for their building programme (Bruyère 1945-1947 (1952): 9). Stela Turin Museum Suppl. 6189 + 6193 (= Tosi and Roccati 50095) is provenanced to the Queens' Valley chapels (Porter and Moss I.2 1964: 706-709) by Bruyère (1930b: 284) but has only Deir el-Medina as the provenance in the Tosi and Roccati catalogue (1972: 129).

The representations on the stelae show Hathor as anthropomorphic, and can most clearly be interpreted as depicting a ceremony in the main Hathor temple. The only stela with an exact find spot, in room 2 of the Khenu-chapel, is DB39 (Plate 5b) of the Workman, Karo/Kel (i). The chapel may have been the location where it was permissible for private individuals to erect stelae that recorded the ceremony that took place within the temple. Stelae recording cult activity at Karnak, such as the stelae depicting ram statues, have been discovered at Deir el-Medina, in or near the Hathor temple precinct (see Chapter 3). This could be the result of regulations regarding the setting up of private records of cult activity. In such a case, permanent divine access, or display of such access, through private inscribed monuments, to the Karnak temple

[1] The latter three respectively: Porter and Moss I.2 1964: 731; Porter and Moss I.2 1964: 697; Porter and Moss I.2 1964: 698.

precinct, was not permissible for the majority of the Deir el-Medina residents, even if occasional actual physical access was. In addition, it may have been of greater significance to the stelae owners to set up their stelae within their own community, where their moment of divine access could be displayed to their contemporaries and descendants.

There is no documentary evidence in the administrative records from Deir el-Medina to support the idea of a personal visit to the temple by Ramesses II. In his survey of visits by dignitaries to the necropolis, Janssen (1997: 152) records only one visit of a king to the West Bank, Seti II, at the time of the Opet festival (O. Cairo 25560). However, the administrative records from the early Ramesside Period are extremely fragmentary, and it is likely that other royal visits will have occurred.

Ramesses II makes an appearance in some of the Deir el-Medina tombs in similar contexts. In TT10 of Penbuy (i) and Kasa (i), both active during the first half of the reign, a scene depicts Ramesses II, his Vizier, Paser and Ramose (i) before Ptah and Hathor, with Penbuy and his brother Penshenabu below offering to Amenhotep I, Queen Ahmes Nefertari, Seti I, Ramesses I and Horemheb (Davies 1999: 81) - the latter three kings are also depicted on stela DB94 of Ramose (i). Ramesses II also accompanies Paser and Ramose (i) in TT4 of Qen (ii) (Davies 1999: 81), and the King and his Vizier appear offering to the Theban triad in TT7 of Ramose (i).[2] Further circumstantial evidence can be found in the stelophorous statue (Cairo JdE 72000) of the Senior Scribe, Ramose (i), which refers to the endowment of a statue on his and the Vizier, Paser's, behalf, from the Ramesseum, in year nine of Ramesses II (see below) - Schmidt (1973: 104) assumes that the king came in person to activate the endowment. If the stelae do record a royal visit, then this body of evidence fills a substantial gap in the textual data.[3]

The individuals dedicating the stelae

Of the named principal dedicators, three are workmen: Karo/Kel (i), Huy (iv) and Nekh(em)mut (i). Nekh(em)mut has been identified as Nekh(em)mut (i) on the basis of the relatives whom he represents and/or lists on the stela: his wife, the Lady of the House, Webkhet (vi)/(viii), his son Khons (v), and his daughters Tameket (ii) and Tasaket (i) (not represented) (Davies 1999: chart 7). Nekh(em)mut (i) must have still been a very young man, despite already having established a family, when his stela depicting Ramesses II was dedicated.[4] His membership of a prominent family, that of Sennedjem (i), and his subsequent promotion to the post of foreman, indicate his importance, which may already have been recognised and so secured his presence at the ceremony. The workman, Huy (iv), buried in TT339, has two stelae in the dataset, with an additional three funerary stelae known.[5] There are in addition several stelae in the dataset dedicated by individuals called Huy who cannot be identified, some of which may belong to this man. His son Wadjmose (i) married Iyemwaw (ii), daughter of the Foreman, Nebnefer (i), and sister of the Foreman, Neferhotep (ii). Thus, despite only carrying the title workman, he was closely connected to one of the most important families in the Village (Davies 1999: 10-11 and chart 6).The workman Karo/Kel (i), buried in TT330, also bears the title Stonemason of Amun in the Southern City, indicating that he, and his father Simut (i), who bore a similar title, may have been employed in building projects on the East Bank (Davies 1999: 274). On a standard-bearer statuette (MMA 65.114; Davies 1999: 274, n. 887) he uses the title Chief Craftsman, which Davies (1999: 274) suggests may have been honorific. He may also have dedicated a stela to Amenhotep I, Queen Ahmes Nefertari and Mertseger, where he identifies himself as a Wab-priest of the Lord of the Two Lands (Davies 1999: 275 and n. 893). He married Takhat (ii), who was the sister of the Foreman, Qaha (i). His daughters were also married to prominent men: Pashedet (i) to the Draughtsman, Nebre (i) (Davies 1999: 149-155), and Henutdjuu (i) to the Foreman, Anhurkhawy (i) (Davies 1999: 275). The group of stelae also

[2] Ramesses II appears in additional tombs in different contexts. For example, in TT217 of the Sculptor, Ipuy (i), the tomb owner is rewarded by Ramesses II at a window of appearances. Ramesses II is also depicted on Elephantine Island in TT216 of the Foreman, Neferhotep (ii).

[3] See Section 4.1(iii), The Visit of the Vizier, To, for an example of the two bodies of material, votive stelae and textual evidence, clearly complementing each other.

[4] Davies (1999: 47) discusses the problem of the apparently extremely long period of service of this man. He appears as an adult with a wife and children on this stela in the reign of Ramesses II, but was Foreman of the Gang in the reign of Ramesses III, a hypothesis first put forward by Bierbrier (1984: 201). Nekh(em)mut (i) is the grandson of Sennedjem (i) and married a granddaughter of the same man, Webkhet (vi/viii) (Davies 1999: chart 7).

[5] Neuchatel Musée d'Ethnographie No. 12, Eg. 238 (Porter and Moss I.2 1964: 719); Turin Museum Suppl. 6148 =Tosi and Roccati 50077 (Porter and Moss I.2 1964: 720); British Museum EA 446 (Porter and Moss I.2 1964: 720).

includes the Guardian, Khawy (ii). Khawy (ii) was active between the years 11 and 38 of Ramesses II and held the position of guardian between the years 21 and 36 (Davies 1999: 192-193). His importance within the community is evident in his appearance in the tombs of other individuals, for example, TT4 of the Sculptor, Qen (ii), TT10 of the Workman, Kasa (i), and the Guardian, Penbuy (i), and TT250, constructed by the Senior Scribe, Ramose (i). In graffiti he associates himself with other important members of the community: in graffito no. 95 with the Senior Scribe, Amenemope (i) or (ii) (Davies 1999: 77), and in graffito no. 849f with the Draughtsman, Nebre (i) (Davies 1999: 154). He dedicates a stela to the ram of Amun with Amenemope (MMA 14.6.183; Davies 1999: 77 and n. 16). In addition, an unnamed Foreman was also present at the ceremony; it may be that the monument of the other contemporary foreman is lost.

The stelae depicting Ramesses II involved in cult activity indicate that the stelae owners witnessed the event (Podemann Sørensen's type (a) divine access; 1989b: 110). They include individuals who, at first, do not appear to be of a particularly high rank and some of whom do not, in this group of stelae, carry titles other than that of workman, though in the context of such stelae the title may have been the most significant. The stelae bear witness to a social group delineating social organisation defined by cult activity, which may partially cut across the professional and lineage hierarchy (Service 1971: 12). This social group centres on the Senior Scribe, Ramose (i), who appears to have been intimately connected with the Hathor cult.

The Senior Scribe, Ramose (i)

Ramose (i) features on reliefs DM87 and DM88 claiming responsibility for the construction of the Khenu chapel, and on stelae DB65 offering to a statue of Ramesses II with the Vizier, Paser. Bruyère discovered a group of stelae and statues dedicated by Ramose (i) in the Khenu-chapel (see, for example, Bruyère 1935-1940 (1952) II: 41-42 and pls. XXXIII-XXXV, XXXIX). There is, in addition, a fragment of a stela to Hathor and Ramesses II dedicated by a scribe (name lost), who may be Ramose (i), from a Ramesside chapel located against the north wall of the Ptolemaic temple precinct (Bruyère 1935-1940 (1952) II: 52-53 and fig. 142 [214]).

The stelophorous statue of Ramose (i) from the Khenu-chapel (Cairo JdE 72000) records an endowment set up by the scribe in year nine under the command of Ramesses II for 'this statue in the [temple] of Hathor, Residing in Thebes' (*n twt pn m [pr?] Ḥwt-ḥr ḥry(t)-tp W3st*) for Ramose (i)'s benefit (Bruyère 1935-1940 (1952) II: 42, pls. XII, XXXV; Porter and Moss I.2 1964: 697 (c); Schmidt 1973: 231-232; Haring 1997: 147). The inscription states that offerings will come from the Ramesseum, and that the endowment has been set up by Ramose (i) and the Vizier, Paser (Haring 1997: 147-149; Hovestreydt 1997: 117-118). The identity of the statue installed by Ramose (i) has been debated,[6] but what is clear is that Ramesses II endowed a statue on behalf of the Senior Scribe, Ramose (i), to be placed in the Hathor temple or Khenu-chapel at Deir el-Medina. Ramose (i)'s link to the Khenu-chapel may in fact be far more personal and personally prestigious than has previously been thought. It is before Hathor, 'Lady of the Southern Sycamore', that Ramose (i) is depicted kneeling in adoration on the relief DM88 from the Khenu-chapel (Figure 3.21). Ramose (i) also depicts Hathor, 'Lady of the Southern Sycamore', on his stela DB89 (Plate 6). In addition, there is a stela fragment, DB101, provenanced to the Queens' Valley chapels, that depicts two cow statues side by side, all epithets lost, with 'Scribe of Truth, Ramose' (*sš m3ʿt Rʿ-ms*) inscribed underneath, which may be related to the Khenu-chapel double Hathor cow cult. Hathor, 'Lady of the Southern Sycamore', does not appear to feature on other extant private monuments from Deir el-Medina. Ramose (i)'s link to the cult of Hathor, 'Lady of the Southern Sycamore', is further supported by a stela in the collection of the Oriental Museum, University of Durham (N1965; Birch 1880: 305-307: Malek 1974: 161-165, pl. XXXIV), which depicts an anthropomorphic Isis-Hathor in the upper register and a cow Hathor in the lower, both identified as Hathor, 'Lady of the Southern Sycamore'. The stela belongs to the Retainer, Amenemheb, who has been identified as the father of Ramose (i) (Malek 1974: 165).

---

6 The statue has been identified as a Hathor-cow statue (Bruyère 1935-1940 (1952) II: 64), the stelopherous statue of Ramose himself (Valbelle 1985: 319), or the wooden statue of a king (Louvre E. 16277) found beneath the Khenu-chapel (Haring 1997: 147-149; Hovestreydt 1997: 117-118). This latter identification is supported by Hovestreydt's discussion (1997) of the letter to the king written on the back of P. Turin 1879, which appears to refer to royal statue cults set up in the vicinity of the Deir el-Medina Hathor temple by private individuals during the Ramesside Period, and indeed may make specific reference to a cult established for Ramesses II by Ramose (i) (1997: 108; 115-116).

The new Hathor cow cult at Deir el-Medina was a state initiative wherein Ramesses II donated the cow statue to serve as as a vehicle for his own royal cult (Pinch 1993: 350; Blumenthal 2000: 57-58). From the evidence it appears that when Ramose (i) was appointed to the post of Senior Scribe in year 5, he brought with him his own northern version of the Hathor cult and installed it alongside the royal southern Hathor cult in the Khenu-chapel. Thus the Khenu-chapel served as the cult centre for a royal cult and for Ramose (i)'s personal cult, from both of which he would have accrued material and spiritual benefits.[7] As Eyre has observed, '[t]here can be little doubt that [the Khenu-chapel] was built by Ramose under the supervision of the Vizier, Paser, and decorated much to their advantage as well as the king' (1980: 118). Alongside the intermittent presence of the Vizier, Paser, Ramose (i) was a state representative within the Village and was responsible for promoting the cult of the king parallel to the established local pantheon.

4.1(ii) Oracular stelae at Deir el-Medina in the reign of Ramesses II

Not only do the stelae and related archaeological evidence indicate that Ramesses II patronised the cult of Hathor at the temple at Deir el-Medina, but he also appears to have interested himself in the cult of his royal predecessor, Amenhotep I, venerated as the founder of the Village (Bierbrier 1982a: 14). The stelae, together with tomb paintings, record the introduction of a new statue of Amenhotep I, known as 'The Favourite (of Amun)' (*pꜣ ib ib*/*pꜣ ḥꜣty* (*n Ỉmn*)), wearing the blue crown, during the reign of Ramesses II. The statue was involved in local oracular decisions, and is connected to the broader phenomenon of the use of oracles that appears to be a characteristic of the reign of Ramesses II. There is a clear evolution in the New Kingdom in the use of oracles: in the 18th Dynasty they were used by kings to legitimise their own appointments, for example, by Tuthmosis III (Černý 1962: 35); but by the 19th Dynasty their use had spread to a far broader demographic (Černý 1962: 35; Frankfurter 1998: 145; Valbelle and Husson 1998: 1056-1071). Oracle statues of deities were carried and addressed during festival processions, and, during the reign of Rameses II, unprecedented numbers of stelae and tomb paintings record such oracular festival processions.

There is a large body of literature dealing with oracles in ancient Egypt. Comprehensive surveys covering historical development, deities, and technical aspects are those of Černý (1962), Kakosy (1982), Valbelle and Husson (1998) and Kruchton (2001). The New Kingdom sources for oracles are of three types: representations of the oracular ceremony on stelae (discussed below) and tomb paintings;[8] textual references from documents[9] and temple wall inscriptions,[10] including temple architectural nomenclature that relates to oracular events taking place in those locations (Cabrol 2001: 727-729); and direct records of the oracular consultation in the form of oracle questions on ostraca.[11] New Kingdom processional oracles take the form of questions addressed to a statue of the god carried by wab-priests in a palanquin (Kees 1960: 45; Černý 1962: 43-46; McDowell 1999: 172). The god in question was the local god of the temple, and there is evidence for the existence of oracles from a number of regional temples.[12] Ryholt has suggested that 'virtually every temple could be consulted for an oracular decision' (1997: 279).

There is some disagreement concerning the period that oracles began to be used in ancient Egypt (Baines and Parkinson 1997: 9-10). It has been suggested by Kruchten (2001) that the Predynastic rocking falcon in the Brooklyn Museum may have acted as an oracular deity, based presumably on later evidence for oracles. There is some evidence for royal use of oracles as early as the 5th Dynasty (Baines and Parkinson 1997). Baines (1987) and Kruchton (2001) discuss possible Middle and early New Kingdom non-royal uses of

[7] See Hovestreydt 1997: 117-118 for a discussion of the motives for and benefits from establishing such cults.

[8] For example, TT19 of Amenmose, depicting Amenhotep 'of the Forecourt' (*n pꜣ wbꜣ*) (Foucart 1932 IV: pls. 28-32; Černý 1962: fig. 9; Wilkinson and Hill 1983: 139 [31.6.5]; Cabrol 2001: 552-553; 608-609, pl. 33).

[9] There are examples in the late Ramesside letters, such as LRL 14, 31, discussed in Pinch 1993: 351; see also Barns 1949; Frankfurter 1998: 145.

[10] 21st Dynasty examples are discussed by Gardiner 1962.

[11] See, for example, Blackman 1926; Černý 1935: 41-58; 1941: 135-141; 1942: 13-24; 1962: 46; Tosi 1988: 174; Sadek 1987: 134; Valbelle and Husson 1998: 1056-1061; McDowell 1999: 172-175.

[12] For example, Amun, Mut, Khonsu and Montu at Karnak, Ptah at Memphis, Seth at Dakhkleh (Černý 1962: 40), Montu at Medamud (Borghouts 1982a: col. 202), Isis at Coptos (Petrie 1896: 15-16 and pl. 19; Černý 1962: 40), Ahmose at Abydos (Legrain 1916: 161-170; Harvey 1992: 3-5; 2004: 4; Valbelle and Husson 1998: 1056), and Amenhotep I at Thebes West (Blackman 1926; Černý 1927: 176-181; 1962: 41-42; McDowell 1990: 107-141; Valbelle and Husson 1998: 1056) and at Karnak (Nims 1956; Wente 1963).

oracles.[13] Based on the later evidence that Amun is designated *nb nṯrw* ('Lord of the Gods') when referring to the portable oracular deity statue, Kruchten (2001: 609) identifies a 12th Dynasty stela (stela Louvre C200) and Deir el-Bahri graffiti where this epithet is employed, and uses this as evidence that oracular statues were processed at this period. However, Kruchten's argument does not allow for an evolution in the meaning of the epithet *nb nṯrw*, which may have begun as an epithet applied to a god in procession, and later expanded to mean a god that gave oracles when in procession. The inscriptions in the 12th Dynasty tomb of Hepdjefai at Assiut refer to statue processions but there is no record of oracular activity (Reisner 1918). As Baines makes clear (1987: 90), there is no direct evidence for oracles prior to the New Kingdom, and the actual practice of petitioning a deity statue in procession may not have occurred prior to the 18th Dynasty. This may be an example of an abstract concept of divine guidance that already existed, made concrete by later kings to demonstrate their relationship with the divine and to support their own authority, which practice was then emulated.

Evidence for oracles at Deir el-Medina

This section draws together the representational evidence for oracles at Deir el-Medina, and contemporary oracles from other locations in Egypt, identifying the iconographical features of oracle representations. There are three explicit representations of oracles dating to the Ramesside Period which are clearly identified as such by the accompanying text. On Wall D (second register) of TT19 of Amenmose (a First God's Servant of Amenhotep I), the statue of Amenhotep I ('of the Forecourt') is depicted carried in his palanquin by wab-priests in a festival procession (the rest of the tomb records episodes from the Valley festival; see Cabrol 2001: 552-553; Figure 4.2). The text records the decision of an oracle asked of Amenhotep I, though the subject is not noted (Foucart 1932 IV: pls. 28-32; Porter and Moss I.1 1960: 33; Černý 1962: fig. 9; Wilkinson and Hill 1983: 139 [31.6.5]; Cabrol 2001: pl. 33).[14]

Figure 4.2 Amenhotep 'of the Forecourt' carried in his palanquin in oracular procession as part of the Valley Festival, in TT19 of Amenmose (after Foucart 1932 IV, *Le Tombeau d'Amonmos*)

On stela Ashmolean Museum 1894/106 from Coptos, Ramesses II offers incense to the bark of Isis carried by wab-priests. The inscription, in 18 columns in the lower register, records a hymn to Isis and the fact of the

[13] Baines (1987: 89-90) notes the general consensus that non-royal oracles do not pre-date the New Kingdom, but goes on to propose a number of possible earlier examples: Ankhtify of Moalla's claim that Horus led him to conquer Edfu is interpreted as a claim made against a 'background of divinatory practice' (9th/10th Dynasty); Haremkhauef of Hierakonpolis (late 13th Dynasty) makes a similar claim on his stela, that Horus sent him to Itjtawy to fetch his new cult image; and in the Story of Sinuhe, Sinuhe claims that 'the god' caused his flight to Palestine. However, Horus, or the god, could in all these cases, be a reference to the king. Further Middle Kingdom evidence has been put forward by Kruchten (2001: 609) where the King's address in viziers' tombs (Middle or early New Kingdom) forbids the use of *bi3yt* (omens or oracles) to decide land disputes (see Kruchten 1988: 826).

[14] TT19 of Amenmose has been dated to the reigns of Ramesses I and Seti I by Porter and Moss (1960 I.1: 33), and to the 20th Dynasty by Černý (1962: 42).

deity statue stopping before the stela dedicator, Nebnakhtef, who has the titles Overseer of Works in the Ramesseum and Chief of the Medjay, Overseer of the Foreign Lands upon the Northern Lands, Charioteer of his Majesty, Royal Messenger to Every Land (Petrie 1896: 15-16, pl. XIX; Porter and Moss V 1937: 129). On stela JdE 43649 from Abydos, the Wab-priest of Osiris, Paser, adores the bark of Ahmose carried by wab-priests. In the lower register, his father, the Wab-priest, Mose, stands adoring, with an inscription recording the decision of a land dispute by the oracle of Ahmose. The stela gives the date as regnal year 14 of Ramesses II (Legrain 1916: 161-170; Porter and Moss V 1937: 93; Harvey 1992: 4; 2004: 4). The defining iconographic element of these oracular representations is the carrying of the deity statue by wab-priests in a bark or palanquin. None of the deities in these representations have the epithets identified by Kruchten as oracular (*nb nṯrw, špsy*; 2001: 609).

The representations listed above are, to my knowledge, the only extant New Kingdom examples where the inscription describes the oracular event depicted. Other stelae that depict the divine bark carried in procession, or depict deity statues defined by the oracular epithets, have generic texts in the form of standard hymns and requests. For example, stela DB114, dating to the middle to second half of the reign of Ramesses II, depicts the Workman, Merwaset (i), kneeling before the bark of Amun-Re carried by wab-priests; Amun-Re is identified as *nb nṯrw*. This is the only example in the dataset where the two types of evidence of an oracular deity, the palanquin and the oracular epithet, appear together, but the text is a generic hymn. Decorum may have restricted the inclusion of texts specifically recording oracular judgements on stelae in the Theban area; alternatively, such stelae may relate to more than one oracular or processional occasion and thus had more value if non-specific in textual content (Morgan 2004: 53-54). Tomb representations are often more personal and less standardised, recording events specific to an individual's life and career.

In this discussion, the criteria used to define an oracular stela are the carrying of the deity statue in a bark or palanquin, and/or the inclusion of oracular epithets. 16 stelae fit the criteria (labeled 'oracle' in the votive stelae tables in Appendix 1). There are, in addition, three non-Deir el-Medina examples: stelae DB271, DB273 and DB300. It should be noted that the stelae recorded as oracular stelae could be interpreted more broadly as representations of festival processions during which oracles may have taken place; the term 'oracle stela/representation' could perhaps be replaced with a broader category such as 'festival stela/representation'. Of the 16 stelae, 11 date to the reign of Ramesses II, nine of which are dedicated to members of the Theban Triad (in the majority of cases including Amun-Re), one to Amenhotep I and one to Taweret. Stela DB1, which pre-dates Ramesses II's reign, is dedicated to the bark-prow of Khonsuemwaset Neferhotep. It may depict a festival occasion rather than an oracular event - the stela shows offerings being given to the bark-prow. There are four 20th Dynasty oracle stelae, two to Amun-Re (DB171, DB183) and one to Amenhotep I (DB174) dating to the reign of Ramesses III, and one Amenhotep I oracle stela (DB206) dating to the reign of Ramesses IV.

The table in Figure 4.3 lists the stelae from Deir el-Medina, and from other sites, which depict or relate to the giving of oracles in the reign of Ramesses II. The deities represented are local gods (the Theban triad at Deir el-Medina/Thebes, Isis at Coptos) or Amenhotep I and/or his father/mother.

Figure 4.3 Oracular representations on stelae dating to the reign of Ramesses II

Stela	Provenance	Dedicator	Deity	Oracle identifier	Date
DB4	Deir el-Medina	Draughtsman of Amun, Pay (i)	Khonsu-em-waset Neferhotep	Epithet: Lord of the Gods	19th Dynasty: Ramesses I-Ramesses II
DB22	Deir el-Medina	Workman, Amenemheb (v)	Theban triad	Divine barks	19th Dynasty: Ramesses II, first half
DB55	Deir el-Medina	Workman, Foreman Nebnefer (i)	Amun-Re, Mut and Hathor	Epithet: Lord of the Gods	19th Dynasty: Ramesses II, first half
DB60	Deir el-Medina	Draughtsman of Amun, Nebre (i) and his son, the Scribe, Khay (i)	Amun-Re	Epithets: The August God who hears prayers...Lord of the Gods	19th Dynasty: Ramesses II, first half

DB86	Deir el-Medina	Senior Scribe, Ramose (i)	Amun-Re	Epithet: The August God	19th Dynasty: Ramesses II, first half
DB95	Deir el-Medina	Senior Scribe, Ramose (i)	Taweret	Epithet: August	19th Dynasty: Ramesses II, first half
DB106	Deir el-Medina	Workman, Thuthirmakhtef (i)	Amun-Re and Taweret	Epithet of Taweret: August	19th Dynasty: Ramesses II, first half
DB114	Deir el-Medina	Workman, Merwaset (i)	Amun-Re	Bark; Epithet: Lord of the Gods	19th Dynasty: Ramesses II, mid-second half
DB126	Deir el-Medina	Wab-priest and Servitor, Amennakht	Amun-Re and Hathor	Epithet: Lord of the Gods	19th Dynasty: Ramesses II (?)
DB128	Deir el-Medina	Wab-priest of Amenhotep I, Atumnakht	Amenhotep I and Tuthmosis IV	Palanquin	19th Dynasty: Ramesses II
DB131	Deir el-Medina	Workman, Neferronpet	Amun-Re and the Ka of Ramesses II	Epithet: Lord of the Gods	19th Dynasty: Ramesses II (?)
DB271	Thebes	First Charioteer of His Majesty, Royal Envoy to All Foreign Lands, Overseer of Foreign Lands in many Foreign Lands, Nui	Amenhotep I and Queen Ahmes Nefertari	Palanquin	19th Dynasty: Ramesses II
DB273	Thebes	Captain of the Bowmen, First Charioteer of his Majesty, Overseer of Foreign Countries, Overseer of Works in the Mansion of Usermaatre Setepenre, Chief of the Medjay, Penre	Amenhotep I	Palanquin	19th Dynasty: Ramesses II
Cairo JdE 43649[15]	Abydos	The Wab-priest of Osiris, Paser, and his father, the Wab-priest, Mose	Ahmose	Divine bark	19th Dynasty: Ramesses II, year 14
Oxford, Ashmolean Museum 1894/106[16]	Coptos	Overseer of Works in the Ramesseum and Chief of the Medjay, Overseer of the Foreign Lands upon the Northern Lands, Charioteer of his Majesty, Royal Messenger to Every Land, Nebnakhtef	Isis	Divine bark	19th Dynasty: Ramesses II

At the Opet festival in Ramesses II's year 1 the new king used the oracle of Amun-Re to designate his son, Nebwenenef, First God's Servant of Amun (Porter and Moss I.1 1960: 267; Černý 1962: 36; Valbelle and Husson 1998: 1056), much in the same way that Nebnakhtef was promoted by Isis at Coptos in the King's presence. It may be that the two non-Deir el-Medina stelae, DB271 and DB273, depicting Ramesses II before Amenhotep I in the palanquin, record new appointments for the high-ranking men dedicating the stelae. These men have similar titles to that of Nebnakhtef on the Coptos stela. Ramesses II seems to have used oracular appointments for more than just royal appointments, as had been the case in the 18th Dynasty, portraying himself as the interpreter of the god's wishes, and he was certainly associated with oracles after his death. In the 20th Dynasty a statue of Ramesses II, 'Ruler of Heliopolis, the Judge' existed at This (P.

[15] Legrain 1916: 161-170; Porter and Moss V 1937: 93; Harvey 1992: 4; 2004: 4.

[16] Petrie 1896: 15-16, pl. XIX; Porter and Moss V 1937: 129.

Harris 61a, 3), which Černý (1962: 43) suggests may have issued oracular judgments. At Abu Simbel, during the 20th Dynasty, a statue of Ramesses II still appointed officials (Černý 1959: 74; 1962: 43).

It is during the reign of Ramesses II that we find the bulk of the extant evidence for oracles being petitioned by what we might term 'ordinary' (non-royal, non-elite) individuals. Oracle questions from Deir el-Medina recorded on ostraca do not pre-date the reign of Ramesses II (though the lack of administrative records of the community for this period in general must be borne in mind). A brief survey of published and dated Deir el-Medina ostraca that may relate to oracles (Černý 1935b: 41-58; 1942: 13-24; 1972: 49-69 and the *Catalogue des Ostraca Hiératiques Non-Littéraires de Deîr el-Médînéh)* brings to light only two relevant ostraca that have been dated prior to Ramesses II. These are no. 824 (O. DM 1736) and no. 825 (O. DM 1737), dated to Seti I on the basis of the inclusion of the shortened prenomen *m3ʿt-Rʿ*, which is taken as a shortened writing of Seti I's prenomen *mn-m3ʿt-Rʿ*. However, it may be that they refer to Ramesses II (*wsr-m3ʿt-Rʿ*).

The new statue of Amenhotep I in the reign of Ramesses II

Redford (1986: 191) has noted that the Ramesside kings, in general, promoted the cults of the royal ancestors to stress their family connection with earlier kings and thus their legitimacy (see also McDowell 1992b: 97). During the reign of Ramesses II cult statues of Amenhotep I at Thebes and Ahmose at Abydos appear on stelae as oracular deities that are petitioned by 'ordinary' people. By linking himself to these deified kings, Ramesses II asserted his legitimacy, increased his visibility amongst the population and involved himself with the lives of a broad demographic group.

During the reign of Ramesses II a number of representations of a statue of Amenhotep I wearing the blue crown, identified by the epithet *p3 ib ib*/*p3 ḥ3ty* (*n'Imn*), 'The Favourite (of Amun)', appear at Deir el-Medina (see Chapter 3).[17] The securely dated representations have been used to date further representations of Amenhotep I in the blue crown to this king's reign. The Ramesside statue of a king wearing the blue crown (statue Louvre E. 16277; Plate 4b and back cover), mentioned in Section 4.1(i) as possibly a statue of Ramesses II, may in fact represent Amenhotep I, or a deliberate conflation or association of the two kings. Irrespective of the identity of this particular statue, it is clear that the villagers supported a separate and new Amenhotep I cult during the reign of Ramesses II, which placed the king at the heart of the cult, and therefore social, activity of the community. More prosaically, the oracular disputes the new Amenhotep I statue initially solved almost always related to property (McDowell 1990: 114-127), which, in the Village, as elsewhere in Egypt, belonged to the state, in the form of royal or temple lands. The new oracle-statue may have been implemented to ensure that property did not become hereditary. The wab-priests and scribes responsible for controlling and recording the oracular responses would have been in a powerful position indeed (Černý 1927: 193; see also Lesko, B. S.: 1994: 23). McDowell (1990: 23) argues that the oracle statue of Amenhotep I resulted in property ownership becoming independent of the state, but the senior scribes who would have been involved in the oracular decision worked closely with the vizier, so this is not necessarily the case. It is possible to relate the depiction of Ramesses II on stelae offering to Amenhotep I in the palanquin (DB271, DB273; non-Deir el-Medina) to the inauguration of an oracular process that became part of the juridical process in the Village.

Further evidence supporting the existence of a new Amenhotep I cult statue introduced alongside an existing popular cult statue can be seen in the apparently restricted access to this new cult: the dedicators of stelae to the new statue are either high-ranking or have a related priestly rank (see Chapter 3). In addition, the lay priesthood of Amenhotep I represents a local elite within the Deir el-Medina community (Černý 1973: 126, 146, 223; Janssen 1992: 84; Lesko B.S.: 1994: 23), who would have wielded significant influence given their involvement in property dispute decisions and related issues decided by the Amenhotep I oracle. The members of the lay priesthood of Amenhotep I listed on the column base JdE 25111/51512 (see Chapter 3, note 20) can all be linked to the Senior Scribe, Ramose (i), through inclusion in TT250 and on other monuments.[18]

---

[17] For example, stela DB79 of Qen (ii), and TT2 of Khabekhenet (i), east wall representation.

[18] Qen (ii)'s tomb (no number given in Davies 1999) contains a scene of Ramesses II followed by the Vizier, Paser, the Senior Scribe, Ramose (i) and Qen (ii). Three of his sons are listed on the column base as wab-priests; Nebre (i) appears in the tombs of Qen (ii) (Davies 1999: 153, n. 68) and Ramose (i) (TT250; Davies 1999: 153), in the latter in his role as lector priest performing the

This brief survey of the oracular/festival stelae reveals an increase in the depiction of festival processions of the deity statue and the use of oracles in the reign of Ramesses II, both of the Theban triad and a new statue of Amenhotep I. The increased emphasis on festival oracular processions is supported by tomb representations of festivals dating to the reign of Ramesses II, and by the hundreds of ostraca recording oracular questions and decisions which appear in the reign of Ramesses II. In order to definitively assess the increase in the use of oracles during Ramesses II's reign a full survey of all tomb representations and stelae over the New Kingdom from all sites in Egypt would be necessary, a task that is beyond the scope of this book. The database of Theban stelae does contain 'oracular' stelae of Amenhotep I from later periods (for example, DB174 of the Foreman, Anhurkhawy (ii), in post during the reigns of Ramesses III-IV; Černý 1927: 190-191, fig. 15), demonstrating a continuing trend.

4.1(iii) The visit of the Vizier, To, to the Queens' Valley chapels

The seven rock-cut chapels located on the way to the Valley of the Queens are decorated with royal stelae (Chapels B, C and E) and royal representations (Chapel D) containing coronation iconography and texts, referring to Ramesses III and his father Sethnakht (Bruyère 1930b: 13-48; Kitchen *forthcoming:* 4, notes that in Chapel E Sethnakht's name usurps that of Seti II). There are a number of private stelae *in situ* that contain similar iconography (for example, stelae DB187 and DB188 in Chapel A, discussed below). Chapels F and G contain reliefs depicting a number of deities. In Chapel G there is a stela *in situ* with representations of Ramesses III and his son Amenkherkhopeshef (Bruyère 1930b: 47 and fig. 28; Kitchen *forthcoming*: 18). There are 35 datable fragments (stelae, offering tables etc.; Bruyère 1930b: 283-299) from the chapels that illustrate that they were in use as a cult centre from the early 19th Dynasty, with 16 dating to the first half of the reign of Ramesses II, and five more dating to the reign of Ramesses II in general. Ten fragments date to the 20th Dynasty, six to the reign of Ramesses III. The remaining four fragments date to the 19th Dynasty. In addition, there are five fragmentary stelae which include cartouches from this area that date to Ramesses I – Ramesses II.[19] Holes for stelae cut into the walls obscuring earlier painted decoration demonstrate continued use of Chapels F and G over a period of time (Bruyère 1930b: 42-48), but the majority of the datable evidence seems to bear witness to a lapse in the use of these chapels following the reign of Ramesses II until Ramesses III had the neighbouring caves (Chapels A-E) decorated in his and his father's honour.

A study of the monuments from the seven chapels suggests that the name given by Bruyère, the Chapels to Ptah and Mertseger ('L'Oratoire de Ptah et Mérseger'), may be a misnomer. The stela base of the Workman, Penniut (Bruyère 1930b: 48; pl. XII, no. 4), discovered during the excavations of French Institute in 1926, states that a stela was placed on the behalf of, or placed by (*iry*) Penniut 'in the Chapels of all the Gods next to the Place of Beauty' (the Valley of the Queens) (*m ḥwwt nṯrw r-gs tꜣ st-nfrw*). The chapels may have been known anciently as 'The Chapels of all the Gods'. Bruyère gives a total of 29 objects inscribed for various forms of Ptah (1930b: 283-299), suggesting that a form of Ptah was indeed one of the principal deities worshipped here. In addition there are three database stelae depicting Ptah: stelae DB179 and DB187, *in situ* in Chapel A, and stela DB221, listed by Bruyère in the finds from this area. However, only six private votive stelae to Mertseger can be provenanced to this site: DB23 of the Workman, Amennakht (xi), which may have come from here (see Bruyère 1930b: 11-13 and fig. 8; Tosi and Roccati 1972: 96), DB188 of the Foreman, Khons (v) (*in situ* in Chapel A; Plate 7), and (not included in the dataset), a faint remnant of a stela *in situ* in Chapel G, of which only the name of the goddess in the upper register remains and part of someone's name, ending in *–ḥtp* (Bruyère 1930b: 47, fig. 28; Kitchen *forthcoming*: 18). The other three are fragments listed in

---

opening of the mouth ceremony. His brother Pendua (iii) is listed as a wab-priest on the column base; Amenemwia (i) has the as yet unexplained title *ꜥꜣ n ꜥ* (see Davies 1999: 206), which is hereditary. He appears in TT250 of Ramose (i) (Davies 1999: 207); Penshenabu (ii) is the brother of the Guardian, Penbuy (i), who is closely associated with Ramose (i) – Penbuy (i) appears in TT250 and on stela Cairo JdE 21604 with Ramose (i); Neferronpet can be tentatively identified as Neferronpet (ii), whose tomb (TT336) includes Ramose (i) offering to Huy (x), Neferronpet (ii)'s brother-in-law and Ramose (i)'s father-in-law (Davies 1999: 88-89). This Neferronpet appears in TT4 of the sculptor Qen (ii), and on a libation basin of the *ꜥꜣ n ꜥ* Harnefer (i), a contemporary of Ramose (i) (Davies 1999: 183). There is an Apehty who was active in year 40 of Ramesses II (O.BM5634, rto. 12; Davies 1999: 37), who may be the same individual as the man listed on the column base, but about whom nothing further is known.

[19] Bruyère 1930b: 39, 283, Porter and Moss I.2 1964: 708, Tosi and Roccati 1972: 125-126, 301 [50089]; Bruyère 1930b: 284, Porter and Moss I.2 1964: 731, Tosi and Roccati 1972: 129, 304 [50095]; Bruyère 1930b: 284, Porter and Moss I.2 1964: 725, Tosi and Roccati 1972: 130, 305 [50098]; Bruyère 1930b: 285, Tosi and Roccati 1972: 140, 313 [50124], and Bruyère 1930b: 288 [6005].

Bruyère's Appendix A (1930b: 286 [6014]; 292 [10]; 297 [12]). There are large images of Hathor and Ptah in Chapel D (Bruyère 1930: 37-39) but nothing as significant of Mertseger. Bruyère (1930b: 6; 43) states that stelae featuring Ptah and Mertseger had been removed from the chapels by Schiaparelli. Mertseger may have been associated with this cliff face and the chapels as an ancient snake goddess (Yoyotte 2003: 293), but by the Ramesside Period the chapels seem to have had a more general cult function, and cult activity associated with Mertseger was not confined to this location, and may not have predominated here.

The datable inscribed material indicates that the chapels were in use from the early 19th Dynasty, but perhaps initially had a less official status than the Hathor temple in the Village. The decoration in Chapel G depicting a king, his vizier and a foreman, all unnamed, may have represented Ramesses II and his Vizier, Paser (Bruyère 1930b 45-48). The second peak of stelae production in the dataset spans the reigns of Ramesses III-Ramesses IV, which is possibly related to royal activity at Thebes, perhaps the coronation of Ramesses III. By the reign of Ramesses III, the Queens' Valley chapels may have formed the most important official cult centre for the community at Deir el-Medina, and the location for events such as the appointment of individuals to posts within the gang. By the 20th Dynasty, Mertseger had replaced Hathor as the female deity of the West Bank *par excellence*, and it is Mertseger who appears on the royal stelae of Sethnakht/Ramesses III. This can be linked to 20th Dynasty royal patronage of the Queens' Valley chapels, and of the ancient snake cult which can be set within a context of a widening gap between the royal household and the East Bank Amun-Re clergy (Häggman 2002: 191-192). The king may have felt the need to make more direct contact with the West Bank communities.

Stelae recording a visit of the Vizier, To, to Deir el-Medina

The Vizier, To succeeded the Vizier, Hori (Helck 1958: 22-24), in the second half of the reign of Ramesses III. There are three private stelae from the Queens' Valley chapels dating to the reign of Ramesses III that depict the Vizier, To, described in the table in Figure 4.4.

Figure 4.4 Private stelae from the Queens' Valley chapels dating to the reign of Ramesses III depicting the Vizier, To

Stela	Provenance	Description
DB179	Chapel E	Round-topped stela, two registers. 1st register: the Vizier, To, offers a bouquet to Amun-Re and Ptah; 2nd register: the Scribes, Bay (ii) and Amennakht (v), kneel, adoring
DB187	Chapel A *in situ*	Round-topped stela, two registers: 1st register: the Vizier, To, before Ptah and Amenhotep I, and the cartouches of Ramesses III; 2nd register: the Wab-priest, Iyernutef, and three sons, stand, adoring
DB188	Chapel A *in situ*	Round-topped stela, two registers. 1st register: the Vizier, To, before the cartouches of Ramesses III and Mertseger who holds *rnpt*-signs; 2nd register: the Foreman, Khons (v), and members of his family, stand, adoring

The stelae depict To in traditional vizerial costume before the deities represented in the Queens' Valley chapels, who may also have been represented by statues at the time. Stela DB188 (Plate 7) depicts Mertseger holding the *rnpt*-signs before the cartouches of Ramesses III. Images of deities holding these signs abound in the chapels dedicated for the coronation of Ramesses III: the royal stela in Chapel C has Re-Harakhti holding the *rnpt*-signs and stela Turin 50091 from Chapel D has a deity, now lost, in the same pose. DB187 and DB188 are set into the wall of Chapel A, next to each other, with the Vizier facing inwards, thus creating a tableau of Amenhotep I, Ptah, Mertseger and the cartouches of Ramesses III. Ramesses III is represented emblematically, perhaps indicating that he was not present at the ceremony commemorated; the cartouches represent the king, or the office of the king (Baines 1985: 278).

Stela DB179 depicts the Scribes, Bay (ii) and Amennakht (v). They are both described simply as 'scribe' though both are known to have been senior scribes, Bay (ii) until year 16 (and so overlapping with

Wennenefer (v)) of Ramesses III and Amennakht (v) from year 16 (Davies 1999: 99; 105) or year 24 (Davies 1999: 283) of Ramesses III until year 6/7 of Ramesses IV (Davies 1999: 283). Stela DB187 depicts the Wab-priest, Iyernutef (Kitchen *forthcoming*: 18), and his three sons. This may be Iyernutef (iii) who elsewhere also has the titles workman, craftsman and sculptor, and is active (if they are all one and the same man) from year 14 of Ramesses III into the reign of Ramesses IV (Davies 1999: 185).

There are two possible interpretations of the dates and individuals on stela DB188. One interpretation is that the individuals depicted following the Foreman (of the right side), Khons (v), who has the epithet *mꜣꜥ ḫrw*, are his son, the Foreman, Nekh(em)mut (vi), Khons (v)'s brother, the Deputy, who therefore must be Amenkhau (i), and Amenkhau (i)'s son, Nekh(em)mut (ii), here given the title workman (known elsewhere with the title draughtsman). Khons (v) was in post for the latter half of Ramesses III's reign (years 15-31; see the table in Figure 4.5, below), as was Amenkhau (i) as deputy (year 17 of Ramesses III until year 7 of Ramesses IV), and Nekh(em)mut (vi) and (ii) were both active from the start of the reign of Ramesses IV (Davies 1999: 279; 281). This would place the stela right at the end of Ramesses III's reign, and indeed involve bringing Nekh(em)mut (ii)'s tenure as foreman forward one or two years in order to place it in the reign of Ramesses III. The second interpretation of the stela is that the Nekh(em)mut behind Khons (v) is his father, the Foreman, Nekh(em)mut (i), in post years 11-15 of Ramesses III, from whom Khons (v) inherited the post, with the other two individuals retaining the same identity. That Nekh(em)mut (ii) has the title workman and not draughtsman suggests that this stela was indeed set up early in his career. This latter identification of the individuals would date the stela to around year 15 of Ramesses III, when Nekh(em)mut (i) ceded his post to his son. The fact that Khons (v) precedes his father, and his names and titles are larger, suggests that he may be marking his new professional status. The years that all these individuals have in common are years 15 or 16 of Ramesses III.

Figure 4.5 Years of known active service of the individuals on the stelae listed in Figure 4.4

Stela and individuals represented	Period of known active service*		
	Ramesses III	Ramesses IV	Later
DB179			
Senior Scribe, Bay (ii)	(Siptah) to 16		
Senior Scribe, Amennakht (v)	16	6 or 7	
DB187			
Wab-priest, Iyernutef (iii)	14	5	
DB188			
Foreman, Nekh(em)mut (i)	11 to 15		
Foreman, Khons (v)	15 to 31		
Deputy, Amenkhau (i)	17	7	
Workman (later Draughtsman), Nekh(em)mut (ii)		1	Ramesses IX, year 8?

* *In the case of the Foremen, Deputy and Senior Scribes, this is the period of service in this post.*

Two graffiti, Western Theban Graffito no. 1111 and Černý Graffito no. 1143 (Černý 1956: 4, 7; Kitchen *forthcoming*: 18), provide supporting evidence for a visit of the Vizier, To, in year 15 or 16 of Ramesses III to officiate at a ceremony at which the men depicted on the stelae were present. These two graffiti record the appointment of the Scribe, Amennakht (v) as senior scribe by the Vizier, To, in year 16 of Ramesses III. Year 16 is To's first certain year in post as vizier in Thebes,[20] and it is from this date that work in the Valley of the Queens is securely attested in the Deir el-Medina archive (Wolterman 1996: 164 and n. 100). In his

[20] The date of his appointment is still under debate: it may be as early as year 12 (see Wolterman 1996: 164 and nn. 95-99).

survey of visits to the necropolis by dignitaries, Janssen (1997: 156) notes that there is a gap in the record until year 15 of Ramesses III.

Janssen discusses the ostraca of years 22 onwards that refer to a vizier visiting a place called 'the Settlement (of) the Tomb' (*tꜣ wḥyt (n) pꜣ ḫr*), which may be a reference to an area near the Valley of the Queens (Černý 1973: 92; for an alternative explanation, see Ventura 1986: 184, n. 44) as this is where the workman were working at this period (Janssen 1997: 157). On the occasions when the reason for the vizier's visit is given it is stated that he is there to 'receive the work' (*šsp bꜣk*). It may be that the work of the gang in the Queens' Valley area at this time was connected with the decoration of the Queens' Valley chapels in honour of Ramesses III and his father Sethnakht. The iconographic evidence in the Queens' Valley chapels and the stelae therein make it clear that certain ceremonies took place here during this reign, and that this location was a professional and social focus.

The ostracon known as O. Nash 11 [1] (BM EA 65933) records a letter from the Foreman, Hay (= Hay (iv), in post years 1-22 of Ramesses III; Davies 1999: 279) to an unnamed vizier, informing him that the work is going as planned and a request that he come for 'the appearance of the god Amun' (*ḫꜥy Ꞽmn*) (Kitchen 1983b: 583-584). O. Florence 2619 (reverse) may be relevant here, though the text is obscure. Initial interpretations of the texts, by Erman (1880) and Černý-Gardiner (1957), argued that the document was 'a business document of the utmost obscurity' (Wolterman 1996: 147). Wolterman (1996: 158-161) argues that O. Florence 2619 (reverse) records the appointment of a vizier called Herwernef in year 15 of Ramesses III by the oracle of Amun, and the reporting of this appointment to the chiefs at Deir el-Medina by a man called Khons, whom he identifies with an *ꜣtw*-officer of this name known from years 13 and 14 of Ramesses III (Wolterman 1996: 158-161). In addition to Khons, who could perhaps be the Foreman, Khons (v), the text mentions a number of other individuals, some of whom are present on the stelae: the Foreman (of the left side), Hay (=(iv)), the Foreman (of the right side), Nekh(em)mut (i), and the Scribe, Wennenefer, who must be Wennenefer (v), Senior Scribe during years 11 – 24 of Ramesses III (Davies 1999: 283).

The ostraca and graffiti either specifically refer to the Vizier, To's visit to promote members of the gang, or more generally support the function of the Queens' Valley chapels as a focus for work-related cult activity during the latter part of the reign of Ramesses III. The vizier was in charge of the organisation of the workforce at Deir el-Medina, and it may be that in his first full year in post To installed a new set of chiefs, or at least filled some of the posts. The ceremony of the promotions took place in the Queens' Valley chapels, the cult focus of the Deir el-Medina community at this period. On this occasion, To appointed a new senior scribe, Amennakht (v) and a new foreman of the right side, Khons (v). The stela of Iyernutef, DB179, may record his appointment as a wab-priest. The relationships between individuals depicted, such as Khons (v) and Nekh(em)mut (i), are reflected in their location, or order, on the stela: Khons (v) iconographically precedes Nekh(em)mut (i) as he is now senior to him in the professional hierarchy at Deir el-Medina.

4.2 Private events on votive stelae

Private events are here defined as events relating to the domestic, social or professional sphere of non-royal individuals. The events are of two kinds: they either relate to the growth and development of an individual and his/her attendance at various significant cultural events, and can be termed 'rites of passage'; or the events may be unexpected and relate to circumstances such as illness or ethical lapses.

Rites of passage in ancient Egypt; sources

Van Gennep's classic work on rites of passage (1909 [1960]) outlines a series of events of which some or all occurred in most societies in some form or other. He defines a rite of passage as a device which incorporated an individual into a new status in a group (1909 [1960]: xiii), and the life of an individual as 'a series of passages from one age to another and from one occupation to another' (1909 [1960]: 2-3). Male rites of passage are more socially visible and include birth, social puberty, marriage, fatherhood, advancement to a higher class, occupational specialisation, and death, and can include betrothal and initiation into religious societies (1909 [1960]: 3). Female rites of passage are less well documented. Laurence (2000: 444-445) notes that, for the Roman world, evidence for the female life course is almost entirely lacking. This may be because, in antiquity, female sexual and social roles began much earlier and there was a less marked transition from puberty to adulthood (Foxhall 1994: 135-136; Meskell 2000: 425; 2002: 89-90), and the fact that they were enacted within the domestic sphere (Pinch 1995: 378). In addition, the nature of the surviving evidence - inscribed monuments - relates to what Foxhall, in the context of the ancient Greek world, has described as the 'adult, free, male citizen' (1994: 136). Such monuments were not used to record the domestic environment and activities in which women were predominantly active.

Traditional divisions, such as those of Van Gennep, have been called into question by Meskell who suggests that the concept 'lifecycle' might be a more accurate template for life experience, rather than the 'eurocentric...rites of passage' (2000: 425; see also Meskell 2002: 14; 88; 93). However, she herself suggests a series of states or events which may have demarcated stages in an individual's life - birth, menarche, circumcision, love and marriage - and it seems safe to work on the premise that certain life-stages or -events are universally significant. In addition, the lifecycle and rites of passage concepts are not mutually exclusive: the lifecycle consists of a series of states (childhood, adolescence, etc.) and rites of passage mark transitions between states, or certain events within states. Pinch (1993: 351) has noted that it is 'notoriously difficult to find traces of 'rites of passage' in Egypt' other than death related ones (see also Pinch 1995: 378), but she goes on to suggest that '[i]t may have been felt that prayers relating to important stages in a person's life...were best made to the prestigious hypostases of deities in the state temples instead of, or as well as, to the deities manifest in community and household shrines' (1993: 351). If this is the case, it may be possible to trace rituals relating to rites of passage in the record of such cult activity.

Three general sources from New Kingdom Egypt can provide information on a number of different life stages: the ostraca and papyri from Deir el-Medina, elite autobiographies, and tomb paintings. More opaquely, funerary rituals may reflect significant activities from life. Many of the ostraca and papyri from Deir el-Medina belong to the genre now known as the 'Journal of the Necropolis', the records of the day-to-day activity of the gang, recording work completed, absences and deliveries. The most complete set are the papyrus records published by Botti and Peet as *Il giornale della necropolis di Tebe* (1928), covering the later years of Ramesses III and the early years of Ramesses IV. Many further ostraca and papyri belonging to the same genre have since come to light, a number of which have been listed by Janssen (1990; see also Janssen 1997: 111-129).[21] Using these records a number of life events can be identified that absented a workman from duty. A search at the time of writing of the Deir el-Medina database of non-literary ostraca produces 99 'hits' when the word 'absence' is used as a search term. The majority of absences are due to illness, but other reasons include a workman absent on account of 'his daughter' (O.Cairo CG 25503), a burial (O.Cairo CG 25506), a mention of a birth (O.Cairo CG 25531), a personal feast (O.Cairo CG 25532), and making an offering and pouring water (O.Cairo CG 25779). Janssen (1980: 127-152) has analysed the reasons for absence, the most detailed record of which is O.BM 5634, dating to year 40 of Ramesses II (see also Janssen 1997: 87-98). He (1980: 128) notes the frequency, and apparent unimportance for the work, of absence. According to Janssen's study, the most frequent reasons for absence are illness, death of a relative, mourning, private feasts, making offerings to gods and deceased relatives, and carrying out work elsewhere than the tomb, with the occasional mention of a birth.

Elite autobiographies can provide a framework of professional events, such as entry into a profession, and promotion from low to high rank, which may have occurred across a number of educated professions. Such biographical events outline a life structure that may be applicable to a range of male individuals of the middle and upper classes. Elite autobiographies occur in tombs and on statues of high-ranking male individuals. An example contemporary with our dataset is the block statue of the First God's Father of Amun at Karnak, Bekenkhons (GL WAF 38, Staatliche Sammlung Ägyptischer Kunst, Munich; Porter and Moss II 1972: 215; Janssen and Janssen 1990: 73, fig. 29), in post during the reign of Ramesses II. The inscription records the owner's four years in 'primary school', eleven years of apprenticeship in the royal stables, four years as a (wab?-) priest and a rise through the priestly hierarchy until reaching the post of first god's father (Janssen and Janssen 1990: 72). Elite New Kingdom tombs record important events such as state festival attendance, and royal rewards, in the lives of their owners.[22] In addition, Assman (1989: 144-145) has interpreted parts of the funerary ritual, in particular the examinations to enter the afterlife, as versions of initiation rituals which took place in life. He regards the rituals as similar to the initiations into the 'secrets'

[21] At the time of writing, many of the Journal ostraca are available on the Deir el-Medina database, http://www.leidenuniv.nl/nino/dmd/dmd.html.

[22] For studies of 18th Dynasty tomb scenes of such events, see Radwan 1969 and Myśliwiec 1985; for receiving of the Gold of Honour, see Schulman 1988: 116-117; for records of attendance at festivals, see Cabrol 1995a; 1995b; 2001.

of a profession, as a 'typical craftsman's examination', for example, the professions of net-makers, bird-catchers, embalmers, priests, and so on.

The sources highlight the following as significant events in a (male) individual's life: births, burials, personal feasts, the making of offerings and attendance at festivals, initiation into a profession and promotion at work, and rewards received on account of professional achievement. The events discussed in this section have been chosen because some votive stelae appear to relate to them, while the historical actuality of the occurrence of such events is supported by related texts and representations, and/or associated artefacts. These events are:

- attendance at state festivals and the consultation of oracles;
- conception and birth;
- entry into/promotion within a profession and rewards for the completion of work;
- entry into a religious organisation/participation in a local religious festival;
- illness/ethical lapse.

These events are related to the more traditional 'rites of passage' of Van Gennep, rather than the 'lifecycle' concept of Meskell, as stelae are more likely, as significant commemorative documents, to record an event rather than a state of being. However, they do indicate a state in the sense that they mark the transition of the individual from one state to a (generally) more socially prestigious one.

Two socially significant events are omitted: marriage and death. Although the event of death and the funeral is a significant and clear rite of passage in ancient Egypt, the data from this study, votive stelae, which commemorate events during an individual's life, are not relevant to the event of an individual's death. As for marriage, the general consensus is that in ancient Egypt it was a juridical, legal and economic event, not marked by a religious ceremony (Pestman 1961: 6-7; Toivari 1998: 1157; 1162-1163; Szpakowska 2008: 214-216). The lack of involvement of any state/religious authority sets it within the private or domestic, rather than the public, realm (Toivari 1998: 1157). Despite the high literacy rate at Deir el-Medina, there is no documentation about the reasons behind partner choice, dates of 'weddings' or related celebrations (Meskell 2002: 95-96; but see Allam 1974; Janssen 1974). Toivari sees marriage at Deir el-Medina as 'an ongoing process rather than a limited act' (1998: 1160), where the giving of a 'dowry' indicated the intention to marry. Marriage as an economic and legal process rather than a single marked event perhaps suffices to inform us that, although the married state was a desired one, in ancient Egypt a marriage ceremony was not seen as necessary. Ancient marriage was conceptually different from marriage in the West today (Toivari 1998: 1157);[23] any surprise at this state of affairs reflects the bias of our own cultural expectations, and indicates the care needed when attempting to reconstruct ancient lives and society.

The offerings

In addition to the iconographic criteria that can reference the event commemorated on the stela, the offerings represented may relate to a specific ritual or action. The offerings have been divided into the following categories: offering stand (most frequently holding a water pot and lotus flower, though sometimes with additional offerings such as loaves), loaded offering table (a larger table with vegetables, meat, flowers, beer etc.), and/or dedicators offering or carrying incense, water, festival offerings - such as musical instruments and ducks -, lotus flowers, or bouquets (or bouquets placed in front of the deity statue) (see the table in Figure 4.6). Sometimes there are no offerings, which in itself may be significant. Sadek (1987: 215) has commented on the lack of variety in the offerings depicted on votive stelae.

The offering stand enjoys a relative increase in popularity in the 20th Dynasty, in comparison with the loaded offering table, depictions of which decrease, as do festival offerings. The offering stand and loaded offering table occur together on only two stelae: stelae DB74 and DB133. In these two instances the loaded offering table occurs before the 'popular' deity, and the offering stand before the 'state' deity. However, this relationship does not hold true for the rest of the stelae, and the stand or table may indicate different ceremonies, rather than differentiating the approaches to a local or state deity. On stelae categorised according to the five life events discussed below, the offering stand appears more frequently on stelae relating to personal or local approaches to the deity.

---

[23] See Blackman 2000: 92 for notes on early 20th century marriage amongst the fellahin in Upper Egypt, which seems to have been conceptually similar to that of the ancient Egyptians.

Figure 4.6 Offerings depicted on the Deir el-Medina stelae

	Total	19th Dynasty	20th Dynasty	Notes
Offering stand	89	54	21	
Loaded offering table	49	40	6	
Incense offered	60	42	13	*In some cases this may be burnt offerings*
Water offered	32	24	4	*In 29 cases this is offered by women*
Festival offerings	19	17	0	*E.g. ducks and musical intruments, carried by individuals*
Lotus flowers	24	16	7	*Carried by individuals*
Bouquet	56	50	3	
Nothing	74	39	28	*The stelae with no additional offerings may include a bouquet depicted near the hypostase*

NB Other than the offering tables and stands, and the bouquets, the offerings are only those offered or held by the dedicators, not by the intermediaries.

Where incense (or sometimes burnt offerings) and water are offered, the foremost dedicator is almost invariably a man who offers the incense, whilst the women offer or carry water. The offering of incense may be the indicator of the primary or principal dedicator. Where there are examples of women on the second register offering incense, this may be an example of the influence of decorum controlling the order of the representation, where women cannot be shown above or in front of men, so their status as principal dedicator is iconographically indicated through the depiction of the incense - for example, stela DB33 of Irynefer (i) and his wife Mehykhati (ii) (see Figure 4.7).[24]

Figure 4.7 Stela of Irynefer (i) and his wife Mehykhati (ii), Deir el-Medina, r. Ramesses II, first half (DB33; The British Museum EA 284; © Trustees of the British Museum)

When no offerings are depicted this may indicate that that the ceremony was an oral one (Baines 2004: 35), or that the participants were passive witnesses rather than active participants. The lack of offerings occurs frequently on type B (intermediary) stelae, where it is the intermediary who may make an offering while the dedicator(s) in the lower register adore(s). The only exception in the Deir el-Medina dataset is stela

[24] See Robins 1994 for a discussion of compositional dominance and gender on stelae.

DB133 where an intermediary offers in the upper register and the dedicators offer in the lower register, but to a secondary deity, and therefore the act of offering relates to a ceremony distinct from that shown in the upper register.

Water offerings are almost exclusively given by women, other than on stela DB182, where the Vizier, Hori, libates before a statue of Amenhotep I and his mother. The stela is dedicated by Hay (vii), using the title Servitor of the Lord of the Two Lands. He is shown in the company of his 'tutor', the Foreman, Hay (iv) and his real father, the Chief Craftsman, Amennakht (x), who precede him. A similar water vessel, a hawk headed jar, can be seen on stela DB87 of the Senior Scribe, Ramose (i), of which only a section of the lower register remains. The administrative records from Deir el-Medina record instances of 'pouring water' (*w3ḥ mw*) for Amenhotep I. Stela DB182 can be related to such a ceremony, where the high rank of all these individuals indicates the relative exclusivity of the ceremony. Men seem to be depicted on stelae making water offerings only in ceremonies connected to Amenhotep I, a context that seems to have precluded the presence of women. The meaning of the female use of water offerings remains obscure, though water offerings have a domestic connection in the sense that the workmen and their families 'poured water' for their deceased relatives (Janssen 1980: 149).

Figure 4.8 Large columnar bouquet (left), mid-size bouquet (centre) (after Dittmar 1986: Abb. 100, Abb. 105) and small bouquet (right), not to scale (© Wolfram Grajetzki). These examples are from stelae dating to the reign of Ramesses II

Bouquets occur on 56 stelae, either held by the hypostasis, placed in front of the hypostasis on a loaded offering table or on the ground, or, more rarely presented by the intermediary or dedicator. The vast majority of the dated examples are from the 19th Dynasty, 38 dating to the reign of Ramesses II. *ʿnḫ*-bouquets were traditionally offered at the Valley festival, where the flowers were first dedicated to Amun-Re at Deir el-Bahri and subsequently purchased by private individuals to be dedicated at family tombs (Bell 1997: 183). Two of the bouquet stelae depict a king giving a large columnar bouquet to the funerary deity Osiris: DB21 of the Outline Draughtsman, Pashed (vii), and DB78 of the Foreman, Qaha (i), both early 19th Dynasty. Both of these stelae come from the tombs of their owners, TT323 of Pashedu (vii) and TT360 of Qaha (i). The bouquets that have been identified as such take three different forms: a tall, columnar bouquet represented as being as tall as the hypostase, which is depicted either in front of (sometimes behind) the hypostase or being offered by a high-ranking intermediary; a smaller version of the same bouquet held by individuals represented on the stelae; and a squat version, perhaps just the head of the bouquet, depicted in front of the zoomorphic forms of the deity (rams and geese of Amun-Re, Hathor cow, Seth hippopotamus) (see Figure 4.8). One interpretation may be that the large columnar bouquet was the bouquet presented during the official ceremony, parts of which were then taken by individuals, and may have been later placed before accessible deity statues. Single lotus flowers, or slim bunches of two or three, which are not elaborately bound, have not been identified as bouquets.

4.2(i) Attendance at state festivals/oracles (47 stelae)

A number of Deir el-Medina ostraca refer to the great Theban festivals, the Valley (e.g. O. Cairo CG 25598, O.DeM 0127), and the Opet (e.g. O. DeM 0046, O. DeM 0354). Some make cryptic references to the 'crossing' (e.g. O. Turin 57034, O. Turin N. 57044) which may refer to the crossing of the river by the Theban triad on the occasion of the Valley festival. O.Cairo CG 25538 refers to a procession of Amun at Thebes and O. DeM 0354 refers to the festival of Mut and Amenhotep [I]. The ostraca concern themselves primarily with supplies and preparations for these festivals (e.g. McDowell 1999: 97, no. 68), while the journal of the necropolis records the workmen as having days off for the state festivals (Sadek 1987: 176). Comparing festival lists such as that on the exterior wall of Medinet Habu with the necropolis journal, Helck (1964: 160-161) noted that the main festival day of a large festival takes place is day 10, the day off for those who work, thus allowing them to attend, and that this is the day the god appears in procession and gives oracles. Graffiti at Deir el Bahri indicate that people visited the Hathor shrines at festival time (Meskell 2002: 171).

Elite tomb paintings depict participation in state festivals and include representations of parts of Karnak temple.[25] Cabrol (2001: 613, n. 169) has suggested that the festival scenes in TT31 of Khonsu may be complementary to the scenes in TT19 of Amenmose, which depict parts of the Valley festival (Cabrol 2001: 553).[26] Representations of whole temple complexes, such as that in TT2 of Khabekhenet (i) of the temple of Mut, indicate that the tomb owner had first hand knowledge of at least the buildings and statuary within the

[25] The principal Deir el-Medina examples and two relevant non-Deir el-Medina examples are listed here:

TT2 of Khabekhenet (i) (Deir el-Medina), Ramesses II (first half): scene depicting the bark of Mut on the lake of Asheru, with a dromos of rams to the north, a representation of the Mut temple complex and two colossal statues of Amun-Re (?) (Cabrol 1995b: 53; 2001: 262-268); two scenes of two different statues of Amenhotep I carried in a palanquin (Černý 1927: figs 13 and 14); Khabekhenet (i) offers to two rows of royal ancestors (Porter and Moss I.1 1960: 7 at (10)); Khabekhenet (i) before Amenhotep I, Queen Ahmes Nefertari and Princess Meryatum (Porter and Moss I.1 1960: 7 at (12));

TT5 of Neferabu (i) (Deir el-Medina), Ramesses II (mid): fragmentary representation of festival activity at Karnak South, including a dromos of rams (Cabrol 1995b: 51-57; 2001: 268-269);

TT217 of the Sculptor, Ipuy (i) (Deir el-Medina), Ramesses II (first half): the barks of the Theban triad (Davies 1927: pl. XXVIII; Cabrol 2001: 625);

TT19 of Amenmose, God's Servant of Amenhotep I 'of the Forecourt' in the reigns of Ramesses I and Seti I: Valley festival scene, with the barks of Mut and Amun-Re towed on a canal, a statue of Amenhotep I 'of the Forecourt' carried by wab-priests, a bark with a statue of Queen Ahmes Nefertari dragged from the temple; further scenes of the barks of Amenhotep I, Queen Ahmes Nefertari and Tuthmosis III before the temple of Tuthmosis III, Amenmose before two rows of royal ancestors, two statues of Amenhotep I in palanquins before the temple (Foucart 1932 IV: pls. 28-32; Černý 1962: fig. 9; Wilkinson and Hill 1983: 139 [31.6.5]; Cabrol 2001: 552-553; 608-609; pl. 33);

TT31 of Khonsu, First God's Servant of Tuthmosis III in the reign of Ramesses II: festival of Montu, barks of Montu and Tuthmosis III in festival procession, the latter before the temple of Tuthmosis III (Cabrol 2001: 608-614).

[26] Identifying elements from these named festival scenes in tombs and mapping them on to stelae representations can, as with the reading of the offerings depicted, aid the interpretation of the event depicted, but care must be taken. For example, TT31 has a representation of the bark of Khonsu with an enclosed deck-house, decorated with djed- and tit-glyphs. If this tomb does represent parts of the Valley festival, then stelae depicting such barks may also relate to this festival, for example, stela DB22, which depicts the river barks of the Theban triad with such a deckhouse. The process can work in reverse. For example, the text on stela DB300 explicitly refers to the Opet festival. The bark of Mut on this stela has a two-tier deckhouse. This same form of deckhouse appears on stela DB183, whose scene is iconographically similar to that found in TT2 of Khabekhenet (Cabrol 1995b: 53; 2001: 262-266), and this may inform us that the unnamed festival depicted in this tomb is the Opet festival. Such a deckhouse is also found on temple representations of boats taking part in the Opet festival. In TT19 of Amenmose, however, where the Valley festival is identified (*Imn-Rꜥ nsw nṯrw m ḥb.f nfr n int*), the bark of Amun has a two-tier deckhouse, indicating perhaps that both forms of bark were used at this festival.

precinct walls. Stelae depicting hypostases found only at certain temples indicate access at some point to these hypostases. A festival occasion may have been used in order to petition particular hypostases (Pinch 1993: 351), and a record of this event created in the form of a stela to sustain the relationship between devotee and divine image. Stelae such as those depicting the Theban triad in barks, or Amun with temple- or festival-related epithets ('opet'; 'kamutef', the oracular epithets 'Lord of the Gods' or 'August') can be related to the appearance/petitioning of these gods on specific festival occasions.

Two of the dataset stelae make explicit reference, in text and/or iconography, to state festivals: stela DB183 of Hesysunebef (i) (r. Ramesses III) depicts a statue of the Foreman, Neferhotep (ii) (in post during the reigns of Ramesses II to Seti II), standing on the bark of Mut, with Hesysunebef (i)'s family in the registers below (Plate 8); stela DB300 of the Overseer of the Temple of Maat, Merymaat records parts of the Opet festival of Ramesses VI's year seven. Stela DB183 can be related to stela DB206 of the Workman, Patjauemdiamun (ii), in post during the reign of Ramesses IV (Davies 1999: 225; see Raven 2000: 300 for a date at the end of the 19th Dynasty), which depicts the statues of Amenhotep I and Nebnefer. This Nebnefer may be the Foreman, Nebnefer (i), in post during the first half of the reign of Ramesses II. The cult of Nebnefer is known from a number of other monuments (Raven 2000: 301), on two of which he is referred to as *s3 nsw*, 'prince', and on occasion his name is written in a cartouche. A prince Nebnefer is not known from other sources, and it may be that Nebnefer acquired post-mortem royal status through his association with the royal ancestors - on stela Cairo JdE 41469 he is shown in the company of Amenhotep I and Queen Ahmes Nefertari (Raven 2000: 301). It may be that stelae DB183, DB206 and Cairo JdE 41469 depict state festival processions which included eminent ancestors from the workmen's community. Both the venerated foremen were in post during the reign of Ramesses II.

The table in Figure 4.9 lists stelae with identified state hypostases (see Chapter 3) with one or more of the following state festival/oracular-related criteria:

- the depiction of the portable statue of the god;
- the use of an oracular epithet;
- the depiction of a high ranking intermediary;
- festival offerings;
- the inclusion of family and/or colleagues - indicating that the event was significant to a large number of people, and not exclusive to distinct groups within the Deir el-Medina community.

Morgan (2004: 53) has concluded, after Kessler (1999), that the ear (and eye) stelae may be connected to festival processions of Amenhotep I, and indicate the dedicators' participation in such festivals. Only one of the stelae in the festival stelae subset, DB4 dedicated to Khonsuemwaset Neferhotep, has ears and eyes. Pinch (1993: 257-259) has argued that the ears on such stelae, as with the eyes, are those of the deity.

The majority of the stelae date to the 19th Dynasty, reign of Ramesses II. The Hathor and the ram of Amun stelae frequently include family and colleagues. In addition, three of the ram of Amun stelae include festival offerings, and/or bouquets. This, together with the high frequency of family/colleague inclusion on these stelae, suggests that the statues depicted were approached as part of a festival occasion. The Hathor, 'Residing in Thebes', stelae, include high frequencies of family (eight) and colleagues (one) and incense (seven). Incense occurs twice on the ram of Amun stelae, and once on the Amenhotep I stelae (where he is in a palanquin). It may be that incense, as well as denoting the principal dedicator, is an identifier of specific, more formal, festival activity. The Amenhotep I stelae are characterised by few offerings other than standard offering tables. This lack of offerings is also the case with the Ptah stelae, which may indicate that the ceremony commemorated was oral, and/or that the dedicators of the stelae were witnesses rather than participants. Three of the oracular deity stelae have no offerings; 12 include family and/or colleagues, a high frequency. The two stelae which meet the most criteria are DB13 (Plate 5a) and DB107, which depict a Hathor hypostasis from a temple geographical list, possibly originally in the Ramesseum, and clearly depict festival celebrations with the inclusion of musical instruments and numerous family members.

Figure 4.9 Attendance at state festivals/oracle stelae*

Hypostases approached as part of a festival or oracle occasion	Stelae
Ram statue of Amun	12, 17, 20, 63, 77**, 117, 151, 229, 255
Amenhotep I in the Blue Crown	54, 79**, 127, 237
Amenhotep I in the Nemes Headdress	27
Hathor, 'Residing in Thebes'	10, 15, 28, 32, 40, 71, 77**, 79**, 105, 110, 165, 227
Hathor, 'Lady of Gebelein'	13
Hathor, 'Lady of Mededu'	107
Hathor, 'Lady of the Southern Sycamore'	89
Ptah, 'Creator of Craftsmen/ship'	135, 138, 179, 205

Hypostases with processional/oracular iconography or epithets	Stelae
Amun-Re	55, 60, 86, 114, 126, 131, 171
Theban Triad	22
(Amun-Re) and Taweret	95, 106
Amenhotep I	128, 174
(Amenhotep I) and Nebnefer	206
Khonsuemwaset Neferhotep	1, 4
Mut (and Neferhotep (ii))	183

**The stelae listed are identified as festival/oracle stelae in the tables in Appendix 1, where further details can be found.*
***Occurs twice.*

Oracular approaches to deity statues could take place on the occasion of festivals. In the dataset two gods have emerged as the primary oracle givers: Amenhotep I and Amun-Re (see Section 4.1(ii)). There are 16 Deir el-Medina stelae that may, by the inclusion of the oracular criteria such as the depiction of gods in procession and the use of oracular epithets, be related to the occasion of oracles. Only one of these stelae has a lone petitioner, stela DB60 of Nebre (i) (Plate 9), which has a long non-generic text and is discussed below as an example of approaching the god at times of personal crisis. The majority of the stelae depict Amun-Re, and/or other members of the Theban triad, or local gods such as Amenhotep I or Taweret, often in procession, and are dedicated by groups of individuals, indicating the public nature of the festival procession, and supporting Kessler's suggestion (1999: 187) that professional groups or societies would make an approach to a deity, allowing a level of access via the group leader that an individual would not have had.

Festivals in the reign of Ramesses II

Representations of statues of deceased kings, a feature of the Ramesside Period (Redford 1986: 45), may be connected to festivals. Redford (1986: 191) notes that, according to the ancient sources, offering to the royal ancestors takes place in three contexts: the daily liturgy of Amenhotep I; the Min festival; and the Valley festival. Redford (1986: 191) places the resurgence of interest in the royal ancestors in the Ramesside Period in the context of the historical background to these dynasties, where the hereditary principle had been superseded by right of appointment, and therefore the Ramesside kings felt the need to stress their family connection to their royal ancestors. Redford describes the Min festival and Valley festival in the 19th Dynasty as 'fashionable' (1986: 196), ensuring that royal legitimacy and pedigree remained in the collective consciousness, and demonstrating it. TT19 of Amenmose, the only explicitly labeled festival depiction extant in a private tomb at Thebes at this period, which includes parts of the Valley festival, depicts deceased kings (Cabrol 2001: 608-609; 612-616; pl. 33). In Redford's list of 26 Theban private depictions of statues of deceased kings (1986: 46-51), 11 can be securely dated to the reign of Ramesses II.[27] There are a further seven dated to the Ramesside Period in general, some of which may date to the reign of Ramesses II. All of

[27] According to additional precise dating after Davies 1999, for a number of the examples.

the remaining principal sources for depictions of the royal ancestors - the reliefs of the Min festival at the Ramesseum, the Turin example of the liturgy of Amenhotep I, the offering tables of the Scribe, Qenhirkhepeshef (i), and the Foreman, Paneb (i) (Redford 1986: 34-44) - date to the reign of Ramesses II. The Medinet Habu reliefs of the Min festival (Redford 1986: 36) may copy those at the Ramesseum.

In relation to the Theban (non-Deir el-Medina) stelae, it may be that stelae that depict deceased kings, and in particular those that also depict funerary deities, can be connected with the Valley festival, where the depictions are representations of cult statues (Redford 1986: 53; McDowell 1992b: 97). Redford notes that '[t]he royal ancestors are, of course, divine and on a par with the gods; both are "Lords of Eternity," and receive equal veneration at the festival which probably provides the *raison d'être* for most of the tomb scenes, viz. the Feast of the Valley' (1986: 52). The scenes of the Valley festival set within the temple of Tuthmosis III in TT19 of Amenmose provide a context for the stelae representations. In TT19 sequences of scenes depict elements of the Valley festival, including rows of royal ancestor statues and the carrying of statues of Amenhotep I and Queen Ahmes Nefertari in palanquins. The stelae depict parts of these occasions in an iconographic short hand (Schulman 1984a) whose lack of specific detail, in particular the identification of the festival, may be due to the pressures of decorum affecting this different medium, the possibility that these stelae were used more than once (Morgan 2004: 54), and the requirement that the stelae function for perpetuity, thus necessitating a lack of specificity in their content. The use of the wab-priest title, indicating involvement in the carrying of the portable statue, may also be connected with festival activity. There are 17 Deir el-Medina stelae dating to the reign of Ramesses II which include references to, or depictions of, the royal ancestors and/or the funerary deities Hathor and Osiris.[28] Hathor accompanies the royal ancestors on stelae dating to the first half of the reign of Ramesses II. Of note is the high frequency of chiefs of the gang (six), and of wab-priests (three), in this subset. In addition, incense is offered seven times.

The Senior Scribe, Ramose (i), frequently the touchstone for events and changes at Deir el-Medina during this period, dedicated a stela, DB94, to the reigning king and his ancestors Horemheb, Ramesses I and Seti I. The scene is repeated in TT10 of Penbuy (i), with Ramesses II, the Vizier, Paser, and Ramose (i), as well as Amenhotep I and Queen Ahmes Nefertari. On stela DB65 Ramose (i) follows the Vizier, Paser, in the lower register, before a statue of Ramesses II. The upper register, most of which is lost, depicted a row of seated deities who may have been deceased kings. One of Ramose (i)'s reliefs from the Khenu-chapel, DM88 (Cairo JdE 72017; Porter and Moss I.2 1964: 697; Figure 3.21), includes the cartouches of Ramesses II, Tuthmosis IV and Horemheb. Ramose (i), the only member of the Deir el-Medina community at this time who came from a truly aristocratic background, is the only one who has representations of royal ancestors other than Amenhotep I/Queen Ahmes Nefertari on votive, as opposed to funerary, monuments. In addition, at the entrance to one of his tombs, TT7, Ramose (i) is shown adoring Amenhotep I, together with Queen Ahmes Nefertari, Horemheb and Tuthmosis IV (only the cartouches remain; Černý 1927: 175; Porter and Moss I.2 1964: 15).

The cult of the royal ancestors, on Deir el-Medina stelae and in tomb representations, is focused in the reign of Ramesses II, and more precisely in the first half of the reign. Cabrol (2001: 707) has noted the concentration of representations of a statue of Tuthmosis III during the reign of Ramesses II, whose cult she describes as being most likely a Ramesside creation (2001: 745, n. 80). The possibly complementary Valley festival scenes from TT19 and TT31 support the theory of a major version of the Valley festival in the early Ramesside Period. If this is the case, the date of TT19 must be pushed forward to Ramesses II rather than Ramesses I – Seti I (?), as it is currently dated in Porter and Moss (I.1 1960: 32). In terms of representations of Ramesses II himself, on private stelae with the royal ancestors, the only depictions in the Theban (non-Deir el-Medina) dataset are on the two stelae dedicated to Amenhotep I in the palanquin, by high-ranking military men. Ramesses II appears far more frequently on the Deir el-Medina stelae (nine times), but in relation to deceased kings only on three stelae: DB127 of the Wab-priest and God's Father of Amun, Anhotep (unidentified), where Ramesses II offers to Amun-Re and Mut, while Anhotep adores Re-Harakhti, Amenhotep I and Queen Ahmes Nefertari below; DB94, and possibly DB65, of the Senior Scribe Ramose (i), in the company of Ramesses I, Horemheb and Seti I (DB94) - the figures are lost on DB65. On stela DB78 Ramesses II offers flowers to Osiris, with his Vizier, Paser following. The Foreman, Qaha (i), in post during the first half of Ramesses II's reign, kneels with his wife below. The funerary associations of this stela, together with the high rank of the dedicator, and flower offerings, may link this stela to the Valley festival.

[28] DB9, DB27, DB42, DB54, DB73, DB77, DB79, DB82, DB98, DB112, DB120, DB121, DB124, DB125, DB127, DB128, DB132.

Earlier in this chapter it was argued that Ramesses II, or a statue of the king, visited the Hathor temple at Deir el-Medina to inaugurate the temple and chapel following its renovation. The relief DM88 of the Hathor cow from the Khenu-chapel, which includes the cartouches of dead kings, suggests a link with the Valley festival - Hathor's centrality to the Valley festival is well known (Schott 1952). It has also been argued that the form of Hathor called 'Foremost in Thebes' (*ḥry(t)-tp W3st*) that was venerated at Deir el-Medina came originally from Deir el-Bahri, the ancient focus of the Valley festival (Schott 1952: 5-7; 108-109; Pinch 1993: 9). It is tempting to suggest that Ramesses II, or his statue, visited Deir el-Medina to inaugurate the Hathor temple on one occasion of the Valley festival (or another festival). This royal visit, and participation in the festival, was of such importance, or presented as such by the (relatively) new king, that commemoration of attendance at the event were made, in the form of stelae and tomb representations, depicting Ramesses II, the state temple deities and/or the deceased ancestors and funerary deities.[29]

4.2(ii) Conception (and birth) (12 stelae)

Literary (e.g. Papyrus Westcar; Lichtheim 1975: 220-222) and medical (see David 1986: 123-131) texts inform us of aspects of fertility and birth. The medical texts are much preoccupied with gynaecology: barrenness was considered a tragedy, whilst pregnancy and childbirth were threatened by physical dangers (David 1986: 125; Szpakowska 2008: 31-33). It is clear from the records of absence from work due to child birth that such an event was of great importance to the community (see, for example, O. Cairo CG 25503; Janssen 1980: 142). The event of a birth was surrounded by rituals and related artefacts to ease the birth for the mother and protect the newborn child (Janssen and Janssen 1990: 9 describes spells, amulets and apotropaic wands used at births; see also Szpakowska 2008: 26-30); birth- and fertility-related artefacts have survived in the archaeological record,[30] and ostraca from Deir el-Medina depict birth arbors (Meskell 1999: 100). The *lit clos*, or enclosed beds (Bruyère 1934-1935 (1939) III: 54-64), located in the first room of the houses at Deir el-Medina may have been associated with the birth process (for an alternative explanation, see Meskell 1999: 99-100). A number of fertility and birth-related artefacts were discovered together in a house at Amarna, in a cupboard-space under the stairs. They consisted of naked female terracotta figure, two painted pottery beds and a stela of a woman and a girl adoring Taweret (Janssen and Janssen 1990: 10; Meskell 2002: 71-72).

The childless Senior Scribe, Ramose (i) dedicated a large inscribed limestone phallus (Cairo TN 29/4/26/3) to Hathor with two lines of rather obscure inscription: 'Cause that I receive the rewards of your house'; 'Cause an endurance in your house from me/my hand' (*imi šsp.i b3kw n pr.ṯ; imi mn m pr.ṯ m-ʿ.i*).[31] Pinch observes that 'the inscription may contain only a standard type of request for the Ka of the donor to dwell in a temple, sharing in the offerings of the goddess' (1993: 242), which is possible given Ramose (i)'s close association with the cult of Hathor in the temple at Deir el-Medina. The phallic form of the monument as a symbol of the male donor, or of hoped for regeneration in the temple, remains theoretical, and it is not clear whether we can relate this to fertility in this life, or the next (Pinch 1993: 242). However, the inscription may indeed be a *double entendre* with a sexual connotation. Two monuments of Ramose (i) that are directly relevant to his childlessness are stela DB83, dedicated to the triad of Qadesh, Min-Amun-Re and Reshep, where Min represents ithyphallic male fertility, and stela DB95, to Taweret, where Taweret represents female fertility. On both of these, Ramose (i) is shown with his wife, Mutemwia, where she is absent from his other 19 stelae in the dataset. The inclusion of wives on stelae dedicated to known fertility deities may indicate the function of these stelae.

---

[29] The Min festival reliefs at the Ramesseum that relate Ramesses II's coronation include the royal ancestor statues (Redford 1986: 35), supplying a second interpretation of some or all of the royal ancestor reliefs and stelae, and festival stelae: the coronation of Ramesses II. Helck (1964: 164-165) has observed that the coronation of the king was celebrated by a statue of the (living) king being carried in procession on the West Bank. The coronation could be linked to the Opet festival, which Ramesses II celebrated at Thebes in his year 1. Ramesses II's donation of the statue of himself /Amenhotep I (see Section 4.1(ii)), discovered in the Khenu-chapel, may be linked to this event.

[30] Examples of birth-related artefacts include birthing bricks (Szpakowska 2008: 24-25, fig. 4.1), apotropaic wands and amulets, principally of Taweret, in the form of a pregnant hippo holding the *s3*-amulet, and the dwarf god, Bes (hundreds of examples are extant in museum collections). Examples of fertility-related artefacts include the wooden, stone and faience phalli from Deir el Bahri (Pinch 1993: 235-345).

[31] For the hieroglyphs, alternative translations and a discussion of the difficulties of the text, see Pinch 1993: 242.

Although Hathor is the goddess believed to be most closely associated with fertility in New Kingdom Egypt, there are only two Hathor stelae in the dataset with women as the primary dedicators: DB13 to a state temple hypostasis (see p. 57; Plate 5a) and DB152, dedicated by a Weshbet-mourner and her daughter, to Hathor as the Good Cat. Pinch's survey (1993) of votive offerings to Hathor indicates that stelae were only one of a large repertoire of votive offerings dedicated to the goddess, and it may be that women in search of fertility would have dedicated another type of votive object, such as a figurine, or an organic artefact that has not survived in the record - though a few votive textiles are extant (Pinch 1993: 103-134). In addition, the Hathor cult at Deir el-Medina was a royal and state cult, accessible only to high-status individuals, therefore perhaps not to general petitions for fertility, whereas the cult at Deir el-Bahri, which Pinch has studied, had, by the late New Kingdom, evolved into a centre for popular worship (Pinch 1993: 25).

From the supporting evidence, the criteria that may indicate that a stela is related to (hoped for) conception and a safe birth are: inclusion of women (either women alone dedicating the stela, or depicted with their husbands), and the inclusion of the fertility or birth related deities Taweret or Min, or Min in his triad of Qadesh-Min-Reshep. There are 12 stelae that meet these criteria.[32] On ten of the 12 stelae the dedicators are a couple, with only two stelae dedicated by women alone: DB154 and DB233. Neither of the women depicted has a title. Stela DB33 (Figure 4.7) is dedicated by the Workman, Irynefer (i), and his wife, Mehykhati (ii). On this stela Mehykhati (ii) holds the incense, and it has been argued above (p. 85) that this indicates her role as the primary dedicator. These stelae have a high frequency (six of the 12) of water offerings, all of which are offered or held by women. The stelae form a fairly clearly defined subset within the dataset.

4.2(iii) Entry into/promotion within a profession (21 stelae)

Janssen and Janssen (1990: 107-108, fig 39) have identified the phrase 'I knotted the girdle' referring to the wearing of the 'gala-kilt' as the indicator of taking up a man's first office (Old and Middle Kingdoms) where it refers to wearing the ceremonial dress of the civil servants (see Pinch 1995: 379). Elite autobiographies are careful to record the offices attained in their owner's lifetimes. Professional achievement was highly regarded and recorded in tombs and on stelae with greater clarity and emphasis than domestic achievements such as marriage and children, which were not regarded as public achievements and must often be deduced from the decorations. Assman (1989: 144-145) has suggested that certain funerary rites reflect initiation rites into professions.

At Deir el-Medina, ostraca with anxious petitions regarding whether young men would gain places in the gang bear witness to the fierce competition for such posts (see, for example, McDowell 1999: 229 no. 180). Posts frequently ran in the family, with important positions such as foreman staying in the same family for generations (Černý 1973: 125-126; Davies 1999: 12-13). The stelae from Section 4.1(iii) provide us with some criteria for stelae that relate to entry into, or promotion within, a profession:

- stelae dedicated to Ptah (alone, or with other deities) as patron of the royal workmen;
- the inclusion of a vizier;
- (and/or) the dedicator alone or with his male relatives and/or colleagues.

One stela that clearly belongs in the realm of an individual's professional career, though not to promotion at work (and so not specifically to this section), is DB175 of the Foreman, Anhurkhawy (ii), which depicts the Vizier, Hori, bringing a message from the Ramesses IV, rewarding the Foreman for completing the tomb. A similar representation occurs on the fragmentary stela DM151 (Bruyère 1935-1940 (1952) II: 44, 86 and pl. XVII), of which the lower register is lacking (Janssen 1963: 64-70). This event may also be the one recorded on O. DeM 41 vs. 10, where the Vizier, Hori, brings rewards (*mkw*) to the crew at the start of the reign of Ramesses IV (Janssen 1997: 161). The concept of recording the giving of rewards on private stelae has a parallel in the private stelae recording the giving of reward gold by the king, which were traditionally dedicated by high elite individuals (Schulman 1988: 116-147).

In this group of 21 stelae[33] there is a high frequency of stelae (eight) with no offerings, indicating the oral nature of the ceremony depicted. There are no instances of water offerings as the professional nature of the

32 DB10, DB17, DB29, DB33, DB72, DB70, DB74, DB83, DB95, DB154, DB160, DB233.

33 DB11, DB24, DB26, DB31, DB39, DB43, DB50, DB51, DB53, DB69, DB88, DB105, DB116, DB135, DB153, DB162, DB170, DB179, DB188, DB192, DB262.

ceremony recorded precluded the presence of women. On 11 stelae the men are alone before the deity statue, on the remaining 10 they are shown with male relatives or colleagues, perhaps indicating different kinds of ceremonies. A vizier appears three times, on DB179 and DB188 alone, and on DB39 where the Vizier, Paser, follows Ramesses II (Plate 5b). The inclusion of the king indicates that this stela records a state ceremony. Stela DB153 (Plate 10) depicts the Quarryman, Huy, in formal dress, adoring Ptah in a shrine, with a water pot and lotus before him. Behind him stands his young son, Mose, dressed as a priest. This may be a record of Mose's entry into the gang, or, alternatively, his initiation into a lay-priesthood. As such it is also discussed in the next section.

4.2(iv) Entry into a religious organisation/participation in a local religious ceremony (18 stelae)

Administrative records and private monuments record individuals using priestly titles, most frequently wab-priest, with instances of god's servant (*ḥm-nṯr*), lector priest (*ẖry-ḥbt*) and the problematic *ꜥꜣ-n-ꜥ* (Davies 1999: 206). The religious organisations discussed here are not the priesthoods that existed within the state temples and which can be regarded as professions, but rather the voluntary organisations staffed by workmen (and their wives) (McDowell 1999: 95). Van Gennep (1909 [1960]: 96-104) identified initiation into religious brotherhoods as a typical 'rites of passage' event, and they have been defined by Service (1971: 12) as cutting across the existing social structure, and articulating it. Certainly, membership of a lay priesthood at Deir el-Medina, at least that of the deified king Amenhotep I, was much sought after, and remained within a limited group of high-status families (Lesko B.S., 1994: 23; see Section 4.1(ii)). The juridical role of the oracle of Amenhotep I, as well as the cult's central role in the community, would have made membership of the lay-priesthood attractive.

An ostracon from the Valley of the Kings is the only extant piece of evidence for the method of selecting priests. It is an oracle question reading, 'Shall one appoint Seti as a god's servant?' (McDowell 1999: 95, no. 65). Lay priesthoods seem to have passed from father to son (McDowell 1999: 95), perhaps a reflection of the organisation of the state priesthoods at East Thebes at this time (see Bierbrier 1975), and entry into them may have involved a period of initiation, with or without an initiation ceremony. Stelae that depict individuals dressed as priests (shaven headed, and/or wearing a sash), and identified by a priestly title rather than by their professional title, may be related either to the ceremony of initiation into the priesthood, or to participation in a local religious ceremony. Stelae depicting large groups of men and one deity may relate to ceremonies of that god, and represent an existing lay-priesthood. The ebony stela discovered by Bruyère in the kitchen of the house NEIV depicts Anukis seated in a shrine on a sledge (?) with two double rows of men below (Bruyère 1934-1935 (1952) III: 247-249 [1] and fig. 127). The principal dedicator named in the horizontal text at the base is the Draughtsman of Amun, Merysekhmet (i). The stela is in fragments so many of the names of individuals cannot be discerned.

The stelae connected to local religious ceremonies may also relate to personal feast days. A personal feast day was a day dedicated to a god to whom an individual, family or group had a special relationship (Van Walsem 1982b: 223: Sadek 1987: 193-197), perhaps a god in whose lay-priesthood they, or another member of their family, served (McDowell 1999: 92). Janssen (1980: 145-146) defines a personal feast day as one referred to as *ḥb.f*/*pꜣy.f ḥb* ('his festival'; see Van Walsem 1982b: 223 for a differentiation of meaning of these two terms), or with the addition of the god's name, for example, *ḥb.f n Ḥwt-ḥr* ('his festival of Hathor'; see Pinch 1993: 344). The papyri and ostraca from Deir el-Medina record absences of workmen for several days at a time to prepare for and celebrate certain 'private', or personal, feasts (Janssen 1980: 146-148). Often men were absent to brew beer for a god. Janssen (1980: 134) notes that in the fairly complete sequence of 'journal' ostraca from Ramesses III-Ramesses IV, only 70 out of the 280 days were working days, with many of the days off relating to 'feasts'. It may be impossible to distinguish between stelae relating to personal feasts and local festivals,[34] and some or all personal feasts and local festivals may, in fact, be one and the same event, or have occured simultaneously. The frequency and regularity of personal feast days are evidence against the erection of a stela on the occasion of such a feast day.

[34] See Meskell 2002: 173-175 for a discussion of the difficulty of distinguishing whether ostraca describing gifts of food and gatherings of people relate to personal feast days or larger festivals. Janssen (1997) interprets the ostraca as relating to personal feasts.

The use of religious titles and/or the wearing of priestly dress have been used as the criteria to identify stelae relating to ceremonies involving the lay-priesthoods, which may include initiation into the priesthood and/or presence at local religious ceremonies. Full priestly dress consists of a shaven head (or skull cap), a sash and a kilt. The sash may have been painted on and, on a number of stelae in this group, is no longer visible, or it is simply not visible in the reproduction of the stela.

The stelae in the group[35] are dedicated to Amenhotep I (and other royal ancestors) (eight stelae), Amun-Re alone or with other gods (six stelae), and one each to Isis, Mertseger, Mut, Hathor and Min, Reshep, Anat and Isis. The priestly titles refer to the lay priesthoods of Amenhotep I (11), Amun-Re (six), Mut (one), with three titles not specifying the priesthood. The lack of Hathor lay-priesthood titles relates to the fact that the Hathor cult at Deir el-Medina was a state-run organisation (Pinch 1993: 350), though it remains unclear who would have performed the rituals in the temple. On nine of the stelae individuals wear full or partial priestly dress. Ten of the stelae have no offerings, suggesting that an oral ceremony is being depicted. No water is offered by dedicators, which reflects the almost total absence of women on the stelae - the 20th Dynasty stela, DB190, dedicated to Mertseger includes the wife of the dedicator in the text. However, water is offered on two occasions by the intermediary, on DB127 of the unidentified Wab-priest and God's Father of Amun, Anhotep, and on DB182 of the Servitor of the Lord of the Two Lands, Hay (vii). Both of these stelae may relate to the royal ancestor cult, a context precluding the presence of women, perhaps necessitating that men carry out the libations.

4.2(v) Illness/personal crisis (4 stelae)

Absences from work due to illness are frequent in the record of the day-to-day activities of the gang. As noted above, illness accounts for the majority of cases of absence recorded on the Deir el-Medina database (Janssen 1980: 135-136). Life in the Village, as elsewhere in Egypt, was hazardous, with dangers ranging from scorpion and snake bites, to child-birth and disease (see Szpakowska 2008: 31-35; 150-175). Healing and protection against future misfortune incorporated both what we term magic and medicine (Pinch 1994: 133-146; Nunn 1996: 96). The village doctor, scorpion charmer (see McDowell 1999: 117) or local wisewoman (Borghouts 1982a: 25-26; Meskell 1999: 179-182) may have been called upon in the first instance, but it seems that in times of emergency, or when an individual had pulled through against extreme odds, the villagers paid a visit to hypostases of state gods to ask for help or express their thanks (Pinch 1993: 351). The best-known example of this is stela DB60 the Draughtsman, Nebre (i), who, in a long and non-generic inscription, thanks Amun-Re for saving the life of his son (Kitchen 2000: 653-655; see Sadek 1987: 226). The non-generic nature of this stela extends to the representation, where Amun-Re is shown as a colossal statue situated, unusually, before temple pylons (Schulman 1988: 44-45; Plate 9).[36]

A kind of illness, though probably closer to a moral or ethical lapse rather than a physical ailment, is that referred to by the Egyptians as 'seeing darkness' (*m33 kkw*). Stela DB116 (Plate 11a) of the Workman, Neferabu (i), asks forgiveness of the god Ptah for swearing falsely by his name. A second stela of this man, DB115, asks forgiveness for being lazy (Sadek 1987: 233-236) and warns against the power of the goddess Mertseger (McDowell 1999: 101). Both of these stelae texts are notable for their length and non-generic nature, and suggest that Neferabu (i) must have suffered some fairly extreme misfortune as a result of his behaviour - whether the stelae refer to one occasion of misfortune, or several, is unclear. The criteria used to define the stelae in this group are the inclusion of a non-generic text and/or image.

The four stelae in the illness/personal crisis group[37] are dedicated by two workmen and an outline draughtsman. They include no offerings other than offering tables, indicating the oral nature of the act, the petitioning of the deity statue. The stelae depict male dedicators, alone, apart from stela DB60 which includes Nebre (i)'s son Khay (i), and, in the text, Nakhtamun (iii), the son rescued from illness by Amun-Re. DB116 of the Workman, Neferabu (i), includes ears and eyes and the 'seeing darkness' formula.

---

[35] DB5, DB8, DB25, DB27, DB99, DB126, DB127, DB128, DB140, DB182, DB187, DB190, DB192, DB199, DB214, DB224, DB232, DB242.

[36] This kind of representation is more common in tomb paintings, for example, in TT19 and TT31 (Cabrol 2001: pl. 33; 608-614).

[37] DB60, DB115, DB116, DB196.

***

The stelae discussed in Section 4.2 illustrate that votive stelae can be categorised according to criteria which can be linked to specific events or activities. The rigid conventions within which the stelae are created control the form and content to the extent that, to the eyes of the 21st century viewer, or indeed any viewer living outside the cultural milieu of Ramesside Egypt, or perhaps even of Deir el-Medina at this period, they appear generic and almost indistinguishable from one another. To a contemporary, local, Egyptian, the stelae contain the necessary information, in the offerings, dress, deity, location and positioning of the individuals, and other iconographic content, to convey clearly whether a stela commemorates presence at a festival, of promotion and work, or another such event.

4.3 Writing Biographies

The table in Figure 4.10 lists individuals with more than three stelae in the dataset, and attempts to categorise their stelae according to the events identified discussed in Section 4.2.

Six of the stelae, DB17, DB60, DB77, DB79, DB83, and DB116 (marked in bold) appear in more than one category. DB77 and DB79 both belong to festival categories. Of the remaining four, DB17, DB60 and DB83 can be related both to state festivals and personal petitions to a deity that may have taken place at these festivals. Only DB116 remains enigmatic in its intent. In general, the early part of the reign of Ramesses II is the most populated, particularly by votive stelae relating to state festival attendance. Stelae become sparser into the 20th Dynasty, where few conclusions can be drawn from the three stelae categorised here other than that festival attendance was still marked.

The Senior Scribe, Ramose (i) has eight of his 21 stelae categorised. By reading only these stelae, it would seem that Ramose (i)'s life was characterised by attendance at state festivals, and petitions to fertility deities, whose involvement in such activities is supported by supplementary evidence. Ramose (i)'s aristocratic background and high rank at Deir el-Medina would have afforded him a higher level of access to state festivals than the majority of the community. In addition, it is well known that Ramose (i) and his wife Mutemwia (i) were childless (Černý 1973: 325; Pinch 1993: 242; Davies 1999: 81-82). The relative paucity of Ramose (i)'s stelae that can be categorised is due to a loss of cultural context and supplementary information for ritual activity. The sheer number of the stelae, indicating broad divine access, formally marks his high social status.

Penbuy (i), Guardian in the first half of the reign of Ramesses II (Davies 1999: 194-195) has all of his six database stelae categorised. From these stelae we can trace a life experience that included attendance at festivals, professional advancement, and pleas for fertility. He was certainly married twice, to Amentetwosret (i) and Iretnofret (i) (Davies 1999: 194), and according to Davies (1999: chart 29) he had five children by his first wife Amentetwosret (i), but perhaps just one by his second wife. The three stelae of Penbuy (i)'s colleague Irynefer (i) (Davies 1999: 263 and Chart 26) have also all been categorised, indicating a set of life stages similar, if less marked, to that of Penbuy (i). The Workman, Neferabu (i) (Davies 1999: 149-151; 155; 157-161; 177; 180; 184; 219; 264), had a more unusual life, plagued by misfortune for which he attempted to atone on two separate occasions.

From an initial attempt at applying a personal reading to private votive stelae which lack overt biographical information, it is possible to place a number of stelae within certain life event categories, and begin to construct possible biographies. Situated alongside other sources of information, such as administrative records and graffiti, they can contribute to the evidence for the past lives of certain individuals.

Figure 4.10 Deir el-Medina individuals with three or more stelae, showing the stelae categorised according to life events

Name	**Title**	**Date in post**	**Attendance at state festivals (r. Ramesses II)/oracular events**	**Conceptio n/birth**	**Entry into/promoti on within a profession**	**Entry into a religious organisation /particip-ation in a local religious ceremony**	**Illness/ personal crisis**	**Total dataset stelae of the individ-ual**
Pay (i)	Draughtsman	19th D: RI – RII, first half	1, 4					**3**
Neferronpet (i)	Workman	19th D: SI – RII, first half	15, **17**	**17**				**3**
Irynefer (i)	Workman	19th D: RII, first half	32	33	31			**3**
Maaninakht-uf (i)	Draughtsman	19th D: RII, first half	(42)		43			**3**
Nebre (i)	Draughtsman	19th D: RII, first half	**60**				**60**	**5**
Penbuy (i)	Guardian	19th D: RII, first half	71, (73)	70, 72, 74	69			**6**
Qaha (i)	Foreman	19th D: RII, first half	**(77)**					**4**
Qen (ii)	Sculptor	19th D: RII, first half	**(79),** (82)					**4**
Ramose (i)	Senior Scribe	19th D: RII, first half	**83**, 86, 89, 95, (98)	**83**, 97	88	99*		**21**
Neferabu (i)	Workman	19th D: RII, mid	117		**116**		115, **116**	**3**
Neferhotep (ii)	Foreman	19th D: RII, second half - SII	(124).					**3**
Anhurkhawy (ii)	Foreman	20th D: RIII - RVI	174					**5**
Hay (vii)	Deputy and Servitor of Amenhotep I	20th D: RIII - RV				182		**3**
Nekh(em)mut (vi)	Foreman	20th D: RIV - RIX	205					**3**

4.4 Summary

The votive stelae are complex multivalent monuments which can be located at the nexus of public and private activity, existing in the public domain and commemorating, within the constraints of their genre, both wider phenomena that affected the workmen, and their own bounded life experience. In terms of social identity, they present an individual as meeting society's normative expectations whilst simultaneously promoting his status and his individuality (Woolf 1996). Members of the community at Deir el-Medina were aspirational (Hulin 1989), keen to present themselves in a relationship to the king that was, prior to the reign of Ramesses II, a prerogative of the elite ruling class. The Middle Kingdom votive/commemorative stelae from Abydos form a comparable example, where individuals marked their presence at the Abydos rituals in order to benefit from participation in the rituals, and to display their level of divine access, sometimes as a result of a relationship with a higher-ranking individual. The private votive stelae depicting Ramesses II draw together a group of contemporary individuals who were present at a royal visit, in person or statue form, to the Hathor temple. Such individuals represent a social elite whose focal point was the Senior Scribe, Ramose (i), and their activity represents a form of social organisation centred on the rituals and ceremonies, with their associated economic benefits, taking place at the Hathor temple and associated Khenu-chapel - the cult of the king and the cult of Ramose (i). The monumental record in the form of reliefs and stelae situates Ramose (i) at the centre of this social phenomenon in the first half of the reign of Ramesses II, creating a local focus for ritual practice in addition to the king. Ramose (i) benefits through association with and access to the royal cult and the state Hathor cult, and by acting as the intermediary for others to these cults.

The Amenhotep I lay priesthood are a social group of considerable influence within the community, focusing on a local cult statue. Ramesses II astutely situates himself at the heart of this cult, diverting the focus back to the kingship, and reasserting control on Village activity by means of the oracle decisions, an example of state intervention in local ritual practice, and a means by which social structure could be perpetuated (Pinch 1993: 357; Frankfurter 1998: 146). As with a number of social practices which take their model from the central ideology, the use of oracles demonstrates support for the ideology of the king as the intermediary, the interpreter of the god, and simultaneously sets up alternate structures wherein the king is omitted: emulation of royal practice has the potential to undermine it. This is a feature of the monumental record of private social practices evident throughout the dataset. In form and content, the stelae both cleave to the conventions of decorum in their style and restricted content, and apparently offer such an alternate ideology, by representing direct access to deity hypostases, through the use of type A and C stelae. Representational 'direct access' is, by the Ramesside Period, conventionally acceptable. It is unlikely that a community as aspirational as that at Deir el-Medina would have knowingly established an alternate structure, but numerous accessible representations of individuals displaying apparent 'direct access' to a deity (though to the hypostasis and not the divine presence), with no recourse to the king, in a semi-literate environment where images were a powerful means of transmitting information, may have had an such an outcome. Alongside this, Ramesses II's presence on a number of the stelae, unusual at this social level, demonstrates an astute awareness by the king of the power of images, and of the status associated with the use of his image. Such stelae can be understood as a royal manipulation of conventions to stress the centrality of the kingship at a time when its authority in the public consciousness was waning. The stelae with the royal image are the highest status artefacts.

The stelae relating to the visit of the Vizier, To, illustrate with the greatest clarity the historical aspect of votive stelae. The complementary sources - ostraca, graffiti and votive stelae - all record aspects of a single event that emerges clearly in the record, illustrating how it is possible to link stelae lacking in overt historical content to a single fixed historical event (Schulman 1980: 97-102; 1988: 197) whilst acting as permanent records of such an event (Woolf 1996: 27). A related example is that of stela DB175, recording the rewarding of the Foreman, Anhurkhawy (ii), for which related stelae and documentary evidence exist. As a record of a ritual related to the dedicator's professional activity, the stelae are much more specific than a record of abstract piety, suggesting that many stelae, for which we have no supplementary evidence, may have similarly specific motives behind their creation. The identification of a number of events in an individual's life that we might term 'rites of passage', due to their traditional role as elements of 'folk religion' (Pinch 1993: 351), may also be revelatory in terms of identifying social organisation, in the sense of the organisation and activity of a community at a local level. A careful study of elements of the content and design of stelae can contribute to an understanding of social practices, which take the form of the 'religious' rituals recorded on the stelae.

The categories discussed leave 61% (162/264 stelae) of the dataset stelae unaccounted for. Further analysis of different aspects of stelae iconography may make it possible to link the stelae to particular events, in particular, to festivals, and perhaps specifically to a large festival early in the reign of Ramesses II. However, there may be events whose occurrence it is impossible to interpret from the iconographic content of the votive stelae due to the loss of cultural context, and the concomitant loss of knowledge of the nature and significance of such events.

***

A historical reading of the votive stelae leads us from a glimpse of royal activity in the Village, to a record of social organisation centring on the cult of Amenhotep I, and the implicit role of Ramose (i) within the Hathor cult, that contrasts with, and complements, the documented social structure of the Village recorded in the administrative record. Chapter 5 continues the social and historical analysis of groups of Ramesside Period votive/commemorative stelae at four contemporary sites: Abu Simbel and Wadi es-Sebua in Lower Nubia, Qantir/Pi-Ramesses in the Eastern Delta and Zawiyet Umm el-Rakham in the Western/Libyan desert. The analysis will determine whether the use of votive stelae at Deir el-Medina is a representative Ramesside Period phenomenon, or whether it represents activity limited to the workmen's community at Thebes, and will assess the extent to which stelae can reflect social structure and/or social organisation on a pan-Egyptian scale during the Ramesside Period.

5. BEYOND THEBES: SOLDIERS, SAILORS AND SANDALMAKERS

Chapter 5 looks at private votive stelae and cult activity during the Ramesside Period from four additional sites: the Lower Nubian sites of Abu Simbel and Wadi es-Sebua, the Delta site of Qantir/Pi-Ramesses, and Zawiyet Umm el-Rakham in the Western (Libyan) Desert. The sites have been chosen due to the relatively large numbers of Ramesside Period votive stelae extant from them. Section 5.1 describes the sites - their location, function, excavation and cult structures; Section 5.2 analyses the comparative dataset stelae as one body, according to the number, date, compositional form and the deities on the stelae; Section 5.3 discusses the stelae and cult images in detail site by site, with a discussion of the findings in Section 5.4.

5.1 The Sites

Abu Simbel (Lower Nubia)

Abu Simbel is located 280 kilometres south of Aswan, on the west bank of the Nile. The site consists of two rock cut temples, constructed in the reign of Ramesses II, referred to here as the Great Temple and the Small Temple. The Great Temple is the largest of the seven Nubian temples constructed by Ramesses II.[1] The original site was regarded as sacred long before the construction of the Ramesses II temples, indicated by the existence of Old and Middle Kingdom graffiti on the cliffs (Lepsius 1913 V: 167-168; Porter and Moss VII 1951: 117-118). Christophe (1961: 303-304) suggests that a cult to Horus of Meha (*mḥꜣ*) predates the Ramesses II temples at this location; this deity occurs in both Abu Simbel temples. In the Small Temple a number of inscriptions mention that the temple was cut into the 'Holy Mountain' (*ḏw wꜥb*; Habachi 1969a: 7; Kitchen 1996: 507, 508). In the South Chapel a text refers to Amun-Re residing in the 'Pure Mountain of Napata' (*ḏw wꜥb npt*; Kitchen 1996: 495), perhaps indicating that Abu Simbel was regarded as a 'mirror' site to the Amun-Re temple further south at Gebel Barkal.

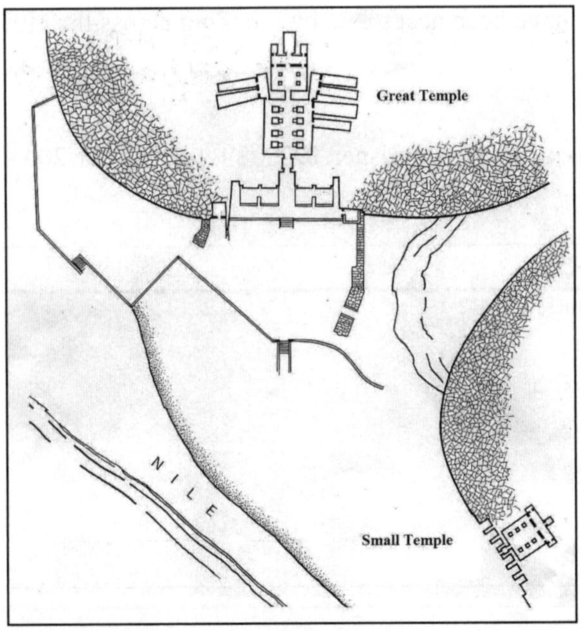

Figure 5.1 Plan of the temples at Abu Simbel (after Fouchet 1965: 207)

The temples were rediscovered in 1813 by the Swiss traveller Johann Ludwig Burckhardt and first entered in August 1817 by Giovanni Belzoni (Otto 1975: col. 25; Desroches-Noblecourt 1986: 1), after which

[1] For the dimensions and description of the Great Temple, see Habachi 1969a: 2; for the Small Temple see Desroches-Noblecourt 1968: 4-5.

numerous travellers made the difficult journey to the distant temples (Fouchet 1965: 206). Champollion recorded parts of the temples in his volumes *Monuments de l'Égypte et de la Nubie* (4 vols., 1835-1845 [1970]). In the early part of the 20th century Maspero published reports on the Nubian temples, including Abu Simbel (1911b; 1912 [1920]). These reports describe the condition of the temples and the restoration work carried out by the Antiquities Service at that time. The temples were later threatened by the construction of the High Dam at Aswan and, from 1963 to 1968, were raised 64 metres as part of the UNESCO rescue project in Nubia (Otto 1975: col. 27; Säve-Söderbergh 1987: 64-126).

The ancient name of the Great Temple was 'The House/Estate of Ramesses Beloved of Amun (the Town)' (*Pr-Rᶜ-ms-sw mry-Ỉmn (pꜣ dmi)*; Habachi 1969a: 2; Otto 1975: col. 25). The principal gods of the temple are Re-Harakhti, Amun-Re and Ramesses II himself, who, with Ptah, are present as seated statues in the sanctuary (Porter and Moss VII 1951: 110 (115); Habachi 1969a: pl. Vb). Habachi (1969a: 2) suggests that Ramesses II is assimilated to the temple gods; Amun-Re and Ptah have the form 'of Ramesses' (*n Rᶜ-ms-sw*; Kitchen 1982b: 177; Uphill 1984: 235-236). Ramesses II is therefore the principal deity in the temple. From an inscription on one of the rock cut stela, stela DB320, which describes the Great Temple as a 'Temple of Millions of Years' (*ḥwt-nṯr ḥḥ rnpwt*) for Ramesses II, Kitchen (1982b: 65; 67; 177) concludes that the Great Temple is a memorial temple for the king under the patronage of Amun-Re and the sun god Re in his various aspects. Ramesses II is most clearly depicted as a form of Re-Harakhti in the Second Court and Sanctuary, where his bark has a hawk-headed prow (Porter and Moss VII 1951: 109 (98); 110 (114); Habachi 1969a: 4-7, figs. 4 and 5). On a pillar in the Second Hall the king as a hawk-headed god is embraced by Anukis (pillar IX; Porter and Moss VII 1951: 109; Kitchen 1996: 501). This concept is reflected on one of the stelae, DB331, found in front of the Great Temple and now in the Cairo Museum, where the Wab-priest, Huy, adores a hawk-headed god identified as Ramesses II, while his wife adores Anukis below (Maspero 1911a: fig. 14).

The Small Temple is located 150 metres to the north of the Great Temple (Otto 1975: col. 26). It is most frequently described as being dedicated to Hathor of Ibshek (Faras) and to Queen Nefertari, the principal wife of Ramesses II (Otto 1975: col. 26; Kitchen 1982b: 66; 99). Desroches-Noblecourt, in her detailed study of the decorative scheme of the temple, proposes that the temple celebrates the flood - Hapy - as the united male (Ramesses II) and female (Hathor-Queen Nefertari) principles, and, by association, the rejuvenation of the king (Desroches-Noblecourt 1968: 109-120). Prior to the UNESCO project, the temple was situated directly on the bank of the river, and in winter would only have been accessible by climbing across the cliff face (Desroches-Noblecourt 1968: 2) or by boat.

Figure 5.2 King's Sons of Kush during the reign of Ramesses II (after Reisner 1920: 39-47; Raedler 2003: 132-133)

King's Son of Kush	**Year in post**
*Yuni	Seti I-Ramesses II 1-2
*Hekanakht	Year 3-24
*Paser II	Year 24/25-34
Huy	Year 34-38
*Setau	Year 38-63
Anhotep	?
*Mernudjem	?

* *Indicates that they feature at Abu Simbel.*

The exact date of the completion of the temples has caused much debate. Schmidt has noted that 'not one temple in Nubia contains a regnal date to indicate the exact time of its construction' (1973: 172). The general consensus, based on inscriptional and iconographic evidence, is that the Great Temple was completed during the first half of the reign of Ramesses II (Habachi 1969). The temple completion date is discussed in detail in Section 5.4(i), below. Desroches-Noblecourt (1968: 119) places the start of the construction of the Small Temple at the beginning of Ramesses II's reign, a theory she supports with the extreme youth of the representations in the temple of the king and queen (1968: 119), and, more securely, with the stela of the King's Son of Kush, Yuni, carved into the rock face north of the temple façade (DB320; Desroches-Noblecourt 1968: pls. X, XX; Habachi 1969a: 11). Yuni was in post for only one or two years at the start of the reign of Ramesses II (see the table in Figure 5.2, above). In addition, the only reference to the deified Ramesses II occurs in the Sanctuary, the last part to be completed (Habachi 1969a: 11). It is not clear whether the two temples were constructed simultaneously or consecutively.

Wadi es-Sebua (Lower Nubia)

Wadi es-Sebua is located about 150 kilometres south of Aswan at the start of a great bend in the Nile. From here, roads branched out into the desert, making it an area of strategic importance (Firth 1927: 236; Habachi 1967: 16; Helck 1975: 100). The site consists of two semi-rock cut temples, the small mud brick construction of Amenhotep III (Firth 1927: 235-237 and pl. 3; Porter and Moss VII 1951: 63-64), later restored by Ramesses II (Habachi 1967: 52; Gundlach 1984: col. 768), and the larger stone construction of Ramesses II, located 200 metres to the north (Gauthier 1912; Porter and Moss VII 1951: 53-64; Gundlach 1984: col. 768).

The temple of Ramesses II was excavated from 1909 by Alexandre Barsanti for the Department of Antiquities (Barsanti and Gauthier 1911; Gauthier 1912; Firth 1927: 236). Robert Mond uncovered the small temple of Amenhotep III in the early 1900s, and cleared and recorded the paintings, before re-covering the temple to preserve it. In the meantime, local villagers had heard of the temple and subsequently destroyed some of the mud brick for *sebakh*. During the 1910-1911 season of the Archaeological Survey of Nubia, the temple was once again uncovered, planned and photographed, and the finds recorded (Firth 1927: 235-237).

During the reign of Amenhotep III the small temple was dedicated to a form of Horus. In his plate list Firth suggests this was Horus of Edfu (*bḥdt*) and later, in the description of the temple, Horus of Baki (*b3ky* = Quban; Firth 1927: 236; see also, Helck 1975: 99-100). A hawk head can be discerned under the later head of the god Amun in the wall painting at the rear of the sanctuary (Firth 1927: pl. 34). The change to Amun worship here occurred prior to the reign of Akhenaten as the figures and names of this god have been destroyed and later restored (Firth 1927: 236). The form of Amun worshipped here was Amun, 'Lord of the Ways' (*'Imn nb n p3 mṯnw*; Gundlach 1984: col. 768).

The large temple of Ramesses II, called the 'Temple of Ramesses Beloved of Amun in the House of Amun' (*ḥwt-nṯr Rʿ-ms-sw mry-'Imn m pr 'Imn*; Habachi 1969a: 12; Helck 1975: 99; Gundlach 1984: col. 768) is dedicated to Amun-Re, Re-Harakhti and the deified Ramesses II, along with numerous other deities, particularly forms of Horus: the four hawk-headed sphinxes in the Second Court represent Horus of Meha (Abu Simbel), of Miam (*miʿm* = Aniba), of Baki (Quban) and of Edfu (Porter and Moss VII 1951: 57 [vii-x]; Kitchen 1996: 480-481). Horus of Buhen (*bhn* = Wadi Halfa) also appears in the reliefs (Porter and Moss VII 1951: 60 (85-86)). Statues, now destroyed, of the three principal deities were situated in the sanctuary (Porter and Moss VII 1951: 62 (122)). The sanctuary reliefs depict Ramesses II offering to the barks of Amun-Re and Re-Harakhti, but in the accompanying text the latter is described as the bark of Ramesses II, as at Abu Simbel (Habachi 1969a pl. 17; Kitchen 1982b: 177). On the autobiographical stela of the King's Son of Kush, Setau (DB350), from the Ramesses II temple at Wadi es-Sebua, this temple is described as being 'in the estate of Amun of Ramesses, Beloved of Amun, Lord of Ways… [and] Horus of Baki' (*m-s3ḥ 'Imn n Rʿ-ms-sw mry-'Imn nb n p3 mṯnw… Ḥr b3ky*; Helck 1975: 91; Kitchen 2000: 65). This has been interpreted as meaning that the Ramesses II temple was built by Setau as a chapel to the cult of the living king in the estate of the existing Amenhotep III temple to Amun, Lord of the Ways, and Horus of Baki (Helck 1975: 100). The Nubian temples of Ramesses II, where he places himself amongst the gods as the recipient of the cult, have been used as evidence for the self-deification of Ramesses II (Habachi 1969a: 1-17; see Moftah 1985: 252-265). However, Kitchen (1982b: 177-178) has argued that these temples functioned as additional memorial temples to Ramesses II and as cult centres to the kingship rather than the king in the person of Ramesses II.

The construction of the larger Ramesses II temple and the restoration of the Amenhotep III temple were most likely the work of Setau who held the post of King's Son of Kush during the latter half of the reign of Ramesses II (Reisner 1920: 44; Helck 1975: 102-112; Kitchen 1982b: 136-138; Raedler 2003: 132; see the table in Figure 5.2). Setau's autobiographical stela (DB350) is dated to year 44, first month of Peret, day 2, and states that 'I made the Temple of Ramesses II, in the House of Amun, being excavated in the Western (?) Mountain…I (re)built all the temples of this land of Kush, that had formerly gone to ruin' (*ir.n.i ḥwt-nṯr (Rʿ-ms-sw mry-'Imn) m pr 'Imn m šd m p3 ḏw imnt…ḳd.i r-prw nbw n t3 pn n K3š wnw w3sy ẖr-ḥ3t*; Kitchen 2000:

65; see also Helck 1975: 85-102). Setau also oversaw the building of the temple at Gerf Hussein where he carved his name and titles deep within the temple (Habachi 1967: 58-59; Gundlach 1984: col. 168). Numerous monuments dedicated by him, and by others which include him, were found at Wadi es-Sebua in and around the two temples.[2] Setau's claim that he oversaw the construction of the Wadi es-Sebua is supported by the stela DB347 of the *sk*-officer, Ramose,[3] which has the same date as Setau's autobiographical stela, and states that Ramesses II charged Setau with taking Libyan captives 'to build in the Temple of Ramesses II in the House of Amun' (*r kd m ḥwt-nṯr* (*Rʿ-ms-sw mry-Ỉmn*) *m pr Ỉmn*; Kitchen 2000: 66; see also Helck 1975: 100; Kitchen 1982b: 138).

At Wadi es-Sebua there is little in the way of agricultural land to support a community, and the lack of known New Kingdom burials suggests that in fact there was no fixed Egyptian community living here at this period (Firth 1927: 236), though here may have been a settlement in the river valley that is now lost. Habachi (1967: 12) suggests that Setau may have been stationed here with his wife Mutnofret and a company of soldiers. There are monuments from Wadi es-Sebua that include Mutnofret, including the life-size dyad base discovered by Habachi in 1959 in the small temple (Habachi 1969b: 51-56) and a stela, DB344, dedicated by a woman named Mutnofret (Raedler 2003: 164-167).

Qantir/Pi-Ramesses (Eastern Delta)

Based on archaeological, textual and geographical evidence, it is now generally accepted that Qantir, located in the north-east Delta, is the site of the Ramesside capital city of Pi-Ramesses. The city covered both this area and the older Middle Kingdom and Hyksos capital, Avaris, located two and a half kilometres to the south at Tell ed-Dab'a (Hamza 1930: 68; Habachi 1954: 444; 557-559; 1969a: 27-28; Bietak 1981: 273-283; 1984: cols. 128-129; Uphill 1984: 1-3; Pusch 2001: 48). The archaeological evidence indicates that the complete re-planning and re-building of the whole site took place at the start of the Ramesside Period (Bietak 1981: 268; Uphill 1984: 193; Pusch 2001: 48). The area had been inhabited throughout the Middle and New Kingdoms, but it was the Ramesside kings, and in particular Ramesses II, continuing the work of his father and grandfather, who enlarged and elaborated both the military capacity and cult buildings of the city. Easy access to the east and routes to the Red Sea, and possibly a canal link to the equally strategically located Tanis, at the mouth of the Tanitic Nile branch made the location strategically important (Römer 1986: col. 195; Dorner 1999: 77). Surrounded by branches of the Nile, the city had a formidable defence capability. The agricultural hinterland provided wine, vegetables, fish and grain to the troops stationed in the city, and also supplied the Theban temples, which owned land here (Dorner 1999: 77).

The city of Pi-Ramesses no longer exists, having been deconstructed by the rulers of the 21st and 22nd Dynasties to provide building material for residences and temples principally at Tanis and Bubastis (Uphill 1984: 223-224). The site is currently under excavation by the Pelizaeus-Museum, Hildesheim and the Bayerisches Landesamt für Denkmalpflege, Munich, under the direction of Edgar Pusch. Pusch's recent work in the northern zone, using a caesium magnetometer (SMARTMAG SM4G Special), has revealed vast living quarters, lake beds, a harbour (?), and possibly parts of temples, palaces or administrative buildings (Pusch 1999: 13-15; 2001: 50).[4] During the Ramesside Period, the site consisted of two major zones. The northern zone, modern Qantir, housed the palace with stables and troop accommodation, bronze, glass and other craft workshops, a central major city temple, and a number of additional temples (Kitchen 1982b: 123, fig. 40; Uphill 1984: 190-191; pls. 5 and 6; Dorner 1996; 1999: 78-79; plan 2; Aufrère and Golvin 1997: 304, 307; Pusch 2001: 48-49). Two structures called the 'Houses of the Sed-Festival', mentioned on a bronze brazier found in the tomb of Psusennes (Uphill 1984: 56; 218) and on a granite block from Tanis (Uphill 1984: 36; 218), may also have stood in the northern zone. The block inscription states that the 'great limestone temple' was located 'to the north of the Sed-Festival Houses' (Uphill 1984: 36; Kitchen 1982b: 123, fig. 40). The southern zone, modern Tell ed-Dab'a, housed the Seth temple complex (Uphill 1984: 190-193; Dorner 1999).

---

[2] For the list of Setau's monuments from here see Habachi 1967: 59-60; a complete list of Setau's monuments can be found in Raedler 2003: 140-145.

[3] For a discussion of this title, see A Note on the Military Titles on p. 116.

[4] See also the work of the Austrian Archaeological Institute, directed by Manfred Bietak, at Tell el-Dab'a/Qantir. Recent accounts of the mapping of areas of the site can be found in Forstner-Müller 2009 and Bietak 2009.

Reconstructions of the city have been attempted by Kitchen (1982b), Uphill (1984), Dorner (1996; 1999) and Aufrère and Golvin (1997: 300-301). Dorner bases his reconstruction (1999: plans 1 and 2) on a sequence of drill cores and the archaeological fieldwork carried out by the Austrian Mission directed by Manfred Bietak, who has been working at the site of Tell ed-Dab'a since 1966 (see Uphill 1984: 1 and Pusch 2001: 48 for brief excavation histories). Kitchen and Uphill have drawn together textual evidence, such as the Hittite Treaty of Ramesses II's year 21 (Kitchen 1982b: 75) and Papyrus Anastasi III (BM EA 10246), a letter of Pabasa to his master Amenemope, describing the city (Gardiner 1937: 21-23; Habachi 1969a: 28; Uphill 1984: 130). Other evidence has come from inscribed blocks and statuary now at Tanis and Bubastis. Reconstructions of individual temples have been attempted by Habachi (1969a: 32, fig. 20), Uphill (1984: 206-211; pls. 9-11) and Dorner (1996). Another of the Anastasi papyri, Papyrus Anastasi II, 1, 4-5 and IV, 6, 4-5, describes the city of Pi-Ramesses as having a temple to Amun in the west, a temple to Seth in the south, a temple to Astarte in the east and one to Wadjyt in the north (Bietak 1984: col. 135). Stela Cairo JdE 34504, discovered in 1907 at Manshiyet es-Sadr, just south of Heliopolis, dates to Ramesses II's year 8, and records the making of statues for the temples of Amun of Ramesses Meryamun and of Ptah of Ramesses Meryamun, in Pi-Ramesses (Hamada 1938: 217-230; Habachi 1954: 551-552; Uphill 1984: 191). The Hittite Treaty (Uphill 1984: 191) suggests that there were at least four main temples or complexes: Amun-Re-Harakhti-Atum, Lord of the Two Lands of Iunu; Amun of Ramesses; Ptah of Ramesses; and Seth Aphehty, son of Nut. Uphill (1984: 194) argues that these gods would all have had temples in the Ramesside Period. The textual references all agree that there was a temple of Amun, the stela and Hittite treaty that there was a temple to Ptah, and the stela and Papyrus Anastasi II that there was a temple to Seth.

The Seth temple or complex located to the south at Tell ed-Dab'a is well known from the archaeological and textual evidence (Bietak 1981; Dorner 1999: 81-82). A lintel from this temple (Bietak 1984: col. 139) with the name of Horemheb gives the earliest date for a New Kingdom Seth temple construction. The 400-Year Stela found at Tanis, and originally from Qantir, depicts Ramesses II in the upper register and records the 400-year anniversary of the cult of Seth of Ramesses (Bietak 1981: 270-271; 1984: cols. 129-130; Uphill 1984: 84-85; 152; 233-234; Gnirs 1996: 117; Kitchen 1996: 116-117). Bietak (1981: 271) suggests that the cult of Seth was practiced at Tell ed-Dab'a in the 13th Dynasty/Hyksos Caananite temples discovered here.

Archaeological evidence for other temples and structures from Pi-Ramesses at the site of Qantir and Tell ed-Dab'a is fragmentary. Combining statuary and architectural pieces with survey results and archaeological evidence, Uphill (1984: 206-211) and Dorner (1996: 70; 1999: 80; plan 2) agree that the principal temple at Pi-Ramesses was dedicated to a composite god Amun-Re-Harakhti-Atum and that it was located in the centre of the city. This is the temple that Kitchen calls the Temple of Re (1982b: 123, fig. 42). Dorner (1996: 79-80; Plan 2) suggests that a structure to the north-west at Tell Abu esh-Shaf'ei may have been the temple of Amun (of Ramesses), as mentioned in Papyrus Anastasi II, 1.1-2.5 (see also Kitchen 1982b: 123, fig. 40). It was here that, in 1955, Shehata Adam discovered the base of a colossal seated statue of Ramesses II, inscribed with his cartouches and Horus name, which he estimated to have originally stood around 10 metres in height. Around the statue were the remains of a mud brick floor and pylon, but the stone of the temple had been removed in antiquity (Shehata Adam 1958: 306; 318-319; Bietak 1984: col. 140). Bietak later discovered a second matching base around 40 metres south east of the first one (Bietak 1975: 45, pl. XLIV; Uphill 1984: 105; 156; 211). The existence of a Ptah temple in the area of Pi-Ramesses dating back to the Middle Kingdom is evident from the inscribed architectural fragments originally from the site (Uphill 1984: 211). The existence of a Ramesside cult to Ptah of Ramesses is also supported by the monumental inscriptions (Uphill 1984: 194; 212) and the textual references on the Manshiyet es-Sadr stela and the Hittite Treaty. Temples to Wadjyt and Astarte, mentioned in Papyrus Anastasi II, are referred to on a number of inscribed blocks, architectural fragments and some statuary (Uphill 1984: 212-213; Pusch 2001: 50). At Gezira Sama'na three kilometres east of Tell ed Dab'a, Habachi discovered a well of Ramesses II, which he suggested may have been a temple well, together with stone fragments (Habachi 1954: 479-489). This could be the site of the Astarte temple, if this site was integrated with the city of Pi-Ramesses, and may have been the centre of an Asiatic military colony (Bietak 1984: col. 141). Kitchen (1982b: 123, fig. 42) places a small Astarte temple next to the main city temple, and a small temple to Wadjyt (Uto) next to the Ptah temple to the north-east. Uphill (1984: 212-213) has also collated a number of inscriptions that mention or depict Monthu, Lord of Thebes, Sekhmet and Thoth, Lord of Eshmunein, and suggests there may also have been temples or chapels to Houroun and Re (Uphill 1984: 195).

Zawiyet Umm el-Rakham (Western/Libyan Desert)

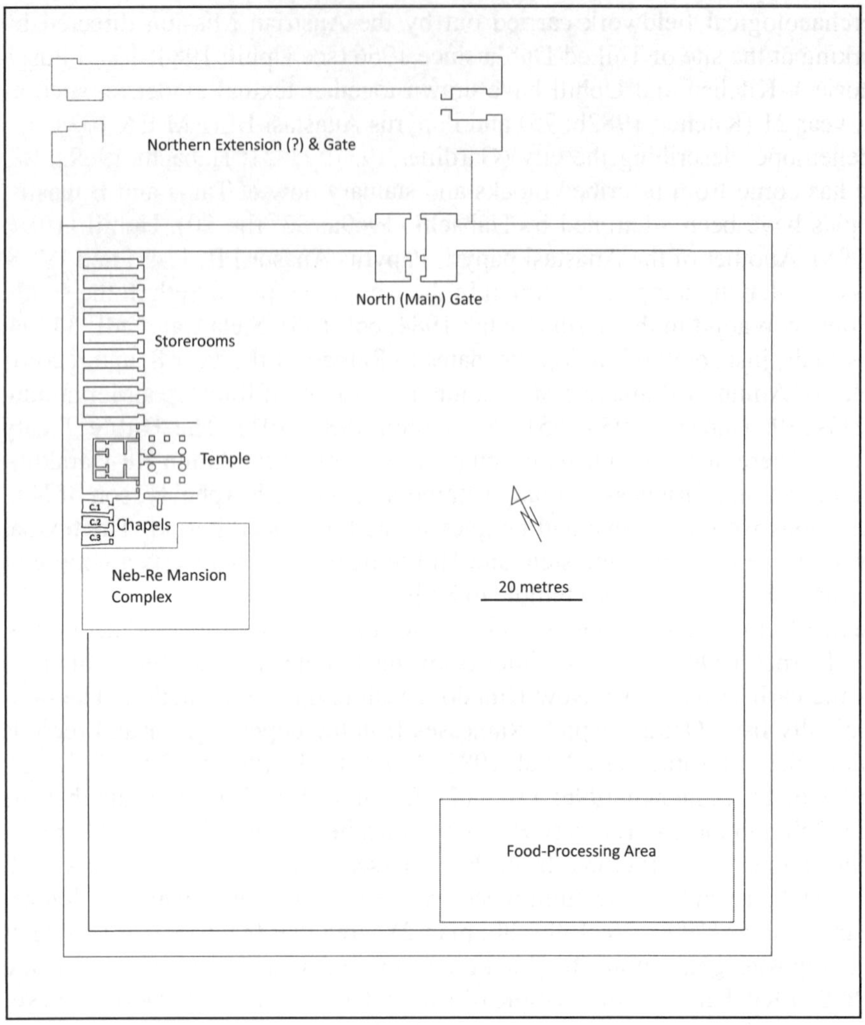

Figure 5.3 Plan of the temple-fort at Zawiyet Umm el-Rakham (© Steven Snape)

Zawiyet Umm el-Rakham is located c. 320 kilometres west of Alexandria, and about 25 kilometres west of Mersa Metrouh (Habachi 1980: 13; Helck 1986: col. 845; Simpson 2002: 12). The temple-fort is located on the western outskirts of the modern village, in the middle of a two kilometre wide fertile coastal strip between the desert to the east and the coast to the north (Simpson 2002: 15). The site consists of a vast mud brick rampart wall around four-five metre thick surrounding a precinct with an area of c. 20,000 metres^2. It contained a number of structures, including a temple and associated chapels. The site of Zawiyet Umm el-Rakham is currently under excavation by the University of Liverpool, under the direction of Steven Snape, who has been working at the site since 1994. A series of monographs presenting the recent work are in the process of being published, the first volume of which, *Zawiyet Umm el-Rakham I. The Temple and Chapels* (2007), by Steven Snape and Penelope Wilson, is available; *Zawiyet Umm el-Rakham II. The Monuments of Neb-Re*, by Steven Snape and Glenn Godenho, is under preparation at the time of writing.[5] At the time of writing, an overview of work at the site can be found at the website created by Geoff Edwards as part of his Masters dissertation at UCL (1998-1999), with the permission of Steven Snape.[6] The website includes (currently) unpublished images of the site and finds, as well as a comprehensive bibliography. Fiona Simpson's unpublished PhD, *Evidence for Late Bronze Age Libyan Culture at the New Kingdom Egyptian*

[5] My thanks to Glenn Godenho for pre-publication access to his work on the Nebre inscriptions.
[6] http://www.geocities.com/zurdig/HomeFrame.htm

Fortress of Zawiyet Umm el-Rakham (Liverpool 2002) includes descriptions of the archaeology and finds from the site.[7]

In 1946, Alan Rowe, the Keeper of the Graeco-Roman Museum, Alexandria, and Inspector of the Western Desert, visited the site of Zawiyet Umm el-Rakham after being informed of the discovery of some inscribed blocks (Snape and Wilson 2007: 1). His sketch map has been reproduced by Habachi (1980: 13) and Snape and Wilson (2007: 2), which latter note the difficulties in reconciling the Rowe map with later plans of the site. Habachi excavated at the site for a number of weeks between 1952 and 1955, discovering the north-facing and east-facing gate complexes and the Main Temple (his 'Temple D'), as well as approximately 16 stelae in its vicinity (Habachi 1980: 15; Snape 2004: 149; Snape and Wilson 2007: 3-5). In 1991 the Mersa Matruh inspectorate of the Egyptian Antiquities Organisation re-cleared the temple (Snape and Wilson 2007: 5), and from 1994 the University of Liverpool have been carrying out a programme of fieldwork to 'explore the nature of Egyptian (particularly Ramesside) activity in 'Libya', and especially at Zawiyet Umm el-Rakham (Snape 1998: 1082; 2003a).

The Liverpool University team has uncovered a number of additional structures in the precinct (Snape 2003a: 101; 2003b: 65-69; 2003c: 2-5 and fig. 2 (plan); 2004: 149-159; Snape and Wilson 2007). The site is now understood to include a main gateway in the wall to the north-east (Habachi's Gate B; Habachi 1980: 13); a limestone temple ('Main Temple') with a peristyle court, two offering rooms and a triple sanctuary; three small chapels fronted by a courtyard and covered portico, located to the west of the temple (it is from here, in the 1950s, that the inscribed limestone doorjambs and stelae were removed, located originally at the rear of the chapels); a smaller second temple to the east of the chapels with inscribed doorways naming the deities Ptah and Sekhmet, and the commander Nebre (*ḥry pḏt imy-r ḫ3swt nb-Rʿ;*[8] Kitchen 1996: 294; see also Habachi 1980: 14-15) worshipping the cartouches of Ramesses II, associated elite residential and storage quarters ('Nebre temple'; Simpson 2002: 20, 72; figs. 1.3, 1.4, 3.1); nine mud brick storage magazines north of the main temple, with inscribed limestone doorways bearing the name of Ramesses II and in one case that of the commander Nebre; a post-Egyptian occupation Libyan squatter settlement (Simpson 2002); a residential area to the south-east; and the enigmatic 'Southern Building'. This originally two storey structure was inscribed with the names of Ramesses II and the Commander, Nebre, and two inscribed lintels for Nebre and his wife Meryptah were discovered here. The buiding includes three long hallways within which stood at least four single standing stones with rounded tops and pottery around the base, and may have been a place of worship for non-Egyptians (Snape 2003c: 5; 2004: 151).

The temple-fort at Zawiyet Umm el-Rakham forms the most distant outpost of what may have been a series of stations stretching down the western edge of the Delta and along the coast westward from modern Alexandria (Habachi 1980: 28-30; Kitchen 1982b: 71-72, 262; 1990: 18; Snape 1998: 1081; Simpson 2002: 15). The evidence for the forts has been summarised and discussed by Edwards[9] (see also Simpson 2002: 15), who concludes that the only certain fortified sites in this area are Zawiyet Umm el-Rakham and Kom el-Abqa'in. Traditional interpretations of these forts have taken them to be an early warning system that served to protect Egypt from the encroaching threat of the Sea Peoples (Habachi 1980: 28-30), or the existing Libyan threat (Snape 1998: 1083; O'Connor 1990; Kitchen 1990: 18; Spalinger 2005: 202; 235). Kitchen (1990: 17-18; see also Simpson 2002: 8) lists the sparse written evidence for Ramesses II in Libya, of which only one piece is dated, a stela at Aswan of year 2, and notes that 'our explicit written sources do not adequately reflect the nature and extent of this Egyptian presence' (1990: 18). In turn, the lack of Egyptian textual references to the Libyans has led scholars to assume that they were not a real threat (Kitchen 1990: 17-18; Spalinger 2005: 202). However, O'Connor's analysis (1990: 85) concludes that Libyan society in the later New Kingdom was organised for war (see also Spalinger 2005: 202). Libyan presence at the Egyptian border may have become more aggressive at this period as a result of climate changes and overcrowding in their homeland (Spalinger 2005: 197). It has been suggested that the incursion of new aggressive Libyan groups, such as the Libu (Rebu) and the Meshwesh, into the area traditionally inhabited by the Tjemehu/Tjehenu Libyans, was the source of the new Libyan threat to the Egyptians.[10]

---

[7] See Snape and Wilson 2007: 6, note 26, for additional theses based on archaeology and finds from Zawiyet Umm el-Rakham.

[8] On his standard-bearer statue found at the site, Nebre also has the titles Overseer of Foreign Lands (*imy-r ḫ3s(w)t*); First Charioteer of his Majesty, the Leiutenant of Chariotry, the Chief of the Medjay in the foreign land of Libya (*kḏn tpy n ḥm.f, idnw n nt-ḥtrw, wr n mḏ3yw ḥr ḫ3st ṯmḥ*) (Snape and Godenho *forthcoming*).

[9] http://www.geocities.com/zurdig/Other_Forts_Frame.htm

[10] For a discussion of the various terms for Libyans, see Kitchen 1990: 16-17. For a recent discussion of Egyptian-Libyan relations during the reign of Ramesses II, see Simpson 2002.

Snape (1998: 1083; 2003c: 5) argues that the massive defence capability at Zawiyet Umm el-Rakham was in place to safeguard wells, which are described in a fragmentary inscription on the northern face of the eastern wing of Habachi's gate B as being within a fortress in Tjemeh. The wells could have supplied an Egyptian garrison in case of siege, whilst allowing the Egyptians to control access to such a resource. The forts could easily be bypassed and so could only provide an early warning system, not withstand an attack on Egypt (Snape 1998: 1083). More recent interpretations of the forts have focused on their economic function (Snape 1998: 1082; 2003b: 69; 2003c: 5; 2004: 149). During the 1995 and 1996 seasons of the University of Liverpool's work at Zawiyet Umm el-Rakham the magazines to the north of the temple were explored. The ceramic vessels found in the magazines were of non-Egyptian form, and suggest that the temple-fort had another function as a trading station or port of call for trans-Mediterranean traders (Snape 1998: 1082; 2003b; 2004: 149; see also Snape and Wilson 2007: 64-65). Kitchen (1990: 16-17) suggests that Ramesses II constructed the Western Delta forts following the campaign of his father Seti I against the Tjehenu Libyans, recorded as part of a sequence of military victories on the north exterior wall of the Hypostyle Hall at Karnak (Porter and Moss II 1972: 56 (169); Kitchen 1990: 17; Spalinger 2005: 187-197). This campaign, in which Ramesses II may have taken part as a prince (Kitchen 1990: 18), paved the way for Egyptian occupation and control of the Western Desert along Egypt's north-west border, and the establishment of control of this area to access trade routes. This can be compared to the aggressive policy of the early Middle Kingdom rulers in Nubia, which led to the construction of a sequence of massive mud brick forts whose primary function was control of the trade routes. An extension of this function may have been to supply the Egyptian armies, as the forts along the Ways of Horus to the East and those in Nubia did. In terms of socio-economic activity, the fort(s) may have regulated trade contacts between local Libyans and foreign merchants coming in to the North African coast.

The inscriptions on the standard-bearer statue of the commander Nebre found in one of the chapels south of the temple throw further light on the relationship between the Egyptians and certain Libyan groups in the early Ramesside Period. The inscription on the rear of the dorsal pillar states that the complex at Zawiyet Umm el-Rakham, described as the 'town/location' (*pꜣ dmi*) of Rameses II was built for the Libyan people (*ṯk*) 'who had been living upon the desert like jackals' (*wn ḥms.sn ḥr ḫꜣst mi wnš*); the Libyans are described as being in charge of the horticulture and agriculture of the settlement (Godenho in Snape and Godenho *forthcoming*). Godenho suggests that the Libyan group referred to as the *ṯk* (possibly short for *ṯktn*) were an existing garrison of Libyan scouts loyal to pharaoh for whom the settlement was constructed. Such a situation would perhaps explain the evidence for non-Egyptian cult practices and material culture at the site.

The site was occupied during the reign of Ramesses II; there is no evidence for Egyptian occupation post-Ramesses II (Kitchen 1990: 19; Snape 2003a: 104; 2003b: 69). Snape (2003b: 69) suggests that the occupation dates to early in this king's reign, citing as evidence the version of the king's name found at the site which is that used at the start of his reign, and the late 18th Dynasty style of the standard-bearer statue of Nebre. Helck (1986: col. 845) suggests that the temple-fort may have been constructed by Nebre.

The extant titles used on the Zawiyet Umm el-Rakham stelae are all military (see Snape and Wilson 2007: 128). The community at Zawiyet Umm el-Rakham was therefore a military unit, stationed here for a period of time, under the command of Nebre. The depiction of two army standard-bearers on one of the stelae has lead Snape to suggest (2003a: 103) that 400 - 500 men were stationed here, as each army standard-bearer would have been in charge of 200 - 250 men (Schulman 1964: 27; Raedler 2003: 157; Spalinger 2005: 252-256), though the number may be higher if the standard bearers mentioned served contemporaneously (Wilson in Snape and Wilson 2007: 128).

5.2 Comparative data: data analysis

There are 117 stelae in the dataset from the four sites: Abu Simbel (21), Qantir (74), Wadi es-Sebua (15) and Zawiyet Umm el-Rakham (7). It should be noted that the Qantir stelae that depict individuals offering to statues of Ramesses II have all been dated to the reign of Ramesses II on the (perhaps erroneous) assumption that the cults did not continue beyond the end of his reign. The majority of the stelae (113 = 96%) date to the 19th Dynasty, with only three (=3%) dating to the 20th Dynasty; one (= 1 %) is not assigned a dynasty. The Abu Simbel and Zawiyet Umm el-Rakham stelae all date to the 19th Dynasty, with just two of the 74 Qantir stelae and one of the 15 Wadi es-Sebua stelae dating to the 20th Dynasty. A closer look at the date of these stelae places 110 (94%) of the stelae in the reign of Ramesses II. Five of the stelae have specific dates, listed in the table in Figure 5.4.

Figure 5.4 Dated stelae from the comparative dataset

Stela number	Site	Dedicator	Date
DB327	Abu Simbel	King's Son of Kush, Setau	Ramesses II, year 38
DB339	Abu Simbel	Ambassador to Every Land, Rekhpehtuf	Siptah, year 1
DB345	Wadi es-Sebua	[Standard-bearer], Paherypedjet	Ramesses II, year 44, 1st Month of Peret, Day 1
DB347	Wadi es-Sebua	*sk*-officer, Ramose	Ramesses II, year 44, 1st Month of Peret, Day 2
DB350	Wadi es-Sebua	King's Son of Kush, Setau	Ramesses II, year 44, 1st Month of Peret, Day 2

The Wadi es-Sebua dates of year 44 have provided the date of the second half of the reign of Ramesses II for the remaining undated stelae from this site. These stelae are confined to days 1 and 2 of the first month of Peret in year 44. Three of the dated stelae have texts of a commemorative nature:

- DB339 (Abu Simbel) mentions a visit by Siptah to install Seti as King's Son of Kush (Kitchen 2003: 262);
- DB345 (Wadi es-Sebua), dated to the first month of Peret, day 1, refers to a royal command to the King's Son of Kush, Setau, to carry out an action, now lost (Kitchen 2000: 62);
- DB347 (Wadi es-Sebua), dated to the first month of Peret, day 2, refers to a royal command to the King's Son of Kush, Setau, to capture Libyans for temple-building and instructs the *sk*-officer, Ramose, to raise a 'force' (?) from the company (*sṯs m p3 s3*; Kitchen 2000: 66).

Stela DB350 is Setau's autobiographical stela (Helck 1975; Kitchen 2000: 63-65). Stela DB425 depicts the ritual action where the king smites his enemies before a god, known as the royal smiting-scene, or icon, with a generic hymn of praise to the king (Kitchen 2000: 63-65).

Of the 117 stelae, 82 are type A, 21 are type B, and 14 are type C. Compared to the stelae from Deir el-Medina, there are more type A (69% compared 47%) and type B (19% compared to 8%) in the comparative dataset, and far fewer type C (12% compared to 45%). Because the majority of the stelae in the comparative dataset date to the 19th Dynasty (only Qantir and Wadi es-Sebua have any stelae dating to the 20th Dynasty) the numbers and percentages of the compositional types of the 19th Dynasty at Thebes are almost identical to those of the full comparative dataset. There are striking differences in the types of stelae left at the different sites, and between these sites and the Deir el-Medina material.

The type A stelae occur most frequently at Abu Simbel (14/21) and Qantir (64/74). They do not occur at all at Zawiyet Umm el-Rakham, where there are six type C and one type B, and at Wadi es-Sebua the three type A stelae form a distinct and separate group to the 12 type B stelae. This latter group, all from the Ramesses II temple, are large (68 to 190 centimetres tall), granite stelae, with 10 dedicated by military men and the King's Son of Kush, Setau, or Setau alone. The type A stelae, all from the Amenhotep III temple, are smaller (between 40 and 42 centimetres tall), and are dedicated to Amun-Re and a variety of deities. The stelae from this site illustrate the distinction that became apparent in the Deir el-Medina dataset between type A (and some type C) stelae, which relate to popular cults, and type B stelae, which relate to an official cult or event. This same phenomenon occurs at Qantir, where the majority of the stelae (65 of the 74) depict individuals before a statue of Ramesses II, which had become the focus of a popular cult.

The frequency of type B stelae, most of which come from Abu Simbel and Wadi es-Sebua, has been noted above. In all but one case the intermediary is Ramesses II; on stela DB340 the intermediary is Siptah. In the Deir el-Medina dataset, the unusually high occurrence of type B stelae in the reign of Ramesses II (11/22 = 50%) was noted; of the 19th Dynasty examples, the figure is 11/13 = 85%. The material from the comparative sites reveals that type B stelae were also a feature of Ramesses II's reign elsewhere in Egypt. The type B stelae, in particular those with the living king as the intermediary, commemorate an event, a ritual public action carried out by the king. This is supported by the existence at both sites of dated stelae that depict the king (see the table in Figure 5.4, above), and which are clearly commemorative.

Type C stelae are far less frequent than at Deir el-Medina, where they made up almost half the dataset (12% compared to 47%). The Deir el-Medina dataset figures revealed that there were relatively more type C stelae produced during the first half of the reign of Ramesses II, and that this was partly the result of the 18 stelae of this type dedicated by the Senior Scribe, Ramose (i). The percentage of type C stelae in the comparative datasets is somewhat misleading: the 10% at Abu Simbel amounts to just three stelae, and the 86% at Zawiyet Umm el-Rakham amounts to six. At Zawiyet Umm el-Rakham, four of the seven stelae have the royal smiting-scene with the dedicator, in military uniform holding the standard of his company, kneeling below. There is just one example of this scene on the Deir el-Medina stelae, stela DB93, dedicated by the Senior Scribe, Ramose (i). Again it is a type C stela, indicating that the scene influences the format of the stelae.

Deities on the comparative dataset stelae

As a percentage, Ramesses II, either in statue form or as the living king, receives 52% (93/192) of the dedications. Amun-Re receives 13% (25/192) compared to 19% (51/264) of the Deir el-Medina stelae (20% of the Theban dataset: 65/319), and is still the largest recipient after Ramesses II. The next most frequently occurring are Ptah (13 = 7%) and Re-Harakhti (11 = 6%).

The cult of Ramesses II at these sites is evident, with the statue cults limited to Qantir and the living king cult to the remaining sites. The one representation of a living king at Qantir is of Ramesses III (DB429). This demarcation of royal statue cult and living king cult stelae is also indicated by the rank of the dedicators. At the border sites the majority of the dedicators are high-ranking military men; at Qantir they are lower ranking military men and individuals with priestly and administrative titles. Women also make dedications at Qantir (for a discussion of the rank of the dedicators see the individual site sections below). Ramesses II is the only king to feature at Wadi es-Sebua and Zawiyet Umm el-Rakham, which is to be expected given the activity of the king at these sites; stelae to other kings are small in number at Abu Simbel and Qantir. In comparison to the Deir el-Medina material, representations of Ramesses II either as a statue or as the living king are frequent. At Deir el-Medina, Ramesses II was not one of the featured deities: there are just four Deir el-Medina stelae (DB65, DB93, DB94, DB134) with representations of a statue or icon (smiting-scene, cartouches) of Ramesses II, rather than the king as intermediary. The lack of representations of Ramesses II as a cult object suggests that, at Thebes, Ramesses II did not establish primary cults to himself within the domain or estate of Amun-Re. Instead, he utilised existing cult infrastructures, such as that of Amenhotep I and Hathor.

Amun-Re is the only other deity to have a significant number of representations (25 = 13%), and he is also the only deity to receive cult attention across all four sites, with the most dedications at Wadi es-Sebua. Wadi es-Sebua has the most diverse number of deities; Zawiyet Umm el-Rakham the most limited. At Wadi es-Sebua it is the King's Son of Kush, Setau, who both features on many of the stelae (Barsanti and Gauthier 1911: 64; Habachi 1967: 59; Raedler 2003: 151) and who dedicates the largest number of stelae himself, to a wide variety of deities. This phenomenon of wide-ranging cultic dedications is comparable to the votive activity of the Senior Scribe, Ramose (i), at Deir el-Medina, who dedicates, or is co-dedicator, on 21 stelae (in the dataset) to a wide variety of gods. At Zawiyet Umm el-Rakham, the soldiers dedicate stelae to Ramesses II as the living king, Amun-Re, Sekhmet and Seth only.

Figure 5.5 Recipients of the votive stelae[11]

		Total	Abu Simbel	Qantir	Wadi es-Sebua	Zawiyet Umm el-Rakham
Kings						
Forms of Ramesses II	Statue: Montu in the Two Lands	**52**		52		
	Living King	**30**	15		10	5
	Statue: Re of the Rulers	**2**		2		
	Statue: The God	**2**		2		
	Statue: Ruler of Rulers	**1**		1		
	Unidentified statue	**8**		8		
Other Kings	Amenmesse	**1**	1			
	Siptah	**1**	1			
	Ramesses III	**1**		1		
Deities	Amun-Re	**28**	8	3	13	4
	Ptah	**13**		7	6	
Forms of Horus	Re-Harakhti	**12**	6		6*	
	Horus	**6**	4		2	
	Harmachis	**1**			1	
	Harsiese	**1**			1	
	Seth	**5**	1		3	1
	Sobek(-Re)	**5**		5		
	Thoth	**4**	4			
	Maat	**2**		1	1	
	Atum	**2**			2	
	Mut	**2**	1		1	
	Nekhbet[12]	**2**			2	
	Reshep	**2**		1	1	
	Renenut	**2**			2	
	Sekhmet	**2**				2
	Shepsy	**2**	2			
Private Individuals	King's Son of Kush, Setau	**5**			5	

**Or forms of, e.g. Amun-Re-Harakhti (2), Re-Harakhti-Atum (1).*

[11] Plus one each of Anukis (Abu Simbel), Bes (Wadi es-Sebua), Hathor (Qantir), Khnum (Wadi es-Sebua), Nehemtawy (Abu Simbel), Osiris (Qantir), and Wadjyt (Wadi es-Sebua).

[12] Tentatively identified by Gauthier (1911: 66) as Osiris but more likely to be Nekhbet, who appears in the temple reliefs at Wadi es-Sebua wearing the atef-crown, for example, in the Pronaos (or Pillared Antechamber) and Antechamber (Gauthier 1912: pls. XLIX (A), LVI (A)).

5.3 The stelae from the individual sites

Abu Simbel (21 stelae; see Appendix 1, Table 3 for a list of the Abu Simbel stelae)

There are numerous stelae and rock inscriptions carved into the cliffs north, south and between the two temples (Porter and Moss VII 1951: 117-119; Otto 1975: col. 26). These date to the Middle and New Kingdoms, with the majority dating to the reign of Ramesses II. The rock cut stelae are given the numbers 1-27 in Porter and Moss (no. 27 is two stelae; Porter and Moss VII 1951: 119), of which 15 are included in the dataset. In addition, Kitchen adds a stela which he numbers 23a (Kitchen 1996: 510), also included. Those omitted are either outside of the date range, are inscriptions or statue texts, such as that of the King's Son of Kush, Paser II (Porter and Moss VII 1951: 117 (1)), or do not retain non-royal dedicators (Abu Simbel 7, 12, 13 - see Schulman 1994: 275 (8), fig. 9 - 16, 19 and 23). The dataset also includes the two stelae, DB339 and DB340, carved into the walls on the north and south of the façade of the Great Temple, and three free-standing round-topped stelae: stela DB331 of the Wab-priest, Huy, discovered in front of the Great Temple, and stelae DB323 and DB326, belonging to the King's Son of Kush, Paser II, found in the sand between the two temples (Gauthier 1936: 50). Additional free-standing stelae must surely have been lost from the site given that those extant were found in the drifting sand. The stelae that remain, therefore, are unlikely to be representative of the full range of cult activity at Abu Simbel. The Abu Simbel dataset comprises 21 stelae in total.

Ramesses II's presence is writ large at Abu Simbel, his colossal statues dominating the façades of the temples. These statues, four seated in front of the Great Temple and four standing in front of the Small Temple, are differentiated by their names, and are found again in the form of Osiride statues within the Great Temple (Porter and Moss VII 1951: 100-101; 104-106; 111-113; Desroches-Noblecourt 1968 II: pls. VI, VII, IX; Habachi 1969a: 3, 8-11). Within the temples Ramesses II interacts with the gods as dedicator and deity (Porter and Moss VII 1951: 95-117). The majority of the stelae (18/21) include Ramesses II in some form.

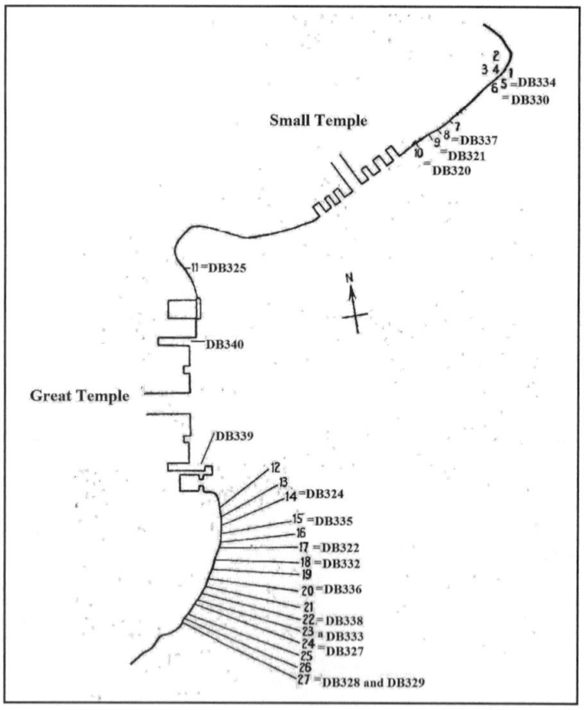

Figure 5.6 Location of the majority of the rock cut stelae at Abu Simbel (after Porter and Moss VII 1951: 111)

The local god at Abu Simbel was a form of Horus, known as Horus, 'Lord of Meha', who is mentioned on stela DB321 of the First Royal Cupbearer, Ramesses-Asha-hebu-sed, when he describes the construction of the temples. On this stela, Ramesses II is said to have performed 'benefactions for his father, Horus, Lord of Meha, in making for him his Temple of Millions of Years, it being excavated in the Mountain of Meha' (*m irt 3ḫw n it.f Ḥr nb mḥ3 m irt n.f ḥwt.f m ḥḥ m rnpwt m šd m ḏw n mḥ3*; Kitchen 2000: 142). Kitchen (1982: 67) states that Meha was the name of the south bluff into which the Great Temple was cut, and Ibshek the name of the north bluff, into which the Small Temple was cut. Horus, 'Lord of Meha', is depicted as a hawk-headed man in the Pillared Hall of the Small Temple, on the right of the entrance, with Ramesses II smiting enemies before him (Porter and Moss VII 1951: 114 (21); Desroches-Noblecourt 1968 II: pls. XXXV, XXXVI). He is represented in a number of places in the Great Temple, for example, on a stela of Ramesses II in the South Recess of the Terrace (Porter and Moss VII 1951: 98 (10)), on an Osiride pillar in the Great Hall (Porter and Moss VII 1951: 105 (VII)) and in the doorway to the Vestibule (Porter and Moss VII 1951: 110 (104)). Hathor of Ibshek appears in both temples (for example, at Porter and Moss VII 1951: 105 I (a) in the Great Temple and throughout the Small Temple; Porter and Moss VII 1951: 111-117; Desroches-Noblecourt 1968). Other local Nubian forms of Horus occur throughout the temples: of Buhen, Miam and Baki.

Ramesses II on stelae (15)
Stelae DB320 - DB322, DB324, DB325, DB327 - DB331, DB333, DB334, DB336, DB337

Of the 21 stelae in the dataset from Abu Simbel, 18 date to the reign of Ramesses II, and 15 of these are dedicated to Ramesses II. The three remaining stelae include him in some form: DB335 has Ramesses II mediating between the King's Son of Kush, Mernudjem, and Thoth, Re-Harakhti and Shepsy; DB323 and DB326 are identical stelae recording a land endowment for a form of Amun, and depict the King's Son of Kush, Paser II, adoring Amun-Re who gives blessings to Ramesses II, not depicted (Gauthier 1936: 49-69 and pl. III). Of the 15 stelae dedicated to Ramesses, only 10 have published images. The stelae dedicated to the king can be divided into the groups discussed below.

(i) Individuals greeting the king (4)
Stelae DB320, DB321, DB324, DB325

The four stelae depict high ranking individuals bending forward and holding one hand out towards the seated king. This is the iconographic representation of the direct reception of a royal command. It informs the 'reader' of the stela that the individual represented has conversed with the king, indicating access to the king, and the concomitant high social status of the dedicator. Three of the stelae are dedicated by the highest ranking men in Nubia, the King's Son of Kush (DB320, DB324, DB325); DB321 is dedicated by the First Royal Cupbearer of his Majesty, Ramesses-Asha-hebu-sed. On stela DB175 from Deir el-Medina, depicting the Royal Scribe and Royal Butler, Hori, greeting Ramesses IV with the same gesture, the text records Hori's royal message of the reward for the Foreman, Anhurkhawy (ii), for completing the royal tomb (Janssen 1963: 64-70). The Abu Simbel stelae in this group are all type A.

The king is shown seated on a throne wearing either the blue crown (DB324, DB325), or the *šwty*-crown (ram horns and double plumes flanked by uraei, DB320; including the atef crown, DB321; Goebs 2001: 323). It may be that the plumed crowns on the stelae are meant to represent the same crown, the *šwty*-crown worn by the northern-most Small Temple façade statue (Desroches-Noblecourt 1968 II: pls. X, XI). The king usually holds emblems of kingship, the crook, flail, ankh-sign, and, on DB324, a sceptre. On DB321 and DB325 his throne base depicts bound enemies. The king's epithets describe him as 'The Perfect God, Son of Re' (*nṯr nfr s3 R'*; DB320 and DB321) and 'Lord of the Two Lands, Lord of Appearances' (*nb t3wy nb ḫʿw*; DB324 and DB325).

Stelae DB320 and DB321 are located north of the entrance to the Small Temple, next to each other (Porter and Moss VII 1951: 112). DB321 of the First Royal Cupbearer, Ramesses-Asha-hebu-sed, describes the construction of a temple in the Mountain of Meha (Plate 12a). The stela also states that Ramesses-Asha-hebu-sed was 'charged to reorganise the land of Kush anew' (*ḫt rdi m-ḥr-n .... r spd t3 n K3š m m3w*[*t*]; Kitchen 2000: 141-142). This stela is carved next to stela DB320 of the King's Son of Kush, Yuni, which abuts the façade of the temple. Both stelae may be iconographically related to the northernmost colossal statue of Ramesses II which wears the *šwty*-crown, though the statue is standing rather than seated, or simply represent the living king. They may have been carved at the same time, at the start of Ramesses II's reign, when construction of the Small Temple (or both temples) began.

Stelae DB324 and DB325 belong to the King's Son of Kush, Paser II, and are located south of the Great Temple (Porter and Moss VII 1951: 112). Ramesses II wears the blue crown on both stelae. The stelae record speeches of the king, suggesting that the representation is of the living king and not of a statue: on DB324, 'Montu praises you and the Spirit of the Pharaoh, LPH, praises you! One is con[tent concerning?] the temple that you have (re?) made' (*Mntw ḥs tw k3 n pr-ʿ3 ʿnḫ wḏ3 snb [ḥs] tw tw h[rw] [...] ḥwt irr.k*; Kitchen 2000: 53); on DB325, 'You are a truly reliable [man], useful to his lord!' (*ntk wy rmṯ mti m3ʿ 3ḫ n nb.f*; Kitchen 2000: 53).

(ii) The king in a chariot (2)
Stelae DB336, DB337

Neither of these stelae has a published image. Stela DB336 depicts the First Charioteer of his Majesty, Meryu, holding the reins of the horses drawing Ramesses II's chariot. Meryu explains his presence at Abu Simbel, saying he has been sent as the 'Royal Envoy to this land of Kush' (*wpwty nsw r t3 pn K3š*; Kitchen 2000: 175). His stela represents his role in the king's entourage. Stela DB337 (Plate 12b) depicts the Royal Scribe, Usimare-Asha-Nakhtu, as a fanbearer following Ramesses II riding in a chariot over enemies (Kitchen 2000: 143). Both stelae are type A and are dedicated by high-ranking individuals, though below the rank of king's son of Kush of the previous group of stelae.

On stela DB337, the foes are described as the 'Great Ruler of Hatti', and the chariot span as '[...] in Thebes' ([..] *m W3st*; Kitchen 2000: 143). Kitchen restores 'Appearing' though 'Victorious' seems more likely, given that the stela appears to reproduce a scene from the Qadesh battle represented inside the Great Temple. The left hand side of the upper register of the Qadesh battle scene, located on the right hand wall of the Great Hall of the Great Temple, depicts a large figure of the king in his chariot surrounded by Hittite foes, a number of whom are in the process of being trampled beneath the hooves of the horses (Porter and Moss VII 1951: 103; Desroches-Noblecourt, Donadoni and Edel 1971: 29-31, pls. IIIa, IV). Here the chariot span is called 'Victorious in Thebes' (Desroches-Noblecourt, Donadoni and Edel 1971: 53 (8)). In the Qadesh battle 'poem' the two horses have the names 'Victorious in Thebes' and 'Mut is Content' (Lichtheim 1976: 70). In one of the war scenes on the left wall of the Great Hall of the Great temple where the king is returning in triumph with Nubian captives (Porter and Moss VII 1951: 103 (39)-(40)) the chariot span is called 'Victory (= 'Victorious'?) in Thebes' (Kitchen 2000: 68).

(iii) The king smiting enemies (DB327)

Stela DB327 (Plate 13) is the largest at Abu Simbel, measuring seven metres high and five metres wide. It is a double stela depicting, on the left, Ramesses II smiting an enemy before Horus, and on the right, the king carrying out the same action before Amun-Re. Amun-Re is 'Lord of the Thrones of the Two Lands' (*nb nsw t3wy*), Horus is 'Lord of Buhen'. The King is 'Lord of the Two Lands' (*nb t3wy*) and 'Lord of Appearances' (*nb ḫʿw*). On the left, the king wears a nemes headdress with double plumes, and, on the right the blue crown. The text here identifies the captives before Amun-Re as the 'chiefs of miserable Kush' (*wrw nw K3š ẖsy*; Kitchen 2000: 71), though they look like Asiatics. The similar looking captives on the left are not identified. In the lower register on both stelae, the King's Son of Kush, Setau, kneels, adoring. Setau held the post of King's Son of Kush during the latter half of the reign of Ramesses II, years 38-63, and maintained a significant presence in Nubia and Upper Egypt, evidenced by his many monuments (Habachi 1967; Helck 1975: 111-112; Raedler 2003). DB327 is a type C stela, as are all known smiting stelae (see Schulman 1994; Snape and Wilson 2007: 129). The smiting-scene stelae were set up by individuals who have in common their high and/or military rank. The smiting-scene as a stela representation is not available to all and indicates social status (see Section 5.4).

The smiting-scene is present in both temples at Abu Simbel, on the right and left interior walls flanking the doorway of the First Hall. On the left in both temples, Amun-Re presents the sword while the king smites a Nubian captive (Porter and Moss VII 1951: 102 (38); 113 (15)). On the right in the Small Temple, the king smites an Asiatic captive before Horus, 'Lord of Meha' (Porter and Moss VII 1951: 114 (21)). On the right in the Great Temple, he smites a Libyan before Re-Harakhti (Porter and Moss VII 1951: 101 (37)). The scene is repeated on the gateway in the enclosure wall (before Amun-Re (?)) (Porter and Moss VII 1951: 97

(1)). The stela of Setau is not identical to the temple representations of this scene, but comes closest to that in the Small Temple, and is oriented as if the observer were looking at the scenes from within the temple, looking out. This scene, and the scene of the king crushing Hittite captives under his chariot on stela DB337, reference Abu Simbel temple reliefs and place them in publicly accessible areas. Such stelae indicate that the dedicator had access to the interior of the temple, and royal sanction to reproduce restricted royal texts and icons. In addition, it is of note that the double stela is a royal prerogative (Raedler 2003: 151).

Stela DB338, dating to the reign of Amenmesse (Schulman initially dated this stela to Seti II; 1994: 271), also depicts the royal smiting-scene. The stela is dedicated by the Deputy of Wawat, Mery, and depicts the king smiting a Nubian(?) captive before Amun-Re. The stela is located just north of that of Setau (Porter and Moss VII 1951: 112), and may be a copy of the right side of this stela. There are in addition two more royal smiting stelae at Abu Simbel, AS12 and AS13, which are not included in the dataset due to their poor preservation.

(iv) Ramesses II in temple scenes (5)
Stelae DB322, DB330 - DB333

On these five stelae the king is represented as an object of worship, as his deified self, and is shown in the company of deities who appear in the temples. He is seated or standing with groups of the following deities: Thoth, Amun-Re, Re-Harakhti, Shepsy, Nehemtawy and Horus. The king wears the blue crown (DB330), the nemes headdress with sun disc (DB322) (indicating a deified form of the king that occurs frequently at Wadi es-Sebua; see, for example, Gauthier 1912: pl. LV (A); pl. LXII (A)), and is hawk-headed (DB331). There are no published images or photographs of DB332 and DB333. The hawk-headed form of Ramesses II is the form of the deified king peculiar to Abu Simbel, and occurs on a pillar in the Second Hall where the king as a hawk-headed god is embraced by Anukis (pillar IX; Porter and Moss VII 1951: 109; Kitchen 1996: 501) and on the bark of the king in the Second Hall and Sanctuary of the Great Temple (Porter and Moss VII 1951: 109 (98); 110 (114); Habachi 1969a: 4-5, figs. 3 and 4). The deified king has no epithets.

The stelae are dedicated by the King's Son of Kush, Hekanakht, and four other individuals: a Scribe, a Wab-priest and two Stablemasters. The Scribe, Wab-priest and one Stablemaster dedicate type A stelae, the other two, type B. The location of the stelae and their compositional form are informative with regard to the function of the stelae. The two type B stelae, DB322 and DB332, are located next to each other south of the Great Temple (Porter and Moss VII 1951: 112). The stela of Hekanakht, DB322, is discussed below in Section 5.4(i), in relation to its possible depiction of the inauguration of one of the temples. It may be that the Stablemaster, Iwefenamun, was present at and involved in this same royal visit, and was granted the special privilege of a rock cut stela at Abu Simbel. It may also indicate the high status of the rank of stablemaster in a society where horses were the privilege of the few, and limited to royal and military use. The stelae are commemorative.

The type A stela, DB333, is located to the south of the temples. It commemorates a group of deities - Thoth, Re-Harakhti and Shepsy - also found on stela DB335 of the King's Son of Kush, Mernudjem. Kitchen (1996: 510) describes the position of the king as seated in the upper register, indicating that the king is not acting as a mediator. Stela DB330 is located in the northernmost group of rock-cut stelae (Porter and Moss VII 1951: 112). DB331 of the Wab-priest, Huy, is a free-standing round-topped stela which was found at the north end of the façade of the Great Temple. It is tempting to link stela DB331 with the Sun Chapel ('North Chapel'; Maspero 1911a; Porter and Moss VII 1951: 99-100) which is dedicated to the various aspects of the sun god, including Thoth and Re-Harakhti (= Ramesses II). It may be that Huy served as a wab-priest for the sun cult in this chapel. His wife Tabes is a chantress and is depicted with her sistrum before a form of Anukis described as 'of Amun of Hery' (*n Ỉmn hri*), possibly a local form of the deity (Valbelle 1981: 109). The Scribe, Hatiay (DB330), worships the deities of the temple proper, and their inclusion on his rock cut stela, despite its distant location, suggests a certain status. There is a deputy known as Hatiay who left an inscription at Wadi el-'Allaqi (Kitchen 2000: 80), who may be the same man in later life.

(v) The king as a cartouche (3)

Stelae DB328, DB329, DB334

On stela DB334 the cartouche of Ramesses II is placed before the figure of the Horus falcon as an isolated icon and focus of the worship. On stelae DB328 and DB329 the cartouche forms part of the dedicatory text. The king's name has no epithets. DB334 is dedicated by a Troop Commander (see Schulman 1964: 53-64 for a discussion of this title), DB328 by a Temple Scribe and DB329 by a First God's Servant. They are all type A, and were carved into the cliff face at the most distant northern (DB334) and southern (DB328 and DB329) locations flanking the temple (Porter and Moss VII 1951: 112).

DB328 and DB329 consist of inscriptions giving praise to Ramesses II with a representation of the dedicator in the centre. This representation can be interpreted as the determinative for the text, where the dedicator's name is the last word in the text. More dramatically, the temple façade with its colossal statues of the king can be regarded as the equivalent of a stela scene as the stelae are oriented towards the façade. Stela DB334 can be interpreted in two ways: as a representation of one of the falcon statues that stand in front of the Great Temple (Porter and Moss VII 1951: 98; Fouchet 1965: pls. 116, 123, 127), and, on a more complex level, as a symbolic representation of the carving of a temple of Ramesses II, represented by the cartouche, in the sacred Mountain of Meha, represented by the Horus falcon.

(vi) Stelae dating to Ramesses II but not dedicated to him (3)

Stelae DB323, DB326, DB335

Stela DB335 depicts Ramesses II offering to Thoth, Re-Harakhti and Shepsy on behalf of the King's Son of Kush, Mernudjem, whose time in post is unknown (Raedler 2003: 133). Stelae DB323 and DB326 are identical round-topped, free-standing stelae depicting the King's Son of Kush, Paser II, adoring Amun-Re who praises Ramesses II (not depicted). These stelae record the endowment of some land for the cult of a form of Amun-Re (Gauthier 1936: 49-69). They may have been boundary stelae, set up to mark the extent of the land; their lower portions are bare and unfinished, indicating that they were set into the ground. They are almost identical, leading Gauthier (1936: 53) to suggest that the speech of Amun may continue from one to the other. The form of Amun is that of the god of Faras (Gauthier 1936: 54), located to the south of Abu Simbel. It is not clear why they are at Abu Simbel, unless they act as a record of the endowment at the official state centre in Nubia. This was the place where, later, the Vizier, Seti (r. Siptah), recorded his appointment, and the King's Sons of Kush may have set up stelae here to mark their appointment.

Other deities: Horus (4),[13] Amun-Re (8) and Re-Harakhti (5)[14]

The Horus stelea are all included in the discussion of the Ramesses II stelae. Four forms of Horus appear, the local Nubian forms, 'Lord of Buhen', 'Lord of Miam' and 'Lord of Meha' (two occurrences), and Horus, 'Lord of the Two Lands, Great God, Lord of Wenet' (*nb t3wy nṯr ꜥ3 nb wnt*). Horus, 'Lord of Meha', appears as a falcon-headed man (DB330) and a falcon (DB334), both wearing the double crown. Horus, 'Lord of Miam', is also a falcon headed man wearing the white crown on DB330. Horus, 'Lord of Buhen', is the focus of the text dedication on DB328. Horus, 'Lord of the Two Lands, Great God, Lord of Wenet' (DB333), appears on the lower register below Thoth, Re-Harakhti, Shepsy, Nehmet(awy) and a seated king. The stelae can all be classified as type A and have in common their relatively distant location from the temples. For example, DB330 and DB334 are in the northernmost area of inscriptions north of the Small Temple, and DB328 and DB333 are located in the southernmost group south of the Great Temple (see Porter and Moss VII 1951: 112; Kitchen 2000: 510). This suggests that the cult of Horus, in his different forms, was a popular one at Abu Simbel, supported by the existence of an original cult of Horus at Abu Simbel, prior to the construction of the state temples, which then incorporated the deity. The cult is not patronised by the King's Sons of Kush.

---

[13] DB328, DB330, DB333, DB334.

[14] DB322, DB323, DB329, DB330, DB333, DB335, DB327, DB338, DB339, DB340.

Amun-Re and Re-Harakhti appear four times together on the same stela (underlined in note 14), with the reigning king. Re-Harakhti has no stelae to himself alone whereas Amun-Re has three: DB323 and DB326, the land endowment stelae of the King's Son of Kush, Paser II (discussed above), and stela DB339, which is a pair with DB340. These latter two stelae, located in the recesses north and south of the entrance to the Great Temple (Porter and Moss VII 1951: 96; 98-99, (9), (11)), record the installation of the Vizier, Seti, in year one of Siptah, and a visit of Siptah to the temple during Seti's period of service; the two events may have taken place at the same time (Kitchen 2003: 262-263). Stela DB338 (r. Amenmesse), with the royal smiting-scene, has been discussed above. There is no cult to either of these gods as individual deities; they are the state deities also celebrated in the Ramesses II temple at Wadi es-Sebua.

The offerings

The stelae in the Abu Simbel subset are characterised by a lack of offerings. On stela DB322, of Hekanakht, both registers have offering tables which appear, from Champollion's drawing (1835-1845 [1970] I: pl. IV (3)) and the stela itself, to be stylised and elaborate versions of the offering stand with the water pot and lotus (upper register) and a loaded offering table in the lower register. The offering stand appears on the two land endowment stelae of Paser II, DB323 and DB326. On DB340 Siptah offers incense. The general lack of offerings indicates that the majority of the stelae set up at Abu Simbel represent individuals present at official, rather than popular, ceremonies, in which they may have been witnesses or oral participants.

Wadi es-Sebua (15 stelae; see Appendix 1, Table 4 for a list of the Wadi es-Sebua stelae)

In clearing the First Court of the Ramesses II temple with its avenue of sphinxes, the excavators, Barsanti and Gauthier, found 11 stelae (Porter and Moss VII 1951: 55), now in the Cairo Museum, seven of which were discovered *in situ* leaning against the mud brick wall of the first court (Barsanti and Gauthier 1911: 64 and pl. V). A twelfth stela, DB348, has been provenanced to this site (Gauthier 1912: 37 [5]). Amongst the finds from the Amenhotep III temple were eight sandstone stelae, and one of steatite (Porter and Moss VII 1951: 63-64), which were published by Firth (1927: 237, and fig. 10; pl. 27 (f)) together with material from Quban, but without stating which stelae came from which site. Habachi (1960: 45-52) published five of the stelae as being definitely from Wadi es-Sebua, now in the Aswan Museum, and of these the three of Ramesside date have been included in the dataset (DB344, DB354, DB355).

The original gods of Wadi es-Sebua were Amun, 'Lord of the Ways', and Horus, 'Lord of Baki', to whom the Amenhotep III temple was dedicated (Gundlach 1984: col. 768), and to which temple Ramesses II's temple was affiliated. When Ramesses II built here, he dedicated his temple in part to a deified form of himself, and as such he appears on 10 of the stelae. The reliefs in the Pronaos (Pillared Antechamber) of the Ramesses II temple depict Ramesses II wearing the nemes headdress with double plumes and horns (for example, Gauthier 1912: pl. XLIX), and in the Antechamber and the rooms flanking the Sanctuary most frequently the nemes headdress with modius and sun-disc (for example, Gauthier 1912: pl. LV (A); pl. LXII (A)). He is also shown in the Antechamber wearing the nemes headdress with the double crown (Gauthier 1912: pl. LVI (A)) or simply the nemes headdress (Gauthier 1912: pl. LVII (A)). On the stelae the deified Ramesses II wears either the blue crown when in a palanquin (for example, stela DB341), or the modius and sun disc when not (for example, stela DB343). The temple of Ramesses II retains extensive statuary in the form of four standing statues of Ramesses II and fourteen sphinx statues: two large and two small of Ramesses II outside the temple entrance; six of Ramesses II for Amun-Re in the First Court, and four of forms of Horus in the Second Court (Gauthier 1912: pls. I-XII; Porter and Moss VII 1951: 55-57; Kitchen 1996: 479-481). The Ramesses II statues are called 'Ramesses Meryamun in the House of Amun' (*Rʿ-ms-sw mry-Ỉmn m pr Ỉmn*; Kitchen 1996: 479, 481). Unlike the statues at Qantir, the statuary is not represented on the stelae, and there is no evidence that they were the focus of cult attention. The temple of Amenhotep III retains only the sanctuary images of Amun-Re where he has the epithet Lord of the Sky (*nb pt*) (Firth 1927: pl. 34). Other epithets are not clear. Other hypostases must be reconstructed from the images on stelae as there is no clear evidence for cult attention at any particular reliefs or statues.The deities represented on the stelae from the Ramesses II temple have been collated from Barsanti and Gauthier's publication (1911) and Kitchen's translation (2000) of the texts.

There is a clear distinction between the stelae from the Ramesses II temple, which are all type B and have Ramesses II as the intermediary, and those from the Amenhotep III temple, which are all type A. The dedicators of the stelae from the Ramesses II temple underpin the coherency of this group: 10 are dedicated by the King's Son of Kush, Setau, alone or with colleagues. Four are dedicated by army Standard-bearers, three of whom include Setau in the dedicatory texts. The twelfth stela is dedicated to Thoth by the Sculptor, Pentaweret. Habachi (1967: 59) suggests that this may be the man responsible for carving the other eleven stelae. This coherency renders a discussion of rank and compositional form of the stelae from the Ramesses II temple almost redundant, so these sections have been kept brief with a note of anything exceptional. The dedicators of the three stelae from the Amenhotep III temple are more diverse, and are discussed below.

A note on the military titles

(i) Army standard-bearers

The rank and role of the army standard-bearer has been extensively discussed.[15] The Egyptian title is *ṯ3y sryt* (Snape and Wilson 2007: 128). The standard-bearer on stelae is depicted holding the standard, a tall pole with a square at the top, which may include the name or emblem of the company to which he belonged (Faulkner 1941: 12-13; Snape and Wilson 2007: 128). Schulman (1964: 71) argues that there is no direct evidence to support the idea that the man with the title 'standard-bearer' actually carried the standard. The role of the standard-bearer was commander of a company, with each company consisting of 200 or 250 men (Schulman 1964: 27, 71; Raedler 2003: 157; Spalinger 2005: 252-256; Snape and Wilson 2007: 128). Raedler (2003: 157) suggests that, as four standard-bearers are recorded on the stelae from the Ramesses II temple at Wadi es-Sebua, there were 1000 men (4 x 250) stationed here.

There is some disagreement about the rank of the standard-bearer. Schulman (1964: 70), with Yoyotte and Lopez (1969: 8), argue that he is the same rank as a troop commander, and in fact was a troop commander who may have had the additional duties associated with the standard, or that this may have been an honorific title. Faulkner (1941: 17), after Helck (1939: 37) places him subordinate to a troop commander. Gnirs (1996: 163) describes standard-bearers as being the lowest members of the officer corps.

(ii) *sk*-officer

The transliteration *sk* for the title of Ramose on stela DB347 is taken from Kitchen (2000: 66), where he does not offer a translation. Raedler (2003: 157) transliterates the title as *s3kw*, again without a translation, but groups Ramose with the standard-bearers, although he is not depicted holding a standard. The hieroglyphs, which are not entirely clear, may be  or . Such a word does not appear in Hannig (2001). Schulman (1964: 57-58) lists a *skt* but does not give the hieroglyphs. He translates the word as 'assault officer', relating the title to *skt*, 'battle-line', and *ski*, 'to destroy', and suggests that this is a functional title of a man who may also have held the title standard-bearer. It indicates the standard-bearer's role of leading the foremost battle-lines (Schulman 1964: 58). This is supported by the Wadi es-Sebua stelae where the *sk*-officer, Ramose, dedicates stelae alongside the standard-bearers. Schulman has only 18th and 20th Dynasty sources for the title (1964: 161). In their critique of Schulman's work, Yoyotte and Lopez (1969: 6) state that the *skt*-officer is more likely to be a military policeman, but give no references.

The stelae from the Ramesses II temple

As noted above, the stelae dedicated at the Ramesses II temple form a coherent group: they are all large rectangular granite stelae of compositional form B, with Ramesses II as intermediary to himself as Ramesses II 'in the House of Amun' (*Rʿ-ms-sw mry-Ỉmn m pr Ỉmn*) in nine cases, to Ramesses II, 'Lord of

[15] See, for example, Helck (1939), Faulkner (1941), Schulman (1964), Yoyotte and Lopez (1969), Gnirs (1996), Raedler (2003), Spalinger (2005), Snape and Wilson (2007).

Appearances' (*Rꜥ-ms-sw mry-Ỉmn nb ḫꜥw*) once, to Ptah-Tatenen and Harsiese once, and to Thoth once (with two other deities whose representations are lost). On 10 of these stelae, the King's Son of Kush, Setau, features, either as the sole dedicator (four times) or with high-ranking colleagues as co-dedicator and/or recipient of the benefits (six times).

Amun-Re, 'Lord of the Thrones of the Two Lands' (*nb nsw tꜣwy*), and Re-Harakhti only appear on stelae featuring the deified Ramesses II, indicating that they do not have independent cults.

Ramesses II 'in the House of Amun' (9)

Stelae DB341 - DB343, DB345, DB347, DB348, DB351, DB353 + Ramesses II, 'Lord of Appearances' (stela DB350)

All the stelae that depict Ramesses II as a recipient of worship are from the Ramesses II temple. On the Ramesses II 'in the House of Amun' stelae the deified king is shown three times in a palanquin in the company of three other deities and four times standing with two other deities. On two occasions he is simply mentioned in the text. On the Ramesses II, 'Lord of Appearances', stela, DB350, the deified king is enthroned, alongside Amun-Re, Mut and Maat. In the palanquin, the deified king appears to be wearing the blue crown. On stela DB343 of the Overseer of God's Servants, Mernudjem, with Setau, the king wears the nemes headdress with a sun disc. This is identical to representations of the deified king in the reliefs in the Antechamber of the Ramesses II temple. The representation of the three gods in the upper register of this stela is similar to a relief in the Ramesses II temple Antechamber, west wall, where Ramesses II offers wine to Amun-Re, the deified Ramesses II and Mut, all enthroned (Gauthier 1912: pl. LV (A); Porter and Moss VII 1951: 60 (87), with Khons listed instead of Ramesses II). Ramesses II is shown here wearing the nemes headdress with a disc on a modius. In the relief, Mut wears the double crown; on the stela Horus, 'Lord of Buhen', replaces her wearing this crown. Horus, 'Lord of Buhen', appears elsewhere in the Antechamber in the double crown (Gauthier 1912: pl. LIV (A); Porter and Moss VII 1951: 60 (86)), as does Ptah (Gauthier 1912: pl. LIV (B); Porter and Moss VII 1951: 60 (84)), who also appears on stela DB343. Stela DB351 has lost part of the upper register, but could be reconstructed as Amun-Re, the deified Ramesses II, and Mut (named as Renenut), in which case the representation would match exactly representations of these deities in the temple (for example, on the south wall of the South-West Room; Gauthier 1912: pl. LXIII (A); Porter and Moss VII 1951: 62 (126)).

Amun-Re, 'Lord of the Thrones of the Two Lands' (6, including 1 from the Amenhotep III temple; 3 possible)

Stelae DB341, DB342, DB344, DB345, DB350, DB352; possible: DB343, DB351, DB353

Amun-Re is represented six times on the Ramesses II temple stelae as 'Lord of the Thrones of the Two Lands' (*nb nsw tꜣwy*). There are two unidentified forms, DB351 and DB353, and on stela DB343, Amun-Re has the epithet 'Lord of the Sky' (*nb pt*). This group includes seven of the stelae discussed in the section above. It is clear from the stelae that Amun-Re, 'Lord of the Thrones of the Two Lands', was the deity of the Ramesses II temple, and Amun, 'Lord of the Ways', was the original deity of the Amenhotep III temple, and that by the Ramesside Period the Amenhotep III temple had become a centre for popular worship.

Stela DB344 is the only stela from the Amenhotep III temple depicting Amun, 'Lord of the Thrones of the Two Lands'. It is compositional type A with deities on both registers. It is the only stela dedicated by a woman, Mutnofret, in the Wadi es-Sebua group. Mutnofret has been identified as the wife of the King's Son of Kush, Setau (Habachi 1967: 56; Raedler 2003: 164-167). Her stela also depicts an unnamed hawk-headed deity, presumably Re-Harakhti, in the upper register. It is worth noting that stela DB355 depicts a similar scene of Amun seated opposite a god identified as Seth, and it may be that the hawk-headed deity is in fact the beaked Seth. Mutnofret adores Ptah, Wadjyt and Khnum in the lower register. The organisation of the representations is illustrative of the gender-related constraints on cult access: Mutnofret depicts the deities of the Ramesses II temple, by this period the major active temple at Wadi es-Sebua, but dedicates the stela at the Amenhotep III temple, by then a centre for popular worship, and only shows herself having direct access to the 'lesser' hypostases of Ptah, Wadjyt and Khnum.

Ptah (5)

Stelae DB341, DB342, DB343, DB349, DB353; + stela DB344 of Mutnofret from the Amenhotep III temple.

Ptah has his usual iconography, appears standing, and can be shown in a shrine. Where his epithets are retained he is called 'Lord of Truth' (*nb mꜣꜥt*), plus 'King of the Two Lands' (*nsw tꜣwy*) once, and 'Lord of the Sky' (*nb pt*) once. He is depicted in the lower register on the five stelae that retain his image, alone or with Re-Harakhti and/or Amun-Re. Ptah's cult may have been a secondary cult, to which individuals had direct access, as at Thebes (see pp.48-52) and Qantir (see pp.121-122), while the king mediated to other deities depicted in the upper register. Five of the stelae are from the Ramesses II temple and are therefore type B with Ramesses II as the intermediary. Four include Setau; DB342 of the Standard-bearer, Iuy, does not. The stela from the Amenhotep III temple is that of Mutnofret, DB344.

Other deities: Horus (2)[16] and Renenut (2)[17]

Horus appears relatively infrequently given that, in the form 'Lord of Baki' (Quban) he was one of the original gods of the area. He may have featured in the Amenhotep III temple, and he appears in various local regional forms within both temples. Both of the stelae are from the Ramesses II temple and have been discussed above. On stela DB399 Horus is represented as a hawk-headed man wearing the double crown and has the epithet 'Lord of Buhen.' He is represented alongside Amun-Re and Ramesses II, with Ptah in a shrine in the lower register. On stela DB348, three forms of Horus are mentioned in the text: Horus 'of Baki', 'of Miam' and 'of Buhen', all of whom are gods with hypostases in the Ramesses II temple - they are either represented by a hawk-headed sphinx in the Second Court of the temple (Gauthier 1912: pl. IV (B); Porter and Moss VII 1951: 57 [vii-x]), or by reliefs at other locations within the temple (Porter and Moss VII 1951: 60-61).

The Renenut stelae include the deified Ramesses II (and other deities) and were both dedicated by Setau. Renenut has the epithet 'Lady of Sustenance' (*nb(t) kꜣw ꜥšꜣw*). The stelae were the only two found in the sand near the south wall of the outer court of the Ramesses II temple (Gauthier 1911: 75-77; Porter and Moss VII 1951: 55), that is, opposite the location of the majority of the stelae. Little remains of the mud brick wall surrounding this outer court (Gauthier 1912: pl. I (B)), so there is no evidence for any reliefs that may have decorated it, and there is no extant relief of Renenut in the temple (see Gauthier 1912; Porter and Moss VII 1951: 53-64). Gauthier's plan (1912: plan A) indicates a doorway through the southern wall, and there is a water tank nearby, both of which, if the water tank is *in situ*, could possibly have been associated with a secondary cult chapel. There is a water tank and possibly an altar near the north wall of the First Court, near the find spot of the majority of the stelae (Gauthier 1912: plan A).

The three stelae from the Amenhotep III temple

DB344, DB354, DB355

Amun, 'Lord of the Ways' is represented on two stelae (DB354, DB355) from the Amenhotep III temple, and is mentioned in the text of stela DB347 from the Ramesses II temple. This latter stela belongs to the *sk*-officer Ramose and records the work of Setau constructing the Ramesses II temple. It depicts Ramesses II offering incense and water before a palanquin in which four unnamed gods stand. They may by identified by means of their iconography as Amun-Re, Ramesses II, Atum (?) and Hathor (?). Amun, 'Lord of the Ways', and Ramesses II 'in the House of Amun', are mentioned in the framing texts. The other two stelae are type A: DB354, dating to the 20th Dynasty, depicts the First God's Servant and Mayor, Pia, adoring Amun alone; DB355 depicts Amun and Seth ('Great of Strength') in the upper register and Reshep (see Schulman 1984b: 861) in the lower register. The dedicator of the stela is a foreigner without a title called Matybaal/Kemabaal, who appears to have brought his own god, Reshep, with him to Nubia. Seth, 'Great of Strength', also occurs

---

[16] Stelae DB343, DB348.

[17] Stelae DB348, DB451.

in the text of two stelae from the Ramesses II temple, DB351 and DB353. DB344 of Mutnofret has been discussed above.

The offerings

On the 12 stelae from the Ramesses II temple, the offering tables are depicted in the upper register between Ramesses II and the principal deities of the stelae. The text publications (Gauthier 1911: 70-73; 81-86; Kitchen 2000: 60-67) of six of the stelae, where images are not available (DB342, DB345, DB346, DB348, DB349, DB352) do not mention offerings other than those given by the king as intermediary, usually wine, and the offering tables. On stela DB349 the representations are lost. The offerings of the mediating king are not discussed here; it is the offerings of the dedicator that inform us of the role of that dedicator in the event recorded. According to the available data on the 12 stelae, 11 of the dedicators offer nothing. On DB343, the Overseer of God's Servants, Mernudjem, holds lotus (?) flowers as he follows Setau, with Ramesses II above, who both offer nothing. The Deir el-Medina data suggested that, on type B stelae, where the intermediary makes an offering, the dedicator does not. The general lack of offerings indicates the official nature of the event recorded, at which the dedicators were witnesses, rather than active participants. On the three stelae from the small temple the dedicators again offer nothing, but include offering tables, on two occasions loaded with vegetables and bread, placed between themselves and the gods they adore. This suggests an active participation in a (popular?) cult, and perhaps the existence of an active system of reversion of offerings.

There are no water offerings, reflecting the almost total absence of women dedicating stelae at Wadi es-Sebua, and no bouquets, supporting the suggestion that stelae with bouquets may be related to the Theban Valley festival (see Section 4.2(ii)).

Qantir/Pi-Ramesses (74 stelae; see Appendix 1, Table 5 for a list of the Qantir/Pi-Ramesses stelae)[18]

Following illicit digging early in the 19th century a collection of 64 stelae said to be from Horbeit in the Delta was sold to W. Pelizaus who placed them in the eponymous museum in Hildesheim (Habachi 1954: 516; Kayser 1973; Schmitz 1998). These stelae have been convincingly argued by Habachi (1954: 518-519) to originate in Qantir, on the grounds that they are remarkably similar to two stelae, DB396 and DB426, which he himself discovered at Qantir in 1942, and two further stelae, DB395 and DB418, which a dealer claimed had come from Qantir. The stelae are iconographically related, the majority depicting a named statue of Ramesses II. A number of additional stelae were added to the group in Hildesheim through this iconographic similarity: stelae in Brussels, Cairo, Lund, Leipzig, Munich, Paris and Stockholm (Habachi 1954: 528-529). Habachi lists 76 stelae in his 1954 publication of the stelae; the dataset from Qantir has 74, as stelae without dedicators are omitted.

The stelae in the Qantir dataset are characterised by their depiction of colossal statues of Ramesses II. Five separate statues can be identified by the epithets:

1. Usermaatre Setepenre, 'Montu in the Two Lands' (*wsr-m3ꜥt-Re stp-n-Rꜥ Mnṯw-m-t3wy*);
2. Ramesses Meryamun, 'The God' (*Rꜥ-ms-sw mry-Ỉmn p3 nṯr*);
3. Usermaatre Setepenre, 'Beloved of Atum' (*wsr-m3ꜥt-Re stp-n-Rꜥ mry-Ỉtm*);
4. Ramesses Meryamun, 'Re of the Rulers' (*Rꜥ-ms-sw mry-Ỉmn Rꜥ ḥḳ3w*) (Habachi 1954: 549-550; see also Clère 1950: 27-28; Habachi 1969a: 28-29; Uphill 1984: 130);
5. Ramesses Meryamun, 'Ruler of Rulers' (*Rꜥ-ms-sw mry-Ỉmn ḥḳ3 ḥḳ3w*) (Scharff 1934: 47-51; Habachi 1954: 555; 1969a: 33-35, fig. 21 and pl. XIIIb).

Papyrus Anastasi II.1 describes four such statues at Pi-Ramesses (Habachi 1969a: 28; Uphill 1984: 130). The letter from Pabasa to his master Amenemope, in Papyrus Ansastasi III, describes Pi-Ramesses at festival time and refers to the residents petitioning the statue 'Montu in the Two Lands' (twice) and Ramesses Meryamun, 'The God' (Gardiner 1937: 23; Habachi 1969a: 28). The Manshiyet es-Sadr stela describes the

[18] There is an additional Qantir stela in the collection in the Rijksmuseum van Oudheden in Leiden (inv. no. F 1963/2.1), depicting Ramesses II offering to his statue 'Montu in the Two Lands' (Schneider 1971). This stela has not been included in the discussion as it lacks a non-royal dedicator.

commissioning of a statue of Ramesses II as Ramesses Meryamun, 'The God', as well as the two further statues for the temples of Amun 'of Ramesses' and Ptah 'of Ramesses', referring to cults in Pi-Ramesses (Hamada 1938: 217-230; Habachi 1954: 551-552; Uphill 1984: 191).

Uphill (1984: 206) has tentatively suggested that three colossal statues from Tanis (his T.25, T.26 and T.175), averaging 21 metres in height, may, due to their size, equate to three of these four statues. The pink granite statue T.25 (Uphill 1984: 13; 129-131), now in fragments, retains the name Usermaatre Setepenre, 'Re of the Rulers' (Uphill translates 'Sun of the Princes'). The epithet is the same but the cartouche name is different, a discrepancy which could be resolved if the other cartouche name had been inscribed elsewhere on the statue (Uphill 1984: 131). This statue name is not peculiar to Pi-Ramesses, as statues with this name are known from Luxor, the Ramesseum and possibly Abu Simbel (Clère 1950: 28-29; Uphill 1984: 131). The grey granite statue T.26 (Uphill 1984: 13-14; 132) is also fragmentary, and statue T.175 (Uphill 1984: 55; 146-147) is a sandstone foot fragment.

Habachi (1969a: 32, fig. 20) has reconstructed a temple at Pi-Ramesses that has the four statues of Ramesses II in front of the pylon. He places the two seated statues, 'Beloved of Atum' and 'Re of the Rulers' on the left and right of the two standing statues, 'Montu in the Two Lands' and 'The God'. This is based on stelae that depict more than one statue:

- Stela DB394, depicting 'Montu in the Two Lands' (centre) and 'The God' (left) as two standing statues. Stela DB369 also depicts these two statues;
- Stela H. 410 (omitted from the dataset due to the lack of dedicator) depicting 'Beloved of Atum' (left), seated, and 'The God' (right), standing.

This reconstruction is also based on the Great Temple at Abu Simbel with its four colossi located before the temple entrance (Uphill 1984: 209; see Habachi 1969a: 3, fig. 2). Uphill (1984: 209) notes that the Great Temple was dedicated to the same group of deities as the gods he suggests are the focus of the temples at Qantir, Amun, Re-Harakhti, Ptah and Ramesses II, proposing that Abu Simbel may in fact copy elements of the main temple at Qantir. Uphill (1984: 207) reads the stela of Mose, DB379 (Plate 14), as a sequence of events taking place in the main temple at Qantir (see also Dorner 1996: 70), matching a number of architectural elements to known pieces. He suggests that the three fragmentary colossal statues, T.25, T.26 and T.175, are from the façade of this temple. In the upper register the stela depicts Ramesses II in the blue crown offering Maat to Ptah 'Who Hears Prayers' (*sḏm nḥwt*). The king then stands at a Window of Appearances and hands rewards to Mose, the Infantryman of the Great Regiment of Ramesses Meryamun, 'Beloved of Atum'. The lower register shows the king standing next to (above, on the stela) a seated statue of himself as 'Re of the Rulers' (Uphill 1984: 207 incorrectly has 'Beloved of Atum'), dispensing rewards to Mose and the army. Dorner (1999: 70) places the main temple next to the palace and suggests that the open court depicted on the Mose stelae was that of the palace. The statue 'Ruler of Rulers' is not included in these reconstructions. Based on the inscription on the Qantir stela in Leiden (F 1963/2.1.), which mentions the 'Field of Tjaru', Schneider (1971: 20-21) locates a sanctuary to Ramesses II housing the statues at Sile (ancient Tjaru), 50 kilometres to the east of Qantir. However, we cannot say for certain in relation to which temples or sanctuaries the colossal statues stood, and they may well have stood at more than one location (Bietak 1984: col. 142).

The statue 'Montu in the Two Lands' is clearly the focus of popular attention, with 52 of the dataset stelae dedicated to it. The statue known as 'The God' only appears on stelae with the statue 'Montu in the Two Lands', that is, it does not appear to have an independent cult. The stela featuring the statue 'Ruler of Rulers' (DB393) is dedicated by the Vizier, Rahotep, and has Ramesses II as the intermediary. The statue 'Re of the Rulers' appears on two stelae, one of which is stela DB379 of Mose, the other is stela DB406 of Tiy, Scribe of the Altar/Table of the Lord of the Two Lands. This latter is therefore the only anomalous stela, in that it is dedicated to a statue other than 'Montu in the Two Lands' but does not have Ramesses II as intermediary or a vizier as the dedicator. If we ignore this anomaly for the present, we can say that 'Montu in the Two Lands' is the focus of popular worship and 'Ruler of Rulers' and 'Re of the Rulers' are statues related to royal or elite activity, and perhaps to particular ceremonies. This corresponds with the letter of Pabasa which describes individuals petitioning the statue 'Montu in the Two Lands' (Papyrus Anastasi III; Gardiner 1937: 23; Habachi 1969a: 27-28; Uphill 1984: 130).

'Montu in the Two Lands' (52)
Stelae DB357 - DB363, DB365 - DB375, DB377, DB378, DB380, DB381, DB383, DB386, DB388, DB389, DB392, DB394, DB395 - DB405, DB407, DB410, DB413 - DB416, DB419, DB420, DB422 - DB424, DB426, DB427

The statue stands on a pedestal wearing the white crown with the ureaus, false beard and sometimes a necklace. He wears the shendyt-kilt and holds an object ('handkerchief'; Habachi 1954: 549) in each hand. In 35 cases he has no epithets. Otherwise, he can be known as 'Great God' , 'Who Hears Prayers', 'Lord of the Sky', 'Dual King', 'Perfect God', 'Lord of the Two Lands' and 'Given Life (like Re)' (*nṯr ꜥꜣ, sḏm nḥwt, nb pt, nsw bity, nṯr nfr, nb tꜣwy, di ꜥnḫ (mi Rꜥ)*).

47 of the stelae are type A, indicating the popular nature of this cult. There are three type B stelae, two of which, DB363 and DB405, have Ramesses II as the intermediary and one, DB358, which has one of his sons, Meryatum, in the role. The two stelae with Ramesses II as the intermediary are dedicated by military men. Two of the stelae, DB400 and DB407, are type C, with stela DB400 including family members. Only five of the Qantir dataset stelae (DB380, DB384, DB400, DB409 and DB412) include family, in all cases wives and in four cases children. Two of these are dedicated to the statue 'Montu in the Two Lands', two to an unidentified statue of Ramesses II and one to Ptah and Hathor. In addition, stela DB389, dedicated to 'Montu in the Two Lands', has a man and a woman carved on the sides of the stela but there are no filiations.

The stelae are dedicated by military men, individuals connected with the royal household, if this is how we are to understand titles followed by 'of the Lord of the Two Lands' (*n nb tꜣwy*), individuals with priestly titles and five women. A significant number (12) have no titles, and, on two stelae, the titles are lost. Those of notable rank are the Royal Butler Ramessu-men (DB394), a Royal Fanbearer (DB427), a vizierial title, whose dedicator's name is unfortunately lost, a Royal Scribe of the Altar/Table of the Lord of the Two Lands, name also lost (DB369), and two army Standard-bearers, Any/Inwya and Ramose (DB363 and DB395). An army standard-bearer of this name is known at Zawiyet Umm el-Rakham (stela DB412) and there is a *sk*-officer Ramose on a stela at Wadi es-Sebua (DB347).[19] The stela of Any/Inwya names his regiments as 'Re of the Rulers', suggesting that the regiment was connected to the cult statue of that name. Stela DB379 of the Infantryman, Mose (dedicated to the statue, 'Re of the Rulers'), tells us that he belonged to the 'Great Regiment' (*sꜣ ꜥꜣ*) of Ramesses Meryamun, 'Beloved of Atum', which may have been another statue-related regiment.

A number of individuals on the stelae and other monuments have titles which may connect them to the cult of 'Montu in the Two Lands': Stela DB370 (Plate 15a) is dedicated by Isis, a singer of 'Montu in the Two Lands', and a woman called Tentopet, the wife of the Fanbearer of the Lord of the Two Lands, Kaemwaset, has the title Royal Sistrum Player of 'Montu in the Two Lands,' on dyad of the pair (Kitchen 1996: 279 at C).

The epithet 'Great God' (*nṯr 'ꜣ*) occurs on three stelae, DB359, DB365 and DB393, applied to the statue 'Montu in the Two Lands' on the first two, and to the statue 'Ruler of Rulers' on the third. Stela DB391 is dedicated by Penweret, Overseer of the Goldworkers and 'one greatly praised of the Great God' (*ḥsy ꜥꜣ n nṯr ꜥꜣ* - this phrase may be connected to the Sobek cult at Pi-Ramesses; see below). The epithet 'Perfect God' (*nṯr nfr*) occurs on six stelae in the dataset, five occurrences of which are in relation to the statue 'Montu in the Two Lands': stelae DB357, DB363, DB365, DB404 and DB424. This suggests that the statue 'Montu in the Two Lands' may have been known by this epithet in particular, and that titles using the epithet may relate to the statue's cult. On stela DB428 the Prince, Setekh-Herkhopshef, has the title the Sem-priest of the Perfect God, relating directly to his father, or to this statue cult. On stela DB365 both epithets, 'Great God' and 'Perfect God', are applied to the statue 'Montu in the Two Lands'.

Other deities: Ptah (7)[20] and Sobek(-Re) (6 occurrence on 5 stelae)[21]

Ptah and Sobek-Re are the only deities with stelae dedicated to them either alone or in the company of other deities, suggesting that active cults to these deities may have existed. Of the Ptah stelae, DB428 dates to the reign of Ramesses III, the rest to the reign of Ramesses II. Ptah is depicted once seated, in a shrine, and six

[19] See *A Note on the Military Titles* on p. 116, for a discussion of the relationship of this title to that of standard-bearer.
[20] DB379, DB384, DB385, DB390, DB400, DB408, DB428.
[21] DB356, DB364, DB387, DB391, DB425.

times standing, three times in a shrine, in his usual form: mummiform, shaven-headed, or wearing a skull cap, and holding the composite sceptre. On stela DB400 Ptah is depicted in the company of the statue 'Montu in the Two Lands'; on stela DB408 (Plate 15b) the deity is depicted in the company of an unidentified statue of Ramesses II. On stela DB385 he is shown in front of a pylon with a column behind him; his epithet is 'upon the Column' (*ḥry p3 wḫ3;* Leitz 2000 II: 527). He is also shown twice with Amun-Re, on stelae DB400 and DB428. His epithets are either standard: 'Lord of Truth', 'King of the Two Lands', 'Beautiful of Face', 'Father of the Gods' (*nb m3ꜥt, nsw t3wy, nfr ḥr, it nṯrw*) or local/popular: 'upon the Column', 'Who Hears Prayers' (*sḏm nḥwt*), and 'of Warep' (*w3rp*). Together with the depiction of Ptah before a temple pylon and pillar and, in association with statues of Ramesses II, this suggests that the form of Ptah venerated on the Qantir stelae is an accessible popular form of Ptah at a temple entrance, similar to the Ptah in the Eastern High Gate at Medinet Habu (Medinet Habu IV: pl. 245). Such secondary cult foci were often inlaid, and this may have been the case at Qantir with the statue of Amun-Re depicted on stelae DB389, who is identified as 'of True Lapis Lazuli' (*ḫsbḏ m3ꜥ*; Leitz 2000 V: 952). On stela DB379 Ptah appears with Hathor, 'Lady of the Southern Sycamore' (*nbt nht rsy*), as a cow in the marshes, where Hathor may also be a subsidiary deity. At Deir el-Medina, Hathor, 'Lady of the Southern Sycamore', is depicted in this form in the Khenu-chapel attached to the Hathor temple (see, for example, relief DM87; Figure 3.21).

Six of the seven Ptah stelae are type A, indicating the popular, accessible nature of the cult. There is one type C stela (DB400), which has been discussed above, in the section on the statue 'Montu in the Two Lands'. The stelae were dedicated by people of the same demographic as the 'Montu in the Two Lands' stelae: military men, palace administration, a temple worker, and also include a craftsman (DB408) and a son of Ramesses II, Setekh-kherkhopshef (DB428). As in the Deir el-Medina and Theban datasets, no women dedicate stelae to Ptah.

Sobek(-Re) appears six times on five stelae, four times as a crocodile-headed man (DB356, DB387, DB391, DB425; Plate 16) and twice as a crocodile (DB364, DB391). As a crocodile-headed man, he is shown standing or seated wearing the *šwty*-crown, and holding the was-sceptre and ankh-sign. As a crocodile he is depicted upon a pedestal wearing a more ornate version of the same crown, flanked by uraei. Behind the recumbent statue is a large curved shape that may be a sun-shade or a sand bank. On stela DB364 where Sobek(-Re) appears as a crocodile, he has no epithets, though the top of the stela is damaged so they may have been lost. The depictions of Sobek(-Re) as a crocodile-headed man have the following epithets: DB356: 'Perfect God' (*nṯr nfr*); DB387: 'Lord of the Sky' (*nb pt*); DB391: 'Lord of "Saty"' (*nb si3ty*, perhaps 'The Mutilator' or 'The Swindler'); DB425: 'The Guilty One' (*p3 ꜥḏ3*). There are four type A, no type B and one type C stelae, indicating the popular nature of the cult. The stelae are dedicated by two Craftsmen, a Sailor and two Scribes associated with the palace. As with the Ptah stelae, no women dedicate stelae to Sobek(-Re). Three of the individuals describe themselves as being '(greatly) praised of the (Great/Perfect) God' (*ḥsy* (*ꜥ3*) *n p3 nṯr* (*ꜥ3/nfr*)), an epithet that is restricted in this subset to stelae dedicated to Sobek(-Re), suggesting that some special privilege of cult access or reward has been bestowed on the dedicators.

The offerings

Figure 5.7 Offerings depicted on the Qantir votive stelae

	Total	19th Dynasty	20th Dynasty	Notes
Offering stand	43	43	0	
Loaded offering table	16	16	0	
Incense offered	11	11	0	
Water offered	1	1	0	*By the wife of a dedicator*
Festival offerings	3	3	0	
Lotus flowers	12	11	1	
Bouquet	0	0	0	
Nothing	17	16	1	*All type A*

In comparison to the Deir el-Medina dataset, there are many more stelae with offering tables holding the water pot and lotus. Water is offered only once, by a woman, whilst her husband offers incense, reflecting the male dominated nature of the subset. There are no bouquets featured on the stelae, once again supporting the suggestion that stelae with such depictions relate to the Theban Valley festival. The existence of 14 stelae with no offerings may be evidence for an oral ceremony, or one at which the stelae dedicators were witnesses rather than participants, and the four type B stelae follow the expected pattern where the dedicator gives no offerings because, or whilst, the intermediary does.

Zawiyet Umm el-Rakham (7 stelae; see Appendix 1, Table 6 for a list of the Zawiyet Umm el-Rakham stelae)

During Habachi's original excavations at this site a number of stelae and door jambs were discovered in the chapels to the west of the main temple (see Figure 5.3). Habachi published only three of the stelae found at Zawiyet Umm el-Rakham (1980: 16-18 and pls. V-VI; two are included in the dataset, stelae DB430 and DB432). Based on Habachi's publications, The *Lexikon der Ägyptologie* lists the number of stelae as 16 (Helck 1986: col. 845); they have more recently been catalogued by Snape and Wilson (2007: 98-125) as amounting to possibly 21 stelae, or parts thereof. Snape and Wilson have collated the information on the stelae found at Zawiyet Umm el-Rakham from a number of sources: the Habachi article in *BIFAO* 1980; Habachi's photographs now housed in Chicago House, Luxor; the actual stelae in the SCA office at Mersa Matrouh; the register book for Habachi's work, and the stelae left on site. Snape and Wilson publish the Habachi photographs of the stelae, as well as photographs of the stelae *in situ*. These latter photographs (A25, C14, C17, D20, D21; see Snape and Wilson 2007: figs. 5.2, 5.3) show the stelae leaning up against one another and against the main temple wall and temple enclosure wall. As Snape and Wilson (2007: 93, n. 1; 94) note, this is similar to the location of the eight stelae found propped against the enclosure wall of the sphinx avenue at Wadi es-Sebua (Barsanti and Gauthier 1911). In 2000, the Liverpool team excavating at Zawiyet Umm el-Rakham, discovered a cache of monuments belonging to the commander Nebre in the southernmost of the rear three rooms of the smaller temple ('Nebre temple'; Snape 2001a: 19; Simpson 2002: 20). The cache consisted of two stelae depicting Nebre offering to deities[22] (Sekhmet on one; Snape 2001a: 20, fig. 4), a naos with integral statues of Ptah and Sekhmet (Snape 2004: 159, fig. 13), and a beautiful two-thirds life-size limestone statue of Nebre as a standard-bearer of Sekhmet, currently on display in the Luxor Museum (Snape 2001a: 20, figs. 1-3; Snape and Godenho *forthcoming*). On all of these monuments attempts had been made to erase Nebre's name, as well as his figure on the stelae (Snape 2001a: 19). In addition, one of Nebre's lintels from the Southern Building had been reused face-down as a threshold (Snape 2001a: 19). Snape (2001a: 19) has suggested that Nebre may have come to regard Zawiyet Umm el-Rakham and its surrounding area as 'his own personal fiefdom' and was ultimately disgraced and replaced. The two Nebre stelae found with the standard-bearer statue have not been included in the dataset as they are, at the time of writing, in the process of being fully published (Snape and Godenho *forthcoming*). The Zawiyet Umm el-Rakham dataset stelae amount to just seven stelae, due to the poor preservation of many of the stelae, and, in one case, the lack of a dedicator (Snape and Wilson 2007: 98 (Stela 1), figs. 5.4, 5.5).

It is the stelae which provide the richest source for information on the deities to whom the temples and chapels at Zawiyet Umm el-Rakham may have been dedicated. In the main temple there are no extant reliefs - the walls stand to only one metre, and the only remaining decoration is the names of Ramesses II on the side of a pillar (Habachi 1980: 16). Other decorated architectural elements at the site are the scenes on the passage walls at Gates A and B (on Habachi's plan; 1980: 13), which depict Ramesses II getting out of his chariot to smite Libyans (Habachi 1980: 16; Helck 1986: col. 845), the lintels and doorjambs from the chapels, magazines and Southern Building, inscribed for Ramesses II and Nebre, and the statue of Nebre and the naos of Sekhmet and Ptah discovered by the Liverpool team. Habachi (1980: 18) disagrees with Rowe's attribution of the main temple to Ptah, on the basis of the inscriptions on the first blocks found here. These inscriptions include Ptah's epithets '[of Ankh]tawy (Memphis), Beautiful of Face in his Great Place' ([*nb ꜥnḫ*]-*tꜣwy nfr ḥr ḥry st wrt*; Cairo JdE 10384). Habachi maintains that the inclusion of the god's name in an inscription is not sufficient proof that this god was the focus of the cult. He tentatively suggests (1980: 18)

[22] On one of the stelae there is some indication that the monument has been re-used, and the identity of the original dedicator is not certain (G. Godenho, *pers. comm.*)

that the temple was dedicated to the Memphite triad, following Rowe's statement that the name of the district was *ḥwt-hꜥpi* and the inclusion of Sekhmet on a number of the objects. This attribution is supported by the more recent discoveries of the Liverpool team of the naos and standard-bearer statue of Nebre, and the smaller temple, dedicated to the Memphite gods of Ptah and Sekhmet; Snape (2001a: 19) suggests that the troops stationed here may have come from Memphis. The chief deity on the stelae is Ramesses II himself, and it may be that the chapels west of the main temple were constructed to worship the deified Ramesses II. Ramesses II is depicted smiting enemies or making offerings before gods, in particular Amun-Re and Sekhmet (Snape and Wilson 2007: 96). Seth and Horus also appear on the stelae (though Horus does not appear on any of the dataset stelae).

Ramesses II (6)
Stelae DB430-DBDB433, DB435, DB436

The form of Ramesses II receiving cult attention at Zawiyet Umm el-Rakham is the living king. On four of the stelae (DB430, DB433, DB435, DB436; see Figure 5.8), Ramesses II is depicted participating in the royal smiting-scene, where he slaughters captives before a god. The king has the epithets 'Lord of Appearances, Given Life/Lord of the Thrones of the Two Lands' (*nb ḫꜥw di ꜥnḫ/nb nsw tꜣwy*). He carries out the ritual before Amun-Re on three occasions (epithets lost), Sekhmet, 'Lady of the West' (*nbt imnt*), and a deity who may be Seth, identified by the epithet 'Great of Strength' (*ꜥꜣ pḥty*; Leitz 2000 II: 22 - Leitz lists two New Kingdom instances of this epithet applied to Amun-Re and 34 where it is applied to Seth). The smiting-scene stelae are all type C. Schulman's list of stelae with this scene (17 examples; 1994: 271-295) does not include the Zawiyet Umm el-Rakham stelae. These additional stelae add an interesting group to the known stelae with this scene in terms of dedicators, whose extant titleholders are all standard-bearers (the dedicator title is lost on stela DB435; for a discussion of the standard-bearers at Zawiyet Umm el-Rakham, see Snape and Wilson 2007: 128).

Figure 5.8 Sketch of the stela of the Standard-bearer, Amenmessu, showing Ramesses II smiting, Zawiyet Umm el-Rakham, r. Ramesses II, first half (DB430; ZUR 2; © Christiane Müller-Hazenbos)

On stela DB432, Ramesses II offers flowers to Sekhmet while the Royal Scribe and Great Chief of the Army, Panehsy, kneels below. Schulman (1964: 49-50) argues that the title great chief (*wr ꜥꜣ*) has the same rank as standard-bearer. The upper register of the remaining stela, DB431, is too damaged to read the scene. Separating the upper from the lower register are three rows of hieroglyphs which contain the cartouches of Ramesses II, and possibly a reference to the part of the army in which the two officials served. In the lower register two Standard-bearers stand facing each other with the cartouches of Ramesses II in the centre. The right-hand Standard-bearer is called Djehutyemheb, and the standard of the man on the left may relate to the regiment of the 'Aten' (*Itn*) (Snape and Wilson 2007: 109).

Other deities: Amun-Re (4)[23] and Sekhmet (2)[24]

Other than stela DB434, which is too damaged to make out the scene, the stelae in this section are included in the section above. The principal role of Amun-Re on the Zawiyet Umm el-Rakham stelae is as the god offering the sword to the smiting king. He has his standard iconography of double plumes and short kilt; any epithets he may have had are lost. On stela DB433 a damaged figure of a god, identified as Seth on account of the epithet 'Great of Strength', offers the sword, although, as this ritual is depicted before Amun-Re on all the other stelae, the god on stela DB433 may in fact be Amun-Re. Sekhmet is depicted standing, as a lioness-headed woman, with a sun disc and ureaus on her head. She has the epithet 'Lady of the West' (*nbt imnt*). On stela DB432 she is offered flowers by Ramesses II; on stela DB436 she stands behind the king as he smites the enemy. On stela ZUR 13 (Snape and Wilson 2007: 116, fig. 5.17), not included in the dataset due to its fragmentary condition, a female goddess who may be Sekhmet stands on the right with a figure of the king on the left.

The offerings

The only offerings depicted are those on stela DB432 of Panehsy, where the king offers flowers to Sekhmet, before whom is an offering stand with a water pot cooled by a lotus flower. This indicates that the stelae depict an official ritual event at which the stelae dedicators were witnesses rather than active participants.

5.4 Summary and discussion of the comparative data stelae

The military outpost at Zawiyet Umm el-Rakham is restricted temporally to the reign of Ramesses II. At the other three sites, the cult activity measured is concentrated in the reign of this king. The sites located in Egyptian Nubia, Wadi es-Sebua and Abu Simbel, have temples dedicated to the Ramesside Period state deities of Amun-Re, Re-Harakhti, Ptah and Ramesses II himself, deities who are celebrated at Qantir, the new dynastic capital. The extant material at Zawiyet Umm el-Rakham indicates that Ptah and Sekhmet, the gods of Memphis and of the Western Delta and desert, were pre-eminent here, alongside Ramesses II in association with Amun-Re.

The stelae from Wadi es-Sebua and Zawiyet Umm el-Rakham are dedicated almost exclusively by military men. The martial emphasis is characteristic of all the comparative dataset stelae. The inclusion of the Qadesh battle scenes and other war scenes, as well as repetition of the smiting-scene, in the Great Temple at Abu Simbel, underline the bellicose nature of the temple in contrast to the Small Temple. A number of the Abu Simbel stelae reflect the military emphasis of Ramesses II's early years, in both text and representation: on stela DB321 Ramesses II has the epithet 'who slays the Nine Bows' (*smꜣ pḏtyw*; Kitchen 2000: 203-204); on stela DB325 Paser II describes the king as a 'warrior who protects his army, (being) their rampart on the day of combat' (*ḏw mk mšꜥ.f pꜣy.sn inb hrw ḏw*; Kitchen 2000: 53); and on stela DB324 of the same man, Ramesses II is described as 'doughty with his sword, hero, valiant like Montu, slaying Syria (Khurru) and trampling down Nubia' (*ṯnr ḥr ḫpš.f pri-ꜥ ḳni mi Mnṯw smꜣ ḫꜣrw ptpt Kꜣš*; Kitchen 2000: 53).

At Qantir, dedicators range from royal princes to craftsmen and washermen, aligning them in range of ranks with the Deir el-Medina dedicators. At Abu Simbel, Wadi es-Sebua (except for the Amenhotep III temple) and Zawiyet Umm el-Rakham, the dedicators are almost exclusively high-ranking military men. The compositional form at Qantir (64/74 stelae are type A) is also comparable to the Deir el-Medina stelae. At Wadi es-Sebua (excluding stelae from the Amenhotep III temple) and Zawiyet Umm el-Rakham the lack of type A stelae indicates the official nature of the cults here. Given the military nature of the sites it is unsurprising that very few women dedicate stelae in the comparative dataset. At Qantir, a city site, a small number of women both dedicate stelae (five examples) and are included on stelae of their husbands (five examples). At Wadi es-Sebua, Mutnofret, the wife of the King's Son of Kush, Setau, dedicates one stela (DB344).

[23] DB430, DB434 - DB436.
[24] DB432, DB436.

The individuals dedicating stelae at Abu Simbel can be contrasted with the dedicators at the other sites, in that they are not groups of contemporaries, but principally sequences of high-ranking individuals such as the five King's Sons of Kush, the highest rank in the region. In addition, though there is some evidence of popular cult activity focusing on a local Horus, the majority of the stelae mark a relationship with the king, in the form of an iconographic representation of greeting the king, or indicate temple access by reproducing restricted royal temple reliefs. Two thirds (14/21) of the stelae from Abu Simbel are type A, but the high-rank of the dedicators, and the fact that many of the stelae represent the living king, serve to indicate a relationship with the king, rather than participation in a popular cult. The Abu Simbel Great Temple seems to have been used as a centre for administrative appointments and thus had a consistently official role. Access to the temple and its environs would have been more restricted than at the smaller and more distant locations of Wadi es-Sebua and Zawiyet Umm el-Rakham. At Abu Simbel the status of the dedicator appears to be connected to the location of the stela, one of the three factors indicative of 'divine access.' Stelae distant from the temples, in the flanking cliff faces to the north and south, generally (though not in the case of the double stela of the King's Son of Kush, Setau, DB327) belong to individuals of a lower rank than those closer to the façades. Stelae DB324 and DB325 of the King's Son of Kush, Paser II, flank the façade of the Great Temple, whilst stela DB320 of the King's Son of Kush, Yuni, abuts the façade of the Small Temple. In addition, certain stelae generate fields of influence of their own, so that we find the Stablemaster, Iwefenamun, carving his stela (DB332) next to that of the King's Son of Kush, Hekanakht (DB322), and the Deputy of Wawat, Mery, carving his smiting-scene stela (DB338) next to the earlier smiting-scene stela of the King's Son of Kush, Setau (DB327). Status is also indicated by the stela representation: the 'greeting the king' gesture is used only by the King's Sons of Kush; individuals of this rank and lower reproduce temple scenes.

In terms of offerings, the relatively frequent depiction of the offering table with water pot and lotus at Qantir suggests that this could relate to a particular ceremony, though without further evidence it is only possible to conclude that that this form of offering table is a feature of the reign of Ramesses II. The remaining three sites are characterised by a lack of offerings, indicating the official nature of the ceremonies commemorated.

The Deir el-Medina dataset stelae are much closer in nature to those from Qantir than to those from the other comparative dataset sites. Put simply, there were organised popular cults at Deir el-Medina and Qantir, both established settlement sites, and official cults and events at the remaining sites, which can be characterised as official/state military encampments.

It seems certain that some of the stelae, in particular those from Abu Simbel and Wadi es-Sebua, are decorated with versions of temple reliefs. The smiting-scene may be one such example. The scenes of the king offering to his deified self, seated or standing amongst deities, are, in many cases, similar or identical to reliefs from within the temples. Whether the stelae depict an actual event of the king offering, or are copies of a temple scene, both types of stelae representation encode status as such temple scenes belong to a restricted iconographic repertoire. Their use on stelae of non-royal individuals implies actual and symbolic 'divine access', and as a result they display status. When stelae depict royal offering scenes, differentiating between copies of restricted temple reliefs and depictions of actual events is problematic. One suggestion is that offering scenes where the king offers to gods in a palanquin, i.e. portable processional statues used at festival time, they represent an actual event. In addition, royal offering scenes including specific details or individuals, such as the stela of the King's Son of Kush, Hekanakht (DB322), at Abu Simbel, on which the Princess Meryatum and Queen Nefertari are also depicted, may be related with more confidence to a single event.

The smiting-scene is present in reliefs and stelae at Abu Simbel and Zawiyet Umm el-Rakham and on one stela from Qantir (r. Ramesses III). A version of the scene occurs on stela DB93 of Senior Scribe, Ramose (i), from Deir el-Medina (Schulman 1994: 54-55). Schulman (1994: 267-269) has discussed the meaning of the scene of offering the sword and smiting enemies. He argues that the scene on stelae is related to that found on temple walls (the 'triumphal scene') where the king slaughters captives before one or more gods, and is brought more captives by the god, as well as being offered the sword. On a temple wall this scene indicates the end of a battle where the king has been successful. According to Schulman (1994: 268-269) the stelae version of the icon represents the event of the king slaughtering captives at the start of a battle, with a priest playing the role of the god. An alternative explanation is that the stelae may copy temple relief versions of this icon.[25] Whether the representation is of a historical action (see Snape and Wilson 2007: 129 for a discussion of this possibility in relation to the smiting-scene stelae at Zawiyet Umm el-Rakham) or a copy of a relief, the stela representation had the symbolic function of protecting the (extended) borders of Egypt. It can be interpreted as both a warning and an apotropaic device, functioning in a smiliar way to the magical execration texts written on smashed prisoner figurines found at the Middle Kingdom fort at Mirgissa in Lower Nubia (Ritner 1993). Schulman (1994: 270) states that the known dedicators are members of the high-ranking colonial administration of Nubia, with one exception, a mercenary shieldbearer from Qantir (DB429). The dedicators of the stelae with this scene at Zawiyet Umm el-Rakham are all army standard-bearers. At Abu Simbel they are the King's Sons of Kush and the Deputy of Wawat.

Historical events commemorated on the stelae

(i) Temple inauguration at Abu Simbel and Wadi es-Sebua

The clearest iconographic representation of a royal visit which may be linked to the temple inauguration at Abu Simbel is the representation of Ramesses II on stela DB322, of the King's Son of Kush, Hekanakht, a view put forward by Kitchen (1982b: 99-100; 135; Raedler 2003: 132). This would fix the completion date at year 24 at the latest, the last known year in post of Hekanakht. The stela of Hekanakht depicts Ramesses II and his daughter Meryatum adoring Amun-Re, Ramesses II and Re-Harakhti in the upper register while Hekanakht kneels adoring Queen Nefertari below. The text is a generic request for a long life for the King's Son of Kush (Kitchen 2000: 49). Kitchen (1982b: 100) suggests that Meryatum took Nefertari's role in this inauguration ceremony, at which Hekanakht was present, because by this date Nefertari was too ill to participate in the long rituals. Kitchen's reading of the representations on this stela as a historical record is of note. Habachi (1969a: 10) interprets this stela as indicating that Hekanakht was more concerned with the Small Temple, the temple of Nefertari, than with the Great Temple. The Hekanakht stela is flanked by two further stelae, DB332 of the Stablemaster, Iwefenamun, and DB335 of the King's Son of Kush, Mernudjem, representing the king as intermediary, that is, participating in official temple ceremonies. Whilst it is unlikely that there were two King's Sons of Kush in post at the same time (Reisner 1920: 40), Iwefenamun could have been present with Hekanakht on the occasion of a royal visit. It is of note that these are the only type B stelae at Abu Simbel dating to Ramesses II, and are therefore the only stelae to commemorate a royal visit. The clearest textual reference to building the temples at Abu Simbel[26] is found on stela DB324 of the King's Son of Kush, Paser II, where he states that the king 'is content with regard to [the temple]' that Paser II 'has

[25] An 18th Dynasty stela with the royal smiting-scene depicts a soldier, Mery-Waset, and his wife kneeling adoring a temple pylon on which is depicted the god Ptah and the king smiting (Charles Ede Limited, *Egyptian Antiquities Sale Catalogue*, 2008: no. 3; ex-Hans Goedicke Collection). In this case the stela scene appears to be a direct copy of the temple pylon scene.

[26] Habachi (1969: 78) fixes the construction of the Great Temple to before Ramesses II's year 34, based on the Blessing of Ptah stela (Porter and Moss VII 1951: 106; Schmidt 1973: 46; Kitchen 1996: 99-110; Kitchen 1982b: 136 dates this text to year 33) and the Marriage stela of Ramesses II's year 34 (Porter and Moss VII 1951: 98 (8); Habachi 1969a: 7; Schmidt 1973: 44-45; Kitchen 1996: 86-96; Gohary 1998: 72), both of which were installed after the completion of the internal decoration. In addition, the double stela of the King's Son of Kush, Setau (DB327), dated to year 38, does not make reference to temple construction, suggesting that the temples were already complete by this date (Habachi 1969a: 7). An inscription dating to Ramesses II's year 1 is carved in the door thickness of the entrance to the Second Hall (Reisner 1920: 40; Porter and Moss VII 1951: 108 (92, 93); Schmidt 1973: 23-24), deep within the temple, leading Reisner (1920: 40) to state that the Great Temple was begun under Seti I. There is no additional evidence for this, and Schmidt (1973: 23-34) argues that this may be a retrospective date, or belong to one of Ramesses II's successors. Stela DB321 of the First Royal Cupbearer, Ramesses-Asha-hebu-sed, refers to the king 'making for him [Horus, Lord of Meha] his Temple of Millions of Years, it being excavated in the Mountain of Meha' (*m irt n.f ḥwt.f m ḥḥ m rnpwt m šd m ḏw n mḥꜣ*; Kitchen 2000: 142). Ramesses-Asha-hebu-sed's years in post are not known, but he states on his stela that he was charged with 'reorganizing the land of Kush' (*r spd tꜣ n Kꜣš m mꜣw*[*t*]; Kitchen 1996: 142), something that may have happened at the start of Ramesses II's reign. Further evidence for such a date in post is the location of his stela, next to that of the King's Son of Kush, Yuni, who was in post at the start of the reign of Ramesses II. Ramesses-Asha-hebu-sed may have been in post at the same time or shortly afterwards. More circumstantial evidence for the construction date can be found in the Great Temple's reliefs, where, in the later parts of the temple (the inner rooms and the Sanctuary), Ramesses II is overtly deified, a theological evolution that took place over the course of his reign (Habachi 1969a: 8-10; Kitchen 1982b: 177-178; Moftah 1985: 252-265). The inclusion of Nefertari, who died around year 25 (Van Dijk 2000: 299), as the principal wife in the temple also indicates that construction must have taken place in the first part of Ramesses II's reign. Princess Bint-Anath appears just once in the temple in this role, on the rear of pillar III in the Great Hall (Porter and Moss VII 1951: 105; Kitchen 1982b: 99). This dating of the Great Temple to the first half of Ramesses II's reign concurs with Desroches-Noblecourt's suggestion (1968: 119) that it was constructed to celebrate the king's first Sed festival in his year 29/30.

made' (*ỉrr.k*). Kitchen prefers to translate Paser II's statement as '(re-)made (?) the temple' (Kitchen 2000: 53; see Habachi 1969b: 171), and he interprets the Paser II stela as relating to the restoration of the damage that occurred following an earthquake of which he places at around year 30/31. One of the four colossal statues on the front of the Great Temple was partially destroyed by the earthquake (Fouchet 1965: pl. 115).[27]

In relation to the construction and inauguration of the Abu Simbel temples, the stelae of officials Yuni, Hekanakht, Ramesses-Asha-hebu-sed, Mernudjem, Paser II and Setau can be interpreted as follows: Yuni was present when the site was chosen, and his successor Ramesses-Asha-hebu-sed was in post during the period of building the temples, as may have been the undated King's Son of Kush, Mernudjem. Hekanakht and Paser II oversaw and completed the construction. Paser II, in post between years 24 - 34, certainly took the credit for construction work of some kind on the temple(s), and his numerous monuments bear witness to a significant and important presence here.[28] After Setau had spent some time at Abu Simbel in year 38 (possibly his first year in post), when he may have been involved in the alterations to the depictions of the king in the temple in relation to his deification (Habachi 1969a: 9, fig. 7), he moved south and constructed other temples that presented a finished theology of the divine king(ship) of Ramesses II.

Stelae DB345, DB347 and DB350 from Wadi es-Sebua are dated to days 1 and 2 of the first month of Peret, year 44 of Ramesses II. They are dedicated by, or include, the King's Son of Kush, Setau. These stelae are commemorative, recording the building and restoration of the temples at Wadi es-Sebua, and they form the link between all the stelae from the Ramesses II temple at this site. On these stelae, Ramesses II offers to various gods who form two distinct groups: gods in a palanquin, and gods whose images can be found within the Ramesses II temple. The palanquin gods are shown very small, and the statue of the deified king can be differentiated from his other representations by the presence of the blue crown. These are the festival, or processional, statues, and the three stelae with these images, DB341, DB347 and DB353, may represent a part of the event of Ramesses II visiting/inaugurating the Wadi es-Sebua temple (see Yoyotte 1951: 12, n.22). According to the stelae, the king made offerings to the processional or 'festival' deities and to other hypostases within the temple, and these offerings, by means of reversion, came to benefit Setau, for whose benefit the offering formula is dedicated, and by extension the colleagues commemorated on the stelae. Where the titles have survived there are two army Standard-bearers of the company 'Ramesses II is Triumphant', Huy and Yam[…], two additional army Standard-bearers, Iuy and Paherypedjet, the Overseer of God's Servants of all the Gods, Mernudjem, and the Sculptor, Pentaweret.

(ii) The appointment of the King's Sons of Kush at Abu Simbel

The Great Temple at Abu Simbel appears to have been central to the appointment of the officials who oversaw Nubia for the king, during and after the reign of Ramesses II. The King's Son of Kush, Setau's stela of year 38, DB327, is the earliest dated inscription extant for him (Schmidt 1973: 49; Helck 1975; Raedler 2003). Five King's Sons of Kush from the reign of Ramesses II carve stelae at Abu Simbel (Huy, in post years 34-38, is absent): Yuni, Hekanakht, Paser II, Setau and the undated Mernudjem (see Figure 5.2). Later in the 19th Dynasty, at the start of the reign of Siptah, a stela, DB339, was set up to mark the appointment of the King's Son of Kush, Seti, as Vizier (the text on this stela explicitly records this; see Kitchen 2003: 262).

---

[27] Kitchen (1982b: 135) writes that soon after the first Sed festival of Ramesses II an earthquake struck Abu Simbel. The earthquake caused the pillars to crack, the collapse of one of the Osiride figures inside the Great Temple and the north jamb of the main entrance doorway, and severe damage to two of the exterior colossi. Presumably Kitchen places this earthquake in year 30/31 as the Blessing of Ptah stela, dated to year 35, is carved over a restored pillar. Kitchen (1982b: 136) states that Paser II placed two statues, one perhaps being statue BM EA 1376 (Porter and Moss VII 1951: 110) which has the title 'Overseer of the Works of the House of Pi-Ramesses Meryamun (The Town)', within the temple to mark his restoration work. A further text in the South Chapel may relate to restoration work at Abu Simbel: 'he has made the great temple anew in his name for his father Amun-Re residing in Nubia, being cut into the Pure Mountain, of fine white sandstone' (*ir.n.f ḥwt-nṯr ꜥ3 m3ꜥw ḥr rn.f n it.f ỉmn-Rꜥ ḥry-ib t3-sti m šd m p3 ḏw wꜥb m inry ḥḏ nfr*; bandeau text from the South Chapel; Kitchen 1996: 495). Raedler (2003: 132) follows Kitchen in dating an earthquake to year 31/32. She also states (2003: 132) that Setau carried out restoration work at Abu Simbel, which is possible but unproven.

[28] Paser II was related to a powerful family close to the king (Reisner 1920: 45-46; Kitchen 1982b: 135), and this may go some way towards explaining the abundance of his monuments at Abu Simbel: two rock cut stelae (DB324 and DB325), which depict him greeting the king, two free standing stelae (DB323 and DB326), a statue in a niche (Abu Simbel 1; Porter and Moss VII 1951: 117), and two statues found in the Great Temple, a headless sandstone seated statue found in the entrance to the Second Hall (Porter and Moss VII 1951: 108), and a sandstone kneeling statue (BM EA 1376; Porter and Moss VII 1951: 110) holding a pedestal with a ram's head, part found in the Great Hall and part found in the Second Hall.

A second stela, DB340, of the same King's Son of Kush, depicting the king offering to the gods, may relate to the same incident, though the text is generic. A graffito on the east wall in Room III of the Great Temple (Porter and Moss VII 1951: 96) records the appointment of a Scribe of two King's Sons of Kush by Ramesses II (Černý 1969: 71-75). Černý (1969: 74) argues that the epithet applied to Ramesses II, 'Great God' (*nṯr ꜥꜣ*), indicates that he was dead and that the appointment was by means of an oracle in the form of a statue of the king. This same epithet is applied to the colossal statues of Ramesses II at Qantir.

The location of the stelae may indicate associated stelae/dedicators: the Stablemaster, Iwefenamun, dedicates stela DB332 next to stela DB322 of the King's Son of Kush, Hekanakht, which appears to record a royal visit. Both stelae depict the king making offerings and are therefore commemorative. There may be a similar association of the King's Son of Kush, Mernudjem (DB335), and the Stablemaster, Khons[...] (DB333).

(iii) The King rewards individuals

Stela DB379 (Plate 14) from Qantir has been discussed at length by Habachi (1969a: 29-31) and Uphill (1984: 207). The stela depicts a sequence of events where Ramesses II offers to Ptah before rewarding Mose from a Window of Appearances and, then, Mose and other members of the army before the statue of Ramesses Meryamun, 'Re of the Rulers'. Mose has the title Infantryman (*wꜥw*) of the Great Regiment of Ramesses Meryamun, 'Beloved of Atum', which may refer to one of the other Qantir statues. Ramesses II appears as an intermediary on three further stela from this site: on stela DB393 of the Vizier, Rahotep, to the statue called 'Ruler of Rulers'; and on stelae DB363 of the Standard-bearer of the Lord of the Two Lands in the Regiment 'Re of the Rulers', Any, and DB405 of the Scribe of the Army of the Two Lands, Thutmose, both to the statue 'Montu in the Two Lands'. These four type B stelae are all dedicated by the Vizier or military men to three separate statues of the king; whether they depict a related event is hard to determine. There are 14 stelae in the Qantir/Pi-Ramesses dataset of men who have clearly military titles and who choose to depict a statue of Ramesses II: 12 of them depict 'Montu in the Two Lands', the stela of Mose depicts 'Re of the Rulers', and one depicts an unidentified statue. Unlike at Abu Simbel and Zawiyet Umm el-Rakham, the soldiers may have been stationed at Qantir/Pi-Ramesses on a semi-permanent basis, and may have approached the statue of 'Montu in the Two Lands' on a number of occasions. As noted above, the high number of type A stelae indicate the popular nature of this statue cult. Ramesses II celebrated his numerous Sed-festivals at Pi-Ramesses, but there is no certain way of linking any of the stelae to one of these Sed festivals. The only documentary evidence for the petitioning of the statues is the letter of Pabasa to Amenemope, in Papyrus Anastasi III (Gardiner 1937: 21-23). This papyrus copy was completed in year 3 of Merenptah (Gardiner 1937: XIV), the precise date of the original text predating it by a few years, i.e. it dates to sometime in the reign of Ramesses II (R. Parkinson, *pers. comm.*).

Another Qantir stela utilised as a documentary record is stela DB429. The stela depicts Ramesses III smiting an Asiatic captive before Reshep who offers him the sword. The text below records an award of land to the Shield-bearer of the Mountainous Lands, Usermaatre-Nakht. Habachi (1954: 511) suggests that this man had played an important role in a battle to be so rewarded. The identical stelae DB323 and DB326 from Abu Simbel are similarly documentary, recording a land endowment for a form of Amun for the benefit of the Scribe of the Documents, Hay, son of Seba, in perpetuity (Gauthier 1936: 49-69 and pl. III).

***

The comparative dataset stelae record a number of historical events, both explicitly, through the inclusion of dates and documentary-style texts, and implicitly, through representations and iconography. They can be shown to demonstrate individual status and identity, and even ethnicity, through choice of form and content, and titular rank. The stelae can be located at various places in relation to the central ideology, dependent on the rank and social identity of the dedicator. Ramesses II, the god, is a direct beneficiary of a large proportion of the dedications, in contrast to his more traditional role at Thebes as the intermediary between the people and the gods. As symbolic messages transmitting information regarding the central ideology, the stelae present and disseminate the shift in the ideology to incorporate the explicit concept of Ramesses II as a god. The stelae dedicators shape and maintain the ideology, negotiating for themselves concomitant status by association with the king. Whilst situating themselves centrally within the hierarchical social structure, the King's Son of Kush, Setau in Nubia and Commander, Nebre at Zawiyet Umm el-Rakham become the focus of networks of patronage, a form of local centralised social organisation which mirrors the state structure whilst operating in unconscious opposition to it. The situation of Setau and Nebre is comparable to that of the Senior Scribe, Ramose (i) at Deir el-Medina.

6. VOTIVE STELAE, THE INDIVIDUAL AND SOCIETY

The intention of this book was to shift the focus of the interpretation of votive stelae from a purely 'religious,' or pietistic, reading, towards something more socially-based, contextualising votive stelae as the end result of social practices. These social practices can be defined as public ritual actions or events, whose specificity is often concealed by conventions of representational decorum, and the requirement that the stela function in perpetuity. In order to clarify the motivation for the creation of a stela, it has been necessary to assess a large dataset in search of patterning in intrinsic (iconography, design) and extrinsic (provenance, historical context) data, and has necessitated the exclusion of stelae where such data were lacking. What has resulted is an exploration of the role of votive stelae as social artefacts which, through image, text and materiality, were active agents in transmitting information on individual and group social status and identity, normative social structure, and alternative social organisation.

Votive stelae and social practice

The underlying concept is that votive stelae represent what we might regard as secular social practices, such as promotion at work, which take place within what we might term a 'religious' ritual context - an example of modern categorisation creating obstacles to our understanding of ancient practices. The stelae reflect the dense religious landscape inhabited by the ancient Egyptians (Borghouts 1982b; Baines 2001: 25-27), where everyday activity was embedded within the supernatural: religion or religious expression was a cultural phenomenon (Finnestad 1989a). As apparent representations of approaches to the divine, the stelae do not simply indicate high levels of piety, but indicate that the presence of the divine was the normative context for a variety of social activities.

Once the social and cultural nature of such 'religious' practices and expression has been established, it is possible to look for the social motivation for erecting a stela, though there is little extant social context for these monuments (Baines 2004: 5; see also Demarée 1982 for the lack of ancient references to making stelae at Deir el-Medina). At Deir el-Medina the almost unique existence of complimentary sources of information, such as the administrative record, on the lives of the stelae dedicators, can supply instances of individual and group activity that may have formed the impetus for erecting a stela. The numerous sources of information, and the hundreds of stelae extant from this site established it as the testing ground for the concept of votive stelae as markers of social practices. Applying a biographical framework to the data, drawn from elite autobiographies and possible references to examples of 'rites of passage' concealed in parts of the funerary ritual, as well as events recorded in Theban New Kingdom tomb decoration - tomb decoration seems to have been less subject to representational conventions controlling content, allowing the introduction of innovative themes and imagery - has allowed the reconstruction of a series of significant events that the Ramesside residents of the community experienced and recorded.

All of these sources, and the stelae themselves, are concerned almost solely with the lives of elite adult male individuals. A certain public social status, whether continual or momentary, was necessary in order to access and utilise the public monumental record, thus almost always excluding low-ranking men, women and children. Women and children's lives were played out in a domestic context to which few of the stelae relate. Foxhall (1994: 135-136; see also Foxhall 1995) uses the term 'monumentality' to describe the use of such monuments by adult males in ancient Greece, and the need to be aware of the bias in their ancient utilisation. The female and domestic sphere is rarely marked in this type of record, and we cannot expect to find it here. Stelae do include women, but as sole dedicators they are few in number. When men and women are represented on the same monument, convention dictates that even if the woman is the primary benefactor, the man must precede the woman (see below). In other words, female access to 'monumentality' and 'monumental time' (Foxhall 1994: 135-137) was limited, and female 'rites of passage' were not as publicly marked (Laurence 2000: 444-445). As Foxhall (1994: 135) points out, this should not force the conclusion that women's roles were secondary or unimportant - at Deir el-Medina for long stretches of time the men were absent at work, and women may have run the community.

A number of different social motivations are represented by the stelae, linked by an approach to a divine hypostasis, and the commemoration, or display, of this approach. Representations of straightforward petitioning of a deity occur on stelae that are related to personal crises, illness, and fertility. The stelae representing personal crises and illness are characterised by the inclusion of non-standard texts and representations. The fertility stelae are, in turn, characterised by the high frequency of women and the inclusion of fertility related deities such as Taweret, or the Near Eastern triad of Qadesh, Min(-Amun-Re) and Astarte. The clarity with which these groups of stelae emerge from the dataset gives some encouragement to the argument that stelae can include implicit and/or explicit references to the event or social practice which motivated their production. The fertility, and personal crises and illness stelae, most directly fit the standard interpretation of votive stelae as records and representations of direct petitions to the divine. Their existence in terms of markers of social status, and their role in reaffirming social structure or marking alternative social organisation, is less obvious. Such stelae are situated at the 'personal' end of the use of such monuments, though as public monuments they cannot help but operate on a number of different levels.

Perhaps the most 'secular' stelae are those that record promotion at work, or rewards for the completion of work. The one 'reward' stela from Deir el-Medina (DB175) uses the 'greeting the king' gesture, which also occurs several times at Abu Simbel, and iconographically represents the fact of the dedicator receiving a direct royal message, often of congratulation for work on royal building projects. The three stelae discussed in Section 4.1(iii), which record a visit of the Vizier, To, to Deir el-Medina, iconographically represent the promotion of a foreman to replace his father, as well as, possibly, a number of other promotions. The promotions may have taken place as part of a festival, and were certainly performed in a ritual context before a statue of a deity. The stelae texts are generic, but in this case references to such an event in the administrative record provide both clarification of the formulaic texts, and illumination of what might seem anomalies in the representations. It is possible to propose that stelae with similar content - the inclusion of Ptah and male-only dedicators - may refer to comparable events within the community. Contemporary inhabitants of Deir el-Medina would not have needed specific textual references to interpret the motivating factor behind the erection of such stelae, that is, to understand the event commemorated.

More complex are the stelae that refer to festival attendance and oracles. Such stelae may account for far more of the dataset than has been included in the groups (see Chapter 4), and, in fact, it is possible to argue that all stelae relate in a broad sense to festival activity, as a wide variety of social activity - such as the promotions at Deir el-Medina - may have taken place during a festival. An attempt has been made to relate a number of stelae to state festivals such as the Valley and Opet festivals, and others to local festivals. State festival attendance was clearly a significant event in an individual's life, indicated by the inclusion of representations of Theban festivals in tombs. On one level such stelae record approaches to the divine, but much more overtly they record and display public divine access to state deities, and thus an instance of high social status for the dedicator and anyone included on the stela. Kessler (1999: 186-187) has argued that stelae can represent a group approach to the deity by means of a higher-ranking leader, and, in reverse, the dispersal of divine authority via intermediaries into the community, much in the same way that the Middle Kingdom Abydos stelae allowed access to the divine to individuals setting up stelae in chapels of higher-ranking individuals (Simpson 1974; Chapter 1).

The idea of referencing specific activity within standard iconography can be extended to include the offerings depicted. Certain offerings, or items carried by individuals, such as musical instruments, relate to the celebratory aspect of festivals. The stelae depicting the offering of bouquets, or deity statues depicted with bouquets, are, in this dataset, almost wholly restricted to Thebes, suggesting that such bouquets are linked to one of the great Theban festivals, perhaps the Valley festival. There are relatively few offerings depicted at the comparative sites. At the Nubian sites and at Zawiyet Umm el-Rakham, the lack of offerings suggests that the stelae commemorate official ceremonies rather than individual cult or ritual activity; such ceremonies will have allowed little active, personal participation other than for some of the high-ranking individuals. At these locations the demographic consisted primarily of battalions of soldiers and their military commanders, involved in temple construction and foreign trade control.

Interpreting votive stelae as the end result of social practices opens up a potential source and method for the study of social practices in Egypt, and thus an aspect of social history. Ancient Egyptian social history has received relatively little attention, other than attempts to highlight the possibility of such an approach in the 1970s (Redford 1979) and 1980s (Trigger *et al* 1983), and the writing of general books on 'life in Egypt' which conceal social differences of period, status and location (Meskell 2002: 14). The complexity of everyday life in Egypt, and its continual diachronic shifting, remains largely unexplored due to a perceived lack of relevant or accurate sources.

Votive stelae as records of historical events

If votive stelae are the end result of social practices, it may be that in some instances the social practice to which one or more stelae can be related may be a single historical event. The hypostases and cult foci depicted on stelae are representations of statues, reliefs or ritual paraphernalia extant and in use during the lifetime of the stela dedicator. Of relevance in the dataset are the colossal statues of Ramesses II on the Qantir/Pi-Ramesses stelae. The actual colossal statues have not yet been firmly identified (but see Uphill 1984: 206), but such statues, with the same or similar epithets, are known from elsewhere in the country, and monumental records and related sources refer to their installation and cult use (see Section 5.3). An attempt has been made to link the representations on the stelae to the original hypostases, with limited success due to the often generic nature of the iconography and epithets on the stelae. At Deir el-Medina, and more generally at Thebes, the clearest example of correspondence of the archaeology and the images are the stelae representations of the ram-statues and criosphinxes of Amun-Re (see Section 3.2). According to Cabrol (2001: 237-238), who has discussed the function of the ram-statues and criosphinxes in detail, a group of the ram-statues was moved during the reign of Ramesses II, and it is during this reign that the majority of the ram-statue stelae occur, suggesting that the move or reinstallation of the ram-statues was celebrated in some way, perhaps at a festival, at which a number of the Deir el-Medina residents were present.

A second indicator that a stela depicts a fixed historical event may be the inclusion of the living king, or a high-ranking individual, in an active role. These stelae are the type B stelae, demonstrating use of an intermediary, and are almost exclusively dedicated by high-ranking individuals, and installed at official cult locations. Slightly different is the royal smiting-scene (all type C), which may either depict a ritual in which the king took part, or be a copy of the iconic scene. The numerous examples of the royal smiting scene at Zawiyet Umm el-Rakham may relate to a ceremony carried out by the king himself (Snape and Wilson 2007: 129), where the soldiers associated themselves with the protection of their fort, and the power of the king, by depicting the smiting-scene on their stelae. The stelae themselves would then act as apotropaic devices. However, the royal smiting-scene has symbolic value of its own, and may not relate to a specific instance of royal activity - there is an implication that its use held its own meaning and significance (Müller-Wollerman 1988; Baines 1991) and can be regarded as 'iconographic action' (Wilkinson 2002: 345). This may also be the case for a number of the ritual scenes on the stelae from the Nubian sites, where stelae representations appear to be copies of royal offering scenes from the temples. It may be that, in some cases, the stelae depict the king or his statue - in both cases equivalent to a royal appearance - taking part in ritual activity, that is, an actual royal appearance.

The depiction of the living king on private monuments is a feature of the reign of Ramesses II. The discussion in Chapter 4 suggested two motivating factors with regard to the proliferation of images of the living king on Theban stelae: firstly, that the image of the king can only have been used on private monuments as a result of royal sanction; and secondly, that the appearance of the king, or his statue, on stelae may relate to a series of linked events. The events include the royal inauguration of the Deir el-Medina Hathor temple following its renovation, an offering of flower bouquets at tombs belonging to two high-ranking members of the Deir el-Medina community, and the appearance of Amenhotep I in the palanquin in festival procession. Ramesses II visited Thebes early in his reign to bury his father and take part in the Opet festival. Theban tomb paintings depict festival activity at this period, the scenes in two of which Cabrol (2001: 553) has suggested represent the same Valley festival. The stelae, and the tomb paintings, suggest that a festival of some significance, be it the Valley festival, the Opet festival, and/or a festival connected to Ramesses II's coronation, certainly took place at Thebes early in the king's reign and made a significant impact on the local populace. A number of the stelae depict Ramesses II interacting with, or alongside, the royal ancestors, a theme that is repeated in reliefs from the Khenu-chapel at the Deir el-Medina Hathor temple and in Deir el-Medina tombs. Although impossible to prove, it is tempting to suggest that the sudden proliferation of stelae during the first half of the reign of Ramesses II, many of them thematically linked by representations of the living king and festival iconography such as statues of the deceased ancestors, deities in palanquins and divine barks in procession, bouquets, and afterlife deities, may belong to a single activity, a great royal festival, to establish the new king at Thebes.

A number of stelae make direct reference in their text to historical events, for example, the stelae with dated texts from Wadi es-Sebua and Abu Simbel (see Figure 5.4). The majority of the stelae are not as direct, but instead may refer to historical events by means of iconography. Using private votive stelae as sources for historical events provides an additional source for events occurring at local and national level, and their significance in the lives of non-royal and non-elite individuals. The possibility that Ramesses II took part in a large festival that imprinted itself on the lives of those living in the Theban area at the time, the sanctioning of the use of the royal image by non-royal and non-elite individuals, and the royal association with, and utilisation of, popular cults on the West Bank, evidence for which can be discerned in the stelae, is informative of the ideology of the Ramesside kingship and its need to reestablish the value of the kingship across as broad a demographic as possible (Kitchen 1982b: 178). At the comparative sites, the ideology takes a different form, where Ramesses II is promoted as the recipient of the cult as well as the intermediary between the people and the gods. In both cases, the stelae present and promote an ideology, and negotiate the status of the dedicator in relation to that ideology.

Votive stelae and social and representational conventions

One of the reasons that stelae have been relatively underused as social and historical sources is their apparently generic nature, in both text and representation. The representations are controlled by decorum, a set of conventions defined within the context of temples, and which reiterate the state ideology of the centrality of the kingship (Baines 1985; Introduction). The social and historical approach of this book to votive stelae argues that both the conventions and the content contain information on the intent of the stela and the status and social identity of the dedicator (see Chapter 1). The location in which the stela was originally set up also carries status-related information, and is linked to the compositional form, with stelae dedicated close to official cult centres more closely following conventional decorum in their design and content (Baines 1997: 219).

The type B stelae include an intermediary of higher rank than the dedicator - in some cases, the king. They depict access to the divinity via the intermediary, and can be closely related to actual ritual activity. The depiction of the living king as the intermediary indicates, and implies, that the dedicator is of a certain status. It is also possible that type A and C stelae relate to particular events or rituals given that a large number of the type A stelae depict a lone individual before his god, or superior. The form may indicate the 'professional' nature of the ritual or event. The Senior Scribe, Ramose (i), does not use type A stelae, suggesting that as an aristocratic individual, he did not partake in local, professional rituals at Deir el-Medina. Further analysis of the use of type A and C stelae may yield more specific results. At Abu Simbel, where a large proportion of the stelae are dedicated by high-ranking officials, in particular, a number of King's Sons of Kush, the type A stelae indicate proximity to the king, a variation on direct access to the divine and displaying the relationship of the dedicator to their professional superior.

A number of stelae demonstrate how convention can conceal - from the modern viewer - the intent of the monument. Associated information regarding stela DB188 of Khons (v) (Plate 7), discussed in detail in Section 4.1(iii), makes it clear that the stela commemorates the promotion of Khons (v) to the post of foreman at Deir el-Medina, a post previously held by his father, Nekh(em)mut (i). Conventionally, a father will precede his son on a stela, his seniority awarding him the higher social, and, by extension, representational, status. However, on stela DB188, Khons (v) precedes his father, Nekh(em)mut (i), as a mark of his newly acquired higher professional, and therefore social, status. On stela DB33 of Irynefer (i), his wife, Mehykhati (ii), depicted in the second register, offers incense. Incense is almost invariably offered by the primary dedicator, who is usually a man. Convention precluded Mehykhati (ii) from preceding her husband on the stela, but her role as primary dedicator is marked by the offering she is shown making, allowing her indirect access to monumentality. Further analysis of gestures, postures and iconographic content may be revealing regarding the intent of votive stelae (see Wilkinson 2002: 345-346). The oblique nature of votive stelae representations is illustrated by stela BM EA 555 (Plate 11b). This stela, from Deir el-Medina, was initially regarded as more overtly funerary than votive, though this may not be the case, and as a result has not been included in the dataset. The stela depicts the Workman, Khabekhenet (i) adoring the Hathor cow emerging from the mountain with a statue named *P3-rḫ-nw*, in the place of the expected royal statue, before it. Zivie (2003: 75) suggests that the statue represents the Overseer of the Treasury, Netjry-Mes *P3-rḫ-nw*, buried at Saqqara in tomb Bubasteion I.16. The tomb includes references to the workmen of the Place of Truth - Deir el-Medina. Zivie argues that Theban workmen were involved with the decoration of this tomb, and that Khabekhenet (i) references, with the stela depiction, his involvement in the carving of the Hathor cow and royal statue in the Saqqara tomb.

The compositional form a stela takes is influenced by its original location. State cult centres exerted fields of influence with regard to the form of private monuments, which display stricter adherence to the accepted decorum the closer they are to the sacred space. This relates to the status of the individual, with access to such sacred spaces only available to individuals of a certain rank. The dissemination of the central ideology by means of representations can be seen as focused and controlled at major centres such as Thebes, and loosening with the greater distance from such centres. Individuals may have chosen to use monuments displaying strict adherence to convention at a distance from the influential centres in order to display their personal proximity to the state ideology, and thus their own social status. At Deir el-Medina, Ramose (i) chose the more traditional type C stelae, as did the King's Son of Kush, Setau in Nubia. Monuments of influential individuals themselves acted as the centre of fields of influence. This is clear at Abu Simbel where 'copy' stelae are carved next to stelae of higher ranking individuals (see Section 5.4). At Deir el-Medina, Ramose (i)'s numerous monuments discovered in the Khenu-chapel (Davies 1999: 80, n. 38) indicate that this structure may have been the focus for cult attention for the community, via Ramose (i). The same situation is apparent at Wadi es-Sebua, where Setau set up stelae in the courtyard of the Ramesses II temple, and was included as the beneficiary on a number of other stelae. The two unpublished stelae of the Commander, Nebre, at Zawiyet Umm el-Rakham indicate a similar situation: the stelae were discovered in the chapel next to the small temple, with a naos and his standard-bearer statue.

The use of text and image to make a statement regarding divine access has comparisons in other semi-literate societies. During the Middle Ages in Europe, text provided direct access to God for literate individuals; indirect access was possible via images which served as mediators between this world and the supernatural (Moreland 2001: 46-47). By the end of the 15th century CE, images had acquired efficacy in their own right, allowing individuals direct access to the divine (Moreland 2001: 50-51). The votive stelae represent adoration of deity statues, reliefs or icons, the mediated form of the deity to which private individuals had access. The representation of the images on stelae not only recorded the instance of divine access, but perpetuated it, and became the focus of ongoing ritual attention, providing another level of mediated access.

Votive stelae, social status and identity

Votive stelae, through image, text and materiality, are active agents in transmitting information on individual, and group, social status and identity. The previous section outlined how representational conventions, or traditional forms, can be used to demonstrate affiliation to the central ideology, and a claim to authority (Baines 1994b), from which an individual may further benefit. This is an example of Woolf's 'partial remedy to the problem of how to surpass and conform at the same time' (1996: 32; see Chapter 1), in a society where the level of conformity rather than difference indicated status, and was the manner in which identity, be it individual or group, was stressed. The stelae also define and structure aspects of social identity such as masculinity, presenting the acceptable norms for public male activity. By means of conventional form and iconography, and the social practices which they record, votive stelae continually created and recreated accepted social structure, both at a local and state level. They were part of the practice and the memory of their society. Rather than being reflective of externally imposed structure, but actively constituting it, they were open to manipulation at an individual level, providing examples of agency and identity. The votive stelae display two forms of ideological, or structural, manipulation, one intentional, and one perhaps not.

The latter, possibly unintentional, ideological manipulation, or unintended consequence (Giddens 1984: 10), was the proliferation of representations of individuals directly accessing a deity hypostasis. Whilst such representations may have been conventionally acceptable by the Ramesside Period, numerous accessible images of individuals directly approaching deities that did not include a representation of the traditional role of the king as intermediary may have created an 'alternative' ideology that bypassed the necessity of the king. The aristocratic Senior Scribe, Ramose (i)'s choice of the more 'traditional' type C, indirect access, form, for 18 of his 21 stelae in the dataset, may have been intended to display his social status by their knowledge of, and apparent support of the conventions related to the central ideology, but the stelae also displayed him in the presence of the deity many times over without the king's presence. As an aristocratic individual, such stelae, and the sheer number of them, will have been influential on the local community.

Royal control of expressions of personal piety had been felt to be necessary in the 18th Dynasty, when official chapels were constructed for private approaches to the deity (Pinch 1993: 357-358; 360). The almost unprecedented appearance of Ramesses II on votive stelae of non-elite individuals at Deir el-Medina, and at Pi-Ramesses (for example, stela DB379 of the Infantryman, Mose), may constitute an alternative remedy for the situation. Ramesses II certainly seems to have understood the power of images, and the necessity, following the collapse of the 18th Dynasty, of maintaining a high visibility kingship. The stelae relating to a visit of Ramesses II to the Hathor temple (Section 4.1(i)) and the oracular/festival stelae dating to Ramesses II (Section 4.1(ii)) are linked by the relatively frequent depictions of the reigning king. Royal representations of kings on private stelae are known from the 18th Dynasty (see e.g. Schulman 1988), and there is a 17th Dynasty example from Abydos (Clère 1982; Plate 1b), but these are restricted to very high-ranking individuals. The use of the image of the reigning king by the Deir el-Medina royal workmen, and the soldier at Pi-Ramesses, reflects a royally sanctioned change in decorum; it is not an example of appropriation or democratisation. Ramesses II may have officially sanctioned the use of his image, by certain groups of people, to support and disseminate the kingship, and his own cult, by means of increased numbers of accessible images of himself.

Intentional manipulation of the conventions for personal benefit is evident in the prominence of Ramose (i) at Deir el-Medina, Setau at Wadi es-Sebua and Nebre at Zawiyet Umm el-Rakham. The monuments of these individuals, and those of their contemporaries are an example of social organisation and the utilisation of official methods and conventions to express local elite hierarchies. In the New Kingdom, the office of the king was promoted as central to society in the form of statue cults and intermediaries (Pinch 1993: 357; Moftah 1985: 256-264). An offshoot of this situation was that those individuals who chose to promote the royal office became socially prestigious in an unprecedented way. The role of Ramose (i) as the centre of a network of social organisation centring on the Hathor temple and Khenu-chapel, and the cult of Hathor and Ramesses II, has been discussed in Section 4.1(i). Ramose (i)'s aristocratic background, his promotion of Ramesses II's cult, and the installation of his own personal Hathor cult, gave him unprecedented social prestige within the Deir el-Medina community. The individuals that dedicate stelae to the Hathor cult during Ramose (i)'s time in post, and demonstrate their relationship to Ramose (i) by including him, and Ramose (i)'s superior colleague, the Vizier, Paser, in their tombs and on their monuments, form what can be termed a 'patronage group', a group of individuals who would benefit both materially, socially and spiritually from association with Ramose (i). Social organisation is based on networks of contacts, and social status is marked by attendance at status-defining events, as well as association with higher-ranking individuals with whom an individual could display a relationship. In turn, Ramose (i) benefited in a similar fashion by inclusion on monuments of others, confirming his place in the monumental record, and his central position in the community.

At Wadi es-Sebua, Setau is included as an intermediary and/or beneficiary of the offering formula on 10 out of the 12 stelae from the Ramesses II temple (see Section 5.3). The inclusion of the offering formula makes a direct statement with regard to the role of Setau, placing him in the same category of beneficiary as the king. At this distance from the state centres of Pi-Ramesses and Thebes, Setau took the opportunity to confirm and perpetuate monumentally the role he may have played in actuality, as the leader of, and material provider for, the troops in his command. At Zawiyet Umm el-Rakham, one of the two stelae found with his standard-bearer statue depicts a man who may be Nebre (figure erased) offering to Sekhmet whilst a second man kneels below. This stela is similar in format to stela DB432 of the Royal Scribe and Great Chief of the Army, Panehsy, where Ramesses II offers to Sekhmet whilst Panehsy kneels below. The Sekhmet stela of Nebre, if it is him, appears to support Snape's argument (2001: 19) that Nebre adopted royal prerogatives, appearing on stelae in the intermediary role more usually taken by the king, setting up an 'alternate' ideology, and that it was this bold move that caused his name to be erased from the monuments. However, officials acting as intermediaries were a phenomenon of the Ramesside Period, particularly in the reign of Ramesses II (Pamminger 1996: 299). The phenomenon is well-illustrated by the monuments of the Vizier, Paser (Pamminger 1996: 288-290) and the King's Son of Kush, Setau (Pamminger 1996: 296-297; Raedler 2003: 157-163). At Wadi es-Sebua, Setau mediates for military standard-bearers, as Nebre does at Zawiyet Umm el-Rakham. It is open to question whether Nebre's adoption of such a role contributed to a fall from grace, evidenced by the erasure of his name from the monuments, or whether the erasure was perhaps connected to his replacement by a new commander (G. Godenho, *pers. comm.*).

Raedler (2003) employs what she calls network theory ('Theoreme der Netzwerktheorie') in her interpretation of Setau's monuments, which interprets the social networks of an individual in terms of social relationships and interaction, and can also throw light on the structure of power and rulership ('Gesellschaft') within the Egyptian elite (Raedler 2003: 129). She constructs charts depicting the social networks in which Setau played the central role at Wadi es-Sebua (2003: 158, fig. 12) and at other sites where he was active (2003: 163, fig. 15). Instead of a strict vertical hierarchy with the king at the top, and individuals ranked at specified levels below him, some parts of society were organised in groups clustering around community leaders who set up local imitations of the centralised social structure. Setau's central role in a group of individuals' lives is similar to that played by the Senior Scribe, Ramose (i), at Deir el-Medina, whose intermediary role has been noted by Pamminger (1996: 298).

The high status of Ramose (i), Setau and Nebre is also manifested in the monumental record by the large number of monuments dedicated by them, or on their behalf, or simply including them. Raedler (2003: 130-131) lists 100 belonging to Setau, where other king's sons of Kush in the early Ramesside Period (eight), have 62 between them. This compares to the large number of monuments belonging to Ramose (i) at Deir el-Medina (Černý 1973: 317-327; Davies 1999: 77-83), and the Commander Nebre at Zawiyet Umm el-Rakham. Setau's monuments include private chapels at Elkab, Qasr Ibrim and Faras, the large double stela at Abu Simbel and his tomb at Dra Abu el-Naga, Thebes (TT288/289), a burial location more usually restricted to the royal family during the reign of Ramesses II (Raedler 2003: 150-151). It has been noted that it is at Wadi es-Sebua, of all the comparative sites, that we find the largest repertoire of deities. This is not because there was a flourishing group of popular cults at this distant Nubian locale - the three stelae from the Amenhotep III temple are the only evidence for popular worship here. Rather, the stelae record and display the King's Son of Kush, Setau's full access to the temple deities and the integral part he played in building the temple. The stelae of the Senior Scribe, Ramose (i), at Deir el-Medina, also include a broad repertoire of deities. This display of 'divine access' by Setau and Ramose (i) indicates their high socio-political status.

In contrast to Ramose (i) at Deir el-Medina, Setau at Wadi es-Sebua and Nebre at Zawiyet Umm el-Rakham, a locally stationed official developing a central role in local cult activity is not evident in the record at Abu Simbel or Pi-Ramesses. At Abu Simbel only the King's Son of Kush, Paser II, leaves more than one monument, and no individuals dedicate stelae for the benefit of any living individual other than the king. In her study of the social relationships developed by Setau at the places he lived and worked, Raedler omits Abu Simbel as there is no evidence that Setau exerted, or displayed, such influence here (Raedler 2003: 163). Abu Simbel is an official cult and administrative centre, and, in this, comparable to Pi-Ramesses, the capital city. Such centres would not allow a private individual to develop a central role in cult activity; at these two sites it was the king who was the primary beneficiary of the monuments.

The representative nature of the Deir el-Medina stelae

Deir el-Medina provides the core dataset for the analysis of stelae as social and historical documents. The utilisation of material from Deir el-Medina as representative of New Kingdom Egypt has been called into question due to the specialised nature of the community (royal craftsmen and their families), and the proposed high rate of literacy. Such a demographic cannot have been typical for many communities, but it is nonetheless a New Kingdom community of a kind, and representative of literate, skilled individuals and their families, their lives and expectations. With such caveats in place, the material from Deir el-Medina can be clearly assessed.

There are aspects of the Deir el-Medina stelae that are clearly unrepresentative of stelae utilisation in the Ramesside Period: the sheer number, the number that a single individual dedicates (which may suggest that the stelae were less valued at Deir el-Medina, being more easily available), and the generally high quality. In addition, in terms of content, the stelae represent a broad spectrum of deities, and indicate relatively high levels of access to state festivals, and royal ceremonies. These factors can be linked to the nature of the community, in its role of royal tomb-builders, and its residents' skills as sculptors and painters. The difference between Deir el-Medina and Thebes more generally, and between Deir el-Medina and the comparative sites, is in the nature of the community, not the function or nature of the stelae: they all function as records of social practices and events.

The Deir el-Medina material is comparable to that from Pi-Ramesses in terms of the types of cults represented, as well as, to a certain extent, the demographic of the dedicators. Both sites are settlement sites of a fairly long duration, with stelae dedicated by non-elite individuals, and women, as well as individuals with elite connections. The stelae refer to popular cults, rather than simply attendance at official events connected to the state cults, which is the case for the other sites. The stelae from Wadi es-Sebua and Zawiyet Umm el-Rakham represent military communities resident for short periods of time. The stelae from Abu Simbel form a separate group, representing high-ranking officials and a number of priests, and dedicated over a fairly long period of time, rather than a homogenous community or group. Given the official nature of the Abu Simbel site, it is not unexpected that the stelae are informative on social structure, and not social organisation.

The analysis of the Deir el-Medina stelae brought to light a number of characteristics that are typical of the dataset as a whole:

- the proliferation of stelae dating to the reign of Ramesses II, and in particular to the first half of the reign;
- the frequent use of type A, direct access, stelae for local professional events;
- the use of type B, or intermediary, stelae, to indicate presence at an official ceremony;
- the existence of patronage groups centred on a local leader.

The sheer number of stelae at Deir el-Medina serves to conceal the motivation behind the commissioning of many of them. The analysis of the core dataset of 264 stelae has suggested a motivation for 102 (= 39%; see Chapter 4). Broadly speaking, all of the stelae record some kind of social practice that may have taken place in a festival context, but the specific practice or event can be harder to discern. The Theban stelae (55), provided a less cohesive group. 40 (= 73%) have been discussed in more detail, with the suggestion that the majority of them relate to an aspect of state festivals. In the light of the Deir el-Medina analysis, the stelae from the comparative sites have been linked to popular approaches to official hypostases (Pi-Ramesses) or attendance at official ceremonies (Abu Simbel, Wadi es-Sebua and Zawiyet Umm el-Rakham). The Pi-Ramesses stelae are as generic in appearance and content as many of the Deir el-Medina stelae, giving little clue to the motivating occasion, and the lack of data from other sources makes establishing fixed historical events behind their commissioning extremely difficult. Further analysis of offerings and dress may be fruitful with regard to these stelae and the outstanding Deir el-Medina stelae. What can be said for certain is that the stelae do not simply represent a relationship, in the abstract sense, of an individual with a deity, but are a record of social practices taking the form of 'divine access', recorded for perpetuity.

***

This book undertook to establish the reasons why an individual would utilise a votive stela - to discover the event, or story, behind the monument. Interpreting the stelae as the end result of social practices implies that they are, on one level, historical documents - they must relate to an event, and, on another level, that they encapsulate an individual's ideal social identity in terms of social status - the level and form of divine access displayed. The stelae have been discussed as an example of material culture actively creating social structure, and alternative social organisations, both intentionally and unintentionally. The manipulation occurs on a number of levels: Ramesses II promotes the centrality of the kingship, in the traditional role as intermediary to the deity, and as the deity itself; high-ranking individuals utilise stelae for self-promotion; and lower-ranking individuals present themselves in relation to a deity, a local high-ranking individual and, on occasion, the king, to accrue spiritual, social and economic benefits by such an association - again, self-promotion. All of these uses manipulate accepted conventions for the stela dedicator's benefit, presenting a constantly shifting interpretation, by means of iconography, of tradition and ideology, or social structure and organisation.

The study reveals that votive stelae offer a relatively untapped source of social and historical information, and a viewpoint other than the official/royal monumental record, for the writing of a social history of Egypt. The social networks evident in Ramesside Egypt reveal the existence of the cults of private individuals, a form of social organisation at local level that may have had a long history, and certainly evolved into later cults of individuals (see, for example, Jelínková-Reymond 1956). The stelae also offer a window into the lives of private individuals, marking their aspirations and achievements. The monuments of the people of ancient Egypt have much yet to tell us.

APPENDIX 1 THE VOTIVE STELAE

The stelae are arranged chronologically and alphabetically according to the name of the principal dedicator.

Table 1 The Deir el-Medina Votive Stelae (264)

Database no.	Owner	Title	Date	Dedicated to	Brief description*	Representational form	Offerings by the dedicator	Find location	Current location	Repository number	Porter and Moss	Primary publication details
1	Piay (ii) and Pay (i)	Piay: Sculptor in the Place of Eternity; Pay: Sculptor of Amun	18th Dynasty: Horemheb - 19th Dynasty: Seti I	Khonsu-em-Waset Neferhotep and Thoth	Offering to deities (oracle)	A	Incense, bouquet and loaded offering table	Unknown	Kingston Lacy, Bankes Collection	8	Porter and Moss I.2 1964: 733	Černý 1958: no. 8
2	Wennefer (i)	Workman in the Place of Truth	18th Dynasty: Horemheb - 19th Dynasty: Seti I	Soped	Offering to deity (ears)	A	Incense, water (offered by women) and offering stand	Unknown	Turin, Museo Egizio	1543	Porter and Moss I.2 1964: 735	Tosi Roccati 1972: 86, 282 [50051]; Morgan 2004: 120-121
3	Pay (i) (?)	Draughtsman in the Place of Truth	18th Dynasty: Horemheb - 19th Dynasty: Ramesses II, first half	Haroeris	Dedicator in text only	C	Offering stand	Unknown	London, The British Museum	373	Porter and Moss I.2 1964: 731	James 1970: 56, pl. XLIV
4	Pay (i)	Draughtsman of Amun	18th Dynasty: Horemheb - 19th Dynasty: Ramesses II, first half	Khonsu-em-Waset Neferhotep	Offering to deity (ears and eyes; oracle)	A	Incense, bouquet and loaded offering table	Unknown	Turin, Museo Egizio	1553	Porter and Moss I.2 1964: 731	Tosi Roccati 1972: 87-88, 283 [50052]; Morgan 2004: 124-126
5	Amenemope	Servitor of Amun	18th Dynasty (end) or 19th Dynasty	Amun-Re and Seth	Offering to deity	C	Incense, bouquet and loaded offering table	Hathor Temple: Northern Sector: North East Corner of the Ptolemaic Precinct of the Temple			Porter and Moss I.2 1964: 715	Bruyère 1935-1940 (1952) II: 115, fig. 195, pls. XVIII, XX (fig. 195) [271]
6	Smen (?)	No title	18th Dynasty or 19th Dynasty	Re-Harakhti	Dedicator in text only	C		Unknown	Turin, Museo Egizio	1648	Porter and Moss I.2 1964: 736	Tosi Roccati 1972: 58-59, 270 [50025]
7	Khons (i)	Sculptor	19th Dynasty: Ramesse I	Mertseger	Dedicator in text only	C	Offering stand	Unknown (acquired in Cairo, April 1929)	Paris, Musée du Louvre	E. 13935	Porter and Moss I.2 1964: 725	Bruyère 1930b: 123, fig. 63; Kitchen, RITA III, p. 456

8	[Siwadjet (i) (?)]	[Ship's Commander of Amun and Servitor of Amun]	19th Dynasty: Ramesses I - Seti I	Min, Isis, Reshep and Anat (?)	Offering to deities	C	Incense and festival offerings	Ramesseum area	Cambridge, The Fitzwilliam Museum	E9.1896	Porter and Moss I.2 1964: 682	Quibell 1898: 16 [4], pl. XIII [3, 4]; Martin 2005: 113-115 [78]
9	Amenemope (i) (?)	Workman in the Place of Truth	19th Dynasty: Seti I - Ramesses II, first half (?)	Amenhotep I and Queen Ahmes Nefertari	Adoring deities (reverse: painted figure of the Vizier, Hori)	C		Unknown	Turin, Museo Egizio	1452	Porter and Moss I.2 1964: 715	Tosi Roccati 1972: 67-68, 274 [50034]
10	Amenmose (iii)	Workman in the Place of Truth	19th Dynasty: Seti I - Ramesses II, first half	Taweret, Nekhbet and Hathor	Adoring and offering to deities (festival)	A	Water (offered by women), lotus flowers and loaded offering table	Unknown	London, The British Museum	1388	Porter and Moss I.2 1964: 716	Bierbrier 1982b: 32-33, pl. 76
11	Baki (i)	Foreman in the Place of Truth	19th Dynasty: Seti I	Ptah and Hathor		A	Bouquet and offering stand	Unknown	London, The British Museum	265	Porter and Moss I.2 1964: 717	James 1970: 40-41, pl. 35: 2
12	Baki (i)	Foreman in the Place of Truth	19th Dynasty: Seti I	Amun-Re (ram)	Adoring deity (festival)	C	Bouquet	Unknown	Turin, Museo Egizio	1549	Porter and Moss I.2 1964: 717	Tosi Roccati 1972: 90-91, 285 [50055]
13	Bukhanefptah (i) (f.)	Lady of the House	19th Dynasty: Seti I - Ramesses II, first half	Nebethetepet (Hathor)	Adoring deity (festival)	A	ival rings, ouquet and loaded offering table	Unknown	Kingston Lacy, Bankes Collection	7	Porter and Moss I.2 1964: 717	Černý 1958: no. 7; Kitchen 2000: 554-555
14	Huy (ii)	Workman in the Place of Truth	19th Dynasty: Seti I - Ramesses II, first half	Amun-Re, Mut and a female deity	Offering to deities	A	Incense, lotus flowers and bouquet	Unknown	Kingston Lacy, Bankes Collection	2	Porter and Moss I.2 1964: 720	Černý 1958: no. 2
15	Neferronpet (i)	Workman in the Place of Truth	19th Dynasty: Seti I - Ramesses II, first half	Hathor	Adoring deity (festival)	A	Offering stand	Hathor Temple: Northern Sector: North East Corner of the Ptolemaic Precinct of the Temple			Porter and Moss I.2 1964: 729	Bruyère 1935-1940 (1952) II: 122-123, pl. XLIV [285]
16	Neferronpet (i) (?)	Workman in the Place of Truth	19th Dynasty: Seti I - Ramesses II, first half	Re-Harakhti	Offering to deity	A	Incense, water (carried by women), festival offerings and offering stand	Unknown	Copenhagen, The National Museum of Denmark	B.6 (A.A.d.8)	Porter and Moss I.2 1964: 728	Mogensen 1918: 22-23, pl. XV [22]

17	Neferronpet (i) and Huy (ii)	Workman in the Place of Truth	19th Dynasty: Seti I - Ramesses II, first half	Amun-Re (ram), Taweret and Seth	Offering to deities (festival)	A	Incense, festival offerings and offering stand	Unknown	Turin, Museo Egizio	1514	Porter and Moss I.2 1964: 729	Tosi Roccati 1972: 93-94, 286 [50057]
18	Pashedu (i)	Workman in the Place of Truth	19th Dynasty: Seti I	Harmachis, two female deities and Ptah; Hathor	Adoring deities	A	Offering stand	Western Cemetery: TT292	Turin, Museo Egizio	Supp. 6155	Porter and Moss I.1 1960: 375	Tosi Rocatti 1972: 120-121, 298 [50082]
19	Pashedu (i)	Workman in the Place of Truth	19th Dynasty: Seti I	Ptah	Offering to deity	A	Incense and double offering stand	Unknown	London, The British Museum	262	Porter and Moss I.2 1964: 733	James 1970: 40, pl. XXXV
20	Pashedu (vii)	Chief Draughtsman in the Place of Truth	19th Dynasty: Seti I	Amun-Re (ram)	Adoring deity (festival)	A	Loaded offering table	Unknown	Leningrad (St Petersburg), The State Hermitage Museum	8726	Porter and Moss I.2 1964: 732-733	Bogoslovsky 1972/1: 96-103, pl.2
21	Pashedu (vii)	Draughtsman of Amun	19th Dynasty: Seti I	Osiris; Anubis	Royal (Ramesses II and Vizier, Paser) mediating scene	B	Bouquet and offering stand	Western Cemetery: TT323			Porter and Moss I.1 1960: 395	Bruyere 1923-1924 (1925): 86, fig. 15
22	Amenemhab (vi)	Workman in the Place of Truth	19th Dynasty: Ramesses II, first half	Amun-Re, Mut and Khonsu	Festival procession - divine barks (oracle)	C	Water (offered by a woman) and loaded offering table	Unknown	Cambridge, The Fitzwilliam Museum	E. SS.52	Porter and Moss I.2 1964: 715	Martin 2005: 68-70 [44]; Kitchen 2000: 476
23	Amennakht (xi)	Workman in the Place of Truth	19th Dynasty: Ramesses II, first half	The Great Peak of the West (Mertseger); Isis	Adoring deities - four serpent heads in high raised relief	C		Queens' Valley Chapels: Finds (?)	Turin, Museo Egizio	1521	Porter and Moss I.2 1964: 709	Tosi Roccati 1972: 96-97, 287 [50059]; Kitchen 2000: 479
24	Amennakhte (xxi)	Workman in the Place of Truth	19th Dynasty: Ramesses II, first half	Ptah	Offering to deity	A	Incense, bouquet and loaded offering table	Unknown (purchased at Dra Abu el-Naga)	Strasbourg, Université Institut d'Égyptologie	206	Porter and Moss I.2 1964: 724	Spiegelberg and Pörtner 1902: 19, pl. XIX [33]; Kitchen 2000: 548
25	Bennakht	Servitor of Mut	19th Dynasty: Ramesses II, first half (?)	Unidentified deity, Mut	Adoring deities	A	Lost	Unknown	Turin, Museo Egizio	Supp. 6169	Porter and Moss I.2 1964: 738	Tosi Roccati 1972: 144, 316 [50135]; Kitchen 2000: 472
26	Horemwia (i)	Workman in the Place of Truth	19th Dynasty: Ramesses II, first half	Ptah	Adoring deity	A		Hathor Temple: Inside Ptolemaic Temple Precinct: Excavations in South West Part Baraize, 1912	Cairo, The Egyptian Museum	JdE 43565	Porter and Moss I.2 1964: 698	Bruyère 1923-1924 (1925): 78, pl. 1 [1]; Kitchen 2000: 533

27	Huy; Smentawy (i) (?)	Huy: Workman of Amun; Smentawy: Wab-priest, Deputy [wab-priest]	19th Dynasty: Ramesses II, first half	Ahmose, Amenhotep I and Queen Ahmes Nefertari	Adoring deities (festival)	C	Offering stand	Unknown	Cairo, The Egyptian Museum	34037	Porter and Moss I.2 1964: 800	Lacau 1909: 70-72, pl. XXIV; Redford 1986: 49 [17]
28	Huy (iv)	Workman in the Place of Truth	19th Dynasty: Ramesses II, first half	Hathor	Royal (Ramesses II) mediating scene (festival)	B	Incense, bouquet and loaded offering table	Unknown	Turin, Museo Egizio	1463	Porter and Moss I.2 1964: 720	Tosi Roccati 1972: 62-63, 272 [50030]; Kitchen 2000: 529
29	Huy (iv)	Workman in the Place of Truth	19th Dynasty: Ramesses II, first half	Qadesh, Reshep and Min-Amen-Re	Adoring deities	C		Unknown	Paris, Musée du Louvre	C. 86	Porter and Moss I.2 1964: 719-720	Andreu 2002: 266-267 [215]; Kitchen 2000: 530-531
30	Ipuy (i)	[Sculptor] in the Place of Truth	19th Dynasty: Ramesses II, first half	Osiris	Offering to deity	A	Incense, water (offered by women) and offering stand	Western Cemetery: TT217	Zagreb, Arkeoloski Muzej	575 (now 15)	Porter and Moss I.2 1964: 721	Saleh 1970: 31 [15]; Kitchen 2000: 450
31	Irynefer (i)	Workman in the Place of Truth	19th Dynasty: Ramesses II, first half	Ptah	Adoring deity	A	Loaded offering table	Unknown	London, The Petrie Museum of Egyptian Archaeology	UC 14545	Porter and Moss I.2 1964: 722	Stewart 1976: 36, pl. 29.2; Kitchen 2000: 483
32	Irynefer (i)	Workman in the Place of Truth	19th Dynasty: Ramesses II, first half	Hathor	Offering to deity (festival)	A	Incense, bouquet and loaded offering table	Unknown	London, The British Museum	814	Porter and Moss I.2 1964: 722	Bierbrier 1993: 14-15, pls. 36-37; Kitchen 2000: 483
33	Irynefer (i)	Workman in the Place of Truth	19th Dynasty: Ramesses II, first half	Taweret	Adoring and offering to deity	C	Incense (offered by the woman), bouquet and loaded offering table	Unknown	London, The British Museum	284	Porter and Moss I.2 1964: 722	Bierbrier 1993: 13, pls. 36-37; Kitchen 2000: 482-483
34	Khabekhenet (i)	Workman in the Place of Truth	19th Dynasty: Ramesses II, first half	Queen Ahmes Nefertari	Adoring cartouches of Ramesses II (house stela)	A		Village: House S.O.V.			Porter and Moss I.2 1964: 703	Bruyère 1934-1935 (1939) III: 69 [top], 208, 325, 326, 329 [12, 13], figs. 196-197, 200
35	Khabekhenet (i)	Workman in the Place of Truth	19th Dynasty: Ramesses II, first half	Osiris (?); Ptah, another deity	Adoring deities	A		Unknown	Formerly Rustafjaell Collection.		Porter and Moss I.2 1964: 724	Sotheby Sale Catalogue, Dec. 19-21, 1906: pl. X [22], no. 404 (4th item)

36	Khaemwaset (i)	Workman in the Place of Truth	19th Dynasty: Ramesses II, first half	Amun-Re	Adoring deity	A		Hathor Temple: Inside Ptolemaic Temple Precinct: Excavations in South West Part by Baraize, 1912	Cairo, The Egyptian Museum	JdE 43564	Porter and Moss I.2 1964:. 698	Bruyère 1923-1924 (1925): 80-81, pl.1[2]; Kitchen 2000: 491-492
37	Kasa (i)	Workman in the Place of Truth	19th Dynasty: Ramesses II, first half	Hathor	Offering to deity	C	Water (offered by a woman), lotus flowers, festival offerings and bouquet	Unknown	London, The British Museum	369	Porter and Moss I.2 1964: 723	James 1970: 43-44, pl. XXXVII; Kitchen 2000: 555
38	Karo/Kel (i)	Workman in the Place of Truth	19th Dynasty: Ramesses II, first half	Goddess	Lost	A	Water (offered by women), festival offerings and offering stand	Unknown	London, The British Museum	818	Porter and Moss I.2 1964: 723	James 1970: 49-50, pl. XL; Kitchen 2000: 553
39	Karo/Kel (i)	Workman in the Place of Truth	19th Dynasty: Ramesses II, first half	Ptah	Royal (queen) mediating scene	B		Unknown	London, The British Museum	328	Porter and Moss I.2 1964: 723	James 1970: 48-49, pl. XL; Kitchen 2000: 552-553
40	Khawy (ii)	Guardian in the Place of Truth	19th Dynasty: Ramesses II, first half	Hathor	Royal (Ramesses II and Vizier, Paser) mediating scene (festival)	B		Hathor Temple: Khenu-chapel: Room 2	Cairo, The Egyptian Museum	JdE 72021	Porter and Moss I.2 1964: 697	Bruyère 1935-1940 (1952) II: 37, 77-78, pls. X, XXXVII, fig. 157 [63]; Kitchen 2000: 470
41	Khons (ii)	Workman in the Place of Truth	19th Dynasty: Ramesses II, first half	Mertseger and Mertseger-Renenut	Adoring deities	A	Offering stand	Hathor Temple: Sector 4 (interior of the Ptolemaic Temple): Hypostyle Hall			Porter and Moss I.2 1964: 725	Bruyère 1935-1940 (1952) II: 101, pls. XVI, XVIII (fig. 172) [227]
42	[Maani]nakhtuf (i)	[Draughtsman in the Place of Truth]	19th Dynasty: Ramesses II, first half	Amenhotep I and Queen Ahmes Nefertari	Adoring deities	B	Offering stand	Western Cemetery: Chapel 1190	Paris, Musée du Louvre	E. 13989	Porter and Moss I.2 1964: 689	Bruyère 1929 (1930a) II: 39-40 [1], pl. IX
43	Maaninakhtuf (i)	Workman in the Place of Truth, Scribe of Amun	19th Dynasty: Ramesses II, first half	Ptah and Maat	Adoring deities	A	Offering stand	Unknown	London, The British Museum	269	Porter and Moss I.2 1964: 725	Bierbrier 1993: 11-12, pls. 30-31; Kitchen 2000: 443

44	Maaninakhtuf (i)	Draughtsman in the Place of Truth	19th Dynasty: Ramesses II, first half	Iah-Thoth	Adoring deity	C		Unknown	Hanover, Kestner Museum	2937	Porter and Moss I.2 1964: 725	Cramer 1936: 95-96, pl. VII [4]; Kitchen 2000: 442
45	Mery[sekhmet] (i)	Draughtsman	19th Dynasty: Ramesses II, first half	Mertseger	Adoring deity	A	Offering stand	Unknown	Berlin, Ägyptisches Museum und Papyrussammlung, Staatliche Museen zu Berlin-SPK	24029	Porter and Moss I.2 1964: 725	Bruyère 1930b: 99, fig. 42.
46	Mutnofert (iv) (f.), Iyn[nofre]ti (i) (f.)	No titles	19th Dynasty: Ramesses II, first half - mid	Renenut	Adoring deity	A	Bouquet and offering stand	Unknown	Turin, Museo Egizio	Supp. 6138	Porter and Moss I.2 1964: 726	Tosi Roccati 1972: 69, 274 [50035]
47	Nakhtamun (iii)	Draughtsman in the Place of Truth	19th Dynasty: Ramesses II, first half	Mertseger	Adoring deity	C	Offering stand	Unknown	Paris, Musée du Louvre	N 4194	Porter and Moss I.2 1964: 729	Andreu 2002: 151 [94]; Kitchen 2000: 447
48	Nakhy (iii)	Chief Craftsman in the Place of Truth	19th Dynasty: Ramesses II, first half	Harsiesi	Offering to deity	A	Incense and offering stand	Unknown	Stockholm, Medelhavsmuseet	NME 28 (=32,000)	Porter and Moss I.2 1964: 726	Bruyère 1928 (1929) II: 17 [2] (description only); Kitchen 2000: 464-465
49	Nebamentet (i)	Workman in the Place of Truth	19th Dynasty: Ramesses II, first half - mid	Thenent (?), Montu and Ratawy	Adoring and offering to deities	C	Water (offered by women), festival offerings	Unknown	Voronezh, Archaeological Museum of Voronezh State University	157	Porter and Moss I.2 1964: 726	Bogoslovsky 1972/2: 75-80, pl. 5
50	Nebdjefa (i)	Workman in the Place of Truth	19th Dynasty: Ramesses II, first half	Thoth and Ptah	Adoring deities	C	Bouquet and loaded offering table	Unknown	London, The British Museum	807	Porter and Moss I.2 1964: 728	James 1970: 38, pl. XXXIII
51	Nebenmaat (i)	Workman in the Place of Truth	19th Dynasty: Ramesses II, first half	Ptah and Harsiesi	Adoring deities	A		Village: House CV: Room 2			Porter and Moss I.2 1964: 705	Bruyère 1934-1935 (1939) III: 200-201 [10], fig. 90; 307-308, fig. 178; Kitchen 2000: 513
52	Nebnefer (i)	Foreman in the Place of Truth to the West of Thebes	19th Dynasty: Ramesses II, first half	Reshep	Dedicator in text only	C	Loaded offering table	Hathor Temple: Northern Sector: North East Corner of the Ptolemaic Precinct of the Temple			Porter and Moss I.2 1964: 727	Bruyère 1935-1940 (1952) II: 115-116, fig. 196 [272]
53	Nebnefer (i)	Foreman in the Place of Truth	19th Dynasty: Ramesses II, first half	Ptah and Khnum, Satis and Anukis (Elephantine Triad)	Adoring deities	C	Offering stand	Unknown	London, The British Museum	267	Porter and Moss I.2 1964: 727	James 1970: 42-43, pl. XXXVII

54	Nebnefer (i)	Foreman in the Place of Truth	19th Dynasty: Ramesses II, first half	Amenhotep I (blue crown) and Queen Ahmes Nefertari	Adoring deities (festival)	C	Bouquet and loaded offering table	Unknown	Copenhagen, The National Museum of Denmark	B4 (A.A.d.9)	Porter and Moss I.2 1964: 727	Buhl 1974: 24 [10]
55	Nebnefer (i) (?)	Workman in the Place of Truth, Foreman of the Lord of the Two Lands	19th Dynasty: Ramesses II, first half	Amun-Re, Mut and Hathor	Adoring deity (upper register lost) (oracle)	C	Lost	Unknown (purchased in Luxor)	Strasbourg, Université Institut d'Égyptologie	974	Porter and Moss I.2 1964: 727	Spiegelberg and Pörtner 1902: 20-21, pl. XIX [36]; Kitchen 2000: 402-403
56	Nebre (i)	Draughtsman of Amun in the Place of Truth	19th Dynasty: Ramesses II, first half	Haroeris	Adoring deity	C	Offering stand	Unknown	London, The British Museum	276	Porter and Moss I.2 1964: 727	Bierbrier 1982b: 34, pl. 79; Kitchen 2000: 446; Morgan 2004: 92-94
57	Nebre (i)	Draughtsman of Amun in the Place of Truth	19th Dynasty: Ramesses II, first half	Khonsu-em-Waset Neferhotep	Adoring deity	C	Bouquet and loaded offering table	Unknown	Turin, Museo Egizio	1589	Porter and Moss I.2 1964: 727	Tosi Roccati 1972: 70, 275 [50036]; Kitchen 2000: 446
58	Nebre (i)	Draughtsman of Amun in the Place of Truth	19th Dynasty: Ramesses II, first half	Meret	Adoring deity	A		Village	Turin, Museo Egizio	1590	Porter and Moss I.2 1964: 727	Tosi Roccati 1972: 101-102, 290 [50063]; Kitchen 2000: 446
59	Nebre (i)	Draughtsman	19th Dynasty: Ramesses II, first half	The Good Swallow and the Good Cat (Hathor)	Offering to deity	A	Bouquet and loaded offering table	Unknown	Turin, Museo Egizio	1591	Porter and Moss I.2 1964: 727	Tosi Roccati 1972: 92, 285 [50056]; Kitchen 2000: 446-447
60	Nebre (i) and son Khay (ii)	Nebre: Draughtsman of Amun/in the Place of Truth; Khay: Scribe (= Outline Draughtsman)	19th Dynasty: Ramesses II, first half	Amun-Re	Adoring deity (oracle)	A	Offering stand	Ramesseum Area: Brick Buildings: Building A	Berlin, Ägyptisches Museum und Papyrussammlung, Staatliche Museen zu Berlin-SPK	20377	Porter and Moss I.2 1964: 683	Erman 1907: pl. 5; Kitchen 2000: 444-446
61	Paherypedjet (i) (?)	Workman in the Place of Truth	19th Dynasty: Ramesses II, first half	Ptah, Sobek, Isis and Mertseger; Shed	Adoring deities	A		Hathor Temple: Inside Ptolemiac Temple Precinct: Excavations in SW Part by Baraize, 1912	Cairo, The Egyptian Museum	JdE 43569	Porter and Moss I.2 1964: 699	Bruyère 1930b: fig. 90

62	Paherypedjet (i)	Workman in the Place of Truth	19th Dynasty: Ramesses II, first half	Amun-Re	Adoring deity	C	Lost	Village			Porter and Moss I.2 1964: 705	Bruyère 1934-1935 (1952) III: 201, fig. 91
63	Parennefer	Workman in the Place of Truth	19th Dynasty: Ramesses II, first half	Amun-Re (ram) and Mut	Adoring and offering to deities (festival)	A	Water (offered by women), lotus flowers, bouquet and loaded offering table	Unknown	London, The British Museum	283	Porter and Moss I.2 1964: 731	James 1970: 52-53, pl. XLII
64	Paser	Mayor of Thebes and Vizier	19th Dynasty: Ramesses II, first half	Hathor	Adoring deity	A	Offering stand	Unknown	Copenhagen, Ny Carlsberg Glyptotek	AEIN 1553 (Amherst Coll.)	Porter and Moss I.2 1964: 803	Koefoed-Petersen 1948: 34, 29, pl. 35; Kitchen 2000: 18
65	Paser, Ramose (i)	Paser: Vizier; Ramose: [Royal?] Scribe in the Place of Truth	19th Dynasty: Ramesses II, first half	Unidentified deities and Ramesses II	Vizier (Paser) mediating scene (?)	B		Hathor Temple: Hathor Chapel of Seti I: Shrine of Bukentef			Porter and Moss I.2 1964: 695	Bruyère 1935-1940 (1952) II: 129, p. 30, fig. 212 [317]; 149 [421]
66	Pashedu (x)	Foreman in the Place of Truth	19th Dynasty: Ramesses II, first half	Amun-Re and Mut; Wadjmosi	Adoring deity	A	Bouquet	Temple of Wadjmose	Cairo, The Egyptian Museum	JdE 27820	Porter and Moss II 1972: 445	Weigell 1924: pl. on p. 260
67	Penamun (ii)	Workman in the Place of Truth	19th Dynasty: Ramesses II, first half	Iah-Thoth	Adoring deity	C	Festival offerings	Hathor Temple: Khenu-Chapel: Room 9, Pit 1414	Cairo, The Egyptian Museum	JdE 72025	Porter and Moss I.2 1964: 698	Bruyère 1935-1940 (1952) II: 42, 79-81, pl. X (fig. 159) [111]; Morgan 2004: 86-88
68	Penamun (ii) and Shedamun/Amunshed (i)	Penamun: Workman in the Place of Truth	19th Dynasty: Ramesses II, first half	Seth and another deity (?)	Adoring deity	C	Bouquet	Hathor Temple: Sector 4 (interior of the Ptolemaic Temple): Hypostyle Hall	Cairo, The Egyptian Museum	JdE 72020	Porter and Moss I.2 1964: 731	Bruyère 1935-1940 (1952) II: 101-102, pl. XVI, fig. 173 [228]; Kitchen 2000: 493
69	Penbuy (i)	Guardian in the Place of Truth	19th Dynasty: Ramesses II, first half	Ptah	Adoring deity	C	Bouquet and loaded offering table	Unknown	London, The British Museum	1466	Porter and Moss I.2 1964: 731	Bierbrier 1982b: 31-32, pl. 73; Morgan 2004: 104-106
70	Penbuy (i)	Guardian in the Place of Truth	19th Dynasty: Ramesses II, first half	Taweret	Adoring deity	A	Incense, water (offered by women), bouquet and festival offerings	Unknown	Glasgow Museum and Art Gallery, Burrell Collection	EGNN.683 (temp no)		Bierbrier and De Meulenaere 1984: 23-30
71	Penbuy (i)	Guardian in the Place of Truth	19th Dynasty: Ramesses II, first half	Hathor	Adoring deity (festival)	C		Unknown	Leipzig, Ägyptisches Museum	5141	Porter and Moss I.2 1964: 732	Blumenthal 2000: 10, pls. 1, 2

72	Penbuy (i)	Workman in the Place of Truth	19th Dynasty: Ramesses II, first half	Ptah	Adoring deity	A	Offering stand	Unknown	London, The British Museum	65355	Porter and Moss I.2 1964: 732	Bierbrier 1982b: 31 pl. 72; Kitchen 2000: 497
73	Penbuy (i)	Workman in the Place of Truth	19th Dynasty: Ramesses II, first half	Queen Ahmes Nefertari	Offering to deity	A	Incense	Unknown	Turin, Museo Egizio	1449	Porter and Moss I.2 1964: 732	Tosi Roccati 1972: 71-72, 275 [50037]; Kitchen 2000: 497; Morgan 2004: 116-118
74	Penbuy (i)	Guardian in the Place of Truth	19th Dynasty: Ramesses II, first half	Taweret and Hathor-Isis	Adoring and offering to deities	A	Water (offered by women), bouquet, loaded offering table and offering stand	Village: House S.O.VI (of Sennedjem): Room 1	Paris, Musée du Louvre	E 16374	Porter and Moss I.2 1964: 705	Bruyère 1934-1935 (1939) III: 198-199, 334-335 [19], fig. 206, pl. XXII [left]; Kitchen 2000: 497
75	Qaha (i)	Foreman in the Place of Truth	19th Dynasty: Ramesses II, first half	Qadesh, Min and Reshep; Anat	Adoring deity	A	Lotus flowers and loaded offering table	Unknown	London, The British Museum	191	Porter and Moss I.2 1964: 723	James 1970: 47-8, pl. XXXIX; Kitchen 2000: 413-414
76	Qaha (i)	Foreman in the Place of Truth	19th Dynasty: Ramesses II, first half	Osiris and Anubis	Offering to deities	A	Incense, water (offered by women), festival offerings, lotus flowers, bouquet and loaded offering table	Western Cemetery: Courtyard of TT360 (according to Bruyère 1930 (1933) III: 73, though not found here)	London, The British Museum	144	Porter and Moss I.1 1960: 424	James 1970: 46-47, pl. XXXIX; Kitchen 2000: 413
77	Qaha (i)	Foreman in the Place of Truth	19th Dynasty: Ramesses II, first half	Amun-Re (ram); Hathor, Amenhotep I and Queen Ahmes Nefertari	Offering to deities (festival)	A	Incense, lotus flowers and loaded offering table	Unknown	London, The British Museum	291	Porter and Moss I.2 1964: 723	Bierbrier 1982b: 27, pl. 65; Kitchen 2000: 414
78	Qaha (i)	Foreman in the Place of Truth	19th Dynasty: Ramesses II, first half	Osiris	Royal (Ramesses II and Vizier, Paser) mediating scene	B	Bouquet	Western Cemetery: Court of TT360			Porter and Moss I.1 1960: 425	Bruyère 1930 (1933) III: 87, fig. 23; 90- 91, [3, 7]
79	Qen (ii)	Sculptor in the Place of Truth	19th Dynasty: Ramesses II, first half	Hathor, Osiris and Amenhotep I (blue crown)	Dedicator in text only (festival)	C		Unknown	London, The British Museum	815	Porter and Moss I.2 1964: 723	Bierbrier 1982b: 37, pls. 84-85; Kitchen 2000: 462-463
80	Qen (ii)	Sculptor in the Place of Truth	19th Dynasty: Ramesses II, first half	Renenut - Mertseger	Adoring deity	C	Bouquet and loaded offering table	Unknown	Bordeaux, Musée d'Aquitaine	8635		Andreu 2002: 214-215 [166]

81	Qen (ii)	Sculptor of Amun in the Place of Truth	19th Dynasty: Ramesses II, first half	Mertseger and Re-Harakhti	Adoring deity	C		Unknown	London, The British Museum	8493	Porter and Moss I.2 1964: 723	Bierbrier 1982b: 37, pls. 84-85; Kitchen 2000: 507-508
82	Qen (ii)	Workman in the Place of Truth to the West of Thebes	19th Dynasty: Ramesses II, first half	Amenhotep I and Queen Ahmes Nefertari	Offering to deities	C	Incense, water (offered by women), festival offerings, lotus flowers, bouquet and loaded offering table	Unknown	New York, The Metropolitan Museum of Art	59.93	Porter and Moss I.2 1964: 723	Metropolitan Museum of Art, Bulletin XIX (Oct. 1960): 41(fig); Kitchen 2000: 462
83	Ramose (i)	Scribe in the Place of Truth	19th Dynasty: Ramesses II, first half	Qadesh, Reshep and Min	Adoring and offering to deities	C	Water (offered by women)	Unknown	Turin, Museo Egizio	1601	Porter and Moss I.2 1964: 733	Tosi Roccati 1972: 102-103, 290 [50066]; Kitchen 2000: 424
84	Ramose (i)	Royal Scribe in the Place of Truth	19th Dynasty: Ramesses II, first half	Re-Harakhti, Atum and Ptah	Offering to deities	C	Incense and bouquet	Hathor Temple: Sector 2 (north of the pit in the centre of the courtyard)	Paris, Musée du Louvre	E 16340	Porter and Moss I.2 1964: 733	Bruyère 1935-1940 (1952) II: 34, 90-91, pls. XII, fig. 166, pl. XXXVII [35]; Kitchen 2000: 425
85	Ramose (i)	[Administrator?] of the Estate of Amun-Re, Scribe in the Place of Truth	19th Dynasty: Ramesses II, first half	Amun-Re and a King's Son of Kush	Adoring, deity not represented	C		Hathor Temple: Sector 3			Porter and Moss I.2 1964: 734	Bruyère 1935-1940 (1952) II: 99, pl. XII (fig. 166) [207]; Kitchen 2000: 428-429
86	Ramose (i)	Royal Scribe in the Place of Truth	19th Dynasty: Ramesses II, first half	Amun-Re	Adoring, deity not represented (oracle)	C		Unknown	Stockholm, Medleshavsmuseet	MM 18566	Porter and Moss I.2 1964: 734	Kitchen 2000: 567-568
87	Ramose (i)	Secretary of the Prince, Royal Scribe	19th Dynasty: Ramesses II, first half	Lost	Lower register only, making a water offering	C	Water pot	Western Cemetery: Chapelle à Trois Loges (=Chapel DM 1211) (Anthes: am nordlichen Berghang (Grabungsstelle C von 1913))			Porter and Moss I.2 1964: 689	Anthes 1943: 67, pl. 18 [b]
88	Ramose (i)	Scribe of Truth in the Place of Truth	19th Dynasty: Ramesses II, first half	Ptah and Maat	Adoring deity	C	Bouquet and loaded offering table	Ramesseum area	Manchester, The Manchester Museum	1759	Porter and Moss I.2 1964: 682	Quibell 1898: 8 [12], 15, pl. X [4]; Kitchen 2000: 427

89	Ramose (i)	Royal Scribe in the Place of Truth to the West of Thebes	19th Dynasty: Ramesses II, first half	Hathor	Adoring deity (festival)	C	Bouquet and loaded offering table	Hathor Temple: Khenu-Chapel: Room 9, Pit 1414	Paris, Musée du Louvre	E 16345	Porter and Moss I.2 1964: 697 (b) end	Bruyère 1935-1940 (1952) II: 42, 68, fig. 150 [120]; Kitchen 2000: 428
90	Ramose (i)	Scribe in the Place of Truth	19th Dynasty: Ramesses II, first half	Shed	Adoring deity	C		Hathor Temple: Khenu-Chapel: Room 9, Pit 1414	Cairo, The Egyptian Museum	JdE 72024	Porter and Moss I.2 1964: 697	Bruyère 1935-1940 (1952) II: 42, 72-73, pl. XXXIX [118]; Kitchen 2000: 427
91	Ramose (i)	Royal Scribe in the Place of Truth	19th Dynasty: Ramesses II, first half	Horus, Lord of the Desert, Isis and Shed	Adoring deities	C		Hathor Temple: Khenu-Chapel: Room 9, Pit 1414	Paris, Musée du Louvre	E 16343	Porter and Moss I.2 1964: 697 (d)	Bruyère 1935-1940 (1952) II: 42, 73-74, pl XXXIX [119]; Kitchen 2000: 427-428
92	Ramose (i)	Scribe [in the Place of Truth]	19th Dynasty: Ramesses II, first half	Mut	Adoring deity	C	Bouquet and loaded offering table	Hathor Temple: Khenu-chapel: Door between Rooms 3 and 4			Porter and Moss I.2 1964: 697	Bruyère 1935-1940 (1952) II: 38, 79, 80, fig. 158 [78]
93	Ramose (i)	Scribe in the Place of Eternity	19th Dynasty: Ramesses II, first half	Ramesses II	Royal smiting scene	C		Hathor Temple: Khenu-chapel: Door between Rooms 3 and 4	Paris, Musée du Louvre	E 16373	Porter and Moss I.2 1964: 697	Andreu 2002: 232 [187]
94	Ramose (i)	Scribe in the Place of Truth	19th Dynasty: Ramesses II, first half	Ramesses I, Horemheb, Seti I and Ramesses II	Adoring cartouches of Ramesses II	A	Bouquet	Hathor Temple: Khenu-chapel: Door between Rooms 3 and 4	Cairo, The Egyptian Museum	JdE 72023	Porter and Moss I.2 1964: 696	Bruyère 1935-1940 (1952) II: 38, 68-70, pls. XII, XXXVIII [79]; Kitchen 2000: 426
95	Ramose (i)	Scribe in the Place of Truth	19th Dynasty: Ramesses II, first half	Taweret	Adoring and offering to deity (oracle)	C	Water (offered by the woman), bouquet and loaded offering table	Unknown	Voronezh, Archaeological Museum of Voronezh State University	71 = VM 156	Porter and Moss I.2 1964: 733	Bogoslovsky 1972/2: 65-74, pls. 3-4
96	Ramose (i)	Royal Scribe and Foreman of the Gang in the Place of Truth on the West	19th Dynasty: Ramesses II, first half	Thoth	Adoring deity	C	Bouquet and loaded offering table	Unknown	Turin, Museo Egizio	1602	Porter and Moss I.2 1964: 733	Tosi Roccati 1972: 81-82, 280 [50047]; Kitchen 2000: 424
97	Ramose (i)	Scribe in the Place of Truth	19th Dynasty: Ramesses II, first half	Mut	Adoring deity	C	Bouquet and loaded offering table	Unknown	Kingston Lacy, Bankes Collection	3	Porter and Moss I.2 1964: 734	Černý 1958: no. 3; Kitchen 2000: 423
98	Ramose (i)	[Scribe in the Place of Truth]	19th Dynasty: Ramesses II, first half	Amenhotep I	Adoring deity	C	Lost	Unknown	London, The British Museum	813	Porter and Moss I.2 1964: 733	British Museum 1914: 41 [426]; Kitchen 2000: 429

99	Ramose (i), Ptahsankh (i)	Ramose: Scribe in the Place of Truth; Ptahsankh: Servitor of Amun	19th Dynasty: Ramesses II, first half	Hathor	Ptahsankh adoring deity	A		Unknown	Tübingen, Stadtmuseum	1716	Porter and Moss I.2 1964: 734	Andreu 2002: 233 [189]
100	Ramose (i) (?)	Scribe in the Place of Truth	19th Dynasty: Ramesses II, first half	Reshep	Dedicator in text only	C	Lost	Unknown	Lyone, A. Varille Collection		Porter and Moss I.2 1964: 734	Leibovitch 1940: 489-490, pl. XLV
101	Ramose (i) (?)	True Scribe of Truth in the Place of Truth	19th Dynasty: Ramesses II, first half (?)	Hathor	Dedicator in text only (fragmentary)	C	Lost	Queens' Valley Chapels (Italian Mission 1906)	Turin, Museo Egizio	Supp. 6011 + 6027	Porter and Moss I.2 1964: 734	Tosi Roccati 1972: 144, 316 [50134]; Kitchen 2000: 424-425
102	Ramose (i) (?)	Scribe	19th Dynasty: Ramesses II, first half (?)	Atum-Re-Harmachis	Dedicator in text only (fragmentary)	C	Offering stand (?)	Hathor Temple: Sector 3 (against the wall of the Ramesside Chapels to the west of the Great Pit)			Porter and Moss I.2 1964: 734	Bruyère 1935-1940 (1952) II: 35, 81-82, fig. 160 [49]
103	Reweben (iii)	Workman in the Place of Truth	19th Dynasty: Ramesses II, first half	Re-Harakhti	Offering to deity	A	Incense and offering stand	Unknown	London, The British Museum	320	Porter and Moss I.2 1964: 734	Bierbrier 1982b: 35, pl. 81; Kitchen 2000: 525
104	Smentawy (i)	Guardian in the Place of Truth	19th Dynasty: Ramesses II, first half	Amun-Re and Mut; Mertseger	Offering to and adoring deities	A	Incense and offering stand	Unknown	London, The British Museum	279	Porter and Moss I.2 1964: 734	Bierbrier 1993: 17 pls. 50-51; Kitchen 2000: 467
105	Thuthirmakhtef (i)	Workman in the Place of Truth	19th Dynasty: Ramesses II, first half	Ptah and Hathor	Offering to deities (festival)	A	Incense, festival offerings, bouquet and offering stand	Unknown	Florence, Museo Archaologico	2524 (or 1623); Cat. no. 55	Porter and Moss I.2 1964: 718	Bruyère 1933-1934 (1937): 47-49, fig. 23; Kitchen 2000:. 562
106	Thuthirmakhtef (i)	Workman in the Place of Truth	19th Dynasty: Ramesses II, first half	Amun-Re and Taweret	Adoring deities (oracle)	C	Lost	Unknown (purchased in Luxor)	Clère Collection		Porter and Moss I.2 1964: 718	Clère 1929: 178-81 [2], pl. 1 [5]; Kitchen 2000: 561-562
107	Tusa (i)	Workman in the Place of Truth	19th Dynasty: Ramesses II, first half	Hathor and Wepwawet	Offering to deities (festival)	C	Incense, water (offered by women), festival offerings, lotus flowers, loaded offering table and offering stand	Unknown	Turin, Museo Egizio	1512	Porter and Moss I.2 1964: 735	Tosi Roccati 1972: 73-74, 276 [50039]; Kitchen 2000: 258

108	User-setet	No title	19th Dynasty: Ramesses II, first half	Nebethetepet (Hathor)	Dedicator not represented (ears)	C		Unknown	Turin, Museo Egizio	1546		Tosi Roccati 1972: 59, 270 [50026]; Morgan 2004: 114-115
109	Wadjmose (i)	Workman in the Place of Truth	19th Dynasty: Ramesses II, first half	Nebmaat (Ptah) and Net	Adoring deities	C		Unknown	Turin, Museo Egizio	1548	Porter and Moss I.2 1964: 735	Tosi Roccati 1972: 72-73, 276 [50038]; Kitchen 2000: 487
110	Wennekhu (i)	Workman in the Place of Truth	19th Dynasty: Ramesses II, first half	Anubis and Isis, Osiris and Hathor	Offering to [deity] (festival)	A	Incense	Western Cemetery: Near TT290			Porter and Moss I.2 1964: 736 (c)	Bruyère 1922-1923 (1924): 29, fig. 3 (3); Kitchen 2000: 488
111	Couple, names lost	No title	19th Dynasty: Ramesses II, first half	Qadesh	Offering to deity	A	Incense	Unknown	Moscow, Pushkin Museum of Fine Arts	I.1.a.5614	Porter and Moss I.2 1964: 736	Hodjash and Berlev 1982: no. 74
112	Amenemwia (i)	No title	19th Dynasty: Ramesses II, mid	Amenhotep I and Queen Ahmes Nefertari	Adoring deities	C	Lotus and offering stand	Village	Berlin, Ägyptisches Museum und Papyrussammlung, Staatliche Museen zu Berlin-SPK	21538	Porter and Moss I.2 1964: 706	Roeder 1913 II: 394 (text)
113	Khaemope (i)/(ii)	Workman in the Place of Truth	19th Dynasty: Ramesses II, mid - second half	N/A	Adoring, deity not represented - pyramid shaped	C		Workmen's Col Station: Miniature Shrine	Oxford, The Ashmolean Museum	1942.47	Porter and Moss I.2 1964: 590 (?)	Davies, N. d. G. 1935-1938: 248 VI, pls. III [2], IV [2]
114	Merwaset (i)	Workman in the Place of Truth	19th Dynasty: Ramesses II, mid - second half	Amun-Re	Festival procession (oracle)	A		Unknown	London, The British Museum	444		Bierbrier 1993: pl. 69
115	Neferabu (i)	Workman in the Place of Truth	19th Dynasty: Ramesses II, mid	Mertseger	Dedicator in text only	C	Offering stand	Unknown	Turin, Museo Egizio	1593 & 1649	Porter and Moss I.2 1964: 728	Tosi Roccati 1972: 94-96, 286 [50058]; Kitchen 2000: 518-519
116	Neferabu (i)	Workman in the Place of Truth	19th Dynasty: Ramesses II, mid	Ptah	Adoring deity	C	Bouquet and loaded offering table	Unknown	London, The British Museum	589	Porter and Moss I.2 1964: 728	James 1970: 36, pl. XXXI; Kitchen 2000: 517-518; Morgan 2004: 98-100
117	Neferabu (i)	[Workman in the] Place of Truth	19th Dynasty: Ramesses II, mid	Amun-Re (ram)	Dedicator in text only (festival)	C	Bouquet	Unknown	Cambridge, Fitzwilliam Museum	E.GA. 3004.1943	Porter and Moss I.2 1964: 728	Martin 2005: 77 [49]
118	Nekh(em)mut (i)	Workman in the Place of Truth	19th Dynasty: Ramesses II, mid	Hathor and Mut	Royal (Ramesses II) mediating scene	B	Offering stand	Unknown	Kingston Lacy, Bankes Collection	9	Porter and Moss I.2 1964: 729	Černy 1958: no. 9; Kitchen 2000: 524

119	Pendua (i)/(vi)	Workman in the Place of Truth	19th Dynasty: Ramesses II, mid	Goddesses Nefertiti and Iretnofret	Adoring deities	C	Lotus flower and offering stand	Unknown	Turin, Museo Egizio	1565	Porter and Moss I.2 1964: 732	Tosi Roccati 1972: 74-75, 277 [50040]; Kitchen 2000: 463
120	Anupemheb (i)	[Scribe in the Place of Truth]	19th Dynasty: Ramesses II, second half - Siptah (?)	Mertseger, Amenhotep I and Queen Ahmes Nefertari	Adoring deities	C	Festival offering	Ramesside Chapels north of Ptolemaic Temple Precinct: Chapel F			Porter and Moss I.2 1964: 694	Bruyère 1945-1947 (1952): 58-59, pl. IX (I) [12]
121	Kha [= Anhurkhawy (i) ?]	Foreman	19th Dynasty: Ramesses II, second half - Merenptah	Amun-Re and Queen Ahmes Nefertari	Royal ancestor (Tuthmosis IV) mediating scene	B	Bouquet offered by intermediary	East Bank: Karnak: Chapel of Hatshepsut**	London, The British Museum	1515	Porter and Moss II 1972: 278	Bierbrier 1982b: pl. XLV
122	Merysekhmet (i)	[Draughtsma n] of Amun	19th Dynasty: Ramesses II, second half	Anukis	Adoring deity (fragments). Ebony	C	Incense	Village: House N.E.IV: Kitchen				Bruyère 1934-1935 (1939) III: 247-248 [1], p. 249, fig. 127
123	Neferhotep (ii)	Foreman in the Place of Truth	19th Dynasty: Ramesses II, second half - Seti II	Lost	Adoring deity	C	Lost	Queens' Valley Chapels (?)	Turin, Museo Egizio	Supp. 6047	Porter and Moss I.2 1964: 728	Tosi Roccati 1972: 147, 318 [50141]; Kitchen 2000: 403
124	Neferhotep (ii)	Foreman in the Place of Truth	19th Dynasty: Ramesses II, second half - Seti II	Amenhotep I and Queen Ahmes Nefertari	Adoring deities	C	Offering stand	East Bank: Karnak: Chapel of Hatshepsut**	London, The British Museum	1516	Porter and Moss II 1972: 279	Bierbrier 1982b: 27, pl. 64
125	Neferhotep (ii)	Foreman in the Place of Truth	19th Dynasty: Ramesses II, second half - Seti II	Amenhotep I, Sekhmet and Min-Amen-Re-Kamutef	Lost	C	Lost	Unknown	Turin, Museo Egizio	Supp. 6188	Porter and Moss I.2 1964: 728	Tosi Roccati 1972: 128, 303 [50093]; Kitchen 2000: 398
126	[Amennakht]	Wab-priest; servitor	19th Dynasty: Ramesses II (?)	Amun-Re and Hathor	Adoring deities (oracle)	C		Hathor Temple: Area N/N-E/E of Ptolemaic Temple Precinct (Finds 1945-1946)			Porter and Moss I.2 1964: 716	Bruyère 1945-1947 (1952): 41-42, fig. 28 (2) [21]
127	Anhotep	[Wab]-priest, God's Father of Amun	19th Dynasty: Ramesses II	Amun-Re and Mut; Re-Harakhti, Queen Ahmes Nefertari and Amenhotep I (blue crown)	Royal (Ramesses II) mediating scene (festival)	B	Offering stand	Unknown (purchased at a dealers at Luxor)	Private Collection			Corteggiani 1975: 152-154, pl. XXV

128	Atumnakht	Wab-priest of Amenhotep I	19th Dynasty: Ramesses II	Amenhotep I (blue crown), Tuthmosis IV and a goddess	Offering to deities (oracle)	A	Incense and offering stand	Unknown	Turin, Museo Egizio	1454 bis	Porter and Moss I.2 1964: 717	Tosi Roccati 1972: 83-84, 281 [50049]
129	Hay (ii)	Workman in the Place of Truth	19th Dynasty: Ramesses II	Montu	Offering to deity	A	Incense and water (offered by women)	Unknown	Avignon, Musée Calvet	A.16	Porter and Moss I.2 1964: 719	Moret 1913: pl. IV [5], facing p. 196, cf. pp. 48-49; Kitchen 2000: 528
130	Nefer(em)senut (i)	Workman in the Place of Truth	19th Dynasty: Ramesses II	Hathor	Offering to deity	A	Incense and offering stand	Unknown	London, The British Museum	316	Porter and Moss I.2 1964: 729	Bierbrier 1982b: 316, pl. 70; Kitchen 2000: 52
131	Neferronpet	Workman in the Place of Truth	19th Dynasty: Ramesses II (?)	Amun-Re and Ramesses II	Adoring deities (upper register lost) (oracle)	C	Lost	Unknown	Berlin, Ägyptisches Museum und Papyrussammlung, Staatliche Museen zu Berlin-SPK	2093	Porter and Moss I.2 1964: 729	Wiedemann 1884: 471, n. 14
132	Qaha	Workman in the Place of Truth	19th Dynasty: Ramesses II (?)	Amenhotep I	Offering to deity	A	Incense	Unknown	London, The British Museum	274	Porter and Moss I.2 1964: 722	Bierbrier 1982b: 28, pls. 66-67
133	Ramose	'Custodian of the Shrine' (after PM VIII)	19th Dynasty: Ramesses II	Osiris, Anubis and Renenut	Royal ancestor (Amenhotep I) mediating scene	B	Loaded offering table and offering stand	Unknown	The Hague, Rijksmuseum Meermanno-Westreenianum im Haag	47/93	Porter and Moss VIII forthcoming: 803-055-381	Bruyère 1930b: 183, fig. 97
134	No name visible	Second man is a Workman in the Place of Truth	19th Dynasty: Ramesses II	Sobek, Taweret and Hathor; cult statue of Ramesses II	[Lower register lost]	C	Bouquet and loaded offering table	Unknown	Moscow, Pushkin Museum of Fine Arts	I.1.a.5627 (4136)		Hodjash and Berlev 1982: 135 [76]
135	Name lost	Overseer of the Works of the Lord of the Two Lands in the Divine Temples, Foreman	19th Dynasty: Ramesses II	Ptah	Royal (Ramesses II) mediating scene (festival)	B		Hathor Temple: Northern Sector: North East Corner of the Ptolemaic Precinct of the Temple			Porter and Moss I.2 1964: 736	Bruyère 1935-1940 (1952) II: 116-117, fig. 197 [273]
136	Nakhtsu (i), and his son, Panakht (iii)	Nakhtsu: Workman in the Place of Truth	19th Dynasty: Merenptah - Siptah	Amenhotep I and Queen Ahmes Nefertari	Offering to deities	A	Incense, water (offered by women) and festival offerings	Unknown	Turin, Museo Egizio	1454	Porter and Moss I.2 1964: 726	Tosi Roccati 1972: 75-76, 277 [50041]

137	Panehsy	Mayor of Thebes and Vizier	19th Dynasty: Merenptah	Amun-Re, Maat	Adoring deities	A	Bouquet	Temple of Tuthmosis III: Room A	At Deir el Bahri	Inv. no. 7695	Porter and Moss II 1972: 541	Lipinska 1984: 51, fig. 172 [71]; Lipinska 1966: 65, no. 16 and pl. X
138	Vizier (=Panehsy?)	Vizier	19th Dynasty: Merenptah	Ptah [and Maat]	Royal (Merenptah) mediating scene (festival)	B		Hathor Temple: Eastern Sector: Houses			Porter and Moss I.2 1964: 695	Bruyère 1935-1940 (1952) II: 142, 143, fig. 233 [382]
139	Apehty (i)	Deputy of the Gang	19th Dynasty: Seti II - Siptah	Seth	Adoring deity	A		Unknown	London, The British Museum	35630	Porter and Moss I.2 1964: 717	Bierbrier 1982b: 30, pl. 71
140	Kel (iv)	Wab-priest of the Lord of the Two Lands	19th Dynasty: Seti II +	Amenhotep I, Mertseger and Queen Ahmes Nefertari	Adoring deities	A	Lotus flowers and offering stand	Unknown (copied at an antiquities dealer in Luxor)			Porter and Moss I.2 1964: 724	Clère 1929: 182-185, pl IV [4]
141	Nebsmen (i) (?)	Workman in the Place of Truth	19th Dynasty: Seti II - Siptah	Amenhotep I and Queen Ahmes Nefertari	Offering to deities	A	Incense and offering stand	Unknown	Edinburgh, The Royal Museum	UC 52	Porter and Moss I.2 1964: 728	Unpublished
142	Nodjembehdet = Nodjemet-shu (i) (Besy) (f.)	Lady of the House	19th Dynasty: Seti II - Tausret	Isis	Offering to deity	C	Water (offered by the woman), festival offerings, lotus flower, bouquet and loaded offering table	Unknown	Geneva, Musée d'Art et d'Histoire	D55	Porter and Moss I.2 1964: 730	Spiegelberg 1906: 24, pl. VIII [2 called 22]
143	Paneb (i)	Foreman in the Place of Truth	19th Dynasty: Sety II-Siptah	Mertseger	Adoring deity	A		Valley of the Kings	London, The British Museum	273	Porter and Moss I.2 1964: 730	Bierbrier 1982b: 30, pl. 71
144	Paneb (i)	Foreman in the Place of Truth	19th Dynasty: Sety II-Siptah	Mertseger	Adoring deity	A		Unknown	London, The British Museum	272	Porter and Moss I.2 1964: 730	Bierbrier 1982b: 30, pl. 70
145	Yipuy (i)	Guardian of the Lord of the Two Lands in the Place of Truth	19th Dynasty: Seti II	Amun-Re, Amenhotep I and Queen Ahmes Nefertari	Offering to deities	C	Incense, water (offered by women), bouquet and offering stand	Unknown	Cairo, The Egyptian Museum	TN 26.2.25.5	Porter and Moss I.2 1964: 721	Černý 1927: 170-172, pl. III
146	Khaemnun (i)/(ii)/(iii)/(iv)	Workman in the Place of Truth	19th Dynasty: Amenmesse +	Osiris	Adoring deity	A	Loaded offering table	Village			Porter and Moss I.2 1964: 705	Bruyère 1931-1932 (1934): 86 [8], fig. 56

147	Pashedu (xiv)	Workman in the Place of Truth	19th Dynasty: Amenmesse (?)	Amun-Re	Adoring deity	A		Unknown	London, The British Museum	341	Porter and Moss I.2 1964: 732	Bierbrier 1993: 12, pls. 32-33 .
148	[Siwadjyt (iv) (?)]	[Workman of the Lord of the Two Lands in the Place of Truth]	19th Dynasty: Amenmesse - Siptah	Lost	Adoring deity (?)	A	Lost	Unknown	Clère Collection		Porter and Moss I.2 1964: 734	Clère 1929: 188-9 [8], pl. II [3]
149	Pamerihu (i)	Sculptor in the Place of Truth	19th Dynasty: Siptah	Queen Ahmes Nefertari	Dedicator in text only	C	Offering stand	Unknown	Vienna, Kunsthistorische Museum	Inv. 158	Porter and Moss I.2 1964: 730	Bergmann 1887: 38-39 [9] (text)
150	Paneb (ii)	Workman in the Place of Truth	19th Dynasty: Siptah - Tausret	Lost	Adoring deities	C	Lost	Unknown	Clère Collection		Porter and Moss I.2 1964: 730	Clère 1929: 186-7 [6], pl. 1 [4]
151	Bay	Workman in the Place of Truth	19th Dynasty (early)	Amun-Re (ram)	Adoring deity (ears; festival)	C	Offering stand	Hathor Temple: Inside Ptolemaic Temple Precinct: Excavations in South West Part by Baraize, 1912	Cairo, The Egyptian Museum	JdE 43566	Porter and Moss I.2 1964: 698	Sadek 1987: 257, pl. XX, 2; Morgan 2004: 84-85
152	Hemtneter (f.)	Weshbet Mourner	19th Dynasty (early)	The 'Good Cat' (Hathor)	Dedicator in text only	C	Bouquet	Unknown	Turin, Museo Egizio	1600	Porter and Moss I.2 1964: 719	Tosi Roccati 1972:. 88-89, 284 [50053]; Kitchen 2000: 533
153	Huy	Quarryman	19th Dynasty (early)	Ptah	Adoring deity	A	Lotus flower and offering stand	Unknown	Birmingham City Museum	1969W29 78	Porter and Moss VIII forthcoming: 803-055-038	Watson 1994: pl. XLIX
154	Iniahay/Iahy (?)	No title	19th Dynasty (early)	Qadesh, Reshep (?) and Min (?)	Adoring deities	C	Lotus flower and loaded offering table	Unknown	Moscow, Pushkin Museum of Fine Arts	I.1.a.5614 (3177)	Porter and Moss I.2 1964: 736	Hodjash and Berlev 1982: 134 [75]
155	Iyernutef (ii)	Sculptor in the Place of Truth	19th Dynasty (mid)	Queen Ahmes Nefertari	Offering to deity (ears)	A	Incense, bouquet and offering stand	Unknown	Paris, Musée du Louvre	N 662	Porter and Moss I.2 1964:. 722	Andreu 2002: 258-9 [208]; Kitchen 2000: 448; Morgan 2004: 110-112
156	Huy (iii)	Workman in the Place of Truth	19th Dynasty (end)	Anukis	Adoring deity	A	Incense and offering stand	Unknown	Whitehead Collection		Porter and Moss I.2 1964: 720	Valbelle 1975: 139-140, pl. XIX

157	[Huy (iii)]	[Workman in the Place of Truth]	19th Dynasty (end)	Osiris and Mertseger	Adoring deities	C	Bouquet and offering stand	Hathor Temple: Northern Sector: North East Corner of the Ptolemaic Precinct of the Temple			Porter and Moss I.2 1964: 720	Bruyère 1935-1940 (1952) II: 121, fig. 202 [282]
158	Nebnefer	Workman in the Place of Truth	19th Dynasty (end)	Amun-Re	Offering to deity	A	Incense	Unknown	London, The British Museum	65356 = 65336	Porter and Moss I.2 1964: 727	Bierbrier 1982b: 39, pl. 89
159	Amenemone	Workman	19th Dynasty	Mertseger	Dedicator in text only	C	Offering stand	Village: Possibly House S.E.VIII	Turin, Museo Egizio	1519	Porter and Moss I.2 1964: 715	Bruyère 1930b: 137; Tosi Roccati 1972: 33-34; 261[50001]
160	Anuy	Workman in the Place of Truth	19th Dynasty	Qadesh, Reshep and Min	Adoring and offering to deities	C	Water (offered by women)	Unknown	London, The British Museum	355	Porter and Moss I.2 1964: 717	James 1970: 53-54, pl. XLII
161	Harmose	No title	19th Dynasty	Re-Harakhti	Dedicator in text only	C	Loaded offering table	Unknown	Kingston Lacy, Bankes Collection	13	Porter and Moss I.2 1964: 718	Černý 1958: no. 13
162	Huy	No title	19th Dynasty	Amenhotep I (blue crown) and Ptah	Adoring deities	A		Unknown	Turin, Museo Egizio	1453	Porter and Moss I.2 1964: 720	Tosi Roccati 1972: 61-62; 272 [50029]
163	Huy	Workman in the Place of Truth	19th Dynasty	Amun-Re	Adoring deity	C	Bouquet	Unknown	Turin, Museo Egizio	1607	Porter and Moss I.2 1964: 720	Tosi Roccati 1972: 89-90, 284 [50054]
164	Mahu	Workman in the Place of Truth	19th Dynasty	Amun-Re, Mut and Mertseger	Offering to deities	A	Incense	Unknown	Turin, Museo Egizio	1580	Porter and Moss I.2 1964: 725	Tosi Roccati 1972: 60-61, 271 [50028]; Kitchen 2000: 503
165	Nebdjuu/Neb nakht	Workman in the Place of Truth	19th Dynasty	Amun-Re, Mut, Re-Harakhti and Hathor - Re-Harakhti principally	Offering to (?) deities (festival)	C	Incense (?) and offering stand	Unknown	Leiden, Het Rijksmuseum van Oudheden	L XI 3	Porter and Moss I.2 1964: 728	Raven 2000: 298-299 [8], pl. XL
166	Nebwa	Stonemason	19th Dynasty	Mertseger	Offering to and adoring deity	A	Incense and water (offered by women)	Ramesside Chapels north of Ptolemaic Temple Precinct: Chapel F			Porter and Moss I.2 1964: 694	Bruyère 1945-1947 (1952): 57-58, pl. VIII [11]
167	P[…]	Workman in the Place of Truth	19th Dynasty	Reshep	Dedicator in text only	C	Offering stand	Unknown	London, The British Museum	263	Porter and Moss I.2 1964: 730	James 1970: 54-55, pl. XLIII

168	Parennefer	Workman in the Place of Truth	19th Dynasty	Amenhotep I and Queen Ahmes Nefertari	Offering to deities	A	Incense, water (offered by women), festival offerings, lotus flowers, bouquet and loaded offering table	Unknown	London, The British Museum	1347	Porter and Moss I.2 1964: 731	Bierbrier 1993: 14, pls. 38-39
169	Pendua (i)/(vi) (?)	Workman in the Place of Truth	19th Dynasty	Mertseger	Adoring deity	C	Offering stand	Unknown	Turin, Museo Egizio	1564	Porter and Moss I.2 1964: 732	Tosi Roccati 1972: 99, 289 [50061]
170	Pennub (i)/(ii)/(iii)	Workman in the Place of Truth	19th Dynasty	Ptah	Dedicator in text only	C	Offering stand	Unknown	London, The British Museum	8497	Porter and Moss I.2 1964: 732	Bierbrier 1982b: 32, pls. 74-75.
171	Amennakht (v)	Scribe in the Place of Truth	20th Dynasty: Ramesses III +	Amun-Re	Festival procession (oracle)	C		Unknown	New York, Metropolitan Museum of Art	21.2.6	Porter and Moss I.2 1964: 716	Aldred 1988: pl. 53;
172	Amennakht	Scribe of the Place of Truth	20th Dynasty: Ramesses III - Ramesses IV	Mertseger	Adoring deity (arms outstretched)	A	Loaded offering table	Unknown	London, The British Museum	374	Porter and Moss I.2 1964: 716	Bierbrier 1993: 17, pls. 50-51.
173	Amennakht [= Nakht?]	Workman of Amun and Scribe	20th Dynasty: Ramesses III (?)	Ptah	Adoring deity	A	Offering stand	Unknown	Edinburgh, The Royal Museum	1960.908	Porter and Moss I.2 1964: 716	Murray 1900: 29, 55 [ix], no. 446 (called Nekht en Ast)
174	Anhurkhawy (ii)	Foreman in the Place of Truth	20th Dynasty: Ramesses III - Ramesses IV	Amenhotep I and Maat	Festival procession (oracle)	A		Unknown	Paris, Musée du Louvre	N 665 [= N 538 or 338]	Porter and Moss I.2 1964: 721	Černý 1927; 190-191, fig. 15; Bruyère 1930 (1933) III: 110-111, fig. 38 (may be top half of DB178)
175	Anhurkhawy (ii)	Foreman in the Place of Truth	20th Dynasty: Ramesses III - Ramesses IV	Ramesses IV, Maat	Royal butler (Hori) greeting the king scene	B		Western Cemetery: TT359	London, The British Museum	588	Porter and Moss I.2 1964: 721	Bierbrier 1982b: 24-25, pl. 57
176	Anhurkhawy (ii)	Foreman in the Place of Truth	20th Dynasty: Ramesses III - Ramesses IV	Amun-Re, Montu, Amenhotep I; Ratawy, Queen Ahmes Nefertari	Adoring deities	A		Unknown	Turin, Museo Egizio	Supp. 7358	Porter and Moss I.2 1964: 721	Tosi Roccati 1972: 64-66, 273 [50032]

177	Anhurkhawy (ii)	Foreman of the Gang of the Lord of the Two Lands [in the Place of Truth] to the West of Thebes	20th Dynasty: Ramesses III - Ramesses IV	Mertseger	Adoring [deity]	C	Lost	Unknown	Cairo, The Egyptian Museum	TN 21.8.15.5	Porter and Moss I.2 1964: 721	Bruyère 1930b: fig. 133
178	Anhurkhawy (ii)	Foreman in the Place of Truth	20th Dynasty: Ramesses III - Ramesses IV	Amenhotep I	Adoring [deity]	C	Lost	Unknown	Marseilles, Musée d'Archéologie	38	Porter and Moss I.2 1964: 721	Bruyère 1930 (1933) III: 110-111, fig. 39 (may be bottom half of DB174)
179	Bay (ii) and Amennakht (v)	Scribes in the Place of Truth	20th Dynasty: Ramesses III	Amun-Re and Ptah	Vizier (To?) mediating scene (festival)	B	Bouquet offered by intermediary and offering stand	Queen's Valley Chapels: Wall of Chapel E	Stolen after being found in the debris on site		Porter and Moss I.2 1964: 708	Bruyère 1930b: 8-10, fig. 5
180	Hay (vii)	Workman in the Place of Truth, Scribe, Chief Craftsman of the Lord of the Two Lands in the Place of Truth, Deputy of the Gang in the Place of Truth	20th Dynasty: Ramesses III-Ramesses V	Anukis	Adoring deity	A		Unknown	London, The British Museum	O. BM 8494		Valbelle 1975: 134-138, fig. 6, a-b
181	Hay (vii)	Deputy of the Gang in the Place of Truth	20th Dynasty: Ramesses III - Ramesses V	Mertseger and Taweret	Dedicator in text only	C		Unknown	Turin, Museo Egizio	1606	Porter and Moss I.2 1964: 718	Tosi Roccati 1972: 100, 289 [50062]
182	Hay (vii)	Servitor of the Lord of the Two Lands	20th Dynasty: Ramesses III - Ramesses V	Amenhotep I and Queen Ahmes Nefertari	Vizier (Hori) mediating scene	B	Water (offered by intermediary) and offering stand	Unknown	London, The British Museum	317	Porter and Moss I.2 1964: 719	James 1970: 20-21, pl. XVI
183	Hesysunebef (i)	Workman of the Lord of the Two Lands in the Place of Truth	20th Dynasty: Ramesses III	Mut and Neferhotep (ii)	Festival procession (divine bark) (oracle)	C	Incense, water (offered by women) and lotus flowers	Ramesseum area	Manchester, The Manchester Museum	4588	Porter and Moss I.2 1964: 682	Quibell 1898: 8 [12], 15, pl. X [3]

184	Hesysunebef (i)	Workman in the Place of Truth	20th Dynasty: Ramesses III	Reshep	Dedicator in text only	C		Unknown			Porter and Moss I.2 1964: 719	Wilkinson, M and C, Supp., pl. 69 [1]
185	Hori (ix)	Chief Draughtsman in the Place of Truth	20th Dynasty: Ramesses III	Mertseger	Adoring deity	C		KV53 (in tomb shaft or huts built over the entrance)	Cairo, The Egyptian Museum	JdE 38792	Porter and Moss I.2 1964: 587	Bruyère 1930b: 113, fig. 53
186	..y..(?) [=Ipuy (ii)?]	Foreman of the Gang in the Place of Truth	20th Dynasty: Ramesses III, first half	Amun-Re (?)	Adoring deity (not clear). Sandstone	A	Offering stand	Unknown	Turin, Museo Egizio	6172		Tosi Roccati 1972: 108, 293 [50071]
187	Iyernutef	Wab-priest	20th Dynasty: Ramesses III +	Ptah and Amenhotep I	Vizier (To) mediating scene	B		Queens' Valley Chapels: Chapel A	In situ		Porter and Moss I.2 1964: 707	Bruyère 1930b: 14-18, fig. 11
188	Khons (v)	Foreman in the Place of Truth	20th Dynasty: Ramesses III +	Mertseger; Ramesses III	Vizier (To) mediating scene	B		Queens' Valley Chapels: Chapel A	In situ		Porter and Moss I.2 1964: 707	Bruyère 1930b: 14-18, fig. 10
189	Nebnefer (ix)	Scribe [=Draughtsman]	20th Dynasty: Ramesses III - Ramesses VII	Thoth	Adoring deity	A		Hathor Temple: Inside Ptolemaic Temple Precinct: Excavations in South West Part by Baraize, 1912	Cairo, The Egyptian Museum	JdE 43571	Porter and Moss I.2 1964: 699	Bruyère 1923-1924 (1925): 88-91, pl. II [3]
190	Neferhor (vi)	Wab-priest of the Lord of the Two Lands	20th Dynasty: Ramesses III - Ramesses V	Mertseger	Adoring deity	C		Unknown	Chicago, Oriental Institute Museum	11107	Porter and Moss I.2 1964: 728	Cartwright 1929: 188-189, fig. 15
191	Neferhotep	Workman in the Place of Truth	20th Dynasty: Ramesses III (?)	Qadesh-Astarte-Anat	Dedicator in text only	C		Unknown	Ex-Winchester College Museum, sold at Christie's (Christie Sale Catalogue, July 12, 1972, No.153)		Porter and Moss I.2 1964: 728	Edwards 1955: 49-51, pl.III

192	Neferhotep (xi)	Wab-priest of Amun and Lector priest of all the Gods	20th Dynasty: Ramesses III	Mertseger, Ptah, Amenhotep I, Queen Ahmes Nefertari, Amun-Re, Mut, Khonsu and another deity	Adoring deities	C		Hathor Temple: Northern Sector: North East Corner of the Ptolemaic Precinct of the temple			Porter and Moss I.2 1964: 728	Bruyère 1935-1940 (1952) II: 120, fig. 201 [281]
193	Pen(men?)nefer (i)	Guardian in the Place of Truth	20th Dynasty: Ramesses III +	Amun-Re and Werethekau	Adoring deities	C	Bouquet and loaded offering table	Unknown	London, The British Museum	812	Porter and Moss I.2 1964: 732	Bierbrier 1993: 18, pls. 52-53
194	Penmennefer (i)	Workman in the Place of Truth	20th Dynasty: Ramesses III - Ramesses V	Ptah	Offering to deity	A	Incense	Unknown	Turin, Museo Egizio	Supp. 6139	Porter and Moss I.2 1964: 732	Tosi Roccati 1972: 108-109, 293 [50072]
195	Penmennefer (i)	Guardian in the Place of Truth	20th Dynasty: Ramesses III - Ramesses V	Iah	Adoring deity	C		Village: House CVI: Room 2	Paris, Musée du Louvre	E 16371	Porter and Moss I.2 1964: 705	Bruyère 1934-1935 (1939) III: 199-200, pl. XXIII
196	Qenhirkhopshef (iv)	Workman in the Place of Truth	20th Dynasty: Ramesses III - Ramesses V	Hathor (Mut and Amun-Re in text)	Adoring deity	C	Offering stand	Queens' Valley Chapels: Finds (?)	London, The British Museum	278	Porter and Moss I.2 1964: 708 (Finds)	Bierbrier 1982b: 37-38, pl. 86
197	Tarekhanu (ii) (f.)	Lady of the House (?)	20th Dynasty: Ramesses III	Mertseger	Adoring deity	A	Offering stand	Unknown	Paris, Musée du Louvre	E 13084	Porter and Moss I.2 1964: 734	Andreu 2002: 276-277 [223b]
198	Amenemone (iii)	Workman	20th Dynasty: Ramesses IV	Amun-Re, Mertseger, Harsiesi and Wepwawet	Adoring deities	C	Offering stand	Unknown	Brussels, Musées royaux d'Art et d'Histoire	E 755	Porter and Moss I.2 1964: 715	Bruyère 1930b: 153, fig. 83
199	Apatjau (i)	Wab-priest of the Lord of the Two Lands	20th Dynasty: Ramesses IV +	Amenhotep I	Adoring deity	A		Unknown	Turin, Museo Egizio	1451	Porter and Moss I.2 1964: 717 (a)	Tosi Roccati 1972: 109-110, 293 [50073]
200	Apatjau (i)	Workman in the Place of Truth	20th Dynasty: Ramesses IV +	Male and female deities	Adoring deities	A		Workmen's Col Station: Miniature Shrine			Porter and Moss I.2 1964: 589	Davies, N. d. G. 1935-1938 I/1: 247 III, pl V:2
201	Huynefer (x)	Workman in the Place of Truth	20th Dynasty: Ramesses IV +	Ptah	Offering to deity	A	Incense	Unknown	New York, The Brooklyn Museum	16.93	Porter and Moss I.2 1964: 270	Maspero 1882: 103 [cii] (text only)
202	Nakhtmin (vi)	Workman in the Place of Truth	20th Dynasty: Ramesses IV - Ramesses VII	Amenhotep I and Queen Ahmes Nefertari	Offering to deities	A	Incense	Unknown	Paris, Musée du Louvre	C 204 = E 3446	Porter and Moss I.2 1964: 729	Boreux 1932: 94 (text)

203	Nekhemmut (vi)	Foreman in the Place of Truth	20th Dynasty: Ramesses IV - Ramesses IX	Amun-Re	Adoring deity	A		Unknown	Turin, Museo Egizio	1587	Porter and Moss I.2 1964: 729	Tosi Roccati 1972: 107, 293 [50070]
204	Nekhemmut (vi)	Foreman in the Place of Truth	20th Dynasty: Ramesses IV - Ramesses IX	Amenhotep I	Adoring deity	C	Lost	Hathor Temple: Area N/N-E/E of Ptolemaic Temple Precinct (Finds 1945-1946)			Porter and Moss I.2 1964: 729	Bruyère 1945-1947 (1952): 41-42 [18], fig. 28 (1)
205	Nekhemmut (vi) (?)	Foreman in the Place of Truth	20th Dynasty: Ramesses IV - Ramesses IX	Ptah	Offering to deity (festival)	A	Incense	Unknown	Rome, Vatican Museum - Museo Gregoraino Egizio	Inv. 289	Porter and Moss I.2 1964: 729	Botti-Romanelli 1951: 91-92, pl. LXV [136]
206	Patjauemdiam un (ii)	Workman in the Place of Truth	20th Dynasty: Ramesses IV	Amenhotep I and Nebnefer, plus Queen Ahmes Neferatri as a cartouche	Dedicator in text only (oracle)	C	Offering stand	Unknown	Leiden, Het Rijksmuseum van Oudheden	F 93/1.27	Porter and Moss I.2 1964: 731	Raven 2000: 299-302, pl. XLII [9]
207	Penrennut (i)	Workman in the Place of Truth	20th Dynasty: Ramesses IV	Amenhotep I, Queen Ahmes Nefertari and Khonsu - Thoth as a child	Offering to deities	A	Incense, lotus flowers and offering stand	Unknown	Kingston Lacy, Bankes Collection	10	Porter and Moss I.2 1964: 732	Černý 1948: no. 10
208	Qaha (v)	Sculptor in the Place of Truth	20th Dynasty: Ramesses IV +	Ptah and Maat	Offering to deities	A	Incense and offering stand	Unknown	Munich, Staatliche Sammlung Ägyptischer Kunst	27 (=Inv 42)	Porter and Moss I.1 1960: 424 (3)	Bruyère 1930b: 49, fig. 29
209	Qaha (v)	Sculptor	20th Dynasty: Ramesses IV	Amun-Re	Offering to deity	A	Incense and lotus flowers	Workmen's Col Station: Miniature Shrine			Porter and Moss I.2 1964: 589	Davies, N. d. G. 1935-1938: 247 [iv], pl iv [3]
210	Qenamun (i)	Workman in the Place of Truth	20th Dynasty: Ramesses IV +	Queen Ahmes Nefertari	Offering to deity	A	Offering stand	Unknown	London, The British Museum	916	Porter and Moss I.2 1964:. 724	Bierbrier 1982b: 38, pl. 87
211	Qenna (v)	Workman	20th Dynasty: Ramesses IV - Ramesses IX	Osiris	Adoring deity	A	Loaded offering table	Unknown	Zargreb, Arkeoloski Muzej	582	Porter and Moss I.2 1964: 724	Saleh 1970: 32-33 [16]
212	Seti, Nebreneheh, Setimose	Draughtsman (x 2)	20th Dynasty: Ramesses IV - Ramesses V (?)	Amenhotep I and Queen Ahmes Nefertari	Offering to deities (?)	A	Offering stand	Unknown	London, The British Museum	217	Porter and Moss I.2 1964: 734	James 1970: 60, pl. XLVI

213	To (i)/(ii)/(iii)	Workman in the Place of Truth	20th Dynasty: Ramesses IV +	Osiris	Offering to deity	A	Water (offered by the man?), lotus flowers, and loaded offering table	Village	Berlin, Ägyptisches Museum und Papyrussammlung, Staatliche Museen zu Berlin-SPK	20989	Porter and Moss I.2 1964: 706	Brunner Traut 1956: 23, pl. XLVII
214	To/[Tjay] (i), Pentaweret (iv)	To: Wab-priest of the Mistress of the Two Lands; Pentaweret: Scribe of the House of Eternity	20th Dynasty: Ramesses IV	Amun-Re	Royal ancestor (Queen Ahmes Nefertari) mediating scene	B		Unknown	Kingston Lacy, Bankes Collection	12	Porter and Moss I.2 1964: 735	Černý 1958: no. 12
215	Iyi (f.)	Lady of the House	20th Dynasty: Ramesses VI	Anukis	Offering to deity	A	Incense, water (offered by the woman) and offering stand	Unknown	London, The British Museum	370	Porter and Moss I.2 1964: 722	James 1970: 55, pl. XLIII
216	Neferhotep (xi)	Workman	20th Dynasty: Ramesses VI	Amun-Re	Adoring deity	A		Hathor Temple: Inside Ptolemaic Temple Precinct: Excavations in South West Part by Baraize, 1912	Cairo, The Egyptian Museum	JdE 43656	Porter and Moss I.2 1964: 699	Bruyère1923-1924 (1925): 81-82, pl. 1 [3]
217	Wabet (?) (f.)	Lady of the House	20th Dynasty: Ramesses VII - Ramesses X	Mertseger	Adoring deity	C	Offering stand	Unknown	Turin, Museo Egizio	1533	Porter and Moss I.2 1964: 735	Tosi Roccati 1972: 97-98, 288 [50060]
218	Prehotep (ii)	Workman in the Place of Truth	20th Dynasty: Ramesses IX	Amun-Re, Mertseger and Amenhotep I	Adoring deities	C	Loaded offering table	Unknown	Turin, Museo Egizio	1451 bis	Porter and Moss I.2 1964: 730	Tosi Roccati 1972: 66-67, 274 [50033]
219	Amennakht (vi)	Foreman in the Place of Truth	20th Dynasty: Ramesses X	Osiris	Offering, deity not represented	C	Wedjat eyes, offering stand	Ramesside Chapels north of Ptolemaic Temple Precinct: Chapel B			Porter and Moss I.2 1964: 694	Bruyère 1935-1940 (1952) II: 129-130, pl. XXII, fig. 214 [319]

220	Name lost [=Khaemhedjet (i) ?]	Royal Scribe of the Lord of the Two Lands, Overseer of the Houses of Gold and Silver, Overseer of the Works of [...]	20th Dynasty: Ramesses XI	Amun-Re and Mertseger	Royal (?) mediating scene	B		Hathor Temple: Northern Sector: North East Corner of the Ptolemaic Precinct of the Temple			Porter and Moss I.2 1964: 718	Bruyère 1935-1940 (1952) II: 118-120, pl. XLIV [280]
221	Anakhtu (ii)/(iii)/(iv)	Workman in the Place of Truth	20th Dynasty	Ptah	Adoring deity	A	Loaded offering table (or offering stand?)	Queens' Valley Chapels: Finds (?)	Edinburgh, The Royal Museum	1961.439	Porter and Moss I.2 1964: 709	Seyffarth MSS XII, 9793
222	Hay (viii)	Workman in the Place of Truth	20th Dynasty (early)	Amun-Re	Adoring deity	A		Unknown	Glasgow Museum and Art Gallery, Burrell Collection	13.62	Porter and Moss I.2 1964: 718	The Burrell Collection, Exhibition 1949: 16 [219]
223	Hutiyi [=Hutiyi (i)/(ii) (?)] (f.)	No title	20th Dynasty (?)	Mertseger	Offering to deity	A	Incense and offering stand	Unknown	Budapest, Hungarian Museum of Fine Arts	56.54 E	Porter and Moss I.2 1964: 719	Oroszlan and Dobrovits 1939: 42-43 [60]
224	Iyernutef (iii) (?)	First God's Workman of the Lord of the Two Lands	20th Dynasty	N/A	Adoring, deity not represented - pyramid shaped	C		Workmen's Col Station: Miniature Shrine	Oxford, The Ashmolean Museum	1942.46	Porter and Moss I.2 1964: 590	Davies, N. d. G. 1935-1938 I/1: 244-245, 248 V, pls. III:1, IV:1
225	Khaemnun	Workman in the Place of Truth	20th Dynasty	Amenhotep I	Adoring deity	A		Village			Porter and Moss I.2 1964: 705	Bruyère 1931-1932 (1934): 86 [9], fig. 56
226	Khaemope	Chief Craftsman in the Place of Truth	20th Dynasty	Osiris	Adoring deity	A	Lotus flowers and offering stand	Unknown	Berlin, Ägyptisches Museum und Papyrussammlung, Staatliche Museen zu Berlin-SPK	24028	Porter and Moss I.2 1964: 724	Weng 1961: 67
227	Khnummose (i)	Workman	20th Dynasty (early)	Hathor	Offering to deity (festival)	A	Incense, lotus flowers and offering stand	Unknown	Moscow, Pushkin Museum of Fine Arts	I .1.a. 6687		Hodjash and Berlev 1982: 150-152 [91]
228	Minkhau (i) or (ii)	Workman in the Place of Truth	20th Dynasty	Mertseger	Offering to deity	A	Incense	Unknown	Copenhagen, The National Museum of Denmark	B 7	Porter and Moss I.2 1964: 726	Bruyère 1930b: 231, fig. 119

229	Nebamun (iv)	Workman in the Place of Truth	20th Dynasty (mid)	Amun-Re (ram)	Adoring deity (festival). Wood	C	Offering stand	Unknown	London, The British Museum	8485	Porter and Moss I.2 1964: 726	Bierbrier 1982b: 36, pl. 83
230	Nebamun (iv)	Workman in the Place of Truth	20th Dynasty (mid)	Ptah, Amun-Re and Mertseger	Adoring deities	C		Medinet Habu	Chicago, Oriental Institute Museum		Porter and Moss I.2 1964:. 776	Bruyère 1930b: 299, fig.146
231	[Nebnefer (vii) (?)]	[Workman in the Place of Truth]	20th Dynasty (late)	Amenhotep I and Queen Ahmes Nefertari	Offering to deities	A	Incense and lotus flowers	Unknown	London, The British Museum	811	Porter and Moss I.2 1964: 730	Bierbrier 1993: 17-18, pls. 52-53;
232	Pamedunetern akht (i)	Wab-priest of the Lord of the Two Lands in the Place of Truth	20th Dynasty (early)	Amun-Re, Mut and Khonsu	Royal ancestor (Amenhotep I) mediating scene	B		Unknown	Kingston Lacy, Bankes Collection	11	Porter and Moss I.2 1964: 730	Černý 1958: no. 11
233	Sheritre (f.)	No title	20th Dynasty	Taweret	Offering to deity	A	Bouquet	Hathor Temple: Inside Ptolemaic Temple Precinct: Excavations in South West Part by Baraize, 1912	Cairo, The Egyptian Museum	JdE 43573	Porter and Moss I.2 1964: 699	Bruyère 1923-1924 (1925): 88-91, pls. II [3], III [1-3]
234	[…]nefer (?)	Draughtsman in the Place of Truth	20th Dynasty	Mertseger	Adoring deity (festival procession?)	A		Unknown	Rome, Vatican Museum - Museo Gregoriano Egizio	22791 (old no: 296)	Porter and Moss I.2 1964: 736	Bruyère 1930b: 115, n. 1, fig. 55
235	Amenemone	Workman of the Lord of the Two Lands in the Place of Truth	Ramesside Period	Mertseger	Adoring and offering to deity	C	Water (offered by the woman) and offering stand	Hathor Temple: Northern Sector: North East Corner of the Ptolemaic Precinct of the Temple			Porter and Moss I.2 1964: 715	Bruyère 1935-1940 (1952) II: 122, fig. 203 [283]
236	Amenemope	No title	Ramesside Period	Amun-Re (Amunresonther), Mut and Amenhotep I	Offering to deities	A	Incense, bouquet and loaded offering table	Unknown	London, The British Museum	816 (354)	Porter and Moss I.2 1964: 715	Bierbrier 1993: 13, pls. 34-35;

237	Haremwia	Workman of the Lord of the Two Lands in the Place of Truth	Ramesside Period	Bau-neteru	Adoring deity (festival)	C	Bouquet	Unknown	London, The British Museum	356	Porter and Moss I.2 1964: 718	British Museum 1914: pl. 42 [left]
238	Hay (?)	Workman	Ramesside Period	[Amenhotep I] and Queen Ahmes Nefertari	Offering to deities (fragments)	A	Water (offered by women) and festival offerings	Western Cemetery: Chapel 1190			Porter and Moss I.2 1964: 689	Bruyère 1929 (1930a) II: 39-41 [2], fig. 14 [12, 13]
239	Henut (f.)	No Title	Ramesside Period	Mertseger	Adoring deity	C		Unknown	Liverpool, World Museum	M 13830	Porter and Moss I.2 1964: 722	Bruyère 1930b: 273, fig. 140
240	Hori (f.)	Lady of the House	Ramesside Period	Queen Ahmes Nefertari	Offering to deity	A	Water (offered by the woman), bouquet and offering stand	Unknown	Turin, Museo Egizio	1450	Porter and Moss I.2 1964: 719	Tosi Roccati 1972: 85, 299 [50050]
241	Huy	Chief Craftsman in the Place of Truth	Ramesside Period	Hathor (?)	Lost	C	Lost	Hathor Temple: Northern Sector: North East Corner of the Ptolemaic Precinct of the Temple			Porter and Moss I.2 1964: 720	Bruyère 1935-1940 (1952) II: 124, 126, fig. 207 [292] (misnumbered as [293] on the figure)
242	Ipuy	God's Workman of the Lord of the Two Lands	Ramesside Period	Isis	Dedicator in text only	C		Unknown	Vienna, Kunsthistorisches Museum	Inv. 120	Porter and Moss I.2 1964: 722	Bergmann 1892: 17 [XIX] (text only)
243	Iy…	Workman in the Place of Truth	Ramesside Period	Sekhmet [and another deity?]	Adoring deity	A	Offering stand	Unknown	London, The British Museum	810	Porter and Moss I.2 1964: 722	Bierbrier 1982b: 38-39, pl. 88
244	Iyemtapet (f.)	Lady of the House	Ramesside Period	Mertseger	Adoring deity	C	Offering stand	Unknown	London, The British Museum	8501	Porter and Moss I.2 1964: 722	Bierbrier 1982b: 38, pl. 88
245	Iyernutef (ii) or (iii)	Sculptor in the Place of Truth	Ramesside Period	Ptah	Adoring deity	A	Offering stand	Hathor Temple: Sector 2 (north of the pit in the centre of the courtyard)			Porter and Moss I.2 1964: 722	Bruyère 1935-1940 (1952) II: 75, 76, fig. 154 [33]
246	Khanun (?)	Workman in the Place of Truth	Ramesside Period	Hathor	Adoring [deity]	A	Not clear	Unknown (purchased in Luxor)			Porter and Moss I.2 1964: 725	Bruyère 1931-1932 (1934): 100 [1], fig. 65
247	Mutemopet (f.)	No title	Ramesside Period	Renenut	Offering to deity (?)	A	Lotus flowers and offering stand	Western Cemetery: TT1245			Porter and Moss I.2 1964: 726	Bruyère 1931-1932 (1934): 10-11 [3], fig. 6

248	Nebamentet	No title	Ramesside Period	Mut	Adoring deity (?)	A	Festival offerings and offering stand	Unknown	Turin, Museo Egizio	Supp. 6165		Tosi Roccati 1972: 145, 316 [50137]
249	Nebnefer	Workman in the Place of Truth	Ramesside Period	Mertseger	Dedicator in text only	C	Offering stand	Unknown	Liverpool, World Museum	M 13959	Porter and Moss I.2 1964: 727	Bruyère 1930b: fig. 46
250	Panakht	Workman in the Place of Truth	Ramesside Period	Mertseger and Ptah	Offering to deities	A	Incense and offering stand	Unknown	Paris, Musée du Louvre	E 13934	Porter and Moss I.2 1964: 732	Bruyère 1930b: 116, fig. 56
251	Paser	Workman in the Place of Truth	Ramesside Period	Mertseger and Hathor	Dedicator in text only	C	Offering stand	Hathor Temple: Khenu-Chapel: Room 9, Pit 1414	Cairo, The Egyptian Museum	JdE 72018	Porter and Moss I.2 1964: 731	Bruyère 1935-1940 II: 34, 76-77, fig. 156 [34]; Kitchen 2000: 490
252	Pashedu	Workman in the Place of Truth	Ramesside Period	Reshep	Adoring deity	C	Offering stand	Unknown	Cambridge, The Fitzwilliam Museum	E.GA 3002.1943	Porter and Moss I.2 1964: 733	Janssen 1950: 209-212, figs. 18-19; Martin 2005: 74 [46]
253	Pashedu	Workman in the Place of Truth to the West of Thebes	Ramesside Period	Reshep	Adoring deity	C	Loaded offering table	Unknown	London, The British Museum	264	Porter and Moss I.2 1964: 732	Bierbrier 1993: 12, pls. 32-33
254	Pashedu	Workman in the Place of Truth	Ramesside Period	Ptah	Offering to deity	A	Incense	Hathor Temple: Sector 2 (north of the pit in the centre of the courtyard)	Paris, Musée du Louvre	E 16370	Porter and Moss I.2 1964: 732	Bruyère 1935-1940 (1952) II: 34, 75, fig. 153 [32]
255	Pashedu	No title	Ramesside Period	Amun-Re (ram)	Adoring deity (festival)	A		Hathor Temple: Hathor Chapel of Seti I: Room preceding the Pronaos			Porter and Moss I.2 1964: 695	Bruyère 1935-1940 (1952) II: 128, fig. 211 [309]
256	Webkhet (f.)	No title	Ramesside Period	Mertseger	Adoring deity (?)	C		Village	Berlin, Ägyptisches Museum und Papyrussammlung, Staatliche Museen zu Berlin-SPK	21565	Porter and Moss I.2 1964: 706	Roeder 1913 II: 397
257	Wen[…] (?)	Workman in the Place of Truth	Ramesside Period	Harsiesi	Adoring deity	A	Offering stand	Unknown	Paris, Musée du Louvre	E. 16361	Porter and Moss I.2 1964: 720	Unpublished
258	[…]pahapi	No title	Ramesside Period	Mertseger	Adoring deity	A		Unknown	London, The British Museum	371	Porter and Moss I.2 1964: 731	Bierbrier 1993: 13, pls. 34-35

259	[unidentified]	No title	Ramesside Period	Seth 'nub'	Dedicator in text only. Wood	C		Western Cemetery: Chapel 1190, first court			Porter and Moss I.2 1964: 689	Bruyère 1929: 44 [4], fig.18
260	Name lost	Draughtsman	Ramesside Period	Lost	Royal (?) mediating scene	B	Offering stand	Unknown	Turin, Museo Egizio	Supp. 6129		Tosi Roccati 1972: 145, 316 [50136]
261	Name lost	Child of the Tomb	Ramesside Period	Mertseger	Offering to deity	A	Incense and offering stand	Unknown	Vienna, Kunst-Historisches Museum	Inv. 122	Porter and Moss I.2 1964: 737	Bruyère 1930b: 119, 120, fig. 58
262	Name lost	Workman	Ramesside Period	Ptah	Offering to deity	A	Incense and offering stand	Hathor Temple: Eastern Staircase and its Surrounding Area	Cairo, The Egyptian Museum	JdE 43570	Porter and Moss I.2 1964: 698	Bruyère 1935-1940 (1952) II: 45, 75, 77, fig. 155 [161]
263	Name lost	Workman in the Place of Truth	Ramesside Period	Queen Ahmes Nefertari	Adoring deity	A		Western Cemetery: Chapel 1190				Bruyère 1929 (1930a) II: 39, 52, fig. 14 [3]
264	Name lost	Workman in the Place of Truth	Ramesside Period	Ptah	Adoring deity	A	Bouquet and loaded offering table	Unknown	London, The British Museum	286	Porter and Moss I.2 1964: 736	Bierbrier 1993: 14 pls. 40-41

All limestone unless indicated.
*** See Chapter 3, note 18.*

Table 2 The Theban Votive Stelae (55)

Database number	Owner	Title	Date	Dedicated to	Brief description**	Representational form	Offerings by the dedicator	Find location	Current location	Repository number	Porter and Moss reference	Primary publication details
265	Amenmen	Workman	18th or 19th Dynasty	Osiris, Isis and Harsiese; Amenhotep I, Queens Ahmes Nefertari and Sit-Kamose	Adoring deities. Sandstone	A	Offering stand	Unknown	London, The British Museum	297	Porter and Moss I.2 1964: 715-716	British Museum 1914 (VI): pl. 33
266	Nebsu	Scribe	Late 18th Dynasty - 19th Dynasty*	Amenhotep I (blue crown), Queen Ahmes Nefertari, Sitamen and Prince Ahmes Sipair	Seated before deities and offering scene. Granite	C	Loaded offering table	Karnak	Cairo, The Egyptian Museum	34029	Porter and Moss II 1972: 294	Lacau 1909: 63-64, pl. 22
267	Userhat	Scribe of Offerings in the Temple of Amenhotep III, First God's Servant in the Temple of Tutankhmun	Late 18th Dynasty -Early 19th Dynasty	Lost	Adoring in lower register [upper register lost]	C	Lost	West Bank: Deir el Bahri: Mentuhotep Temple	New York, The Metropolitan Museum of Art	05.4.2	Porter and Moss II 1972: 396	Hayes 1959 II: fig. 191

268	Iwefenamun	Stonemason of the Temple of Amun	19th Dynasty: Ramesses II, end	Min of Coptos; Isis	Royal (Amenhotep I) mediating scene	B		Unknown	Private Collection			Altenmüller 1981: 1-7, pl. 1
269	Roma	Prince, Mayor, Overseer of the God's Servants of all the Gods and the God's Servants of Amun, First God's Servant of Amun	19th Dynasty: Ramesses II - Seti II	Re-Harakhti, Maat, Osiris, Isis; Harsiesi, Anubis, Amenhotep I, Queen Ahmes Nefertari and Queen Ahhotep	Adoring deities	C	Offering stand	Unknown	Leiden, Rijksmuseum van Oudheden	No. V.8 (Anastasi Coll.	Porter and Moss I.2 1964: 807	Boeser 1913: pl. XXIV [43]
270	Huy	Wab-priest of the Prow of Amun	19th Dynasty: Ramesses II	Khonsu-em-Waset Neferhotep (?), Ptah (?), another god and goddess; Amenhotep I (blue crown) and Queen Ahmes Nefertari	Adoring deities	A	Loaded offering table	West Bank: Mortuary Temple of the High Priest Nebwenenef: Beneath the temple	London, The Petrie Museum of Egyptian Archaeology	UC 14212	Porter and Moss I.2 1964: 606	Stewart 1976: 47, pl 38.2
271	Nui	First Charioteer of his Majesty, Royal Envoy to all Foreign Lands, Overseer of Foreign Lands in Many Foreign Lands	19th Dynasty: Ramesses II	Amenhotep I (blue crown) and Queen Ahmes Nefertari	Royal (Ramesses II) mediating scene (oracle)	B	Loaded offering table	Unknown	Location unknown			Wente 1963: 30-36
272	Parapanefu	Lector priest of the Vizier, Parahotep	19th Dynasty: Ramesses II	Parahotep	Offering to Vizier	A	Incense, water and offering stand	Unknown	Durham, The Oriental Museum	N1961	Porter and Moss VIII forthcoming: 803-055-275	Bierbrier 1994: 407-410
273	Penre	Troop Commander, First Charioteer of his Majesty, Overseer of Foreign Countries, Overseer of Works in the Mansion of Usermaatre Setepenre, Chief of the Medjay	19th Dynasty: Ramesses II	Amenhotep I (blue crown)	Royal (Ramesses II) mediating scene (oracle)	B	Double offering stand	Unknown (purchased in Luxor)	Chicago, Oriental Institute Museum	10494	Porter and Moss I.2 1964: 802	Nims 1956: 146-149, pl. IX; Kitchen 2000: 191
274	Mahuhy	First God's Servant of Amun	19th Dynasty: Seti II	Amun-Re, Mut and Khonsu	Royal (Seti II) mediating scene	B	Loaded offering table	East Bank: Karnak: Sacred Lake: Fowlyard			Porter and Moss I.1 1960: 222	Chevrier 1936: 140, pl. II (2)
275	Dedia	Overseer of the Draughtsmen of Amun	19th Dynasty: Siptah (?)	Amun-Re, Mut, Khonsu, Min, Isis, Thoth, Maat, Hathor, Wennenefer, Re-Harakhti, Anubis, Hathor and Nepthys	Deities and text only [lower section lost]. Granite	C		West Bank: Deir el Bahri: Mentuhotep Temple: Upper North Colonnade	London, The British Museum	706	Porter and Moss 1964 I.1: 656	Pinch 1993: 87, fig. 7c

276	Amenerhatef	Workman	19th Dynasty	Osiris	Adoring deity	C	Bouquet (?) and loaded offering table	Unknown	London, The British Museum	345	Porter and Moss I.2 1964: 715	James 1970: pl. XLVI
277	Amenmose	Guardian of the Estate of Amun	19th Dynasty	Amenhotep I and Hathor	Offering to deities	C	Incense and water (offered by the woman)	West Bank: Deir el Bahri: Mentuhotep Temple	Philadelphia, University of Philadelphia, Museum of Archaeology and Anthropology	E 11818	Porter and Moss II 1972: 396	Naville 1907: 69-70, pl. XXV [F]
278	Amenmose	Royal Scribe of the Altar/Table of the Lord of the Two Lands, Overseer of the Huntsmen of Amun	19th Dynasty	[Osiris?]	Adoring deity	A	Lost	West Bank: Deir el Medina: Western Cemetery (?): TT149	London, The British Museum	107		Bierbrier 1993: 10, pls. 22-23 [2]
279	Amenope-nakht	Scribe of Troops of the Estate of Amun, Wab-priest of the Prow of Amun, Overseer of Works of all the Monuments of Amun	19th Dynasty	Osiris, Isis, Mertseger, Amenhotep I and Queen Ahmes Nefertari	Adoring deities	A	Loaded offering tables	Unknown	Cairo, The Egyptian Museum	JdE 43134	Porter and Moss I.2 1964: 800	Bruyère 1930b: fig. 79
280	Bek	No title	19th Dynasty	Amun-Re (ram) and Khonsu	Adoring deities. Sandstone	A	Loaded offering table and offering stand	Unknown	Moscow, Pushkin Museum of Fine Arts	I.1.a.5607	Porter and Moss I.2 1964: 810	Hodjash and Berlev 1982: 141 [81]
281	Djau	Workman of Amun	19th Dynasty	Ptah (?)	Adoring deity	A	Double offering stand	Unknown	Brussels, Musées royaux d'Art et d'Histoire	E. 410	Porter and Moss I.2 1964: 799	
282	Huy	Workman	19th Dynasty	Ahmose and Queen Ahmes Nefertari	Offering to deities	C	Incense, festival offerings and double offering stand	Unknown (purchased)	Copenhagen, Ny Carlsberg Glyptotek	AEIN 898	Porter and Moss I.2 1964: 803	Koefoed-Petersen 1948: XXX, 24, pl. 26
283	Khons	[Sculptor?] of Amun	19th Dynasty	Taweret; Mut	Dedicator in text only	C	Offering stand	Unknown	New York, The Metropolitan Museum of Art	47.105.4	Porter and Moss I.2 1964: 725	Hayes 1959 II: fig. 242
284	Mahu	Goldsmith of Amun	19th Dynasty (?)	Re	Adoring, deity not represented. Sandstone	C		Unknown (purchased by Petrie)	London, The Petrie Museum of Egyptian Archaeology	UC 14231	Porter and Moss 1.2 1964: 809	Stewart 1976: 35, pl. 27.2

285	Nebmehyt	No title	19th Dynasty	Khnum	Adoring deity. Wood	C	Loaded offering table	Unknown (purchased in Cairo from a Luxor dealer)	Strasbourg, Université Institut d'Égyptologie	1594	Porter and Moss I.2 1964: 726	Spiegelberg 1918: 65-66
286	Nebwa	Scribe of the Army of the Lord of the Two Lands	19th Dynasty	Wenut and Sobek-Re	Offering to deities	A	Incense, festival offerings, bouquet, water and offering stand	West Bank: Ramesseum Area	Philadelphia, University of Philadelphia, Museum of Archaeology and Anthropology	1567	Porter and Moss I.2 1964: 682	Quibell 1898: 19-20 [2], pl. XXVII [2]
287	Netjermose	Workman of Amun	19th Dynasty	Amun-Re (ram)	Dedicator in text only	C		Unknown	London, The Petrie Museum of Egyptian Archaeology	UC 14605	Porter and Moss I.2 1964: 809	Stewart 1976: 39, pl. 30.2
288	Pairy	Scribe	19th Dynasty	Osiris	Adoring deities	A	Offering stand	Unknown	Moscow, Pushkin Museum of Fine Arts	I.1.a.5633 (4074)		Hodjash and Berlev 1982: 144-145 [86]
289	Parennefer	No title	19th Dynasty	Thoth	Adoring deity	A	Loaded offering table	Unknown	Florence, Museo Archaeologico	7617 (cat. No. 45)	Porter and Moss I.2 1964: 805 (called Sennefer)	Bosticco 1965: 53
290	Rahuy/Rahotep	Medjay of the West	19th Dynasty	Taweret	Offering to deity	A	Incense and offering stand	West Bank: Temple of Tuthmosis III: In the area of rooms A and D	Deir el Bahri cache	Inv. F7757	Porter and Moss II 1972: 541	Lipinska 1984: 49, 118 [69], figs. 168-169
291	Ramery	Overseer of the Magazine	19th Dynasty	Osiris	[Upper register lost], adoring and offering to deity	A	Lotus flowers and double offering stand	Unknown	Durham, The Oriental Museum	N1960		Birch 1880: 299-300
292	Ramose	Mayor … to the West of Thebes	19th Dynasty	Hathor	Adoring deity	C	Lotus flowers	West Bank: Deir el Bahri: Middle and Upper Colonnades Area: Edge of Mound of Amenhotep I bricks, SE Hatshepsut Forecourt	New York, Metropolitan Museum of Art		Porter and Moss I.2 1964: 650	Unpublished; MMA photo M.5.C.143

293	Roy	Soldier of the Ship	19th Dynasty	Osiris	Offering to deity	A	Incense, water, bouquet (?) and loaded offering table	West Bank: Ramesseum Area	Philadelphia, University of Philadelphia, Museum of Archaeology and Anthropology	E 2169	Porter and Moss I.2 1964: 681	Quibell 1898: 20 [4], pl. XXVII [4]
294	Thutnefer	No title	19th Dynasty	Amun-Re (ram)	Dedicator in text only	C		Unknown (purchased in Cairo in 1930)	Copenhagen, Ny Carlsberg Glyptotek	AEIN 1676	Porter and Moss I.2 1964: 803	Koefoed-Petersen 1948: XXXVI, 39, pl. 52.
295	Name lost	Ka-servant of Tuthmosis I (or, in the Ka-service of Tuthmosis I), Scribe of the Divine Offerings	19th Dynasty (?)	Amun-Re	Royal ancestor (Tuthmosis I) mediating scene. Sandstone	B		Unknown	London, The Petrie Museum of Egyptian Archaeology	UC 14466	Porter and Moss VIII forthcoming: 803-055-631	Stewart 1976: 48, pl. 39.1
296	Amenemope	Wab-priest of Amun	20th Dynasty: Ramesses III-VI	Ptah	Vizier (?) mediating scene. Sandstone	B	Lotus flowers	West Bank: Under Tell of Temple of Tuthmosis II			Porter and Moss II 1972: 457	Bruyère 1926 (1952): 22-23, 58 [5], fig. 13, pl. XII [5]
297	Pennestytawy	Steward of the Temple of a Million Years of Usermaatre Meryamun [Medinet Habu] in the Estate of Amun	20th Dynasty: Ramesses III, second half	Osiris	Adoring deity	A	Offering stand	Unknown	Cairo, The Egyptian Museum	JdE 2013		Kitchen and Gaballa 1980: 76-77, pl. 2, fig. 2
298	To	Scribe of the Lord of the Two Lands	20th Dynasty: Ramesses III	Thoth	Adoring deity	A		West Bank: Deir el Medina: East of Ptolemaic Temple Precinct: Great Pit			Porter and Moss I.2 1964: 692	Bruyère 1948-1951 (1953): 41, pl. XI (2) [20A]
299	Montuemtawy	Royal Scribe and Overseer of the Treasury	20th Dynasty: Ramesses IV	Ramesses IV; Serpent headed goddess (Mertseger?)	Adoring deity	A		West Bank: Deir el Medina: Workmen's Col Station: Hut R, Eastern Group			Porter and Moss I.2 1964: 589	Bruyère 1934-1935 (1939) III: 359-360 [R (E)], fig. 209
300	Merymaat	Wab-priest, Divine Scribe and Overseer of the Temple of Maat	20th Dynasty: Ramesses VI, year 7	Amun-Re, Mut and Khonsu; Maat	Festival procession (oracle)	A		East Bank: Karnak: Temple of Maat	Karnak cache	Inv. 1723	Porter and Moss II 1972: 13	Varille 1943: 22-23, 27, pls. LXVIII, LXXII [A]

301	(Paser and) Amen[…]	Paser: God's Father of Amun, Fan-bearer and Mayor of Thebes; Amen[…]: Guardian of the Treasury of Upper and Lower Egypt	20th Dynasty: Ramesses IX	Amun-Re, Mut and Khonsu; Victorious in Thebes	Vizier (Paser) mediating scene	B		Unknown	London, The British Museum	1214		Bierbrier 1982b: 21, pl. 48
302	Bakenwerel	Sculptor	20th Dynasty	Amun-Re	Adoring deity	A	Offering stand	Unknown (acquired in Luxor)	Florence, Museo Archaeologico	7225	Porter and Moss I.2 1964: 805	Bosticco 1965: 67-68 [62]
303	Huy	God's Servant	20th Dynasty	Ptah	Adoring deity	A	Offering stand	West Bank: Under Tell of Temple of Tuthmosis II			Porter and Moss II 1972: 457	Bruyère 1926 (1952): 22, 59 [13], pl. XII [3]
304	Meryptah(em)peramun	No title	20th Dynasty	Amun-Re, Mut and Khonsu; Osiris and Isis, and Amun-Re	Adoring deities	A	Festival offerings, bouquet and (loaded) offering stand	Unknown	London, The British Museum	350	Porter and Moss I.2 1964: 808	Bierbrier 1993: pls. 64-65
305	Pahu	Sculptor	20th Dynasty	Osiris, Isis and Horus, Queen Ahmes Nefertari, Ahmose and Amenhotep I	Adoring deities	A	Offering stand	Unknown	New York, The Brooklyn Museum	37.1503	Porter and Moss I.2 1964: 799	Redford 1986: 51-52, pl. I
306	Suterniut	Prince, Mayor, Fourth God's Servant of Amun at Karnak, Overseer of God's Servants	20th Dynasty	Atum	Adoring deity	A		Unknown	London, The Petrie Museum of Egyptian Archaeology	UC 14356		Stewart 1976: 35, pl 27.4
307	Amenemhat	Sandal-maker of Amun	Ramesside Period	Amun-Re and Ptah	Dedicator in text only. Sandstone	C	Loaded offering table	Unknown	Kingston Lacy, Bankes Collection	15	Porter and Moss I.2 1964: 812	Černý 1958: no. 15
308	Anenna	Guardian of the Estate of Amun	Ramesside Period	Amun-Re and Queen Ahmes Nefertari; Amenhotep I	Adoring deity	C	Bouquet and loaded offering table	West Bank: Funerary Temple of Queen Ahmes Nefertari (Men-Aset)			Porter and Moss II 1972: 422	Northampton 1908: 8-9 [14], pl. IV [7]
309	Hatiay	Scribe	Ramesside Period	Osiris	Offering to deity	A	Bouquet, incense, water (offered by one of the women) and loaded offering table	Unknown	Cairo, The Egyptian Museum	34.138	Porter and Moss I.1 1960: 396	Lacau 1909: 188, pl. LVII

310	Merymaat	God's Servant, Divine Scribe of Maat and Overseer of the Temple of Maat	Ramesside Period	Maat and Thoth	Adoring deities	A	Offering stand	East Bank: Karnak: Temple of Maat: Finds			Porter and Moss II 1972: 13	Varille 1943: pl. LXIX
311	Nefersekheru	Wab-priest of Tuthmosis II	Ramesside Period	Lost	[Upper register lost], adoring and offering to deity. Sandstone?	C	Offering stand	West Bank: Tell of Temple of Tuthmosis II			Porter and Moss II 1972: 457	Bruyère, Rapport 1926 (1952): 56 [1], pl. XI (8), pl. XII (2)
312	Pagar	Chief of the Medjay	Ramesside Period	Amun-Re (ram) and Mut	Adoring deity	A	Offering stand	Karnak (?)	Vienna, Kunsthistorisches Museum	193		Guglielmi 1994: 55-68, pl. 1
313	Pashedu	Scribe of the Chamber of the [unknown word]	Ramesside Period	Osiris	Adoring deity	A	Offering stand	Unknown	Turin, Museo Egizio	1571	Porter and Moss I.2 1964: 733	Unpublished
314	Pashedu	Chief of the Medjay in the West of Thebes	Ramesside Period	Amen-Re-Harakhti-Atum with Mut and Khonsu-em-Waset Neferhotep	Adoring deity. Sandstone	C	Festival offerings, bouquet and loaded offering table	Unknown (purchased in Luxor)	London, The Petrie Museum of Egyptian Archaeology	UC 14576	Porter and Moss VIII forthcoming: 803-055-649	Stewart 1976: 38, pl 30.1
315	Qaha	No title	Ramesside Period	Amenhotep I	Adoring deity	A	Offering stand	Unknown	London, The Petrie Museum of Egyptian Archaeology	UC 14423	Porter and Moss VIII forthcoming: 803-055-622	Stewart 1976: 47-48, pl. 38.3
316	Re (f.)	Follower of Amun-Re, Great Singer of Hathor	Ramesside Period	Amun-Re (ram)	Adoring deity	C	Bouquet (?), loaded offering table and offering stand	Unknown	Hanover, Kestner Museum	2938	Porter and Moss I.2 1964: 806	Cramer 1936: 103-104 [23], pl. IX [3]
317	No name	Measurer of Amun	Ramesside Period	Amenhotep I and Queen Ahmes Nefertari	Adoring deity	C	Bouquet and loaded offering table	Karnak (?)	London, The British Museum	989		Edwards 1939: 54, pl. XLVI
318	Sedjem-wy-amun (f.)	Musician of Amun	20th or 21st Dynasty	Hathor	Adoring deity	A	Lotus flowers, festival offerings and offering stand	Unknown	Moscow, The Pushkin Museum of Fine Arts	I.1.a.5616 (3569)		Hodjash and Berlev 1982: 154 [101]
319	No name (f.)	No title	20th to 22nd Dynasty	Astarte	Offering to deity	C	Incense and double offering table	West Bank: Ramesseum Area			Porter and Moss I.2 1964: 682	Quibell 1898: 20 [6], pl. XXVII [6]

**Likely from content to date to the reign of Ramesses II.*
*** All limestone unless otherwise indicated.*

Table 3 The Abu Simbel Votive Stelae (21)

Database number	Owner	Title	Date	Dedicated to	Brief description*	Representational form	Offerings (by the dedicator)	Find location	Current location	Repository number	Porter and Moss reference	Primary publication details
320	Yuny	Overseer of the Southern Foreign Lands, King's Son of Kush, Overseer of Works in the Estate of Amun, Chief of the Medjay	19th Dynasty: Seti I - Ramesses II, year 2	Ramesses II	Greeting the king gesture	A		North of the Small Temple	In situ	Abu Simbel 10	Porter and Moss VII 1951: 117	Champollion 1835-1845 [1970] I: pl. IV (4); Kitchen 2000: 47-48
321	Ramesses-Asha-Hebu-Sed	First Royal Cupbearer of his Majesty	19th Dynasty: Ramesses II (start of reign)	Ramesses II	Greeting the king gesture	A		North of the Small Temple	In situ	Abu Simbel 9	Porter and Moss VII 1951: 117	Champollion 1835-1845 [1970] I: pl. IX (2); Kitchen 2000: 141-142
322	Hekanakht	King's Son of Kush, Overseer of the Southern Foreign Lands	19th Dynasty: Ramesses II, years 3-24	Amun-Re, Ramesses II, Re-Harakhti and Queen Nefertari	Royal (Ramesses II) mediating scene (and adoring Queen Nefertari)	B	Loaded offering table	South of the Great Temple	In situ	Abu Simbel 17	Porter and Moss VII 1951: 118	Champollion 1835-1845 [1970] I; Kitchen 2000: 49
323	Paser II	King's Son of Kush	19th Dynasty: Ramesses II, years 24/25-34	Amun-Re	Adoring deity	A	Offering stand	Between the two temples	Cairo, The Egyptian Museum	TN 5/12/35/1	Porter and Moss VII 1951: 118	Gauthier 1936: 49-69 and pl. III
324	Paser II	Prince, King's Son of Kush, Overseer of the Southern Foreign Lands, Fanbearer on the King's Right Hand, Royal Envoy to Every Foreign Land, Overseer of Works in Pi-Ramesses, Royal Scribe	19th Dynasty: Ramesses II, years 24/25-34	Ramesses II	Greeting the king gesture	A		South of the Great Temple	In situ	Abu Simbel 14	Porter and Moss VII 1951: 118	Kitchen 2000: 53
325	Paser II	Prince, King's Son of Kush, Overseer of the Southern Foreign Lands, Royal Scribe	19th Dynasty: Ramesses II, years 24/25-34	Ramesses II	Greeting the king gesture	A		Between the two temples	In situ	Abu Simbel 11	Porter and Moss VII 1951: 117	Maspero 1911b: 164-165, fig. 16; Kitchen 2000: 53
326	Paser II	King's Son of Kush	19th Dynasty: Ramesses II, years 24/25-34	Amun-Re	Adoring deity	A	Offering stand	Between the two temples	Cairo, The Egyptian Museum	JdE 65834	Porter and Moss VII 1951: 118	Gauthier 1936: 49-69, pl. III

327	Setau	King's Son of Kush, Overseer of the Southern Foreign Lands, Steward of Amun, Royal Scribe; Prince and Count, God's Father, Chief of Secrets of the King's Domain, Eyes of the Upper Egyptian King and Ears of the Lower Egyptian King, Confidant of Horus in his Palace	19th Dynasty: Ramesses II, year 38	Amun-Re, Re-Harakhti and Ramesses II	Double royal smiting scene	C		South of the Great Temple	In situ	Abu Simbel 24	Porter and Moss VII 1951: 118	Schulman 1994, fig. 3; Kitchen 2000: 72-73
328	Ahmose	Scribe of the Temple	19th Dynasty: Ramesses II	Horus and Ramesses II	Adoring deities	A (?)		South of the Great Temple	In situ	Abu Simbel 27	Porter and Moss VII 1951: 119	Lepsius 1913 V: 167 [VI]
329	Hatia	First God's Servant	19th Dynasty: Ramesses II	Ramesses II	Adoring deity	A (?)		South of the Great Temple	In situ	Abu Simbel 27	Porter and Moss VII 1951: 119	Lepsius 1913: 167 [VII]
330	Hatiay	Scribe	19th Dynasty: Ramesses II	Amun-Re, Ramesses II, Ra-Harakhti, Horus, Lord of Meha and Horus, Lord of Miam	Adoring deities	A		North of Small Temple	In situ	Abu Simbel 6	Porter and Moss VII 1951: 117	Champollion 1835-1845 [1970] I: pl. IV (1); Kitchen 2000: 83
331	Huy	Wab-priest	19th Dynasty: Ramesses II	Ramesses II, Thoth and Anukis	Adoring deities	A		In front of the terrace of the Great Temple, north end	Cairo, The Egyptian Museum	TN 26/8/15/1	Porter and Moss VII 1951: 111	Maspero 1911b: 160, fig. 14; Kitchen 2000: 88
332	Iwefenamun	Stablemaster	19th Dynasty: Ramesses II	Thoth and Ramesses II	Royal (Ramesses II) mediating scene	B		South of the Great Temple	In situ	Abu Simbel 18	Porter and Moss VII 1951: 118	Kitchen 2000: 180
333	Khons[…]	Stable[master]	19th Dynasty: Ramesses II	Thoth, Re-Harakhti, Shepsy, Nehmet(awy), Ramesses II and Horus	Adoring deity	A		South of the Great Temple	In situ	Abu Simbel 23a		Kitchen 1996: 510
334	Maya	?	19th Dynasty: Ramesses II	Horus and Ramesses II	Adoring deity	A		North of the Small Temple	In situ	Abu Simbel 5	Porter and Moss VII 1951: 117	Champollion, 1835-1845 [1970] IV: pl. IV (1); Kitchen 2000: 80

335	Mernudjem	King's Son of Kush, Overseer of the Southern Foreign Lands; Standard Bearer of the Company 'Ruler of the Two Lands', Leader of the En[tourage], Weapon Bearer (?) of His Majesty, King's Son of Kush, Overseer of the Southern Foreign Lands, Fanbearer on the King's Right Hand, Overseer of Granaries, Overseer of the God's Servants of all the Gods of Nubia, Overseer of the Gold Lands of the Lord of the Two Lands, Royal Scribe	19th Dynasty: Ramesses II	Thoth, Re-Harakhti and Shepsy	Royal (Ramesses II) mediating scene	B	Incense/burnt offerings	South of the Great Temple	In situ	Abu Simbel 15	Porter and Moss VII 1951: 118	Kitchen 2000: 77-78
336	Meryu	First Charioteer of his Majesty	19th Dynasty: Ramesses II	Ramesses II	Dedicator holding (?) royal chariot span	A		South of the Great Temple	In situ	Abu Simbel 20	Porter and Moss VII 1951: 118	Kitchen 2000: 175
337	Usimare-Asha-Nakhtu	Royal Scribe	19th Dynasty: Ramesses II	Ramesses II	King in chariot, dedicator following	A		North of the Small Temple	In situ	Abu Simbel 8	Porter and Moss VII 1951: 117	Kitchen 2000: 143
338	Mery	Deputy of Wawat	19th Dynasty: Amenmesse	Amun-Re and Amenmesse	Royal smiting scene	C		South of the Great Temple	In situ	Abu Simbel 22	Porter and Moss VII 1951: 118	Habachi 1978: fig. 4; Schulman 1994, fig. 2; Kitchen 2003: 149-150
339	Rekhpehtef	Ambassador of Every Land, Attendant of the Lord of the Two Lands, Confidant of Horus in his Palace, Charioteer of his Majesty	19th Dynasty: Siptah, year 1	Amun-Re	Adoring deity	A		Great Temple, south recess	In situ	Abu Simbel South Recess (9)	Porter and Moss VII 1951: 98	Kitchen 2003: 262
340	Seti	Prince and Count, King's Son of Kush, Overseer of the Gold Land of Amun, Fanbearer on the King's Right Hand, Royal Secretary of Pharaoh, First Official of Pharaoh, Eyes of the Upper Egyptian King and Ears of the Lower Egyptian King, First God's Servant of Mut and Thoth, Overseer of the Treasury, Overseer of Documents within the Mansion of Ramesses II Meryamun in the Domain of Re; Royal Scribe	19th Dynasty: Siptah	Amun-Re, Mut, Re-Harakhti, Seth and Siptah	Royal (Siptah) mediating scene	B		Great Temple, north recess	In situ	Abu Simbel North Recess (11)	Porter and Moss VII 1951: 99	Kitchen 2003: 262-263

**All sandstone*

Table 4 The Wadi es-Sebua Votive Stelae (15)

Database number	Owner	Title	Date	Dedicated to	Brief description*	Representational form	Offerings by the dedicator	Find location	Current location	Repository number	Porter and Moss reference	Primary publication details
341	Huy (and Setau)	Standard-bearer on the Right of the King, of the company 'Triumphant'	19th Dynasty: Ramesses II, second half	Amun-Re, Ramesses II, Nekhbet (?), Ptah and Re-Harakhti-Atum; Setau (in border text)	Royal (Ramesses II) mediating scene	B	Loaded offering table	Ramesses II temple: against the brick wall surrounding the avenue of sphinxes, furthest to the west	Cairo, The Egyptian Museum	JdE 41405 (?)	Porter and Moss 1951 VII: 55	Barsanti and Gauthier 1911: 65-68, pl. I [I]; Kitchen 2000: 60-61
342	[I]uy	Standard-bearer on the Right of the King	19th Dynasty: Ramesses II, second half	Amun-Re, Ramesses II and Atum; Ptah and Re-Harakhti	Royal (Ramesses II) mediating scene	B		Ramesses II temple: against the brick wall surrounding the avenue of sphinxes	Cairo, The Egyptian Museum	JdE 41399	Porter and Moss 1951 VII: 55	Barsanti and Gauthier 1911: 74-75, pl. V (third from the right - general view of seven of the stelae) [V]; Kitchen 2000: 62
343	Mernudjem (and Setau)	Overseer of God's Servant of all the Gods	19th Dynasty: Ramesses II, second half	Amun-Re, Ramesses II and Horus; Ptah; Setau (in text)	Royal (Ramesses II) mediating scene	B	Lotus flowers	Ramesses II temple: in the sand south of the avenue of sphinxes	Cairo, The Egyptian Museum	JdE 41402	Porter and Moss 1951 VII: 55	Barsanti and Gauthier 1911: 81-82 [VIII]; Gauthier 1912 II: pl. LXVI B; Kitchen 2000: 65
344	Mutnofret (f.)	No title	19th Dynasty: Ramesses II, second half	Amun-Re and Harakhti; Ptah, Wadjyt and Khnum	Adoring deities. Sandstone	A	Offering stand	Amenhotep III temple: unknown	Aswan Museum	15	Porter and Moss 1951 VII: 63	Habachi 1960: 47-48, fig. 3 and pl. XVIb
345	Paherypedjet (and Setau)	Lost [Standard-bearer - after Raedler 2003: 157]	19th Dynasty: Ramesses II, year 44, 1st Month of Peret, Day 1	Amun-Re, Re-Harakhti (in text) and Ramesses II; Setau (in text)	Royal (Ramesses II) mediating scene	B	Offering stand	Ramesses II temple: against the brick wall surrounding the avenue of sphinxes	Cairo, The Egyptian Museum	JdE 41406	Porter and Moss 1951 VII: 55	Barsanti and Gauthier 1911: 70-72, pl. V (on right - general view of seven of the stelae) [III]; Kitchen 2000: 61-62
346	Pentaweret	Sculptor	19th Dynasty: Ramesses II, second half	Thoth and two other deities	Royal (Ramesses II) mediating scene	B		Ramesses II temple: unknown	Cairo, The Egyptian Museum	JdE 41404	Porter and Moss 1951 VII: 55	Barsanti and Gauthier 1911: 85-86 [XI]; Kitchen 2000: 66
347	Ramose (and Setau)	*sk*-officer	19th Dynasty: Ramesses II, year 44, 1st Month of Peret, Day 2	Amun-Re, Ramesses II, a male and female deity; Setau (in text)	Royal (Ramesses II) mediating scene	B	Triple offering stand	Ramesses II temple: in four fragments north of the avenue of sphinxes	Cairo, The Egyptian Museum	JdE 41403	Porter and Moss 1951 VII: 55	Barsanti and Gauthier 1911: 83-85 [IX]; Kitchen 2000: 65-66

348	Setau	King's Son of Kush	19th Dynasty: Ramesses II, second half	Renenut and Ramesses II; Amun-Re-Harakhti, Horus Lord of Baki, Horus, Lord of Miam and Horus, Lord of Buhen (all in text)	Royal (Ramesses II) mediating scene	B		Ramesses II temple: unknown [south wall? See Porter and Moss 1951 VII: 55]	Cairo, The Egyptian Museum	JdE 41394	Porter and Moss 1951 VII: 55	Kitchen 2000: 66-67 ['XII']; see also Gauthier 1912 I: 37 [5]
349	Setau	High Steward of Amun, King's Son; Festival Leader of Amun	19th Dynasty: Ramesses II, second half	[Ptah]-tatenen and Harsiese	Royal (Ramesses II) mediating scene	[B?]	Lost	Ramesses II temple: against the brick wall surrounding the avenue of sphinxes	Cairo, The Egyptian Museum	JdE 41407 (?)	Porter and Moss 1951 VII: 55	Barsanti and Gauthier 1911: 85 [X]; Kitchen 2000:. 66
350	Setau	King's Son of Kush; Superintendant of the Gold Lands of Amun, Fan-bearer to the Right of the King, Overseer of the Treasury, Sem-priest of Amun, Royal Scribe; Overseer of the South Lands, High Steward of Amun	19th Dynasty: Ramesses II, year 44, 1st Month of Peret, Day 2	Amun-Re, Ramesses II, Mut and Maat	Royal (Ramesses II) mediating scene	B		Ramesses II temple: against the brick wall surrounding the avenue of sphinxes	Cairo, The Egyptian Museum	JdE 41395	Porter and Moss 1951 VII: 55	Barsanti and Gauthier 1911: 77-81, pl. V (second from the left - general view of seven of the stelae) [VII]; Gauthier 1912 II: pl. LXVI A; Kitchen 2000: 63-65
351	Setau	King's Son of Kush; High Steward [of the City], Festival Leader of Amun, Overseer of the South Lands, True Royal Scribe, whom he loves	19th Dynasty: Ramesses II, second half	Amun-Re, Ramesses II and a female deity; Seth and Renenutet (in text)	Royal (Ramesses II) mediating scene	B		Ramesses II temple: in the sand south of the avenue of sphinxes	Cairo, The Egyptian Museum	JdE 41396	Porter and Moss 1951 VII: 55	Barsanti and Gauthier 1911: 75-77, pl. III [VI]; Kitchen 2000: 62-63
352	[Setau and Dua-Seba]	[Setau: King's Son of Kush]	19th Dynasty: Ramesses II, second half	Amun-Re, Harmachis (?), Atum (?) and Ramesses II; Amun-Re-Harakhti (in text),	Royal (Ramesses II) mediating scene	B		Ramesses II temple: against the brick wall surrounding the avenue of sphinxes	Cairo, The Egyptian Museum	JdE 41401	Porter and Moss 1951 VII: 55	Barsanti and Gauthier 1911: 72-73, pl. V (centre - general view of seven of the stelae) [IV]; Kitchen 2000: 62

353	Yam …(and Setau)	[Standard-bearer] of the company 'Ramesses II (is) Triumphant'	19th Dynasty: Ramesses II, second half	Amun-Re, Ramesses II, Nekhbet (?) and Ptah; Setau (in border text) and Seth (in text)	Royal (Ramesses II) mediating scene	B	Loaded offering table	Ramesses II temple: against the brick wall surrounding the avenue of sphinxes	Cairo, The Egyptian Museum	JdE 41400	Porter and Moss 1951 VII: 55	Barsanti and Gauthier 1911, 68-70, pl. II [II]; Kitchen 2000: 61
354	Pia	First God's Servant and Mayor	20th Dynasty	Amun	Adoring deity. Sandstone	A	Loaded offering table	Amenhotep III temple: unknown	Aswan Museum	11	Porter and Moss 1951 VII: 63	Habachi 1960: 45-47, fig. 1, pl. XVIa
355	Matybaal (or Kemabaal)	No title	Ramesside Period	Amun-Re and Seth; Reshep	Adoring deities. Sandstone	A	Loaded offering table and offering stand	Amenhotep III temple: unknown	Aswan Museum	16	Porter and Moss 1951 VII: 63	Habachi 1960: 50, fig. 4, pl. XVIII

**Granite unless otherwise indicated.*

Table 5 The Qantir/Pi-Ramesses Votive Stelae (74)

Database number	Owner	Title	Date	Dedicated to	Brief description*	Represen tational form	Offerings (by the dedicator)	Find location	Current location	Reposi tory numbe r	Porter and Moss reference	Primary publication details
356	Aamek	Favoured one of the Perfect God, Scribe of the Lord of the Two Lands	19th Dynasty: Ramesses II	Sobek	Adoring deity	A	Incense	Unknown	Hildesheim, Roemer-Pelizaeus Museum	490		Habachi 1954: 539; Kitchen 2000: 160
357	Aanakht	Chief of Transport (?)	19th Dynasty: Ramesses II	Ramesses II as User-Maat-Re Setep-en-Re Montu-em-Tawy	Adoring deity	A	Loaded offering table	Unknown	Hildesheim, Roemer-Pelizaeus Museum	1105		Habachi 1954: 534; Kitchen 2000: 190
358	Akhpet (?)	Pure of Hands in the Temple of Re	19th Dynasty: Ramesses II	Ramesses II as User-Maat-Re Setep-en-Re Montu-em-Tawy	Royal (Prince Meryatum) mediating scene	B	Loaded offering table	Unknown	Hildesheim, Roemer-Pelizaeus Museum	1102		Habachi 1954: 541, pl. XXXVIII
359	Amenaanak hty	Scribe of the Lord of the Two Lands	19th Dynasty: Ramesses II	Ramesses II as User-Maat-Re Setep-en-Re Montu-em-Tawy	Adoring deity	A		Unknown	Hildesheim, Roemer-Pelizaeus Museum	487		Habachi 1954: 531; Kitchen 2000: 160
360	Amenemheb	Scribe of the Chariotry	19th Dynasty: Ramesses II	Ramesses II as User-Maat-Re Setep-en-Re Montu-em-Tawy	Adoring deity	A	Offering stand	Unknown	Hildesheim, Roemer-Pelizaeus Museum	403		Habachi 1954: 530; Kitchen 2000: 178
361	Amenemope t	No title	19th Dynasty: Ramesses II	Ramesses II as User-Maat-Re Setep-en-Re Montu-em-Tawy	Adoring deity	A	Offering stand	Unknown	Hildesheim, Roemer-Pelizaeus Museum	1095		Habachi 1954: 534

362	Amenemper	Infantryman	19th Dynasty: Ramesses II	Ramesses II as User-Maat-Re Setep-en-Re Montu-em-Tawy	Adoring deity	A	Incense and loaded offering table	Unknown	Hildesheim, Roemer-Pelizaeus Museum	1078		Habachi 1954: 532; Kitchen 2000: 188
363	Any/Inwya	Standard bearer of the Lord of the Two Lands in the Regiment Re-of-the-Rulers	19th Dynasty: Ramesses II	Ramesses II as User-Maat-Re Setep-en-Re Montu-em-Tawy	Royal (Ramesses II) mediating scene	B	Double offering stand	Unknown	Kelekian, Paris			Habachi 1954: 542; Clère 1950, 36-38, pl. III, A; Kitchen 2000: 183
364	Bakenamun	Greatly Favoured one of his God, Overseer of Sculptors in the Temple of Amun-Re, Lord of Ta-Beneret	19th Dynasty: Ramesses II	Sobek-Re	Adoring deity	C	Loaded offering table	Unknown	Hildesheim, Roemer-Pelizaeus Museum	399		Habachi 1954: 537, pl. XXXV, A; Kitchen 2000: 317
365	Djehutyemheb	'Horse Groom' (?) of the Lord of the Two Lands	19th Dynasty: Ramesses II	Ramesses II as User-Maat-Re Setep-en-Re Montu-em-Tawy	Adoring deity	A	Offering stand	Unknown	Hildesheim, Roemer-Pelizaeus Museum	408		Habachi 1954: 530; Kitchen 2000: 185
366	Djehutymes	Scribe of the Table/Altar of the Lord of the Two Lands	19th Dynasty: Ramesses II	Ramesses II as User-Maat-Re Setep-en-Re Montu-em-Tawy	Adoring deity	A	Incense	Unknown	Hildesheim, Roemer-Pelizaeus Museum	430		Habachi 1954: 531; Kitchen 2000: 158
367	Hesyu	Trumpeter	19th Dynasty: Ramesses II	Ramesses II as User-Maat-Re Setep-en-Re Montu-em-Tawy	Adoring deity	A	Offering stand	Unknown	Hildesheim, Roemer-Pelizaeus Museum	397	Porter and Moss IV 1934: 26	Habachi 1954: 529; Roeder 1926: pl. V, 2; Kitchen 2000: 187
368	Hori	No title	19th Dynasty: Ramesses II	Ramesses II as User-Maat-Re Setep-en-Re [Montu-em-Tawy]	Adoring deity	A		Unknown	Hildesheim, Roemer-Pelizaeus Museum	1087		Habachi 1954: 533
369	I…	Royal Scribe of the Tables/Altars of the Lord of the Two Lands	19th Dynasty: Ramesses II	Ramesses II [as The God?] and as User-Maat-Re Setep-en-Re Montu-em-Tawy	Adoring deities	A	Incense and offering stand	Unknown	Hildesheim, Roemer-Pelizaeus Museum	1086		Habachi 1954: 540, pl. XXXVII; Kitchen 2000: 158
370	Isis (f.)	Singer of Montu-em-tawy	19th Dynasty: Ramesses II	Ramesses II as User-Maat-Re Setep-en-Re Montu-em-Tawy	Adoring deity	A	Festival offerings and offering stand	Unknown	Hildesheim, Roemer-Pelizaeus Museum	380		Habachi 1954: 529; Kayser 1973: pl. 53
371	Iumen	Workman	19th Dynasty: Ramesses II	Ramesses II as User-Maat-Re Setep-en-Re Montu-em-Tawy	Adoring deity	A	Offering stand	Unknown	Hildesheim, Roemer-Pelizaeus Museum	404		Habachi 1954: 530; Kitchen 2000: 163
372	Khonsu	Sandal-maker of the Gold-house of the Temple of Ptah	19th Dynasty: Ramesses II	Ramesses II as User-Maat-Re Setep-en-Re Montu-em-Tawy	Adoring deity	A	Offering stand	Unknown	Stockholm, Medelhavsmuseet	E 1450		Habachi 1954: 535; Säve-Söderbergh 1945: 21-38, fig. 3; Kitchen 2000: 318

373	Maamaa	Scribe of the Lord of the Two Lands in the Temple of Re	19th Dynasty: Ramesses II	Ramesses II as User-Maat-Re Setep-en-Re Montu-em-Tawy	Adoring deity	A		Unknown	Hildesheim, Roemer-Pelizaeus Museum	983		Habachi 1954: 532; Kitchen 2000: 317
374	Mahuhy	Scribe of the Table/Altar of the Two Lands	19th Dynasty: Ramesses II	Ramesses II as User-Maat-Re Setep-en-Re Montu-em-Tawy	Adoring deity	A	Lotus flowers and offering stand	Unknown	Leipzig, Ägyptisches Museum der Universität Leipzig	3618		Habachi 1954: 535; Kitchen 2000: 159
375	May	Scribe of the Temple of Maat	19th Dynasty: Ramesses II	Ramesses II as User-Maat-Re Setep-en-Re Montu-em-Tawy	Adoring deity	A	Offering stand	Unknown	Hildesheim, Roemer-Pelizaeus Museum	1083		Habachi 1954: 533, pl. XXXIV, A; Kitchen 2000:317
376	Mentu-Hor	No title	19th Dynasty: Ramesses II	Ramesses II as an unidentified statue	Adoring deity	A	Offering stand	Unknown	Hildesheim, Roemer-Pelizaeus Museum	1084		Habachi 1954: 540
377	Meramun-nakht	Deputy of the Pharaoh	19th Dynasty: Ramesses II	Ramesses II as User-Maat-Re Setep-en-Re Montu-em-Tawy	Adoring deity	A	Offering stand	Unknown	Hildesheim, Roemer-Pelizaeus Museum	1077		Habachi 1954: 532; Kitchen 2000: 162
378	Mesiaia	Washerman (?)	19th Dynasty: Ramesses II	Ramesses II as User-Maat-Re Setep-en-Re Montu-em-Tawy	Adoring deity	A	Offering stand	Unknown	Hildesheim, Roemer-Pelizaeus Museum	405		Habachi 1954: 530; Kitchen 2000: 162
379	Mose	Infantryman of the Great Regiment of (Ramesses Meryamun) Beloved of Atum	19th Dynasty: Ramesses II	Ptah and Ramesses II as Sun of the Rulers	Royal reward scene	A		Unknown	Hildesheim, Roemer-Pelizaeus Museum	374	Porter and Moss 1934 IV: 26	Habachi 1954: 535; Roeder 1926: 65-66, fig. 2; Kitchen 2000: 187-188
380	Nakhtamun (and his wife)	?	19th Dynasty: Ramesses II	Ramesses II as User-Maat-Re Setep-en-Re Montu-em-Tawy	Adoring deity	A		Unknown	Hildesheim, Roemer-Pelizaeus Museum	411	Porter and Moss 1934 IV: 26	Habachi 1954: 538
381	Nakhtu	Doorkeeper (?)	19th Dynasty: Ramesses II	Ramesses II as User-Maat-Re Setep-en-Re Montu-em-Tawy	Adoring deity	A	Lotus flowers	Unknown	Hildesheim, Roemer-Pelizaeus Museum	409		Habachi 1954: 531
382	Nebamun	No title	19th Dynasty: Ramesses II	Osiris	Adoring deity	A	Lotus flowers and offering stand	Unknown	Hildesheim, Roemer-Pelizaeus Museum	1893	Porter and Moss 1934 IV: 26	Habachi 1954: 542; Roeder 1961: pl. IV, 1; Kitchen 2000: 318
383	Neferhor	Scribe of the Army of the Lord of the Two Lands	19th Dynasty: Ramesses II	Ramesses II as User-Maat-Re Setep-en-Re Montu-em-Tawy	Adoring deity	A	Loaded offering table	Unknown	Paris, Musée Rodin	156		Habachi 1954: 535; Kitchen 2000: 183
384	Neferronpet	Royal Scribe	19th Dynasty: Ramesses II	Ptah and Hathor	Adoring deity	A	Offering stand	Unknown	Hildesheim, Roemer-Pelizaeus Museum	492		Habachi 1954: 539, pl. XXXVI, B; Kitchen 2000: 160

385	Neferronpet	Doorkeeper of Pharaoh	19th Dynasty: Ramesses II	Ptah	Adoring deity	A	Incense and offering stand	Unknown	Hildesheim, Roemer-Pelizaeus Museum	1892	Porter and Moss 1934 IV: 26	Habachi 1954: 542; Roeder 1926: pl. IV, 2; Kitchen 2000: 161
386	Nekhu-ib	Workman	19th Dynasty: Ramesses II	Ramesses II as User-Maat-Re Setep-en-Re Montu-em-Tawy	Adoring deity	A	Lotus flowers and offering stand	Unknown	Hildesheim, Roemer-Pelizaeus Museum	1098		Habachi 1954: 534; Kitchen 2000: 229
387	Osiris	Scribe of the Treasury	19th Dynasty: Ramesses II	Sobek-Re	Adoring deity	A		Unknown	Hildesheim, Roemer-Pelizaeus Museum	400		Habachi 1954: 537; Kitchen 2000: 100
388	Paherypedje t	Singer of Pharaoh	19th Dynasty: Ramesses II	Ramesses II as User-Maat-Re Setep-en-Re Montu-em-Tawy	Adoring deity	A	Incense	Unknown	Hildesheim, Roemer-Pelizaeus Museum	494		Habachi 1954: 531; Kitchen 2000: 160
389	Penamun	GBT (unknown word) of the Treasury	19th Dynasty: Ramesses II	Ramesses II as User-Maat-Re Setep-en-Re Montu-em-Tawy	Adoring deity	A	Offering stand	Unknown	Hildesheim, Roemer-Pelizaeus Museum	378		Habachi 1954: 529; Kitchen 2000: 100
390	Pennesytaw y	Chief of Fishermen (?) of the "Sunshade"	19th Dynasty: Ramesses II	Ptah	Adoring deity	A	Offering stand	Unknown	Hildesheim, Roemer-Pelizaeus Museum	1108		Habachi 1954: 541; Kitchen 2000: 317
391	Penweret	Overseer of the Goldworkers and Greatly Favoured one of the Great God	19th Dynasty: Ramesses II	Sobek-Re	Adoring deity	A	Incense and offering stand	Unknown	Hildesheim, Roemer-Pelizaeus Museum	398		Habachi 1954: 536-537; Kayser 1973: pl. 53; Kitchen 2000: 161
392	Rafy/Rofy	Scribe	19th Dynasty: Ramesses II	Ramesses II as User-Maat-Re Setep-en-Re Montu-em-Tawy	Adoring deity	A	Offering stand	Unknown	Hildesheim, Roemer-Pelizaeus Museum	1088		Habachi 1954: 533; Kitchen 2000: 160
393	Rahotep	Prince, Fanbearer to the Right of the King, Mayor and Vizier	19th Dynasty: Ramesses II	Ramesses II as Ruler-of-Rulers	Royal (Ramesses II) mediating scene (ears)	B	Loaded offering table	Unknown	Munich, Staatliche Sammlung Ägyptischer Kunst	287		Scharff 1934: 47-51; Habachi 1969: 33-35, fig. 21, pl. XIIIb; Kitchen 2000: 35
394	Ramessu-men	Royal Butler	19th Dynasty: Ramesses II	Ramesses II as User-Maat-Re Setep-en-Re Montu-em-Tawy and as The God	Adoring deities	A	Lotus flowers and loaded offering table	Unknown	Hildesheim, Roemer-Pelizaeus Museum	1079	Porter and Moss 1934 IV: 26	Habachi 1954: 539-540; Roeder 1961: pl. V, 4; Kitchen 2000: 143
395	Ramose	Standard-bearer	19th Dynasty: Ramesses II	Ramesses II as User-Maat-Re Setep-en-Re Montu-em-Tawy	Adoring deity	A	Lotus flowers and offering stand	Samana Canal (?)	Cairo, The Egyptian Museum	JdE 87832		Habachi 1954: 523-524, pl. XXXIII; Kitchen 2000: 157
396	Rodjekbuti	Armourer	19th Dynasty: Ramesses II	Ramesses II as User-Maat-Re Setep-en-Re Montu-em-Tawy	Adoring deity	A		West of plot 34 dug by Hamza	Cairo, The Egyptian Museum	JdE 88666		Habachi 1954: 519-520, pl. XXX, A; Kitchen 2000: 184

397	Sekhmet(?)emwia (f.)	No title	19th Dynasty: Ramesses II	Ramesses II as User-Maat-Re Setep-en-Re Montu-em-Tawy	Adoring deity	A	Festival offering and lotus flowers	Unknown	Hildesheim, Roemer-Pelizaeus Museum	1080		Habachi 1954: 532
398	Sethnakht	The One Attached to the Balance	19th Dynasty: Ramesses II	Ramesses II as User-Maat-Re Setep-en-Re Montu-em-Tawy	Adoring deity	A	Lotus flowers and offering stand	Unknown	Brussels, Musées royaux d'Art et d'Histoire	E 3048	Porter and Moss 1934 IV: 26	Habachi 1954: 534-535; Kitchen 2000: 101-102
399	Sety (?)	Washerman of the Prince (?)	19th Dynasty: Ramesses II	Ramesses II as User-Maat-Re Setep-en-Re Montu-em-Tawy	Adoring deity	A	Loaded offering table	Unknown	Hildesheim, Roemer-Pelizaeus Museum	1092		Habachi 1954: 533
400	Setyerneheh	No title	19th Dynasty: Ramesses II	Amun-Re, Ptah and Ramesses II as User-Maat-Re Setep-en-Re Montu-em-Tawy	Adoring deities (ears)	C	Offering stand	Unknown	Hildesheim, Roemer-Pelizaeus Museum	375		Habachi 1954: 536, pl. XXXIV, B; Kayser 1973: pl. 56
401	Sha (?) (f.)	Lady of the House	19th Dynasty: Ramesses II	Ramesses II as User-Maat-Re Setep-en-Re Montu-em-Tawy	Adoring deity	A	Offering stand	Unknown	Hildesheim, Roemer-Pelizaeus Museum	376		Habachi 1954: 529
402	Smentiwaset	Follower	19th Dynasty: Ramesses II	Ramesses II as User-Maat-Re Setep-en-Re Montu-em-Tawy	Adoring deity	A		Unknown	Hildesheim, Roemer-Pelizaeus Museum	429		Habachi 1954: 531; Kitchen 2000: 162
403	Sunensu	Royal Workman	19th Dynasty: Ramesses II	Ramesses II as User-Maat-Re Setep-en-Re Montu-em-Tawy	Adoring deity	A	Offering stand	Unknown	Hildesheim, Roemer-Pelizaeus Museum	1081		Habachi 1954: 532; Kitchen 2000: 162
404	Suro (?)	No title	19th Dynasty: Ramesses II	Ramesses II as User-Maat-Re Setep-en-Re Montu-em-Tawy	Adoring deity	A	Offering stand	Unknown	Hildesheim, Roemer-Pelizaeus Museum	1097	Porter and Moss 1934 IV: 26	Habachi 1954: 534
405	Thutmose	Scribe of the Army of the Lord of the Two Lands	19th Dynasty: Ramesses II	Ramesses II as User-Maat-Re Setep-en-Re Montu-em-Tawy	Royal (Ramesses II) mediating scene	B	Bouquet, loaded offering table and offering stand	Unknown	Hildesheim, Roemer-Pelizaeus Museum	377	Porter and Moss 1934 IV: 26	Habachi 1954: 536; Roeder 1926: pl. IV, 3; Kitchen 2000: 183-184
406	Tiy	Scribe of the Altar/Table of the Lord of the Two Lands	19th Dynasty: Ramesses II	Ramesses II as Sun-of-the-Rulers	Adoring deity	A		Unknown	Hildesheim, Roemer-Pelizaeus Museum	1085		Habachi 1954: 540; Kitchen 2000: 159
407	Tjen<er>amun	Trumpeter (?)	19th Dynasty: Ramesses II	Ramesses II as User-Maat-Re Setep-en-Re Montu-em-Tawy and Maat	Adoring deities	C	Loaded offering table and offering stand	Unknown	Hildesheim, Roemer-Pelizaeus Museum	428		Habachi 1954: 538; Kitchen 2000: 187
408	Userhat	Draughtsman of Amun-Re	19th Dynasty: Ramesses II	Ramesses II as an unidentified statue and Ptah	Adoring deities	A	Incense	Unknown	Brussels, Musées royaux d'Art et d'Histoire	E 3049		Habachi 1954: 542-543; Clère 1950: 40-41, pl. IV, B; Kitchen 2000: 317

409	Yafi (and his wife)	Attendant	19th Dynasty: Ramesses II	Ramesses II as an unidentified statue	Adoring deity	A	Incense and water (offered by the woman)	Unknown	Hildesheim, Roemer-Pelizaeus Museum	488	Habachi 1954: 538-539; Kitchen 2000: 162
410	No name	No title*	19th Dynasty: Ramesses II	Ramesses II as User-Maat-Re Setep-en-Re Montu-em-Tawy	Adoring deity	A	Festival offerings and offering stand	Unknown	Hildesheim, Roemer-Pelizaeus Museum	1094	Habachi 1954: 534
411	No name	No title	19th Dynasty: Ramesses II	Ramesses II as an unidentified statue	Adoring deity	C	Offering stand	Unknown	Hildesheim, Roemer-Pelizaeus Museum	1096	Habachi 1954: 541
412	No name	No title, military	19th Dynasty: Ramesses II	Ramesses II as an unidentified statue	Adoring deity (ears)	A	Lotus flower and offering stand	Unknown	Brussels, Musées royaux d'Art et d'Histoire	E 3047	Habachi 1954: 543
413	No name (f.)	No title	19th Dynasty: Ramesses II	Ramesses II as User-Maat-Re Setep-en-Re Montu-em-Tawy	Adoring deity	A	Loaded offering table	Unknown	Hildesheim, Roemer-Pelizaeus Museum	407	Habachi 1954: 530
414	No name	No title	19th Dynasty: Ramesses II	[Ramesses II as User-Maat-Re Setep-en-Re Montu-em-Tawy]	Adoring deity	A		Unknown	Hildesheim, Roemer-Pelizaeus Museum	406	Habachi 1954: 530
415	No name	No title	19th Dynasty: Ramesses II	Ramesses II as User-Maat-Re Setep-en-Re Montu-em-Tawy	Adoring deity	A		Unknown	Hildesheim, Roemer-Pelizaeus Museum	1090	Habachi 1954: 533
416	No name	No title	19th Dynasty: Ramesses II	[Ramesses II as User-Maat-Re Setep-en-Re Montu-em-Tawy]	Adoring deity	A		Unknown	Hildesheim, Roemer-Pelizaeus Museum	1093	Habachi 1954: 533
417	No name	No title	19th Dynasty: Ramesses II	Ramesses II as an unidentified statue	Adoring deity	A	Offering stand	Unknown	Hildesheim, Roemer-Pelizaeus Museum	489	Habachi 1954: 539
418	No name	No title	19th Dynasty: Ramesses II	Ramesses II as an unidentified statue	Adoring deity	A	Lotus flowers and offering stand	Unknown	Cairo, The Egyptian Museum	JdE 86124	Habachi 1954: 521-522, pl. XXXI
419	No name (f.)	No title	19th Dynasty: Ramesses II	Ramesses II as User-Maat-Re Setep-en-Re Montu-em-Tawy	Adoring deity	A	Incense, lotus flowers and offering stand	Unknown	Hildesheim, Roemer-Pelizaeus Museum	1099	Habachi 1954: 534
420	No name	No title	19th Dynasty: Ramesses II	[Ramesses II as User-Maat-Re Setep-en-Re Montu-em-Tawy]	Adoring deity	A	Offering stand	Unknown	Lund, Museum of the History of Civilisations	32156	Habachi 1954: 535; Clère 1950: 41, pl. IV, C
421	No name	No title	19th Dynasty: Ramesses II	Amun-Re, Ramesses II as an unidentified statue and Bes	Adoring deities	C	Offering stand	Unknown	Hildesheim, Roemer-Pelizaeus Museum	426	Habachi 1954: 538; Kitchen 2000: 318

422	No name	Doorkeeper of the Lord of the Two Lands	19th Dynasty: Ramesses II	Ramesses II as User-Maat-Re Setep-en-Re Montu-em-Tawy	Adoring deity	A	Loaded offering table	Unknown	Hildesheim, Roemer-Pelizaeus Museum	427	Porter and Moss 1934 IV: 26	Habachi 1954: 538; Kitchen 2000: 161
423	No name (lost?)	No title (lost?)	19th Dynasty: Ramesses II	Ramesses II as User-Maat-Re Setep-en-Re Montu-em-Tawy	Adoring deity	A	Offering stand	Unknown	Hildesheim, Roemer-Pelizaeus Museum	1082		Habachi 1954: 533
424	Name lost	Infantryman of the Lord of the Two Lands	19th Dynasty: Ramesses II	Ramesses II as User-Maat-Re Setep-en-Re Montu-em-Tawy	Adoring deity	A	Offering stand	Unknown	Hildesheim, Roemer-Pelizaeus Museum	493		Habachi 1954: 531; Kitchen 2000: 161
425	Name lost	Sailor of Pharaoh	19th Dynasty: Ramesses II	Sobek	Adoring deity	A		Unknown	Hildesheim, Roemer-Pelizaeus Museum	401		Habachi 1954: 537; Kitchen 2000: 189
426	Name lost	Title lost	19th Dynasty: Ramesses II	Ramesses II as [User-Maat-Re Setep-en-Re Montu-em-Tawy]	Adoring deity	A	Lost	West of plot 34 dug by Hamza	Cairo, The Egyptian Museum			Habachi 1954: 520-521 and pl. XXX, B
427	Name lost	Royal fanbearer to the Right […]	19th Dynasty: Ramesses II	Ramesses II as User-Maat-Re Setep-en-Re Montu-em-Tawy	Adoring deity	A	Offering stand	Unknown	Hildesheim, Roemer-Pelizaeus Museum	495		Habachi 1954: 532
428	Setekh-Kherkhopshef	King's Son, Prince and Mayor, God's Father, Beloved, Keeper of the Secrets of Pharaoh, Foremost of the Entire Land, the Sem-priest of the Perfect God, the Prince of/in the Judgement Hall, the Leader of the 'flat' lands and the Khaw-nebut, King's Son, who unites the Throne of Horus, Prince and Royal Scribe	20th Dynasty: Ramesses III	Amun-Re and Ptah	Adoring deities	A	Lotus flowers	South of Qantir, near Ezbet Silmi	Cairo, The Egyptian Museum	JdE 87829		Habachi 1954: 501-504 and pl. XXXVIII
429	Usermaatre-Nahkt	Shield-bearer of the Mountainous Lands	20th Dynasty: Ramesses III	Ramesses III (and Reshep)	Royal smiting scene	C		South of Qantir, near Ezbet Silmi	Cairo, The Egyptian Museum	JdE 88879		Habachi 1954: 507-514, pl. XXIX; Schulman 1994: 273 [4], fig. 5

**The stelae without names are either unfinished or would have had the details painted on.*
*** All limestone.*

Table 6 The Zawiyet Umm el-Rakham Votive Stelae (7)

Database Number	Owner	Title	Date	Dedicated to	Brief description*	Represen tational form	Offerings (by the dedicator)	Find location	Current location	Snape and Wilson (2007) number	Primary publication details
430	Amenmessu	Standard-bearer	19th Dynasty: Ramesses II, first half	Amun-Re and Ramesses II	Royal smiting scene	C		Main temple: in the corridor surrounding the temple	Zagazig magazine (?)	ZUR 2	Habachi 1980: 17, pl. VIA; Snape and Wilson 2007: 100-101, fig. 5.6
431	Djehuty-meket/emheb and another man	Standard-bearer	19th Dynasty: Ramesses II, first half	Ramesses II (rest lost)	Upper scene lost; two standard-bearers with inscription below	C (?)		Main temple: in the corridor surrounding the temple	SCA office, Mersa Matrouh	ZUR 6	Snape and Wilson 2007: 108-109; figs. 5.10, 5. 11
432	Panehsy	Royal Scribe and Great Chief of the Army	19th Dynasty: Ramesses II, first half	Sekhmet	Royal (Ramesses II) mediating scene	B		Main temple: in the corridor surrounding the temple	Zagazig magazine (?)	ZUR 3	Habachi 1980: 18, pl. VIB; Snape and Wilson 2007:. 102-103, fig. 5.7
433	Ramose	Standard-bearer	19th Dynasty: Ramesses II, first half	Seth (?) and [Ramesses II]	Royal smiting scene	C		Main temple: in the corridor surrounding the temple	Unknown	ZUR 9	Snape and Wilson 2007: 112-113, fig. 5.14
434	Sobeknebtawy	Standard-bearer	19th Dynasty: Ramesses II, first half	[Amun?]	Surface damaged, man adoring deity (?)	C (?)		Main temple: in the corridor surrounding the temple	In situ	ZUR 18	Snape and Wilson 2007: 122-123, fig. 5.23
435	Name lost	Lost	19th Dynasty: Ramesses II, first half	Amun-Re and Ramesses II	Royal smiting scene	C		Main temple: in the corridor surrounding the temple	SCA office, Mersa Matrouh	ZUR 5	Snape and Wilson 2007: 106-107, fig.5.9
436	Name lost	[Standard-bearer]	19th Dynasty: Ramesses II, first half	Amun-Re, Sekhmet and Ramesses II	Royal smiting scene	C		Main temple: in the corridor surrounding the temple	SCA office, Mersa Matrouh	ZUR 4	Snape and Wilson 2007: 104-105; fig. 5.8

**All limestone.*

APPENDIX 2 THEBAN TOMBS CITED

Theban Tomb	Porter and Moss reference
2	Porter and Moss I.1 1960: 6-9
3	Porter and Moss I.1 1960: 9-11
4	Porter and Moss I.1 1960: 11-12
5	Porter and Moss I.1 1960: 12-14
7	Porter and Moss I.1 1960: 15-16
10	Porter and Moss I.1 1960: 19-21
16	Porter and Moss I.1 1960: 28-29
19	Porter and Moss I.1 1960: 32-34
31	Porter and Moss I.1 1960: 47-49
90	Porter and Moss I.1 1960: 183-185
149	Porter and Moss I.1 1960: 260
181	Porter and Moss I.1 1960: 286-289
217	Porter and Moss I.1 1960: 315-317
215	Porter and Moss I.1 1960: 311
250	Porter and Moss I.1 1960: 336
265	Porter and Moss I.1 1960: 346
277	Porter and Moss I.1 1960: 353-355
290	Porter and Moss I.1 1960: 372-374
292	Porter and Moss I.1 1960: 374-376
323	Porter and Moss I.1 1960: 394-395
330	Porter and Moss I.1 1960: 398
336	Porter and Moss I.1 1960: 404-405
339	Porter and Moss I.1 1960: 406-407
359	Porter and Moss I.1 1960: 421-424
360	Porter and Moss I.1 1960: 424-425

APPENDIX 3 TITLES USED ON THE VOTIVE STELAE[1]

Male Titles	
Royal Envoy of/to Every Land	*wpwty ḫꜣswt nbwt*
Chief Craftsman (in the Place of Truth)	*ḥry ḥmww (m st mꜣꜥt)*
Chief Draughtsman (in the Place of Truth)	*ḥry šs-ḳd (m st mꜣꜥt)*
Chief of Fishermen (?) (of) the "Sunshade"	*ḥry ḥꜣmw pꜣ šwt*
Chief of the Medjay	*ḥry mḏꜣyw*
Chief of Transport (?)	*ḥry šꜣ(s)*
Child of the Tomb	*ms-ẖr*
Deputy of the Gang	*idnw n pꜣ ỉswt*
Deputy of Pharaoh	*idnw n pr-ꜥꜣ*
Doorkeeper of the Lord of the Two Lands	*iry-ꜥꜣ n nb tꜣwy*
Fanbearer on the King's Right Hand	*ṯꜣy šwt / ḫw ḥr nsw ỉmnt*
First Charioteer	*ḳdn tpy*
First God's Servant (of Amun)	*ḥm-nṯr tpy (n Ỉmn)*
First Royal Cupbearer	*wdpw nsw tpy*
Follower/Courtier	*šmsw*
Foreman (in the Place of Truth)	*ꜥꜣ n ỉswt / ḥry ỉswt (m st mꜣꜥt)*
Fourth God's Servant of Amun	*ḥm-nṯr 4 n Ỉmn*
GBT (unknown word) of the Treasury	*gbt n pr-ḥḏ*
God's Father of Amun	*it-nṯr n Ỉmn*
Goldsmith of Amun	*nbỉ n Ỉmn*
Great Chief of the Army	*wr ꜥꜣ n mšꜥ*
Guardian (of the Temple)	*sꜣw / sꜣwty n (ḥwt-nṯr)*
Guardian of the Sword ('Armourer')	*sꜣw m ḫpš*
High Steward (of Amun)	*imy-r pr wr (n Ỉmn)*
Horse Groom (?) (of the Lord of the Two Lands)	*ḳnḳn (n nb tꜣwy)*
Infantryman (of the Lord of the Two Lands)	*wꜥw (n nb tꜣwy)*
Infantryman (of the ship)	*wꜥw n mnḏ / mꜥnḏt*
Ka-prophet	*ḥm-kꜣ*
King's Son of Kush	*sꜣ-nsw n Kꜣš*
Lector priest	*ẖry-ḥbt*
Mayor of Thebes (vizierial title)	*imy-r niwt*
Mayor	*ḥꜣty-ꜥ*
Mayor of Western Thebes	*ḥꜣty-ꜥ n imnt Wꜣst*
Measurer of Amun	*ḫꜣw n Ỉmn*
Medjay of the West	*mḏꜣyw n ỉmnt*
Outline Draughtsman (of Amun/in the Place of Truth)	*sš ḳd (n Ỉmn / m st mꜣꜥt)*
Overseer of Foreign Countries	*ḥry ḫꜣswt*

[1] Excluding a small number of the more unusual titles from the stelae belonging to the high officials at Wadi es-Sebau and Abu Simbel. Many of the stelae are poorly published, and the titles in the text and appendices have been taken from Kitchen's translations (Kitchen 2000).

Overseer of the Goldworkers	*ḥry nbw*
Overseer of God's Servants	*imy-r ḥmw-nṯr*
Overseer of the Granaries	*Iny-r šnwt*
Overseer of the Magazine	*ḥry šnꜥ*
Overseer of Sculptors in the temple of Amun	*ḥry ḳstyw m pr-Imn*
Overseer of the Southern Foreign Lands	*imy-r ḫ3swt rsy(wt)*
Overseer of the Treasury	*imy-r pr-ḥḏ*
Overseer of Works	*imy-r k3wt*
Pure of Hands in the temple of Re (epithet)	*wꜥb ꜥwy m pr-Rꜥ*
Royal Scribe	*sš nsw*
Sailor of the Palace	*nfy n pr-ꜥ3*
Sandalmaker (of Amun)	*ṯbw (n Imn)*
Secretary	*sš šꜥt*
Scribe of the Chariotry	*sš nt-ḥtrw*
Scribe of the Divine Offerings	*sš ḥtpw nṯryw*
Scribe of the Lord of the Two Lands	*sš n nb t3wy*
Scribe of Offerings	*sš ḫt nbt nfrwt*
Scribe of the Table/Altar of the Lord of the Two Lands	*sš n wḏḥw n nb t3wy*
Scribe of the Temple	*sš n ḥwt-nṯr*
Scribe of the Treasury	*sš n pr-ḥḏ*
Scribe of Troops of the Estate of Amun	*sš mšꜥ n pr Imn*
Sculptor	*ḳsty*
Servitor of …	*b3k n…*
Shield-bearer of the Mountainous Lands	*ḳrꜥw ḫ3swt*
sk-officer	*sk*
Stablemaster	*ḥry iḥw*
Standard-bearer	*ṯ3y sryt*
Stonemason	*ḫrty-nṯr*
The One Attached to the Balance	*iry mḫ3t*
Vizier	*ṯ3ty*
Wab-priest (of the Prow of Amun)	*wꜥb (n ḥ3t Imn)*
'Workman'* (in the Place of Truth)	*sḏm ꜥš (m st m3ꜥt)*

Female titles	
Lady of the House	*nbt pr*
Singer (of Montuemtawy)	*ḥsy (n Mnṯw-m-t3wy)*
Great Singer of Hathor	*ḥsy wr n Ḥwt-ḥr*
Musician of Amun	*šmꜥyt n Imn*
Weshbet-mourner	*wšbt*

**Lit. 'one who hears the call'*

BIBLIOGRAPHY

Abd el-Hafeez, A., J-C. Grenier, and G. Wagner. 1985. *Stèles funéraires de Kom Abu Bellou*. Paris: Éditions Recherché sur les Civilisations.

Abdalla, A. 1992. *Graeco-Roman Funerary Stelae from Upper Egypt*. Liverpool: Liverpool University Press.

Aldred, C. 1988. *The Egyptians* (2nd Edition). London: Thames and Hudson.

Allam, S. 1974. An Allusion to an Egyptian Wedding Ceremony. *Göttinger Miszellen* 13:9-11.

Altenmüller, H. 1981. Amenophis I. als Mittler. *Mitteilungen Deutschen Archäologischen Instituts Abteilung Kairo* 37:1-7.

Andreu, G. Editor. 2002. *Les Artistes de pharaon: Deir el-Médineh et la vallée des Rois*. Paris: Éditions de la Réunion des Musées Nationaux.

Anthes, R. 1943. Die Deutschen Grabungen auf der Westseite von Theben in den Jahren 1911 und 1913. *Mitteilungen Deutschen Archäologischen Instituts Abteilung Kairo* 12:1-72.

Arnold, D. 1962. *Wandrelief und Raumfunktion in ägyptischen Tempeln des Neuen Reiches*. Münchner Ägyptologische Studien. Vol. 2. Berlin: Bruno Hessling.

Assmann, J. 1975. *Ägyptischen Hymnen und Gebete*. Zürich: Artemis.

- 1978. Eine Traumoffenbarung der Göttin Hathor. Zeugnisse 'Persönlicher Frömmigkeit' in thebanischen Privatgräbern der Ramessidenzeit. *Revue d'Égyptologie* 30:22-50.

- 1989. "Death and Initiation in the Funerary Religion of Ancient Egypt," in *Religion and Philosophy in Ancient Egypt*. Yale Egyptological Studies. Vol. 3. Edited by W. K. Simpson, pp. 135-159. New Haven, Connecticut: Yale Egyptological Seminar.

- 2001. *The Search for God in Ancient Egypt*. Ithaca and London: Cornell University Press.

Aufrère, S., J.-C. Golvin, and J.-C. Goyon. 1997. *L'Égypte restituée*. Vol. 3. Paris: Éditions Errance.

Austin, M. M. and P. Vidal-Naquet. 1972. *Economic and Social History of Ancient Greece: An Introduction*. Berkeley: University of California Press.

Babić, S. 2005. "Status, Identity and Archaeology," in *The Archaeology of Identity. Approaches to Gender, Age, Status, Ethnicity and Religion*. Edited by M. Díaz-Andreu and S. Lucy, pp. 67-85. London and New York: Routledge.

Baer, K. 1960. *Rank and Title in the Old Kingdom: The Structure of the Egyptian Administration in the Fifth and Sixth Dynasties*. Chicago: The Oriental Institute of the University of Chicago.

Baines, J. 1983. Literacy and Ancient Egyptian Society. *Man* New Series 18:572-593.

- 1985. *Fecundity Figures: Egyptian Personification and the Iconology of a Genre*. Warminster: Aris and Phillips.

- 1986. The Stela of Emhab: Innovation, Tradition, Hierarchy. *Journal of Egyptian Archaeology* 72:41-53.

- 1987. Practical Religion and Piety. *Journal of Egyptian Archaeology* 73:79-98.

- 1988. "Literacy, Social Organization, and the Archaeological Record: The Case of Early Egypt," in *State and Society. The Emergence and Development of Social Hierarchy and Political Centralization*. Edited by J. Gledhill, B. Bender, and M. T. Larsen, pp. 192-214. London: Unwin Hyman.

- 1989. Communication and Display: The Integration of Early Egyptian Art and Writing. *Antiquity* 63:471-482.

- 1990. Restricted Knowledge, Hierarchy and Decorum: Modern Perceptions and Ancient Institutions. *Journal of the American Research Center in Egypt* 27:1-23.

- 1991. Review: *Ceremonial Execution and Public Rewards: Some Historical Scenes on New Kingdom Private Stelae*, by A. R. Schulman. Orbis Biblicus et Orientalis. Vol. 75. Freiburg: Universitätsverlag; Göttingen: Vandenhoeck & Ruprecht 1988. *Bulletin of the American Schools of Oriental Research* 281:91-93.

- 1991. "Society, Morality and Religious Practice," in *Religion in Ancient Egypt: Gods, Myth and Personal Practice*. Edited by B. E. Shafer, pp. 123-200. London: Routledge.

- 1994a. "Contexts of Fate: Literature and Practical Religion," in *The Unbroken Reed: Studies in the Culture and Heritage of Ancient Egypt, in Honour of A. F. Shore*. Edited by C. J. Eyre, M. A. Leahy and L. M. Leahy, pp. 35-52. London: Egypt Exploration Society.

- 1994b. On the Status and Purposes of Ancient Egyptian Art. *Cambridge Archaeological Journal* 4:67-94.

- 1995. "Kingship, Definition of Culture, and Legitimation," in *Ancient Egyptian Kingship*. Edited by D. B. O'Connor and D. P. Silverman, pp. 3-47. Leiden: E. J. Brill.

- 1997. "Temples as Symbols, Guarantors, and Participants in Egyptian Civilization," in *The Temple in Ancient Egypt: New Discoveries and Recent Research*. Edited by S. Quirke, pp. 216-241. London: British Museum Press.

- 2001. Egyptian Letters of the New Kingdom as Evidence for Religious Practice. *Journal of the Ancient Near Eastern Society* 1.1:1-31.

- 2004. "Egyptian Elite Self-Presentation in the Context of Ptolemaic Rule," in *Ancient Alexandria. Between Egypt and Greece*. Columbia Studies in the Classical Tradition. Edited by W. V. Harris and G. Ruffini, pp. 34-61. Leiden and Boston: E. J. Brill.

Baines, J. and C. J. Eyre. 1983. Four Notes on Literacy. *Göttinger Miszellen* 61:65-96.

Baines, J. and R. B. Parkinson. 1997. "An Old Kingdom Record of an Oracle? Sinai Inscription 13," in *Essays on Ancient Egypt in Honour of Herman te Velde*. Edited by J. Van Dijk, pp. 9-26. Leiden: E. J. Brill.

Baraize, E. 1913. Compte rendu des travaux exécutés à Deir el-Médineh. *Annales du Service des Antiquités de l'Égypte* 13:19-42.

Barns, J. 1949. The Neville Papyrus: A Late Ramesside Letter to an Oracle. *Journal of Egyptian Archaeology* 35:69-71.

Barsanti, A. and H. Gauthier. 1911. Stèles trouvées à Ouadi es-Sabouà (Nubie). *Annales du Service des Antiquités de l'Égypte* 11:64-86.

Beard, M. 1991. "Ancient Literacy and the Function of the Written Word in Roman Religion," in *Literacy in the Roman world*. Journal of Roman Archaeology, Supplementary Series, no. 3. Edited by J. H. Humphrey, pp. 35-58. Ann Arbor, Michigan: Department of Classical Studies, University of Michigan.

Bell, L. 1985. Luxor Temple and the Cult of the Royal Ka. *Journal of Near Eastern Studies* 44:251-294.

- 1997. "The New Kingdom 'Divine' Temple: The Example of Luxor," in *Temples in Ancient Egypt*. Edited by B. E. Shafer, pp. 127-184. Ithaca, New York: Cornell University Press.
Berg, D. 1993. Another Look at Ostracon MFA Boston II.1498. *Journal of the American Research Centre in Egypt* 30:57-69.
Bierbrier, M. L. 1975. *The Late New Kingdom in Egypt, c. 1300-664BC*. Warminster: Aris and Phillips.
- 1980. Piay in Cambridge. *Journal of Egyptian Archaeology* 68:85-92.
- 1982a. *The Tomb-builders of the Pharaohs*. London: British Museum Press.
- 1982b. *Hieroglyphic Texts from Egyptian Stelae etc. in the British Museum*. Vol. 10. London: British Museum Press.
- 1987. *Hieroglyphic Texts from Egyptian Stelae etc. in the British Museum*. Vol. 11. London: British Museum Press.
- 1993. *Hieroglyphic Texts from Egyptian Stelae etc. in the British Museum*. Vol. 12. London: British Museum Press.
- 1994. "Rahotep in Durham," in *Hommages à Jean Leclant*. Vol. 1. Edited by C. Berger, G. Clerc and N. Grimal, pp. 407-410. Cairo: Institut Français d'Archéologie Orientale.
- 2000. "Paneb Rehabilitated," in *Deir el Medina in the Third Millennium AD*. Egyptologische Uitgaven. Vol. XIV. Edited by R. J. Demarée and A. Egberts, pp. 51-54. Leiden: Nederlands Instituut voor het Nabije Oosten.
Bierbrier, M. L., and H. J. A. de Meulenaere. 1984. "Hymne à Taouêret sur une stèle de Deir el-Médineh," in *Sundries in Honour of T. Säve-Söderbergh*, pp. 23-32. Uppsala: Uppsala Universitet.
Bietak, M. 1975. *Tell El-Dab`a II: Der Fundort im Rahmen einer archäologisch-geographischen Untersuchung uber das Ägyptische Ostdelta*. Vienna: Verlag der Österreichischen Akademie der Wissenschaften.
- 1981. *Avaris and Piramesses: Archaeological Exploration in the Eastern Nile Delta (Mortimer Wheeler Archaeological Lecture 1979)*. Proceedings of the British Academy, London. Vol. LXV. Oxford: Oxford University Press.
- 1984. "Ramesstadt," in *Lexikon der Ägyptologie V*. Edited by W. Helck and W. Westendorf, cols. 129-145. Wiesbaden: Harrassowitz.
- 2009. Perunefer: The Principal New Kingdom Naval Base. *Egyptian Archaeology* 34:15-17.
Birch, S. 1880. *Catalogue of the Collection of the Egyptian Antiquities at Alnwick Castle*. London: R. Clay Sons and Taylor.
Blackman, A. M. 1926. Oracles in Ancient Egypt. *Journal of Egyptian Archaeology* 12:176-185.
- 1935. The Stela of Nebipusenwosret: British Museum no. 101. *Journal of Egyptian Archaeology* 21:1-9, pl. 1.
Blackman, W. 1927 [2000]. *The Fellāhīn of Upper Egypt* (2nd Edition). Cairo: The American University in Cairo Press.
Blumenthal, E. 2000. *Kuhgöttin und Gottkönig: Frömmigkeit und Staatstreue auf der Stele Leipzig Ägyptische Museum 5141*. Leipzig: Ägyptisches Museum der Universität Leipzig.
Bodel, J. 2001. "Epigraphy and the Ancient Historian," in *Epigraphic Evidence: Ancient History from Inscriptions*. Approaching the Ancient World. Edited by J. Bodel, pp. 1-56. London and New York: Routledge.
Boeser, P. A .A. 1913. *Beschreibung der Aegyptischen Sammlung des Niederländischen Reichsmuseums der Altertümer in Leiden*. Vol. 6. The Hague: M. Nijhoff.
Bogoslovsky, E. S. 1972a. Monuments and Documents from Dêr el-Medîna. *Vestnik drevnei istorii* 119:79-103.
- 1972b. Monuments and Documents from Dêr el-Medîna in the Museums of the USSR (III). *Vestnik drevnei istorii* 120:64-105.
- 1980. Hundred Egyptian Draughtsmen. *Zeitschrift für Ägyptische Sprache* 167:89-116.
Bomann, A. H. 1991. *The Private Chapel in Ancient Egypt: A Study of the Chapels of the Workmen's Village at El-Amarna with Special Reference to Deir el Medina and Other Sites*. London: Kegan Paul International.
Borchardt, L. 1933. "Metallbelag an Steinbauten," in *Allerhand Kleinigkeiten*, pp. 1-11. Leipzig: Privatdruck, August Pries.
Boreux, C. 1932. *Musée National du Louvre: Département des Antiquités Egyptiénnes. Guide-catalogue sommaire*. 2 Vols. Paris: Musées Nationaux.
Borghouts, J. F. 1981. Monthu and Matrimonial Squabbles. *Revue d'Égyptologie* 33:11-22.
- 1982a. "Montu," in *Lexikon der Ägyptologie IV*. Edited by W. Helck and W. Westendorf, col. 202. Wiesbaden: Harrassowitz.
- 1982b. "Divine Intervention in Ancient Egypt and its Manifestation (*b3w*)," in *Gleanings from Deir el-Medîna*. Egyptologische
Uitgaven. Vol. I. Edited by R. J. Demarée and J. J. Janssen, pp. 1-70. Leiden: Nederlands Instituut voor het Nabije Oosten.
Bosticco, S. 1965. *Le stele egiziane del Nuovo Regno*. Rome: Istituto Poligrafo dello stato, Libreria dello stato.
Botti, G. and T. E. Peet. 1928. *Il giornale della necropoli di Tebe*. Turin: Fratelli Bocca.
Botti, G. and P. Romanelli. 1951. *Le sculture del Museo Gregoriano Egizio*. Città del Vaticano: Tipografia Poliglotta Vaticana.
Bourdieu, P. 1980. *Le Sens pratique*. Paris: Éditions de Minuit.
Brand, P. 2003. "Veils, Votives and Marginalia: Adaptations of Existing Monuments for Political and Pious Needs in the Ramesside and Third Intermediate Periods." (Unpublished conference paper) *Sacred Spaces and their Function through Time,* The British Museum, London, 2003.
British Museum. 1911. *Hieroglyphic Texts from Egyptian Stelae etc. in the British Museum*. Part I. London: British Museum Press.
- 1912a. *Hieroglyphic Texts from Egyptian Stelae etc. in the British Museum*. Part II. London: British Museum Press.
- 1912b. *Hieroglyphic Texts from Egyptian Stelae etc. in the British Museum*. Part III. London: British Museum Press.
- 1913. *Hieroglyphic Texts from Egyptian Stelae etc. in the British Museum*. Part IV. London: British Museum Press.
- 1914. *Hieroglyphic Texts from Egyptian Stelae etc. in the British Museum*. Part V. London: British Museum Press.
- 1922. *Hieroglyphic Texts from Egyptian Stelae etc. in the British Museum*. Part VI. London: British Museum Press.
- 1925. *Hieroglyphic Texts from Egyptian Stelae etc. in the British Museum*. Part VII. London: British Museum Press.
Brovarski, E. 1976. Senenu, High Priest of Amun at Deir el-Bahri. *Journal of Egyptian Archaeology* 62:52-73.
- 1989. *The Inscribed Material of the First Intermediate Period from Naga ed-Der*. Ph.D. thesis, University of Chicago (unpublished).
Brunner-Traut, E. 1956. *Die altägyptischen Scherbenbilder (Bildostraka) der deutschen Museen und Sammlungen*. Wiesbaden: Franz Steiner.

- 1979. *Egyptian Artists' Sketches: Figured Ostraca from the Gayer-Anderson Collection in the Fitzwilliam Museum, Cambridge*. Istanbul: Nederlands Historische-Archaeologisch Instituut; Leiden: Nederlands Instituut voor het Nabije Oosten.
Bruyère, B. 1924-1953. *Rapports sur les fouilles de Deir el Medinéh*. 25 Vols. Cairo: Institut Français d'Archéologie Orientale.
- 1925. Stèles trouvées par ME Baraize à Deir el Medinéh. *Annales du Service des Antiquités de l'Égypte* 25:76-96.
- 1930b. *Mert seger à Deir el Medinéh*. Cairo: Institut Français d'Archéologie Orientale.
- 1959. *Tombes thebaines à Deir el Medinéh*. Cairo: Institut Français d'Archéologie Orientale.
Budge, E. A. Wallis. 1893. *Catalogue of the Egyptian Collection in the Fitzwilliam Museum, Cambridge*. Cambridge: Cambridge University Press.
Buhl, M. L. 1974. *A Hundred Masterpieces from the Ancient Near East*: Copenhagen: National Museums of Denmark.
Burke, P. 1991. "Overture: the New History, its Past and its Future," in *New Perspectives on Historical Writing*. Edited by P. Burke, pp. 1-23. Cambridge: Polity Press.
Burrell Collection, Exhibition 1949 (Corporation of Glasgow Art Galleries and Museums, McLellan Gallery).
Cabrol, A. 1995a. Les Criosphinx de Karnak: un nouveau dromos d'Amenhotep III. *CahKarn* 10:1-32.
- 1995b. Une représentation de la tombe de Khâbekhenet et les dromos de Karnak-sud: nouvelle hypothèse. Les béliers du dromos du temple de Khonsou et l'intérieur de l'enceinte du temple de Mout. *CahKharn* 10:32-57.
- 2001. *Les Voies processionnelles de Thèbes*. Orientalia Lovaniensia Analecta. Vol. 97. Leuven: Peeters.
Caminos, R. A. 1978. Review: *Egyptian Stelae, Reliefs and Paintings from the Petrie Collection (Part 1, The New Kingdom)*, by H. M. Stewart. Warminster: Aris and Phillips. 1976. *Journal of Egyptian Archaeology* 64:151-157.
Cannon, A. 1989. The Historical Dimension in Mortuary Expression of Status and Sentiment. *Current Anthropology* 30:437-458.
Cartwright, H. W. 1929 (April). The Iconography of Certain Egyptian Divinities as Illustrated in the Collections of the Haskell Oriental Museum. *American Journal of Semitic Languages and Literature* 45 (1928-1929):179-196.
Černý, J. 1927. Le Culte d'Amenophis Ier chez les ouvriers de la Nécropole thébaine. *Bulletin de l'Institut Francaise d'Archéologie Orientale* 27:159-203.
- 1929a. L'Identité des 'serviteurs dans la place de Vérité' et des ouvriers de la Nécropole royale de Thèbes. *Revue d'Égyptologie* 2:200-209.
- 1929b. Papyrus Salt (British Museum 10055). *Journal of Egyptian Archaeology* 15:243-258.
- 1931. Les Ostraca hiératiques, leur intérêt et la nécessité de leur étude. *Chronique d'Égypte* 12:212-224.
- 1935a. *Catalogue des ostraca hiératiques non-littéraires de Deîr el-Médînéh, nos. 1-113*. Vol. 1. Cairo: Institut Français d'Archéologie Orientale.
- 1935b. Questions addressées aux oracles. *Bulletin de l'Institut Français d'Archéologie Orientale*. 35:41-58.
- 1937a. *Catalogue des ostraca hiératiques non-littéraires de Deîr el-Médînéh, nos. 114-189*. Vol. 2. Cairo: Institut Français d'Archéologie Orientale.
- 1937b. *Catalogue des ostraca hiératiques non-littéraires de Deîr el-Médînéh, nos. 190-241*. Vol. 3. Cairo: Institut Français d'Archéologie Orientale.
- 1939. *Catalogue des ostraca hiératiques non-littéraires de Deîr el-Médînéh, nos. 242-339*. Vol. 4. Cairo: Institut Français d'Archéologie Orientale.
- 1941. Le Tirage au sort. *Bulletin de l'Institut Français d'Archéologie Orientale* 40:135-141.
- 1942. Nouvelle série des questions addressées aux oracles. *Bulletin de l'Institut Français d'Archéologie Orientale* 41:13-24.
- 1951. *Catalogue des ostraca hiératiques non-littéraires de Deîr el-Médînéh, nos. 340-456*. Vol. 5. Cairo: Institut Français d'Archéologie Orientale.
- 1952. *Ancient Egyptian Religion*. London: Hutchinson's University Library.
- 1958. *Egyptian Stelae in the Bankes Collection*. Oxford: Oxford University Press.
- 1962. "Egyptian Oracles," in *A Saite Oracle Papyrus from Thebes*, by R. A. Parker, pp. 35-48. Providence, Rhode Island: Brown University Press.
- 1969. Two King's Sons of Kush of the Twentieth Dynasty. *Kush* 7:71-75.
- 1970. *Catalogue des ostraca hiératiques non-littéraires de Deîr el-Médînéh, nos. 624-705*. Cairo: Institut Français d'Archéologie Orientale.
- 1972. Troisième sèries des questions addressées aux oracles. *Bulletin de l'Institut Français d'Archéologie Orientale* 72:49-69.
- 1973 [2001]. *A Community of Workmen at Thebes in the Ramesside Period*. Cairo: Institut Français d'Archéologie Orientale.
Černý, J., and A. H. Gardiner. 1957. *Hieratic Ostraca*. Vol. 1. Oxford: Oxford University Press.
Champollion, J.-F. 1835-1845 [1970]. *Monuments de l'Égypte et de la Nubie*. 4 Vols. Geneva: Éditions de Belles-Lettres.
Chapman, R. 2003. *Archaeologies of Complexity*. Routledge: London and New York.
Chevrier, H. 1936. Rapport sur les travaux de Karnak (1935-1936). *Annales du Service des Antiquités de l'Égypte* 36:131-157.
Chevrier, H., and E. Drioton. 1940. *Le Temple reposoir de Séti II à Karnak*. Cairo: Imprimerie Nationale, Boulac.
Christophe, L.-A. 1955. *Temple d'Amon à Karnak. Les divinités des colonnes de la grande salle hypostyle et leurs épithètes*. Cairo: Institut Français d'Archéologie Orientale.
- 1961. Quelques remarques sur le Grand Temple d'Abou Simbel. *Le Revue du Caire* 255:303-333.
Clère, J. J. 1929. Monuments inédits des serviteurs dans la place de Vérité. *Bulletin de l'Institut Français d'Archéologie Orientale* 28:173-201.
- 1950. Nouveaux documents relatifs au culte des colosses de Ramsès II dans le Delta. *KÊMI* 11:24-46.
- 1975. Un monument de la religion populaire de l'époque ramesside. *Revue d'Égyptologie* 27:73-76.
- 1982. La Stèle de Sânkhptah, chambellan du roi Râhotep. *Journal of Egyptian Archaeology* 68:60-69, pls. IV-VI.
Corteggiani, J.-P. 1975. Documents divers (VII-X): VIII-Une stèle thébaine de l'époque ramesside. *Bulletin de l'Institut Français*

d'Archéologie Orientale 75:152-154.
Cramer, M. 1936. Ägyptische Denkmäler im Kestner-Museum zu Hannover. *Zeitschrift für Ägyptische Sprache* 72:81-108.
Crocker, P. T. 1985. Status Symbols in the Architecture of El-'Amarna. *Journal of Egyptian Archaeology* 71:52-65.
Cowgill, G. L. 2000. "'Rationality' and Context in Agency Theory," in *Agency in Archaeology*. Edited by M.-A. Dobres and J. E. Robb, pp. 51-60. London and New York: Routledge.
David, R. 1986. *The Pyramid Builders of Ancient Egypt. A Modern Investigation of Pharaoh's Workforce.* London: Guild Publishing.
Davies, B. G. 1999. *Who's Who at Deir el Medina: A Prospographic Study of the Royal Workmen's Necropolis.* Egyptologische Uitgaven. Vol. XIII. Leiden: Nederlands Instituut voor het Nabije Oosten.
Davies, N. d. G. 1927. *Two Ramesside Tombs at Thebes.* New York: Metropolitan Museum of Art.
- 1935-1938. "A High Place at Thebes," in *Mélanges Maspero.* Vol. 1, pp. 241-250. Cairo: Institut Français d'Archéologie Orientale.
Davies, W. V. 1982. The Origin of the Blue Crown. *Journal of Egyptian Archaeology* 68:69-78.
De Botton, A. 2004. *Status Anxiety.* London: Hamish Hamilton (Penguin).
De Cenival, F. 1972. *Les Associations religieuses en Égypte d'après les documents démotiques.* Cairo: Institut Français d'Archéologie Orientale.
De Cenival, J. L., and G. Haeny. 1964. Report préliminaire sur la troisième campagne de fouilles à Ouadi es-Sebouè. *Bulletin de l'Institut Français d'Archéologie Orientale* 62:219-229.
Della Monica, M. 1975. *La Classe ouvrière sous les pharaons: étude du village de Deir el Medinéh.* Paris: Librairie d'Amérique et d'Orient.
De Lubicz, R. A. Schwaller. 1999. *The Temples of Karnak.* London: Thames and Hudson.
Demarée, R. J. 1982. "Remove your Stela (O.Petrie 21=Hier. Ostr. 16, 4)," in *Gleanings from Deir el-Medina.* Egyptologische Uitgaven. Vol. I. Edited by R. J. Demarée and J. J. Janssen, pp. 101-108. Leiden: Nederlands Instituut voor het Nabije Oosten.
- 1983. *The 3kh iḳr n Rᶜ Stelae: On Ancestor Worship in Ancient Egypt.* Egyptologische Uitgaven. Vol. III. Leiden: Nederlands Instituut voor het Nabije Oosten.
- 2001. Deir el-Medina After All? *Göttinger Miszellen* 183:5-6.
Desroches-Noblecourt, C. and C. Kuentz. 1968. *Le Petit temple d'Abou Simbel.* Collection Scientifique. Cairo: Centre de Documentation et d'Étude sur l'Ancienne Égypte.
Desroches-Noblecourt, C., S. Donaldoni and E. Edel. 1971. *Le Grand temple d'Abou Simbel. La Bataille de Qadech.* Collection Scientifique. Cairo: Centre de Documentation et d'Étude sur l'Ancienne Égypte.
Díaz-Andreu, M. and S. Lucy. 2005. "Introduction," in *The Archaeology of Identity. Approaches to Gender, Age, Status, Ethnicity and Religion.* Edited by M. Díaz-Andreu and S. Lucy, pp. 1-12. London and New York: Routledge.
Dittmar, J. 1986. *Blumen und Blumensträuße als Opfergabe im alten Ägypten.* Münchner Ägyptologische Studien. Vol. 43. Munich and Berlin: Deutscher Kunstverlag.
Dobres, M.-A. and J. E. Robb, 2000. "Editor's Introduction," in *Agency in Archaeology.* Edited by M.-A. Dobres and J. E. Robb, pp. 3-17. London and New York: Routledge.
Donohue, V. A. 1988a. "A Gesture of Submission," in *Studies in Pharaonic Kingship and Society.* Edited by A. B. Lloyd, pp. 82-114. London: Egypt Exploration Society.
- 1988b. The Vizier Paser. *Journal of Egyptian Archaeology* 74:103-123.
- 1992. The Goddess of the Theban Mountain. *Antiquity* 66:871-885.
Dorner, J. 1996. "Zur Lage des Palastes und des Haupttempels der Ramssesstadt," in *Haus und Palast im Alten Ägypten.* International Symposium in Cairo, April 8. to 11. 1992. Edited by M. Bietak, pp. 69-71. Vienna: Verlag der Österreichischen Akademie der Wissenschaften.
- 1999. Die Topographie von Piramesse - Vorbericht. *Egypt and the Levant* 9:77-83.
Drenkhahn, R. 1984. "Ramses III," in *Lexikon der Ägyptologie V.* Edited by W. Helck and W. Westendorf, cols. 114 –119. Wiesbaden: Harrassowitz.
Dryoff, K., and B. Pörtner. 1904. *Aegyptische Grabsteine und Denksteine aus süddeutschen Sammlungen.* Vol. 2. Strasbourg: Schlesier & Schweikhardt.
Du Bourguet, P. 2002. *Le Temple de Deir al-Médîna.* Cairo: Institut Français d'Archéologie Orientale.
Dunham, D. 1937. *Naga ed-Dêr Stelae of the First Intermediate Period.* London: Humphrey Milford.
Duquesne, T. 2004. "The Salakhana Stelae. A Unique Trove of Votive Stelae Objects from Asyut." (Unpublished conference paper). *The Ninth International Congress of Egyptologists,* Grenoble, September 2004.
- 2005. "Gender, Class and Devotion: Demographic and Social Aspects of the Salakhana Stelae." (Unpublished conference paper). *British Egyptology Conference I,* Cambridge, September 2005.
Edgerton, W. F. 1951. The Strikes in Ramesses III's Twenty-Ninth Year. *Journal of Near Eastern Studies* 10:137-145.
Edgerton, W. F. and J. A. Wilson. 1936. *Historical Records of Ramesses III: The Texts in Medinet Habu.* Vols. I and II. Chicago: The Oriental Institute of the University of Chicago.
Edwards, I. E. S. 1939. *Hieroglyphic Texts etc. from the British Museum.* Vol. 8. London: British Museum Press.
- 1955. A Relief of Qudshu- Astarte- Anath in the Winchester College Collection. *Journal of Near Eastern Studies* 14:49-51.
Erman, A. 1907. *A Handbook of Egyptian Religion.* London: Constable.
Evers, H. G. 1929. *Staat aus dem Stein.* Vol. II. Munich: F. Bruckmann.
Eyre, C. J. 1980. *Employment and Labour Relations in the Theban Necropolis.* D.Phil., University of Oxford (unpublished).
Fabretti, A., F. Rossi and R.V. Lanzone. 1882 and 1888. *Regio Museo di Torino. Antichità Egizie.* 2 Vols. Turin.
Faulkner, R. O. 1941. Egyptian Military Standards. *Journal of Egyptian Archaeology* 27:12-18.
- 1952. The Stela of the Master Sculptor Shen. *Journal of Egyptian Archaeology* 38:3-5, pl. 1.
Finnestadt, R. B. 1989a. "Religion as a Cultural Phenomenon," in *The Religion of the Ancient Egyptians: Cognitive Structures and*

Popular Expressions. Proceedings of the Symposia in Uppsala and Bergen, 1987 and 1988. ACTA Universitatis Upsaliensis. Edited by G. Englund, pp. 73-76. Uppsala: Uppsala Universitet.
- 1989b. "The Pharaoh and the "Democratization" of Post-mortem Life," in *The Religion of the Ancient Egyptians: Cognitive Structures and Popular Expressions*. Proceedings of the Symposia in Uppsala and Bergen, 1987 and 1988. ACTA Universitatis Upsaliensis. Edited by G. Englund, pp. 89-93. Uppsala: Uppsala Universitet.

Firth, C. M. 1927. *The Archaeological Survey of Nubia. Report for 1910-1911*. Survey of Egypt. Cairo: Government Press.

Fischer, H. G. 1959. Review: *Medinet Habu V*. Oriental Institute Publications. Vol. 83. Chicago: The Oriental Institute of the University of Chicago. *American Journal of Archaeology* 63:195-198.
- 1964. *Inscriptions from the Coptite Nome: Dynasties VI-XI*. Rome: Pontificium Institutum Biblicum.
- 1968. *Dendera in the Third Millennium BC down to the Theban Domination of Upper Egypt*. Locust Valley, New York: J. J. Augustin.
- 1976. "Archaeological Aspects of Epigraphy and Palaeography," in *Ancient Egyptian Epigraphy and Palaeography*, pp. 29-50. New York: Metropolitan Museum of Art.

Forstner-Müller, I. 2009. Providing a Map of Avaris. *Egyptian Archaeology* 34:10-13.

Foucart, G., M. Baud and E. Drioton. 1928-1932. *Tombes thébaines*. Vols. I-IV. Cairo: Institut Français d'Archéologie Orientale.

Fouchet, M.-P. 1965. *Rescued Treasures of Egypt*. London: George Allen and Unwin Ltd.

Foxhall, L. 1994. "Pandora Unbound. A Feminist Critique of Foucault's *History of Sexuality*," in *Dislocating Masculinity*. Edited by A. Cornwall and N. Lindisfarne, pp. 133-146. London and New York: Routledge.
- 1995. "Monumental Ambitions," in *Time, Tradition and Society in Greek Archaeology: Bridging the 'Great Divide'*. Edited by N. Spencer, pp. 132-149. London and New York: Routledge.

Frandsen, P. J. 1992. "The Letter to Ikhtay's Coffin: O. Louvre Inv. No. 698," in *Village Voices: Proceedings of the Symposium "Texts from Deir el-Medina and their Interpretation" Leiden, May 31-June 1, 1991*. Egyptologische Uitgaven. Vol. XI. Edited by R. J. Demarée and A. Egberts, pp. 31-50. Leiden: Nederlands Instituut voor het Nabije Oosten.

Frankfort, H. 1928. The Cemeteries of Abydos: Work of the Season 1925-1926. *Journal of Egyptian Archaeology* 14:235-243.
- 1948. *Ancient Egyptian Religion: An Interpretation*. New York: Columbia University Press.

Frankfurter, D. 1998. *Religion in Roman Egypt. Assimilation and Resistance*. Princeton, New Jersey, and Chichester, West Sussex: Princeton University Press.

Freed, R. E. 1981. "A Private Stela from Naga-ed Dêr and the Relief Style of Amenemhat I," in *Studies in Ancient Egypt, the Aegean and the Sudan*. Edited by D. Dunham and W. K. Simpson, pp. 68-76. Boston: Department of Ancient Egyptian, Nubian and Near Eastern Art, Museum of Fine Arts.
- 1996. "Stela Workshops of the Early 12th Dynasty," in *Studies in Honor of William Kelly Simpson*. Vol. 1. Edited by P. dėr Manuelian, pp. 296-336. Boston: Department of Ancient Egyptian, Nubian and Near Eastern Art, Museum of Fine Arts.

Friedman, D. F. 1994. "Aspects of Domestic Life and Religion," in *Pharaoh's Workers: The Villagers of Deir el Medina*. Edited by L. H. Lesko, pp. 95-118. Ithaca: Cornell University Press.

Frood, E. 2003. Ritual Function and Priestly Narrative: The Stelae of the High Priest of Osiris, Nebwawy. *Journal of Egyptian Archaeology* 89:59-81.

Galán, J. M. 1999. Seeing Darkness. *Cahiers Caribéens d'Égyptologie* 74:18-30.

Gardiner, A. H. 1911. The Goddess Nekhbet at the Jubilee Festival of Ramesses III. *Zeitschrift für Ägyptische Sprache* 48:47-51.
- 1918. The Delta Residence of the Ramessides. *Journal of Egyptian Archaeology* 5:127-138, 179-200, 242-271.
- 1933. The Dakhleh Stela. *Journal of Egyptian Archaeology* 19:19-30.
- 1937. *Late-Egyptian Miscellanies*. Brussels: Édition de la Fondation égyptologique reine Elisabeth.
- 1962. The Gods of Thebes as Guarantors of Personal Property. *Journal of Egyptian Archaeology* 48:57-69.

Gardner, A. 2002. Social Identity and the Duality of Structure in Late Roman-period Britain. *Journal of Social Archaeology* 2:323-351.

Gauthier, H. 1912. *Les Temples immergés de la Nubie. Le Temple de Ouadi es-Sebuâ*. 2 Vols. Cairo: l'Institut Francais d'Archéologie Orientale.
- 1936. Une fondation pieuse en Nubie. *Annales du Service des Antiquités de l'Égypte* 36:49-69.

Giddens, A. 1984. *The Constitution of Society. Outline of the Theory of Structuration*. Cambridge: Polity Press.

Gilchrist, R. 2000. Archaeological Biographies: Realizing Human Lifecycles, - courses and – histories. *World Archaeology* 31:325-327.
- 2004. "Archaeology and the Life Course: A Time and Age for Gender," in *A Companion to Social Archaeology*. Edited by L. Meskell and R. W. Preucel, pp. 142-160. Malden, MA, USA, Oxford, UK and Victoria, Australia: Blackwell Publishing.

Gitton, M. 1975a. *L'Épouse du dieu Ahmes Néfertary: documents sur sa vie et son culte posthume*. Centre de Recherches d'Histoire Ancienne. Vol. 15. Annales Littéraires de l'Université de Besançon.
- 1975b. "Ahmose Nofretere," in *Lexikon der Ägyptologie I*. Edited by W. Helck and E. Otto, cols. 102-109. Wiesbaden: Harrassowitz.

Goebs, K. 2001. "Crowns," in *The Oxford Encyclopedia of Ancient Egypt*. Vol. 1. Edited by D. B. Redford, pp. 321-326. New York: Oxford University Press.

Gnirs, A. M. 1996. *Militär und Gesellschaft. Ein Beitrag zur Sozialgeschichte des Neuen Reiches*. Studien zur Archäologie und Geschichte Altägyptens. Vol. 17. Heidelberg: Heidelberger Orientverlag.

Godron, G. 1959. Un fragment de stèle au nom du *sḏm-ʿš ḫʿy-<m>-bḫnt*. *Bulletin de l'Institut Français d'Archéologie Orientale* 58:81-85.

Gohary, J. 1998. *Guide to the Nubian Monuments on Lake Nasser*. Cairo: The American University in Cairo Press.

Goyon, J.-C., and H. el-Achirie. 1974. *Le Ramesseum VI. La Salle des Litanies*. Cairo: Centre d'études et de la documentation sur l'ancienne Égypte.

Grandet, P. 2000. *Catalogue des ostraca hiératiques non-littéraires de Deîr el-Médînéh, nos. 706-830*. Vol. 8. Cairo: Institut Français d'Archéologie Orientale.

- 2003. *Catalogue des ostraca hiératiques non-littéraires de Deîr el-Médînéh, nos. 831-1000*. Vol. 9. Cairo: Institut Français d'Archéologie Orientale.

Grebaut, E. and G. Maspero. 1890-1915. *Le Musée égyptien: recueil de monuments et des notices sur les fouilles d'Égypte*. Cairo: Institut Français d'Archéologie Orientale.

Guglielmi, W. 1991. Zur Bedeutung von Symbolen der Persönlichen Frömmigkeit: die verschiedenfarbigen Ohren und das Ka-Zeichen. *Zeitschrift für Ägyptische Sprache* 118:116-127.

- 1994. "Die Funktion von Tempeleingang und Gegentempel als Gebetsort: Zur Deutung einiger Widder- und Gansstelen des Amun," in *Ägyptische Tempel-Struktur, Funktion und Programm (Akten der Ägyptologischen Tempeltagungen in Gosen 1990 und in Mainz 1992)*. Hildesheimer Ägytologische Beiträge. Vol. 37. Edited by R. Gundlach and M. Rochholz, pp. 55-68. Hildesheim: Gerstenberg.

Guglielmi, W., and J. Dittmar. 1992. "Anrufungen der persönlichen Frömmigkeit auf Gans- und Widder Darstellungen des Amun," in *Gegengabe - Festchrift für Emma Brünner-Traut*. Edited by I. Gamer-Wallert and W. Helck, pp. 119-142. Tübingen: Attempto.

Gundlach, R. 1984. “Sebua (Wadi-es),” in *Lexikon der Ägyptologie V*. Edited by W. Helck and W. Westendorf, cols. 768-769. Wiesbaden: Harrassowitz.

Gunn, B. 1916. The Religion of the Poor in Ancient Egypt. *Journal of Egyptian Archaeology* 3:81-94.

Gutgesell, M. 1989. *Arbeiter und Pharaonen. Wirtschafts- und Sozialgeschichte im Alten Ägypten*. Hildesheim: Gerstenberg.

Habachi, L. 1954. Khata'na-Qantir: Importance. *Annales du Service des Antiquités de l'Égypte* 52:443-559.

- 1957. The Graffiti and Work of the Viceroys of Kush in the Region of Aswan. *Kush* 5:13-36.

- 1960. Five Stelae from the Temple of Amenophis III at Es-Sebua' now in the Aswan Museum. *Kush* 8:45-52.

- 1967. Setau, the Famous Viceroy of Ramses and his Career. *Cahiers d'Histoire Égyptienne* 10 Nubie:50-68.

- 1969a. *Features of the Deification of Ramesses II*. Glückstadt: J. J. Augustin.

- 1969b. The Administration of Nubia During the New Kingdom with Special Reference to Discoveries Made During the Last Few Years. Actes du symposium international sur la Nubie organisé par L'Institut d'Égypte et tenu au siège de l'Institut les 1er, 2 & 3 Mars 1965. *Mémoires de l'Institut d'Égypte* 59:65-78.

- 1972. Nia, the Wab-Priest and the Doorkeeper of Amun-of-the-Hearing-Ear. *Bulletin de l'Institut Français d'Archéologie Orientale* 71:67-85.

- 1976. Miscellanea on Viceroys of Kush and their Assistants Buried in Dra' Abu el-Naga', South. *Journal of the American Research Center in Egypt* 13:113-116.

- 1978. King Amenmesse and Viziers Amenmose and Kha'emtore: Their Monuments and History. *Mitteilungen Deutschen Archäologischen Instituts Abteilung Kairo* 34:57-67.

- 1980. The Military Posts of Ramesses II on the Coastal Road and the Western Part of the Delta. *Bulletin de l'Institut Français d'Archéologie Orientale* 80:13-30.

- 1985. *Elephantine IV: The Sanctuary of Heqaib*. 2 Vols. Mainz am Rhein: Philip von Zabern.

Haeny, G. 1971. Zu den Platten mit Opfertischszene aus Helwan und Gise. Aufsätze zum 70. Geburtstag von Herbert Ricke. Edited by Schweizerische Institut für Ägyptische Bauforschung und Altertumskunde in Kairo. *Beiträge zur ägyptischen Bauforschung und Altertumskunde* 12:143-164.

- 1997. "New Kingdom 'Mortuary Temples' and 'Mansions of Million Years'," in *Temples in Ancient Egypt*. Edited by B. E. Shafer, pp. 86-126. Ithaca, New York: Cornell University Press.

Häggman, S. 2002. *Directing Deir el-Medina. The External Administration of the Necropolis*. Uppsala Studies in Egyptology. Vol. 4. Uppsala: Department of Archaeology and Ancient History, Uppsala Universitet.

Hamada, A. 1938. A Stele from Manshiyet Es-Sadr. *Annales du Service des Antiquités de l'Égypte* 38:217-230.

Hamza, M. 1930. Excavations of the Department of Antiquities at Qantir (Faqus District). *Annales du Service des Antiquités de l'Égypte* 30:31-68.

Hannig, R. 2001. *Grosses Handwörterbuch Ägyptisch-Deutsch: die Sprache der Pharaonen* (2800-950 v. Chr.). (2nd Edition). Mainz am Rhein: Philip von Zabern.

Hardwick, T. 2003. The Iconography of the Blue Crown in the New Kingdom. *Journal of Egyptian Archaeology* 89:117-142.

Haring, B. J. J. 1997. *Divine Households: Adminstrative and Economic Aspects of the New Kingdom Royal Memorial Temples in Thebes*. Egyptologische Uitgaven. Vol. XII. Leiden: Nederlands Instituut voor het Nabije Oosten.

Hart, G. 1988. *A Dictionary of Egyptian Gods and Goddesses*. London: Routledge and Kegan Paul Ltd.

Harvey, S. 1992. Monuments of Ahmose at Abydos. *Egyptian Archaeology* 4:3-5.

- 2004. New Evidence at Abydos for Ahmose's Funerary Cult. *Egyptian Archaeology* 24:3-6.

Hassan, S. 1932-1960. *Excavations at Giza 1929-1938*. 9 Vols. Cairo: Faculty of Arts of the Egyptian University.

Hayes, W. C. 1953, 1959. *The Scepter of Egypt: A Background for the Study of the Egyptian Antiquities in the Metropolitan Museum of Art*. 2 Vols. Cambridge, Mass.: Harvard University Press.

Helck, W. 1939. *Der Einfluss der Militärführer in der 18. ägyptischen Dynastie*. Leipzig: J. C. Hinrichs'sche Buchhandlung.

- 1955. Zur Geschichte der 19. und 20. Dynastie. *Zeitschrift für Deutschen Morgenländischen Gesellschaft* 105:27-38.

- 1958. *Zur Verwaltung des Mittleren und Neuen Reiches*. Leiden: E. J. Brill

- 1964. Feiertage und Arbeitstage in der Ramessidenzeit. *Journal of Economic and Social History of the Orient* 7:136-166.

- 1966. Zum Kult an Königstatuen. *Journal of Near Eastern Studies* 25:32-41.

- 1968. *Die Ritualszenen auf der Umfassungsmauer Ramses' II. in Karnak*. Ägyptologische Abhandlungen. Vol. 18. Wiesbaden: Harrassowitz.

- 1975. Die Grosse Stele des Vizekönigs *st3w* aus Wadi es-Sabua. *Studien zur Altägyptischen Kultur* 3:85-112.

- 1986. “Umm er-Rahman,” in *Lexikon der Ägyptologie VI*. Edited by W. Helck and W. Westendorf, col. 845. Wiesbaden: Harrassowitz.

Hermann, A. 1940. *Die Stelen der Thebanischen Felsgräber der 18. Dynastie.* Glückstadt: J. J. Augustin.
Hodder, I. 1987. "The Contextual Analysis of Symbolic Meanings," in *The Archaeology of Contextual Meanings.* Edited by I. Hodder, pp. 1-10. Cambridge: Cambridge University Press.
- 2004. "The "Social" in Archaeological Theory: An Historical and Contemporary Perspective," in *A Companion to Social Archaeology.* Edited by L. Meskell and R. W. Preucel, pp. 23-42. Malden, MA, USA, Oxford, UK and Victoria, Australia: Blackwell Publishing, 23-42.
Hodjash, S. and O. Berlev. 1982. *The Egyptian Reliefs and Stelae in the Pushkin Museum of Fine Arts, Moscow.* Leningrad: Aurora Art Publishers.
Hooper, F.A. 1961. *Funerary Stelae from Kom Abou Billou.* Ann Arbor: Kelsey Museum of Archaeology.
Hovestreydt, W. 1997. A Letter to the King Relating to the Foundation of a Statue (P. Turin 1879 VSO). *Lingua Aegyptia* 5:107-121.
Hulin, L. C. 1989. "The Diffusion of Religious Symbols in Complex Societies," in *The Meaning of Things: Material Culture and Symbolic Expression.* Edited by I. Hodder, pp. 90-96. London: Unwin Hyman.
James, T. G. H. 1961. *Hieroglyphic Texts from Egyptian Stelae etc. from the British Museum.* Vol 1 (2nd Edition). London: British Museum Press.
- 1962. Review: *Ceiling Stelae in the Second Dynasty Tombs from the Excavations at Helwan,* by Z. Saad. Suppl. *Annales du Service des Antiquités de l'Égypte* 21 (1957) in *Bibliotheca Orientalis* 19:137-139.
- 1970. *Hieroglyphic Texts from Egyptian Stelae etc. from the British Museum.* Vol. 9. London: British Museum Press.
- 1976. Le Prétendu 'sanctuaire de Karnak' selon Budge. *Bulletin de la Société Française d'Égyptologie* 75:7-30.
Janssen, J. J. 1963. An Unusual Donation Stela of the 20th Dynasty. *Journal of Egyptian Archaeology* 49:64-70.
- 1974. An Allusion to an Egyptian Wedding Ceremony. *Göttinger Miszellen* 10:25-28.
- 1975. *Commodity Prices from the Ramessid Period. An Economic Study of the Village of Necropolis Workmen at Thebes.* Leiden: E. J. Brill.
- 1980. Absence from Work by the Necropolis Workmen. *Studien zur Altägyptischen Kultur* 8:127-153.
- 1982. Gift-Giving in Ancient Egypt as an Economic Feature. *Journal of Egyptian Archaeology* 68:253-258.
- 1982. "Two Personalities," in *Gleanings from Deir el-Medina.* Egyptologische Uitgaven. Vol. I. Edited by R. J. Demarée and J. J. Janssen, pp. 109-131. Leiden: Nederlands Instituut voor het Nabije Oosten.
- 1992. "Literacy and Letters at Deir el-Medina," in *Village Voices: Proceedings of the Symposium "Texts from Deir el-Medina and their Interpretation" Leiden, May 31-June 1, 1991.* Egyptologische Uitgaven. Vol. XI. Edited by R. J. Demarée and A. Egberts, pp. 81-94. Leiden: Nederlands Instituut voor het Nabije Oosten.
- 1997. *Village Varia: Ten Studies in the History and Administration of Deir el-Medina.* Egyptologische Uitgaven. Vol. XI. Leiden: Nederlands Instituut voor het Nabije Oosten.
Janssen, J. M. A. 1950. Une stèle du dieu Reshef à Cambridge. *Cahiers Caribéens d'Égyptologie* 49:209-212.
Janssen, R. M., and J. J. Janssen. 1990. *Growing Up in Ancient Egypt.* London: The Rubicon Press.
- 1996. *Getting Old in Ancient Egypt.* London: The Rubicon Press.
Jelínková-Reymond, E. 1956. *Les Inscriptions de la statue guérisseuse de Djed-Her-le-Sauveur.* Bulletin d'Égyptologie. Vol. 23. Cairo: Institut Français d'Archéologie Orientale.
Kákosy, L. 1982. "Orakel," in *Lexikon der Ägyptologie IV.* Edited by W. Helck and W. Westendorf, cols. 600-606. Wiesbaden: Harrassowitz.
Kanawati, N. 1977. *The Egyptian Administration of the Old Kingdom. Evidence of its Economic Decline.* Warminster: Aris and Phillips.
Kayser, H. 1973. *Die ägyptischen Altertümer im Roemer-Pelizaeus-Museum in Hildesheim.* Hildesheim: Gebrüder Gerstenberg.
Kees, H. 1953. *Das Priestertum im ägyptischen Staat vom Neuen Reich bis zur Spätzeit.* Leiden: E. J. Brill.
- 1958. Review: *Ceiling Stelae in the Second Dynasty Tombs from the Excavations at Helwan,* by Z. Saad. Suppl. *Annales du Service des Antiquités de l'Égypte* 21 (1957), in *Orientalistische Literaturzeitung* 53: 533-535.
- 1960. Webpriester der 18. Dynastie im Trägerdienst bei Prozessionen. *Zeitschrift für Ägyptische Sprache* 85:45-56.
- 1961. *Ancient Egypt: A Cultural Topography.* London: Faber.
Keller, C. A. 2001. "A Family Affair: The Decoration of Theban Tomb 359," in *Colour and Painting in Ancient Egypt.* Edited by W. V. Davies, pp. 25-28, pls. 73-93. London: British Museum Press.
Kemp, B. J. 1989. *Ancient Egypt: Anatomy of a Civilization.* London: Routledge.
Kessler, D. 1999. Dissidentenliteratur oder kultischer Hintergrund? (Teil 2). *Studien zur Altägyptischen Kultur* 27:173-221.
Kitchen, K. A. 1973. A Donation Stela of Ramesses III. *Bulletin de l'Institut Français d'Archéologie Orientale* 73:193- 200.
- 1977. "Historical Observations on Ramesside Nubia," in *Ägypten und Kusch.* Schriften zur Geschichte und Kultur des alten Orients. Vol. 13. Edited by E. Endesfelder, K.-H. Priese, W.-F. Reineke, and S. Wenig, pp. 213-225. Berlin: Akademie.
- 1979a. *Ramesside Inscriptions: Historical and Biographical I.* Oxford: Blackwell.
- 1979b. *Ramesside Inscriptions: Historical and Biographical II.* Oxford: Blackwell.
- 1980. *Ramesside Inscriptions: Historical and Biographical III.* Oxford: Blackwell.
- 1982a. *Ramesside Inscriptions: Historical and Biographical IV.* Oxford: Blackwell.
- 1982b. *Pharaoh Triumphant: The Life and Times of Ramesses II.* Warminster: Aris and Phillips.
- 1983a. *Ramesside Inscriptions: Historical and Biographical V.* Oxford: Blackwell.
- 1983b. *Ramesside Inscriptions: Historical and Biographical VI.* Oxford: Blackwell.
- 1990. "The Arrival of the Libyans in Late New Kingdom Egypt," in *Libya and Egypt.* Edited by M. A. Leahy, pp. 15-27. London: SOAS Centre of Near and Middle Eastern Studies and the Centre for Libyan Studies.
- 1996. *Ramesside Inscriptions: Translated and Annotated II: Ramesses II, Royal Inscriptions.* Oxford: Blackwell.
- 2000. *Ramesside Inscriptions: Translated and Annotated III: Ramesses II, His Contemporaries.* Oxford: Blackwell.
- 2003. *Ramesside Inscriptions: Translated and Annotated IV: Merenptah and the Late Nineteenth Dynasty.* Oxford: Blackwell.

- Forthcoming. *Ramesside Inscriptions: Translated and Annotated V.* Oxford: Blackwell.
Kitchen, K. A., and G. A. Gaballa. 1980. Ramesside Varia III: a Behedite, a Theban and a Thinite. *Serapis* 6:76-77, pl. 2, fig. 2.
Klebs, L. 1915. *Die Reliefs des Alten Reiches (2980-2475 v. Chr.). Material zur ägyptischen Kulturgeschichte.* Heidelberg: C. Winter.
Koefoed-Petersen, O. 1948. *Les Stèles égyptiennes.* Copenhagen: Glyptothèque Ny Carlsberg.
Kruchten, J.-M. 2001. "Oracles," in *The Oxford Encyclopedia of Ancient Egypt.* Vol. 2. Edited by D. B. Redford, pp. 609-612. New York: Oxford University Press.
Lacau, P. 1909. *Catalogue général des antiquités égyptiennes du Musée du Caire. Nos. 34001-34189. Stèles du Nouvel Empire.* Cairo: Institut Français d'Archéologie Orientale.
Lalouette, C. 1995. *L'Empire des Ramsès*: Paris: Flammarian.
Lange, H. O., and H. Schäfer. 1925. *Catalogue général des antiquitiés égyptiennes du Musée du Caire. Nos. 20001-20780. Grab- und Denksteine des Mittleren Reiches in Museum von Kairo.* Vol. 3. Berlin: Reichsdruckerei.
Laurence, R. 2000. Metaphors, Monuments and Texts: The Life Course in Roman Culture. *World Archaeology* 31:442-455.
Le Roy Ladurie, E. 1975. *Montaillou, village occitan de 1294 à 1324.* Paris: Gallimard.
Leahy, M. A. 1977. *Abydos in the Late Period: An Epigraphic and Prosopographic Analysis.* Ph.D. thesis, University of Cambridge (unpublished).
- 1989. A Protective Measure from Abydos. *Journal of Egyptian Archaeology* 75:41-60.
Leader, R. E. 1997. In Death Not Divided: Gender, Family and State on Classical Athenian Grave Stelae. *American Journal of Archaeology* 101:683-699.
Lefebvre, G. 1929. *Histoire des grands prêtres d'Amon de Karnak jusqu'à la XXIe dynastie.* Paris: Librarie Orientaliste P. Geuthner.
Legrain, G. 1904. Notes d'inspection XIV. Sur Mahouhi, premier prophète d'Amon. *Annales du Service des Antiquités de l'Égypte* 5:137-139.
- 1908. *Répertoire généalogique et onomastique du Musée du Caire: monuments de la XVIIe et de la XVIIIe dynasties.* Geneva: Société anonyme des arts graphiques.
- 1916. Un miracle d'Ahmès 1er à Abydos sous le règne de Ramsès II. *Annales du Service des Antiquités de l'Égypte* 16:161-170.
Leibovitch, J. 1939. Quelques nouvelles représentations du dieu Rechef. *Annales du Service des Antiquités de l'Égypte* 39:145-160.
- 1940. Un fragment de stèle dédiée a Rechef. *Annales du Service des Antiquités de l'Égypte* 40:489-494.
- 1961. Kent et Qadesh. *Syria* 38:23-34, pls. I, II.
Leitz, C. Editor. 2002-2003. *Lexikon der ägyptischen Götter und Götterbezeichnungen.* 8 Vols. Leuven: Peeters.
Leprohon, R. J. 1978. The Personnel of the Middle Kingdom Funerary Stelae. *Journal of the American Research Center in Cairo* 15:33-38.
Lepsius, R. 1900. *Denkmäler aus Aegypten und Aethiopien.* Vol. 3. Leipzig: J. C. Hinrichs'sche Buchhandlung.
- 1913. *Denkmäler aus Aegypten und Aethiopien.* Vol. 5. Leipzig: J. C. Hinrichs'sche Buchhandlung.
Lesko, B. S. 1994. "Ranks, Roles and Rights," in *Pharaoh's Workers: The Villagers of Deir el Medina.* Edited by L. H. Lesko, pp. 15-39. Ithaca: Cornell University Press.
Lesko, L. H. 1994. "Literature, Literacy and the Literati," in *Pharaoh's Workers: The Villagers of Deir el Medina.* Edited by L. H. Lesko, pp. 131-144. Ithaca: Cornell University Press.
Lichtheim, M. 1973. *Ancient Egyptian Literature: A Book of Readings. Vol. I: The Old and Middle Kingdoms.* Berkeley: University of California Press.
- 1976. *Ancient Egyptian Literature: A Book of Readings. Vol. II: The New Kingdom.* Berkeley: University of California Press.
- 1988. *Ancient Egyptian Autobiographies Chiefly of the Middle Kingdom.* Orbis Biblicus et Orientalis. Vol. 84. Freiburg: Universitätsverlag; Göttingen: Vandenhoeck & Ruprecht.
Lipinska, J. 1966. List of Objects Found at the Deir el-Bahari Temple of Tuthmosis III, Season 1961/1962. *Annales du Service des Antiquités de l'Égypte* 59:63-98
- 1984. *Deir el Bahri IV: The Temple of Tuthmosis III, Statuary and Votive Monuments.* Warsaw: PWN-Éditions Sciéntifique du Pologne.
Malaise, M. 1977. La Position de la femme sur les stèles du Moyen Empire. *Studien zur Altägyptischen Kultur* 5:184-198.
- 1984. *Les Représentations de divinités sur les stèles du Moyen Empire,* in *Orientalia J. Duchesne-Guillemin emerito oblate* (= *Acta Iranica* 23), pp. 393-420. Leiden: E. J. Brill.
Malek, J. 1974. Two Monuments of the Tias. *Journal of Egyptian Archaeology* 60:161-167.
- 1991. A Stela of the Draughtsman Pashed I at Deir el Medina. *Journal of Egyptian Archaeology* 77:176-180.
Marciniak, M. 1974. *Les Inscriptions hiératiques du temple de Thutmose III.* Warsaw: PWN-Éditions Sciéntifiques de Pologne.
Marée, M. 1993. A Remarkable Group of Egyptian Stelae from the Second Intermediate Period. *Oudheidkundige Mededelingen uit het Rijksmuseum van Oudheden te Leiden* 73:7-22
Mariette, A. 1880. *Catalogue général des monuments d'Abydos découverts pendant les fouilles de cette ville.* Paris: Imprimerie Nationale.
Martin, G. T. 1982. Two Monuments of New Kingdom Date in North American Collections. *Journal of Egyptian Archaeology* 68:81-84.
- 2005. *Stelae from Egypt and Nubia in the Fitzwilliam Museum, Cambridge, c. 3000 BC – AD 1150.* Cambridge: Cambridge University Press.
Maspero, G. 1882. Rapport sur une mission en Italie (suite). *Recueil de travaux relatifs à la philologie et à l'archéologie égyptiennes et assyriennes* 3:102-108.
- 1911a. La Chapelle nouvelle d'Ibsamboul. *Zeitschrift für Ägyptische Sprache* 48:91-96.
- 1911b. *Les Temples immergés de la Nubie. Rapports relatifs à la consolidation de temples.* Cairo: Institut Français d'Archéologie Orientale.

- 1912 [1920]. *Les Temples immergés de la Nubie. Rapports relatifs à la consolidation de temples: documents.* Vol. 1. Cairo: Institut Français d'Archéologie Orientale.
- 1915. *Guide du visiteur au Musée du Caire.* Cairo: Institut Français d'Archéologie Orientale.
- 1916. *Études de mythologie et d'archéologie.* Paris: E. Leroux.
McDowell, A. G. 1990. *Jurisdiction in the Workmen's Community of Deir el-Medina.* Egyptologische Uitgaven. Vol. V. Leiden: Nederlands Instituut voor het Nabije Oosten.
- 1992a. Agricultural Activity by the Workmen at Deir el-Medina. *Journal of Egyptian Archaeology* 78:195-206.
- 1992b. "Awareness of the Past in Deir el-Medina," in *Village Voices: Proceedings of the Symposium "Texts from Deir el-Medina and their Interpretation" Leiden, May 31-June 1, 1991.* Egyptologische Uitgaven. Vol. XI. Edited by R. J. Demarée and A. Egberts, pp. 95-110. Leiden: Nederlands Instituut voor het Nabije Oosten.
- 1994. "Contact with the Outside World," in *Pharaoh's Workers: The Villagers of Deir el Medina.* Edited by L. H. Lesko, pp. 41-60. Ithaca: Cornell University Press.
- 1999. *Village Life in Ancient Egypt: Laundry Lists and Love Songs.* Oxford: Oxford University Press.
Meskell, L. 1994. Deir el Medina in Hyperreality: Seeking the People of Pharaonic Egypt. *Journal of Mediterranean Archaeology* 7:193-216.
- 1998. An Archaeology of Social Relations in an Egyptian Village. *Journal of Archaeological Method and Theory* 5:209-243.
- 1999. *Archaeologies of Social Life: Age, Sex, Class etcetera in Ancient Egypt.* Oxford: Blackwell.
- 2000. Cycles of Life and Death: Narrative Homology and Archaeological Realities. *World Archaeology* 31:423-441.
- 2002. *Private Life in New Kingdom Egypt.* Princeton and Oxford: Princeton University Press.
Meskell, L., C. Gosden, I. Hodder, R. Joyce and R. W. Preucel. 2001. Editorial Statement. *Journal of Social Archaeology* 1:5-12.
Meskell, L. and R. W. Preucel. 2004, "Part II: Identities" in *A Companion to Social Archaeology.* Edited by L. Meskell and R. W. Preucel, pp. 121-141. Malden, USA, MA, Oxford, UK and Victoria, Australia: Blackwell.
Metropolitan Museum of Art, Bulletin XIX (October 1960).
Miller, D. 1995. "Consumption Studies as the Transformation of Anthropology" in *Acknowledging Consumption: A Review of New Studies.* Edited by D. Miller, pp. 264-295. Routledge: London.
Miller, P. 1937. A Family Stela in the University Museum, Philadelphia. *Journal of Egyptian Archaeology* 23:1-6, pls. i-iii.
Moftah, R. 1985. *Studien zum ägyptischen Königsdogma im Neuen Reich.* Mainz am Rhein: Philip von Zabern.
Mogensen, M. 1918. *Inscriptions hiéroglyphiques du Musée National de Copenhague.* Copenhagen: A.-F. Höst & fils.
Moje, J. 2007. *Untersuchungen zur Hieroglyphischen Paläographie und Klassifizierung der Privatstelen der 19. Dynastie.* Studien zu Geschichte, Kultur und Religion Ägyptens und des Alten Testaments. Vol. 67. Wiesbaden: Harrassowitz.
Moreland, J. 2001. *Archaeology and Text.* London: Duckworth.
Moret, A. 1913. Monuments égyptiens du Musée Calvet à Avignon. *Recueil de travaux relatifs à la philologie et à l'archéologie égyptiennes et assyriennes* 35:48-59, 193-206.
Morgan, E. E. 2004. *Untersuchungen zu den Ohrenstelen aus Deir el Medina.* Studien zu Geschichte, Kultur und Religion Ägyptens und des Alten Testaments. Vol. 61. Wiesbaden: Harrassowitz.
Morris, E. 2002. Review: *Archaeologies of Social Life: Age, Sex, Class et cetera in Ancient Egypt*, by L. Meskell. Princeton and Woodstock: Princeton University Press. 2002. *Journal of Egyptian Archaeology* 88:265-267.
Morris, I. 1986. Gift and Commodity in Archaic Greece. *Man* New Series 21:1-17.
- 1987. *Burial and Ancient Society: The Rise of the Greek City-state.* New Studies in Archaeology. Cambridge: Cambridge University Press.
- 1992. *Death-Ritual and Social Structure in Classical Antiquity.* Cambridge: Cambridge University Press.
- 1994. "Everyman's Grave," in *Athenian Identity and Civic Ideology.* Edited by A. L. Boegehold and A. C. Scafuro, pp. 7-101. Baltimore and London: The Johns Hopkins University Press.
- 2000. *Archaeology as Cultural History.* Malden, MA, USA and Oxford, UK: Blackwell.
Müller, H. W. 1933. Die Totendenksteine des Mittleren Reiches, Ihre Genesis, Ihre Darstellungen und Ihre Komposition. *Mitteilungen Deutschen Archäologischen Instituts Abteilung Kairo* 4:165-206.
Müller-Wollermann, R. 1988. Der Mythos vom Ritus "Erschlagen der Feinde". *Göttinger Miszellen* 105:69-76.
Munro, P. 1973. *Die spätägyptischen Totenstelen.* 2 Vols. Ägyptologische Forschungen. Vol. 25. Glückstadt: J. J. Augustin.
Murnane, W. J. 1995. "The Kingship of the Nineteenth Dynasty: A Study in the Resilience of an Institution," in *Ancient Egyptian Kingship.* Probleme der Ägyptologie. Vol. 9. Edited by D. O'Connor and D. P. Silverman, pp. 185-217. Leiden: E. J. Brill.
Murray, M. A. 1900. *Catalogue of Egyptian Antiquities in the National Museum of Antiquities, Edinburgh.* Edinburgh: Printed for the Society of Antiquaries of Scotland.
Myśliwiec, K. 1976. *Le Portrait royal dans le bas-relief du Nouvel Empire.* Warsaw: PWN-Éditions Scientifiques de Pologne.
- 1985. *Eighteenth Dynasty before the Amarna Period.* Iconography of Religions: Egypt, 5. Leiden: E. J. Brill.
Naville, E. 1907. *The 11th Dynasty Temple at Deir el-Bahari.* Vol. 1. London: Egypt Exploration Fund.
Nelson, H. H. 1981. *The Great Hypostyle Hall at Karnak Volume 1, Part 1. The Wall Reliefs.* Oriental Institute Publications. Chicago: The Oriental Institute of the University of Chicago.
Nims, C. F. 1952. Another Geographical List from Medinet Habu. *Journal of Egyptian Archaeology* 38:34-45.
- 1956. A Stele of Penre, Builder of the Ramesseum. *Mitteilungen Deutschen Archäologischen Instituts Abteilung Kairo* 14:146-149.
- 1965. *Thebes of the Pharaohs: Pattern for Every City.* London: Elek.
- 1977. "Ramesseum Sources of Medinet Habu Reliefs," in *Studies in Honor of George R. Hughes.* Studies in Ancient Oriental Civilization. Vol. 39. Edited by J. H. Johnson and E. F. Wente, pp. 169-175. Chicago: The Oriental Institute of the University of Chicago.
Northampton, W., P. E. Newberry and W. Spiegelberg. 1908. *Report on Some Excavations in the Theban Necropolis during the Winter of 1898-9.* London: A. Constable.

Nunn, J. F. 1996. *Ancient Egyptian Medicine*. London: British Museum Press.

Obsomer, C. 1993. "*di.f prt-ḫrw* et la filiation *ms(t).n* / *ir(t).n* comme critères de datation dans les textes du Moyen Empire" in *Individu, société et spiritualité dans l'Égypte pharaonique et copte. Mélanges égyptologiques offerts au Professor Aristide Théodoridès*. Edited by C. Cannuyer and J.-M. Kruchten, pp. 163-200. Brussels: Association Montoise d'Égyptologie.

O'Connor, D. 1985. "The "Cenotaphs" of the Middle Kingdom at Abydos," in *Mélanges Gamal Eddin Mokhtar*. Edited by P. Posener-Kriéger, pp. 161-178. Cairo: Institut Français d'Archéologie Orientale.

- 1997. "Ancient Egypt: Egyptological and Anthropological Perspectives," in *Anthropology and Egyptology, Monographs on Mediterranean Archaeology*. Vol. 8. Edited by J. Lustig, pp. 13-24. Sheffield: Sheffield Academic Press.

Orcurti, P. C. 1852-1855. *Catalogo illustrato dei monumenti egizii del R. Museo di Torino compilato dal Professore Pier-Camillo Orcurti applicator al Museo d'Antichità ed Egizio e pubblicato per ordine del Ministero d'Instruzione Pubblica.* 2 Vols. Turin: Tipografia Nazionale Di G. Bianciardi.

Oroszlan, Z. and A. Dobrovits. 1939. *Az Egyiptomi Gyüjtemény: Vezeto*. Budapest.

Osing, J. 1977. *Der Tempel Sethos I. in Gurna. Die Reliefs und Inschriften*. Vol. 1. Mainz am Rhein: Philip von Zabern.

Otto, E. 1975. "Abu Simbel," in *Lexikon der Ägyptologie I*. Edited by W. Helck and E. Otto, cols. 25-27. Wiesbaden: Harrassowitz.

Page, A. 1973. *Ancient Egyptian Figured Ostraca in the Petrie Collection*. Warminster: Aris and Phillips.

Pamminger, P. 1996a. "Ein Beispiel magistraler Intervention. Zu einem unpublizierten Relieffragment in Chicago," in *Wege öffnen. Festschrift für Rolf Gundlach zum 65. Geburtstag*. Studien zu Geschichte, Kultur und Religion Ägyptens und des Alten Testaments. Vol. 35. Edited by M. Schade-Busch, pp. 184-186. Wiesbaden: Harrassowitz.

- 1996b. Magistrale Intervention: Der Beamte als Mittler. *Studien zur Altägyptischen Kultur* 23:281-304.

Parkinson, R. B. 1999. *Cracking Codes: The Rosetta Stone and Decipherment*. London: British Museum Press.

Pestman, P. W. 1961. *Marriage and Matrimonial Property in Ancient Egypt*. Papyrologica Lugduno-Batava. Vol. 9. Leiden: E. J. Brill.

Peterson, B. E. J. 1965-1966. Two Egyptian Stelae. *Orientalia Suecana* 14-15:3-8.

- 1973. *Zeichnungen aus einer Totenstadt: Bildostraka aus Theben-West*. Stockholm: Medelshavsmuseet.

Petrie, W. M. F. 1896. *Koptos*. London: B. Quaritch.

Pflüger, K. 1947. The Private Funerary Stelae of the Middle Kingdom and their Importance for the Study of Ancient Egyptian History. *Journal of the American Oriental Society* 67:127-135.

Pinch, G. 1993. *Votive Offerings to Hathor*. Oxford: Griffith Institute.

- 1994. *Magic in Ancient Egypt*. London: British Museum Press.

- 1995. "Private Life in Ancient Egypt," in *Civilizations of the Ancient Near East*. Vol. 1. Edited by J. M. Sasson, pp. 363-381. New York: Scribner.

Podemann Sørensen, J. 1989a. "Introduction to Part 1," in *The Religion of the Ancient Egyptians: Cognitive Structures and Popular Expressions*. Proceedings of the Symposia in Uppsala and Bergen, 1987 and 1988. ACTA Universitatis Upsaliensis. Edited by G. Englund, pp. 3-6. Uppsala: Uppsala Universitet.

- 1989b. "Divine Access: The So-Called Democratization of Egyptian Funerary Literature as a Socio-Culturel Process," in *The Religion of the Ancient Egyptians: Cognitive Structures and Popular Expressions*. Proceedings of the Symposia in Uppsala and Bergen, 1987 and 1988. ACTA Universitatis Upsaliensis. Edited by G. Englund, pp. 109-125. Uppsala: Uppsala Universitet.

Porter, B., and R. L. B. Moss. 1934. *Topographical Bibliography of Ancient Egyptian Hieroglyphic Texts, Reliefs and Paintings IV: Lower and Middle Egypt*. Oxford: Clarendon.

- 1937. *Topographical Bibliography of Ancient Egyptian Hieroglyphic Texts, Reliefs and Paintings V: Upper Egypt, Sites*. Oxford: Clarendon.

- 1939. *Topographical Bibliography of Ancient Egyptian Hieroglyphic Texts, Reliefs and Paintings VI: Upper Egypt. Chief Temples*. Oxford: Clarendon.

- 1951. *Topographical Bibliography of Ancient Egyptian Hieroglyphic Texts, Reliefs and Paintings VII: Nubia, the Deserts and Outside Egypt*. Oxford: Clarendon.

- 1960. *Topographical Bibliography of Ancient Egyptian Hieroglyphic Texts, Reliefs and Paintings I.1: Theban Necropolis: Private Tombs*. Oxford: Clarendon.

- 1964. *Topographical Bibliography of Ancient Egyptian Hieroglyphic Texts, Reliefs and Paintings I.2: Theban Necropolis: Royal Tombs and Smaller Cemeteries*. Oxford: Clarendon.

- 1972. *Topographical Bibliography of Ancient Egyptian Hieroglyphic Texts, Reliefs and Paintings II: Theban Temples*. Oxford: Clarendon.

Posener, G. 1975. La Piété personelle avant l'äge amarnien. *Revue d'Égyptologie* 27:195-210.

Pusch, E. B. 1999. Towards a Map of Piramesse. *Egyptian Archaeology*. 14:13-15.

- 2001. "Piramesse," in *The Oxford Encyclopedia of Ancient Egypt*. Vol. 3. Edited by D. B. Redford, pp. 48-50. New York: Oxford University Press.

Quinn, S. 1991. A New Kingdom Stela in Girton College Showing Amenhotep I wearing the *ḫprš*. *Journal of Egyptian Archaeology* 77:169-175.

Quibell, J. E. 1898. *The Ramesseum*. London: B. Quaritch.

Quirke, S. 1992. *Ancient Egyptian Religion*. London: British Museum Press.

Randall-McIver, D., and A. Mace, 1899-1901. *El Amrah and Abydos*. London: Egypt Exploration Fund.

Radwan, A. 1969. *Die Darstellungen des regierenden Königs und seiner Familienangehörigen in den Privatgräbern der 18. Dynastie*. Berlin: B. Hessling.

Raedler, C. 2003. "Zur Repräsentation und Verwirklichung pharaonischer Macht in Nubien: Der Vizekönig Setau," in *Das Königtum der Ramessidenzeit*. Edited by R. Gundlach and U. Rößler-Köhler, pp. 129-173. Wiesbaden: Harrassowitz.

Raven, M. R. 2000. "Objects from Deir el-Medina in the National Museum of Antiquities, Leiden," in *Deir el-Medina in the Third*

Millennium AD. Egyptologische Uitgaven. Vol. XIV. Edited by R. J. Demarée and A. Egberts. Leiden: Nederlands Instituut voor het Nabije Oosten.
Redford, D. B. 1986. *Pharaonic King-Lists, Annals and Day Books: A Contribution to the Egyptian Sense of History*. Mississauga: Benben Publications.
Redford, D. B. Editor. 2001. *The Oxford Encyclopedia of Ancient Egypt*. 3 Vols. New York: Oxford University Press.
Reeves, N. 1984. Excavations in the Valley of the Kings 1905/6: A Photographic Record. *Mitteilungen Deutschen Archäologischen Instituts Abteilung Kairo* 40:227-235.
Reisner, G. A. 1918. The Tomb of Hepzefa, Nomarch of Siut. *Journal of Egyptian Archaeology* 5:79-98.
- 1920. The Viceroys of Ethiopia. *Journal of Egyptian Archaeology* 6:28-55.
- 1936. *The Development of the Egyptian Tomb down to the Accession of Cheops*. Cambridge, Mass.: Harvard University Press.
Richards, J. 2005. *Society and Death in Ancient Egypt. Mortuary Landscapes of the Middle Kingdom*. Cambridge: Cambridge University Press.
Ritner, R. 1993. *The Mechanics of Ancient Egyptian Magical Practice*. Studies in Ancient Oriental Civilization. Vol. 54. Chicago: The Oriental Institute of the University of Chicago.
Robins, G. 1990. While the Woman Looks On: Gender Inequality in New Kingdom Egypt. *KMT* 1/3 (Fall):18-21; 64-65.
- 1994. Some Principles of Compositional Dominance and Gender Hierarchy in Egyptian Art. *Journal of the Americal Research Center in Egypt* 31:33-40.
Roccati, A. 2003. "Les Mutations culturelles à Deir el-Médineh sous les Ramsès," in *Deir el-Médineh et la vallée des Rois: la vie en Égypte au temps des pharaons du Nouvel Empire*. Edited by G. Andreu, pp. 197-208. Louvre: Éditions Khéops-Musée du Louvre.
Roeder, G. 1913. *Aegyptische Inschriften aus den Königlichen Museen zu Berlin II. Inschriften des Neuen Reiches: Statuen, Stelen, Reliefs*. Leipzig: J. C. Hinrichs'sche Buchhandlung.
- 1926. Ramses als Gott nach dem Hildesheimer Denksteinen aus Horbeit. *Zeitschrift für Ägyptische Sprache* 61:57-67.
Römer, M. 1986. "Tanis," in *Lexikon der Ägyptologie VI*. Edited by W. Helck and W. Westendorf, cols. 194-209. Wiesbaden: Harrassowitz.
Roth, A. M. 1991. *Egyptian Phyles in the Old Kingdom: The Evolution of a System of Social Organization*. Studies in Ancient Oriental Civilization. Vol. 48. Chicago: The Oriental Institute of the University of Chicago.
Rowe, A. 1940-1941. Newly Identified Monuments in the Egyptian Museum Showing the Deification of the Dead together with Brief Details of Similar Objects Elsewhere. *Annales du Service des Antiquités de l'Égypte* 40:1-50.
- 1958. A History of Ancient Cyrenaica. A New Light on Aegypto-Cyrenean Relations: Two Ptolemaic Statues Found in Tolmeita. *Supplément aux Annales du Service des Antiquités de l'Égypte* 12.
Ruffle, J., and. K. A. Kitchen. 1979. "The Family of Urhiya and Yupa, High Stewards of the Ramesseum, Parts I and II," in *Glimpses of Ancient Egypt: Studies in Honour of H. W. Fairman*. Edited by G. A. Gaballa, J. Ruffle and K. A. Kitchen, pp. 55-74. Warminster: Aris and Phillips.
Rusch, A. 1923. Die Entwicklung der Grabsteinformen in Alten Reich. *Zeitschrift für Ägyptische Sprache* 58:101-124
Ryholt, K. 1997. Two New Kingdom Oracle Petitions O.BMFA 72.659, 72.666. *Revue d'Égyptologie* 48:279-282.
Saad, Z. Y. 1957. *Ceiling Stelae in the Second Dynasty Tombs from Excavations at Helwan*. Cairo: Institut Français d'Archéologie Orientale.
Sadek, A. I. 1979. Glimpses of Popular Religion in New Kingdom Egypt: I. Mourning for Amenhotep I at Deir el-Medina. *Göttinger Miszellen* 36:51-56.
- 1987. *Popular Religion in Egypt during the New Kingdom*. Hildesheim: Gerstenberg.
Saleh, J. M. 1970. *Les Antiquités égyptiennes de Zagreb*. Paris: Mouton.
Saller, R. P. 2001. "The Family and Society," in *Epigraphic Evidence: Ancient History from Inscriptions*. Approaching the Ancient World. Edited by J. Bodel, pp. 94-117. London and New York: Routledge.
Sandman Holmberg, M. 1946. *The God Ptah*. Lund.
Satzinger, H. 1969. Die Abydos-Stele des *Ipwy* aus dem Mittleren Reich. *Mitteilungen Deutschen Archäologischen Instituts Abteilung Kairo* 25:121-130.
Sauer, E. W. Editor. 2004. *Archaeology and Ancient History. Breaking Down the Boundaries*. London and New York: Routledge.
Sauneron, S. 1950. Deux Mentions d'Houron. *Revue d'Égyptologie* 7:121-126.
- 1959. *Catalogue des ostraca hiératiques non-littéraires de Deîr el-Médînéh, nos. 550-623*. Cairo: Institut Français d'Archéologie Orientale.
Säve-Söderbergh, T. 1945. "Zwei neue Denkmäler des Königskults in der ramessidischen Militärkolonie Horbeit," in *Einige Ägyptische Denkmäler in Schweden, Vilhelms Ekmans Universitetsfond, Uppsala*. Vol. 52, pp. 21-38. Uppsala, Leipzig, The Hague, Cambridge: Almqvist & Wiksells, Otto Harrassowitz, M. Nijhoff, W. Heffer & Sons, Ltd.
- 1987. *Temples and Tombs of Ancient Nubia: The International Rescue Campaign at Abu Simbel, Philae and Other Sites*. Leiden: Thames and Hudson.
Scharff, A. 1934. Ein Denkstein des Vezirs Rahotep aus der 19. Dynastie. *Zeitschrift für Ägyptische Sprache* 70:47-51.
Schmidt, J. D. 1973. *Ramesses II: A Chronological Structure for his Reign*. Baltimore: Johns Hopkins University Press.
Schmitz, B. 1998. "Die Anfänge der Ägypten-Sammlung in Hildesheim: Ein Beitrag zur Geschichte der Ägyptologie," in *Proceedings of the Seventh International Congress of Egyptologists*. Orientalia Lovaniensia Analecta. Vol. 82. Edited by C. J. Eyre, pp. 1029-1036. Leuven: Peeters.
Schneider, H. 1971. Gleanings in the Egyptian Collection at Leiden I. Four Stelae. *Oudheidkundige Mededelingen uit het Rijksmuseum van Oudheden te Leiden* 52:8-21.
Schott, S. 1952. *Das schöne Fest vom Wüstentale*. Wiesbaden: Steiner.
Schulman, A. R. 1962. The Egyptian Chariotry: A Re-examination. *Journal of the American Research Center in Egypt* 2:75-96.
- 1963. A Cult of Ramesses III at Memphis. *Journal of Near Eastern Studies* 22:177-184.

- 1964. *Military Rank, Title and Organization in the Egyptian New Kingdom*. Berlin: B. Hessling.
- 1980. A Memphite Stela, the Bark of Ptah and Some Iconographic Comments. *Bulletin of the Egyptologial Seminar 2*:83-109.
- 1981. "Reshep Times Two," in *Studies in Ancient Egypt, the Aegean and the Sudan: Essays in Honour of Dows Dunham on the Occasion of his 90th Birthday, June 1 1980*. Edited by W. K. Simpson and W. H. Davies, pp. 157-166. Boston: Museum of Fine Arts.
- 1984a. The Iconographic Theme "Opening of the Mouth" on Stelae. *Journal of the Americal Research Center in Egypt* 21:169-196.
- 1984b. "Reshep at Zagazig: A New Document," in *Studien zur Sprache und Religion Ägyptens zu Ehren von Wolfhart Westendorf*. Vol. 2. Edited by F. Junge, pp. 857-863. Göttingen: Seminar für Ägyptologie und Koptologie.
- 1985. The Cult Statue "Reshep, He Who Hears Prayers". *Bulletin of the Egyptological Seminar* 6:89-106.
- 1988. *Ceremonial Execution and Public Rewards: Some Historical Scenes from New Kingdom Private Stelae*. Orbis Biblicus et Orientalis. Vol. 75. Freiburg: Universitätsverlag; Göttingen: Vandenhoeck & Ruprecht.
- 1994. "Take for Yourself the Sword," in *Essays in Egyptology in Honor of Hans Goedicke*. Edited by B. M. Bryan and D. Lorton, pp. 265-280. San Antonio, Texas: Van Siclen Books.

Scott, N. E. 1962. A Stela and an Ostracon: Two Acquistions from Deir el-Medineh. *Bulletin of the Metropolitan Museum of Art* 21:149-153.

Service, E. R. 1971. *Primitive Social Organisation: An Evolutionary Perspective*. (2nd Edition). New York: Random House.

Shoukry, A. 1958. The So-called Stelae of Abydos. *Mitteilungen Deutschen Archäologischen Instituts Abteilung Kairo* 16:292-297.

Sharpe, J. 1991. "History From Below," in *New Perspectives on Historical Writing*. Edited by P. Burke, pp. 24-41. Cambridge: Polity Press.

Shaw, I and P. T. Nicholson. Editors. 1995. *The British Museum Dictionary of Ancient Egypt* London: British Museum Press.

Simpson, F. 2002. *Evidence for Late Bronze Age Libyan Culture at the New Kingdom Egyptian Fortress of Zawiyet Umm el-Rakham*. Ph.D. thesis, University of Liverpool (unpublished).

Simpson, W. K. 1974. *The Terrace of the Great God at Abydos: The Offering Chapels of Dynasties 12 and 13*. New Haven: Peabody Museum of Natural History.
- 1982. Egyptian Sculpture and Two Dimensional Representation as Propaganda. *Journal of Egyptian Archaeology* 68:266-271.

Snape, S. 1986. *Mortuary Assemblages from Abydos*. Ph.D. thesis, University of Liverpool (unpublished).
- 1998. "Walls, Wells and Wandering Merchants: Egyptian Control of Marmarica in the Late Bronze Age," in *Proceedings of the Seventh International Congress of Egyptologists*. Orientalia Lovaniensia Analecta. Vol. 82. Edited by C. J. Eyre, pp. 1081-1084. Leuven: Peeters.
- 2001a. Nebre and the Heart of Darkness: The Latest Discoveries from Zawiyet Umm el-Rakham (Egypt). *Antiquity* 75:19-20.
- 2001b. Nebre. *Ancient Egypt Magazine* 8 (August/September).
- 2003a. "The Emergence of Libya on the Horizon of Egypt," in *Mysterious Lands*. Edited by D. O'Connor and S. Snape, pp. 93-106. London: UCL Press, Institute of Archaeology.
- 2003b. "Zawiyet Umm el-Rakham and Egyptian Foreign Trade in the 13th Century BC," in *Sea Routes...Interconnections in the Mediterranean*. Edited by N. C. Stampolides and V. Karageorghis, pp. 63-70. Athens: University of Crete and the A. G. Leventis Foundation.
- 2003c. New Perspectives on Distant Horizons: Aspects of Egyptian Imperial Administration in Marmarica in the Late Bronze Age. *Libyan Studies* 34:1-8.
- 2004. The Excavations of the Liverpool University Mission to Zawiyet Umm el-Rakham 1994-2001. *Annales du Service des Antiquités de l'Égypte* 78:149-160.

Snape, S. and P. Wilson. 2007. *Zawiyet Umm el-Rakham I. The Temple and Chapels*. Bolton: Rutherford Press.

Snape, S. and G. Godenho. Forthcoming. *Zawiyet Umm el-Rakham II. The Monuments of Neb-Re*. Bolton: Rutherford Press.

Sotheby Sale Catalogue, December 19-21, 1906.

Spalinger, A. J. 1996. *The Private Feast Lists of Ancient Egypt*. Wiesbaden: Harrassowitz.
- 2005. *War in Ancient Egypt: The New Kingdom*. Malden, MA, USA and Oxford, UK: Blackwell.

Spanel, D. B. 1996. "Palaeographic and Epigraphic Distinctions between Texts of the So-called First Intermediate Period and Early 12th Dynasty," in *Studies in Honor of William Kelly Simpson*. Vol. 2. Edited by P. der Manuelian, pp. 765-786. Boston: Museum of Fine Arts.

Spiegelberg, W. 1898. *Zwei Beiträge zur Geschichte und Topographie der Thebanischen Necropolis im Neuen Reich*. Strasbourg: Schlesier & Schweikhardt.
- 1918. Ein Heiligtum des Gottes Chnum von Elephantine in der thebanischen Totenstadt. *Zeitschrift für Ägyptische Sprache* 54: 64-67.

Spiegelberg, W. and B. Pörtner. 1902. *Aegyptische Grabsteine und Denksteine aus süddeutschen Sammlungen I: Karlsruhe, Mülhausen, Strassburg, Stuttgart*. Strasbourg: Schlesier & Schweikhardt.
- 1906. *Aegyptische Grabsteine und Denksteine aus verschiedenen Sammlungen III: Bonn, Darmstadt, Frankfurt, Genf, Neuchâtel*. Strasbourg: Schlesier & Schweikhardt.

Stevens, A. 2003. The Material Evidence for Domestic Religion at Amarna and Preliminary Remarks on its Interpretation. *Journal of Egyptian Archaeology* 89:143-168.

Stewart, H. M. 1976. *Egyptian Stelae, Reliefs and Paintings from the Petrie Collection. Part 1: The New Kingdom*. Warminster: Aris and Phillips.

Strudwick, N. 1985. *The Administration of Egypt in the Old Kingdom. The Highest Titles and their Holders*. London: KPI.
- 1994a. "Change and Continuity at Thebes: The Private Tomb after Akhenaten," in *The Unbroken Reed: Studies in the Culture and Heritage of Ancient Egypt, in Honour of A. F. Shore*. Edited by C. J. Eyre, M. A. Leahy, and L. M. Leahy, pp.

321-336. London: Egypt Exploration Society.
- 1994b. "The Population at Thebes in the New Kingdom: Some Preliminary Thoughts," in *Thebanische Beamtennekropolen: Neue Perspektiven archaeologischer Forschung*. Edited by J. Assmann, E. Dziobek, H. Guksch and F. Kampp, pp. 97-105. Heidelberg: Orientverlag.

Strudwick, N., and H. Strudwick. 1999. *Thebes in Egypt: A Guide to the Tombs and Temples of Ancient Luxor*. London: British Museum Press.

Szpakowska K. 2003. Playing with Fire: Initial Observations on the Religious Uses of Clay Cobras from Amarna. *Journal of the American Research Center in Egypt* 40: 43-53
- 2008. *Daily Life in Ancient Egypt: Recreating Lahun*. Malden, USA; Oxford, UK; Victoria, Australia: Blackwell Publishing.

Te Velde, H. 1982. "Mittler," in *Lexikon der Ägyptologie IV*. Edited by W. Helck and W. Westendorf, cols. 161-162. Wiesbaden: Harrassowitz.

The Oriental Institute of the University of Chicago. 1930-1970. *The Epigraphic Survey. Medinet Habu*. Vols. 1-8. Oriental Institute Publications. Chicago: The Oriental Institute of the University of Chicago.
- 1979. *The Epigraphic Survey. The Temple of Khonsu*. Vol. 1. Oriental Institute Publications. Chicago: The Oriental Institute of the University of Chicago.

Toivari, J. 1998. "Marriage at Deir el Medina," in *Proceedings of the Seventh International Congress of Egyptologists*. Orientalia Lovaniensia Analecta. Vol. 82. Edited by C. J. Eyre, pp. 1157-1163. Leuven: Peeters.

Tosi, M. 1988. "Popular Cults at Deir el Medina," in *Egyptian Civilization: Religious Beliefs*. Edited by A. M. D. Roveri, pp. 162-177. Milan: Edizione Electa.

Tosi, M., and A. Roccati. 1972. *Stele e altre epigrafi di Deir el Medina*. Turin: Edizione d'Arte Fratelli Pozzo.

Traunecker, C. 1979. Manifestations de piété personelle à Karnak. *Bulletin de la Société Francaise d'Égyptologie* 85:22-31.
- 1987. "Une pratique de magie populaire dans les temples de Karnak," in *La magia in Egitto ai tempi dei faraoni*. Edited by A. Roccati and A. Siliotti, pp. 221-242. Milan: Rassegna Internazionale di Cinematografia Archeologica Art e Natura Libri.

Trigger, B. G. 1993 [2001]. *Early Civilizations: Ancient Egypt in Context*. Cairo: The American University in Cairo Press.

Trigger, B. G., B. J. Kemp, D. O'Connor, and A. B. Lloyd. 1983. *Ancient Egypt: A Social History*. Cambridge: Cambridge University Press.

Turner, V. W. 1969. *The Ritual Process: Structure and Anti-structure*. London: Routledge and Kegan Paul Ltd.

Ucko, P. J. 1969. Ethnography and Archaeological Interpretation of Funerary Remains. *World Archaeology* 1/2 (October). *Techniques of Chronology and Excavation*: 262-280.

Uphill, E. P. 1984. *The Temples of Per Ramesses*. Warminster: Aris and Phillips.

Valbelle, D. 1975. Témoignages du Nouvel Empire sur les cultes de Satis et d'Anoukis à Elephantine et à Deir el-Médineh. *Bulletin de l'Institut Français d'Archéologie Orientale* 75:123-145, pls. XVIII-XXIII.
- 1981. *Satis et Anoukis*. Mainz am Rhein: Philip von Zabern.
- 1982. "Mertseger," in *Lexikon der Ägyptologie IV*. Edited by W. Helck and W. Westendorf, cols. 79-80. Wiesbaden: Harrassowitz.
- 1985. *Les Ouvriers de la tombe. Deir el-Médineh à l'époque ramesside*. Bibliothèque d'Étude. Vol. 96. Cairo: Institut Français d'Archéologie Orientale.

Valbelle, D. and. C. Bonnet. 1975. Le Village de Deir el-Médineh: reprise de l'étude archéologique. *Bulletin de l'Institut Français d'Archéologie Orientale* 75:429-446.

Valbelle, D. and G. Husson. 1998. "Les Questions oraculaires d'Égypte: histoire de la recherche, nouveautés et perspectives," in *Egyptian Religion: The Last Thousand Years. Studies Dedicated to the Memory of Jan Quaegebeur*. Vol. 2. Orientalia Lovaniensia Analecta. Vol. 85. Edited by W. Clarysse, A. Schoors, and H. Willems, pp. 1055-1071. Leuven: Peeters.

Van Dijk, J. 2000."The Amarna Period and the Later New Kingdom," in *The Oxford History of Ancient Egypt*. Edited by I. Shaw, pp. 272-313. Oxford: Oxford University Press.

Van Gennep, A. 1909 [1960]. *The Rites of Passage*. London: Routledge and Kegan Paul Ltd.

Van Walsem, R. 1982a. "The God Monthu and Deir el-Medîna," in *Gleanings from Deir el-Medina*. Egyptologische Uitgaven. Vol. I. Edited by R. J. Demarée and J. J. Janssen, pp. 195-214. Leiden: Nederlands Instituut voor het Nabije Oosten.
- 1982b. "Month-names and Feasts at Deir el-Medîna," in *Gleanings from Deir el-Medina*. Egyptologische Uitgaven. Vol. I. Edited by R. J. Demarée and J. J. Janssen, pp. 215-244. Leiden: Nederlands Instituut voor het Nabije Oosten.

Vandier, J., 1952. *Manuel d'archéologie égyptienne I: les époques de formation; les trois premières dynasties*. Paris: A. et J. Picard.
- 1954. *Manuel d'archéologie égyptienne II: les grandes époques, l'architecture funéraire*. Paris: A. et J. Picard.
- 1964. Iousâas et (Hathor)-Nébet-Hétépet (first article). *Revue d'Égyptologie* 16:55-146.
- 1965. Iousâas et (Hathor)-Nébet-Hétépet (second article). *Revue d'Égyptologie* 17:89-176.
- 1966. Iousâas et (Hathor)-Nébet-Hétépet (third article). *Revue d'Égyptologie* 18:67-142.
- 1968. Iousâas et (Hathor)-Nébet-Hétépet (fourth article). *Revue d'Égyptologie* 20: 135-148.
- 1969. Un groupe du Louvre représentant la déesse Hathor sous quatre de ses aspects. *Mélanges de l'Université Saint-Joseph* 45:159-183.

Varille, A. 1943. *Karnak I*. Cairo: Institut Français d'Archéologie Orientale.

Ventura, R. 1986. *Living in a City of the Dead: A Selection of Topographical and Administrative Terms in the Documents of the Theban Necropolis*. Orbis Biblicus et Orientalis. Vol. 69. Freiburg: Universitätsverlag; Göttingen: Vandenhoeck & Ruprecht.

Vernus, P. 1991. "Sur les graphies de la formule 'l'offrande que donne le roi', au Moyen Empire et la Deuxieme Période Intermédiare" in *Middle Kingdom Studies*. Edited by S. Quirke, pp. 141-152. New Malden, Surrey: SIA.
- 2000. "La Grotte de la vallée des Reines dans la piété personelle des ouvrièrs de la tomb (BM278)," in *Deir el-Medina in*

the Third Millennium AD. Egyptologische Uitgaven. Vol. XIV. Edited by R. J. Demarée and A. Egberts, pp. 331-336. Leiden: Nederlands Instituut voor het Nabije Oosten.

Vleeming, S. P. 1982. "The Days On Which the *ḳnbt* Used to Gather," in *Gleanings from Deir el-Medina*. Egyptologische Uitgaven. Vol. I. Edited by R. J. Demarée and J. J. Janssen, pp. 183-189. Leiden: Nederlands Instituut voor het Nabije Oosten.

Vogelsang-Eastwood, G. 1993. *Pharaonic Egyptian Clothing*. Leiden: E. J. Brill.

Von Bergmann, E. 1887. Inschriftliche Denkmäler der Sammlung ägyptischer Altertümer des österreichischen Kaiserhauses. *Recueil de travaux relatifs à la philologie et à l'archéologie égyptiennes et assyriennes* 9:32-63.

- 1892. Inschriftliche Denkmäler der Sammlungng ägyptischer Altertümer des österreichischen Kaiserhauses. *Recueil de travaux relatifs à la philologie et à l'archéologie égyptiennes et assyriennes* 12:1-22.

Walz, C. A. 1994. Review: *Death-Ritual and Social Structure in Classical Antiquity*, by I. Morris. Cambridge: Cambridge University Press. 1992. *American Journal of Archaeology* 98:574-575.

Ward, W. A. 1994. "Foreigners living in the Village," in *Pharaoh's Workers: The Villagers of Deir el Medina*. Edited by L. H. Lesko, 61-85. Ithaca: Cornell University Press.

Watson, P. 1994. "Six Stelae in Birmingham City Museum and Art Gallery," in *The Unbroken Reed: Studies in the Culture and Heritage of Ancient Egypt, in Honour of A. F. Shore*. Edited by C. J. Eyre, M. A. Leahy and L. M. Leahy, pp. 365-378. London: Egypt Exploration Society.

Weigell, A. E. P. B. 1924. *Ancient Egyptian Works of Art*. London: T. F. Unwin Ltd.

Wenig, S. 1961. *Führer durch das Berliner Ägyptische Museum*. Berlin: Staatliche Museen zu Berlin.

Wente, E. F. 1963. Two Ramesside Stelas Pertaining to the Cult of Amenhotep I. *Journal of Near Eastern Studies* 22:30-36.

Wiebach, S. 1981. *Die Ägyptische Scheintür. Morphologische Studien zur den Entwicklung und Bedeutung der Hauptkultstelle in den Privat-Gräbern des Alten Reiches*. Hamburg: Borg.

- 2001. "False door," in *The Oxford Encyclopedia of Ancient Egypt*. Vol. 1. Edited by D. B. Redford, pp. 498-501. New York: Oxford University Press.

Wiedemann, A. 1884. *Ägyptische Geschichte. Teil I: Von den ältesten Zeiten bis zum Tode Tutmes III.* Goltha: Friedrich Andreas Perthes.

Wildung, D. 1977. *Egyptian Saints*. New York: New York University Press.

Wilkinson, K., and M. Hill. 1983. *Egyptian Wall Paintings: The Metropolitan Museum of Art's Collection of Facsimiles*. New York: The Metropolitan Museum of Art.

Wilkinson, M and C, Supp.: see Porter and Moss I.2 1964: 719.

Wilkinson, R. H. 2002. "Symbols," in *A Guide to Egyptian Religion*. Edited by D. B. Redford, pp. 339-347. Oxford: Oxford University Press.

Wolterman, C. 1996. A Vizier of Ramses III Visits an Oracle of Amun and Deir el Medina. *Revue d'Égyptologie* 47:147-170.

Woolf, G. 1996. Monumental Writing and the Expansion of Roman Society in the Early Empire. *Journal of Roman Studies* 86:22-39.

- 2002. Making the Most of Historical Roman Archaeology. *Archaeological Dialogues* 9.1 (July):51-55.

Yoyotte, J. 1951. Un document relatif aux rapports de la Libye et de la Nubie. *Bulletin de la Société Francaise d'Égyptologie* 6:9-14.

- 1960. "Les Pèlerinages dans l'Égypte ancienne," in *Les Pèlerinages*. Sources Orientales. Vol. 3, pp. 17-74. Paris: Éditions du Seuil.

- 2003. "À propos de quelques idées reçues: Mereseger, la butte et les cobras," in *Deir el-Médineh et la vallée des Rois: la vie en Égypte au temps des pharaons du Nouvel Empire*. Edited by G. Andreu, pp. 281-307. Paris: Éditions Khéops-Musée du Louvre.

Yoyotte, J., and J. Lopez. 1969. L'Organisation de l'armée et les titulaires de soldats au Nouvel Empire égyptien. *Bibliotheca Orientalis* 26:3-19.

Zivie, A. 1979. *La Tombe de Pached à Deir el-Médineh [no. 3]*. Cairo: Institut Français d'Archéologie Orientale.

- 2003. "Un détour par Saqqara. Deir el-Médineh et la Nécropole memphite," in *Deir el-Médineh et la vallée des Rois: la vie en Égypte au temps des pharaons du Nouvel Empire*. Edited by G. Andreu, pp. 67-82. Paris: Éditions Khéops-Musée du Louvre.

Plate 1a Middle Kingdom mud brick cenotaphs at Abydos

Plate 1b Stela of Sankhptah, Abydos, 17th Dynasty (BM EA 833)

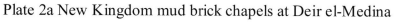

Plate 2a New Kingdom mud brick chapels at Deir el-Medina

Plate 2b The Queens' Valley Chapels at Deir el-Medina

Plate 3a Stela (recto) of the Sculptor in the Place of Truth, Qen (ii), Deir el-Medina (DB80)

Plate 3b Stela of Henut, Deir el-Medina (DB239)

Plate 4a Stela of the Wab-priest, Huy, Thebes (DB270)

Plate 4b Wooden statue of a king, Deir el-Medina (Musée du Louvre E. 16277)

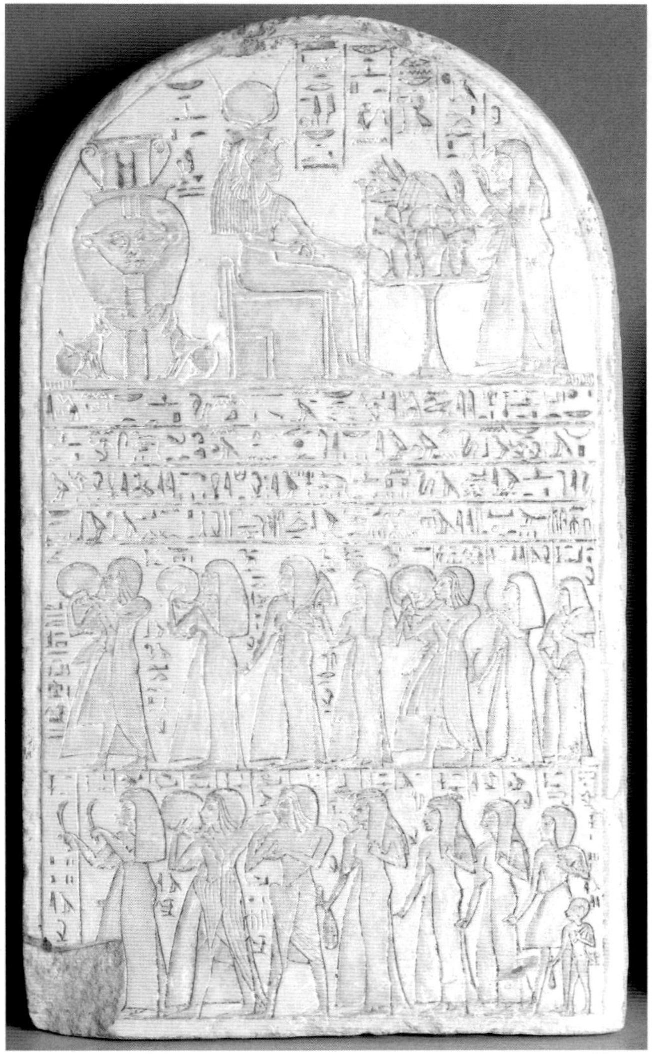

Plate 5a Stela of the Lady of the House, Bukhanefptah (i), Deir el-Medina (DB13)

Plate 5b Stela of the Workman in the Place of Truth, Karo or Kel (i), Deir el-Medina (DB39)

Plate 6 Stela of the Senior Scribe, Ramose (i), Deir el-Medina (DB89)

Plate 7 Stela of the Foreman in the Place of Truth, Khons (v), Queens' Valley Chapels, Deir el-Medina (DB188)

Plate 8 Stela of the Workman of the Lord of the Two Lands, Hesysunebef (i), Ramesseum area (DB183)

Plate 9 Stela of the Draughtsman in the Place of Truth, Nebre (i), Ramesseum area (DB60)

Plate 10 Stela of the Quarryman, Huy and his son, Mose, Deir el-Medina (DB153)

Plate 11a Stela of the Workman in the Place of Truth, Neferabu (i), Deir el-Medina (DB116)

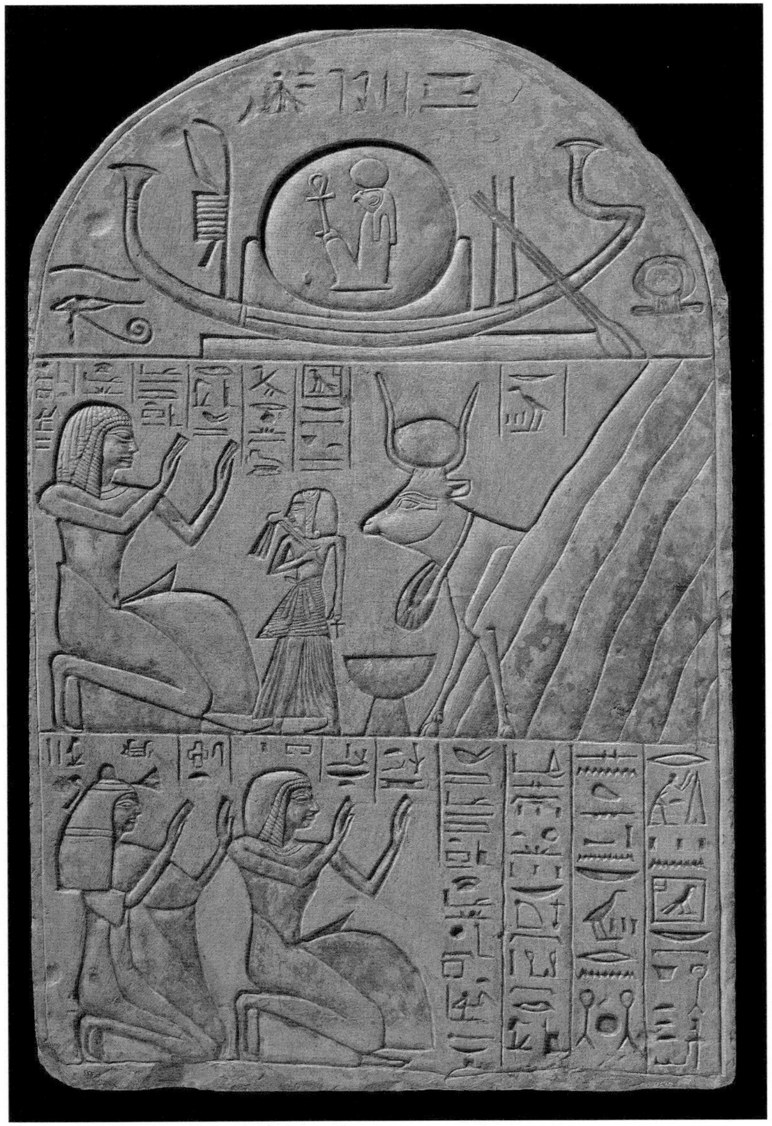

Plate 11b Stela of the Workman in the Place of Truth, Khabekhenet (i), Deir el-Medina (BM EA 555)

Plate 12a Rock-cut stela of the First Royal Cupbearer, Ramesses-Asha-Hebu-Sed, Abu Simbel (DB321)

Plate 12b Rock-cut stela of the Royal Scribe, Usimare-Asha-Nakhtu, Abu Simbel (DB337)

Plate 13 Rock-cut double stela of the King's Son of Kush, Setau, Abu Simbel (DB327)

Plate 14 Stela of the Infantryman of the Great Regiment of (Ramesses Meryamun), Beloved of Atum, Mose, Qantir (DB379)

Plate 15a Stela of the Singer of Montu-em-tawy, Isis, Qantir (DB370)

Plate 15b Stela of the Draughtsman of Amun, Userhat, Qantir (DB408)

Plate 16 Stela of the Overseer of the Goldworkers, Penweret, Qantir (DB391)